Henry Stevens, George Waymouth

The Dawn of British trade to the East Indies

Henry Stevens, George Waymouth

The Dawn of British trade to the East Indies

ISBN/EAN: 9783744730600

Printed in Europe, USA, Canada, Australia, Japan

Cover: Foto ©ninafisch / pixelio.de

More available books at **www.hansebooks.com**

THE COURT RECORDS OF THE
EAST INDIA COMPANY

THE DAWN OF BRITISH TRADE

TO THE EAST INDIES

AS RECORDED IN THE

COURT MINUTES OF THE EAST INDIA COMPANY

1599-1603

Containing an account of the formation of the Company
The first Adventure and Waymouth's Voyage
in search of the North-West Passage

NOW FIRST PRINTED FROM THE ORIGINAL MANUSCRIPT

BY HENRY STEVENS of VERMONT

WITH AN INTRODUCTION BY

SIR GEORGE BIRDWOOD K' CSI MD

LONDON
HENRY STEVENS & SON 115 ST. MARTIN'S LANE
Over against the Church of St Martin in the Fields
MDCCCLXXXVI

CHISWICK PRESS:—C. WHITTINGHAM AND CO., TOOKS COURT,
CHANCERY LANE.

PREFACE

HE original manuscript from which this volume is printed, is preserved in the India Office, London, where it is known as the first volume of the Court Minutes of the East India Company; and consists of 120 leaves foolscap folio, written in the old court hand of the Elizabethan period. Some few years ago it was sent, with other documents, to the Public Record Office to be calendared, and there fell under the notice of my late father, Mr. Henry Stevens of Vermont, who, ever watchful for new materials for history, especially American, immediately recognised its importance. Finding that only a very small portion had ever been quoted, he determined with the sanction of the Authorities of the India Office, to print it in full, and forthwith employed an expert to transcribe it exactly with all its peculiarities of spelling and contraction. This proved a work of time and of considerable difficulty, as the handwriting is extremely illegible in places, and in some cases several opinions were required to decipher certain passages.

The transcript, on completion, was handed to Messrs. Charles Whittingham and Co. of the Chiswick Press, with instructions to follow copy in the minutest particulars of spelling and contractions, a task which somewhat taxed their resources and ingenuity for peculiar types. The proofs, after careful correction with the transcript, were re-read with the original manuscript by an independent expert, and many and curious were the corrections which resulted.

Mr. Stevens's intention was to have written a lengthy essay by way of introduction, but he was unfortunately prevented by failing health and the pressure of other work. I may add, however, that from his memoranda it appears he was probably more interested in the volume from an American than from an Indian point of view. Perhaps this is pardonable when it is remembered how close were his sympathies and studies with the history and geography of the land of his birth; nevertheless, the importance of the British and Indian aspect of the volume must by no means be lost sight of. Finding that his memoranda were not sufficiently detailed to be capable of extension, Sir George Birdwood has kindly assented to my request to write an introduction.

Of the voyage for the discovery of the North-West Passage here recorded, very little has hitherto been known beyond the details given by Waymouth himself in his Journal, printed by Purchas, volume iii. pages 809-814. The present volume tends to contradict some of the statements there given, for in the opening paragraph of the Journal Waymouth says, his ships were "thoroughly victualled and abundantly furnished with all necessaries for a yeere and an halfe, by the right Worshipfull Merchants of the Moscouie and Turkie Companies," whereas we now learn that the expedition was undertaken at the sole instance of the East India Company, and certainly at first with some opposition from the Moscovie Company. George Waymouth was one of my father's most favourite subjects for study, and I have hopes that some interesting particulars respecting him may yet be gleaned from memoranda made for the introduction to an account of another of his Voyages which is also in the press.

Another point which greatly interested Mr. Stevens in this volume is the mention of the 'May flowre,' and I have heard him express a very decided opinion that the vessel here referred to was undoubtedly the veritable Pilgrim Ship. The mention of Hakluyt is also worthy of attention. On the 29th of January 1600 (see page 123) he is referred to as "Mr Hacklett the historiographer of the viages of the East Indies," and "was required to sett downe in wryting a note of the principall places in the East Indies wher Trade is to be had to thend the same may be vsed for the better instruccon of o^r factors in the said voyage," and on the 16th of February (see page 143) we find that £10 was paid to him for his "advyses." The further payment of 30s. for three maps on the same date, raises the delightful query as to what maps they were, whether three different ones or three copies of Molyneux's "true hydrographical description of so much of the world as hath been hitherto discovered and is come to our knowledge," published just about this time and inserted by Hakluyt in some copies of his 'Principall Navigations,' but of which only some nine or ten specimens have come down to posterity. The last copy came to light in 1881, when it realised £131 at public auction. It would indeed be interesting if another copy should turn up amongst the East India Company's records.

The letters printed on pages 265 to 283, are probably draft letters of the "Company of Levant Merchants," and they commence at the opposite end of the manuscript volume to the minutes of the East India Company. From the first letter being dated March, 1599, while the first entry of the East India Company is September, 1599, it would appear that the book originally belonged to the Levant Company, but was afterwards used by both companies in common. This tends to show that the East India Company was partially an outgrowth of the

Levant Company, as several persons mentioned appear to have been prominent members of both Companies, notably Sir Thomas Smith, who held the office of Governor of each (see pages 62 and 281). Under these circumstances it was thought best to print these letters, although they do not pertain directly to the East India Company.

A word as to method of printing. The manuscript has been followed with the greatest possible care, though in one or two instances the greatest experts of the Record Office and others were at variance over a word or figure. The reader's indulgence is therefore requested should he discover an error. The words printed within brackets [ ] are struck through in the original as corrections, but have been printed here, as in many cases they tend to the better understanding of the sentence. The passages printed in italics are interlineated in the manuscript. The Index, which I undertook at my father's request, I have endeavoured to make as copious as possible.

Henry N. Stevens.

INTRODUCTION

"Qui mare teneat, eum necesse rerum petiri."—CICERO, *Ep. ad Att.*, x.

HE History of the East India Company is a work that has still to be written, although from its rise, at the close of the sixteenth century, to its disappearance thirty years ago, the Company was careful to provide all the necessary material for the task, and to place on formal record the simplest acts of its administration, and the reasons which prompted all its decisions. The value of these contemporary annals—for the Court Books, Factory Diaries, Consultations, and general correspondence, really constitute a continuous narrative—has been only impaired in a small degree by the ravages of time, and by the neglect of less careful custodians than the men who originally determined that their successors in office should gain by their example and experience, and that the Company itself should not suffer in the eyes of posterity from any ambiguity as to its proceedings. The present volume, printed as a labour

b

of love under the direction and at the charge of the late Mr. Henry Stevens, is, so far as print can be made a facsimile of manuscript, identical with the first Court Book kept by the adventurers trading to the East Indies, who received from Queen Elizabeth in the last year of the sixteenth century a patent, or charter, recognizing them as the East India Company, with a monopoly of trade and specified privileges for a given term of years.

The first entry is of the names of those persons who subscribed on 22nd September, 1599, to "the pretended voiage to the Easte Indias, the whiche it maie please the Lorde to psper;" and the last is the report of a committee meeting on 28th June, 1603. Within those four years is contained the germ of every triumph subsequently achieved in the seas and lands of the East. The committees to which the adventurers entrusted the guidance of their affairs not merely laid down the countries with which it was desirable to trade, and the English commodities for which their markets might provide a vent, but they dwelt upon the inconveniences of the long sea route by the Cape of Good Hope to India, and listened with approval to any project, however visionary, for bringing London nearer to the wealthy kingdoms of Asia. As will be seen, their hopes centred in the North-West passage, which Robert Thorne had been the first to advocate in Henry VIII.'s reign as furnishing a road to Cathay and India, and which long continued to dangle before the eyes of the Company as a glorious possibility, never realizing its promise until in our time the discovery has been made, and the feat accomplished, not by naval skill and daring, but by the connexion of the two great oceans of the world by a line of railway. The early references to America contained in this volume will be of peculiar interest to the descendants of the Pilgrim Fathers of the *May Flower*,[1] who have so rapidly spread themselves over that mighty continent, and who have so brilliantly carried on the commercial traditions of the Mother Country of us all.

The present volume, the first Court Book, furnishes irrefragable evidence that the managers of the East India Company began their undertaking in a thoroughly practical and businesslike manner. They encountered a rebuff, however, on the very threshold of their enterprise, for after three meetings they were obliged to postpone their first voyage until the following year in consequence of the negotiations then in progress with Spain for the conclusion of a peace. The active life of the Company, therefore, did not commence until the meeting at Founders' Hall, on 23rd September, 1600, whereat it was announced that "it was her Ma^{es} pleasure that they shuld proceade in ther purpose." The first steps taken were the appointment of committees to select and purchase suitable vessels for the voyage, as well as the necessary stores and equipment. The *Susan*, or more

---

[1] The East India Company possessed in 1659 a ship called the *May Flower*, which I believe subsequently foundered in the Bay of Bengal. In my *Report on the Miscellaneous Old Records of the India Office* (H.M.'s Stationery Office, 1879), I ask whether it could have been the same ship as the *May Flower*, which landed the Dutch, Scotch, and English emigrants from Delft Haven, Southampton, and Plymouth, in New England, 25 Dec., 1620.

strictly the *Great Susan*, the *Hector*, and the *Assention*, were the first three vessels purchased, and then, after protracted bargaining with its owner, the Earl of Cumberland, the *Mare Scurge*, afterwards re-named the *Red Dragon*, was procured as the Admiral's ship. These four vessels constituted what is termed "the First Voyage," but a fifth, and much smaller vessel, named the *Guift*,[1] was added to them for the conveyance of some of the indispensable supplies of the squadron, and it was to be cast adrift at the discretion of the commander. The committees had to report to the Court every particular of their transactions with the owners of the ships, and these form the substance of the first half of the present volume. The inventories of the four ships named, given at pp. 15-20, pp. 22-4, pp. 42-4, are exceedingly curious, and mention everything on board from culverins and masts to " 1 pease pott & 2 gridirons." The *Mare Scurge*, of 600 tons burden, and twice the size of the next largest vessel of the fleet, the *Hector*, cost £3,700. The *Susan* was purchased for £1,600; but the prices given for the others are not stated. The *Guift* cost £300. These sums included everything on board, as well as the vessels themselves, and with regard to two of them it was stipulated that the seller should take back his ship at half price on its safe return.

The ships having been procured, the next thing was

---

[1] The received names of the ships here called *Mare Scurge*, and *Guift*, are *Malice Scourge* and *Guest*. The name of the *Assention* is usually spelled *Ascension*.

to make them ready for sea, and this was done with all dispatch—the workmen on the *Mare Scurge* being allowed a barrel of beer a day to prevent their running to the ale-house. They were then provided with their proper companies, the *Mare Scurge* having 200 men, the *Hector* 100 men, the *Susan* 80 men, and the *Assention* 80 men. The sailors received two months' wages in advance, and the officers were treated in an equally liberal manner. Great care was shown in the selection of the latter, and when the Lord Treasurer made a special appeal for Sir Edward Michelborne to be employed in the voyage the Court firmly refused " to imploy anie gent," and requested " leave to sort ther busines wth men of ther owne quality." Captain James Lancaster was appointed Captain of the *Mare Scurge*, and Admiral of the Squadron. Captain John Middleton commanded the *Hector*, with the succession to the chief command in the event of Lancaster's death. Both these officers were also appointed principal factors. The Master of the *Susan* was Samuel Spencer, and of the *Assention*, Roger Hankin.

The Company had difficulties of its own. Some of the adventurers were not prompt in paying up their instalments, and in April, 1601, the Company was £7,000 in default, and had to appeal to the Lords of the Privy Council for special powers to deal with those that " shewe themselves remisse & vnwillinge to furnyshe there promyssed contribucons," and this request was granted. The order is a characteristic one, and will be found at pp. 165-6. The Company issued warrants against the defaulters in accordance with this order, and we may assume that this summary mode of dealing was attended with satisfactory results as the subject gradually disappears from the Court Minutes.

On 1st May, 1601, the Court sanctioned the payment of "twentie merkes" to the King of Heralds for assigning Corporate Arms to the Company, but these were not the same Insignia[1] of Community, with the motto " Auspicio Regis et Senatus Angliæ," which, at a later date, became renowned throughout the East. Very stringent rules were also passed for the maintenance of order in the Court, and some of them would not be without their value in a more august assembly at the present day, as, for instance, the regulation providing that no brother of the Company should speak to any one matter "above three sundry tymes." The penalty of doing so was 3s. 4d., a considerable amount in those days. Penalties of different amounts were inflicted for uncivil or intemperate speeches and behaviour, for interruptions, such as private whisperings, &c., for breaking silence when enjoined by the Governor, for

---

[1] The earliest armorial bearings of the East India Company known to me are those stamped on the back of the bound volumes of the older —seventeenth century—records at the India Office. They are very beautiful, the shield being divided into three bands, the uppermost bearing conventional red and white Tudor roses on a gold ground; the middle the conventional white lilies of France on a blue ground; and the lowermost, three quaint heraldic ships sailing all in a line on an azure sea. The supporters are a blue sea lion on either side. The crest is a terrestrial globe, beflagged right and left; and the motto "Deus indicat." And God did indeed fulfil the expectation of his trustful ones.

leaving the Court without permission, and the refusal to pay these fines or penalties entailed a term of imprisonment. For further information on these points the reader must be referred to pp. 201-4.

It was in June, 1603, that news was received through a Frenchman that left the English fleet at sea of its safe return to European waters, but the first Court Book contains only special reference to the arrival of the *Assention*, from the officers of which vessel several letters were read in the General Court held on 6th June, 1603. Ten days later the reward of five pounds was assigned to Mr. Midleton of Plymouth " for his paines ryding hether wth the first report of the coming of the *Assention* out of the East Indies." Special orders were sent down to Plymouth that the ship was not to break bulk until anchored in the Thames. Warehouses suitable for the reception of its cargo were taken, tithes were paid to the Lord High Admiral for a prize captured at sea, and on the 16th June the entrance of the vessel into the river was publicly announced. Six pounds had then to be paid for pilotage and £917 for customs to the King (for James I. had succeeded " Good Queen Bess "), before the adventurers were in a position to know how their first journey had prospered. The Court Book says modestly that it afforded encouragement for a second venture, but for more exact and detailed information concerning the return of the East India Company's first squadron from Asia the reader will refer to the passages themselves.

Very soon after the sailing of the first fleet for India

by the Cape of Bona Speransa, the project of discovering a route to the East Indies by the North-West Passage was brought before the Court by " one George Waymoth[1] a navigator." The subject was considered in a dual form—first, whether the Company would take it up and be at the charge of fitting out two or three pinnaces, and secondly, if it would not accept this direct responsibility, would it leave the matter to private men, and reward their discovery by the surrender of the trade by this route for certain years? Whether from fear of losing any of the privileges and advantages of the monopoly of trade with China and the East Indies, or from pure public spirit, it was determined that " the findinge out of the Northwest passage " shall be " consented unto for a voyage." The readiness of the Court to undertake this quest, and to seriously take up George Waymouth's idea can only be understood by realising the state of geographical knowledge at the time, and the hopes of the commercial classes of the discovery of new and short routes to the Indies as well as of new countries.

The discovery of the North-West Passage had been the first ambition of English navigators. Henry VIII.'s letters patent to John Cabot and his three sons in 1496 were for the discovery of this very route.[2] In the next reign Robert Thorne advocated the same project which Sebastian Cabot revived under Edward VI. and Mary, and the expedition of Sir Hugh Willoughby and Richard

---

[1] His name is afterwards spelt Waymouth and Waymouthe.
[2] See my *Report on the Miscellaneous Old Records of the India Office*, particularly p. 75 and pp. 91-92.

Chancellor to the White Sea, partly a failure and partly a success, was really another attempt to solve the same problem. The voyages of Martin Frobisher, in 1576-8, were the first to give any tangible ground of hope in the discovery of an inlet on the coast of Labrador running westward, and he was "highly commended of all men for the great hope he brought of a passage to Cathaia." These different attempts made in the course of a century, were so many endeavours to realise the predictions of Seneca and Pulci.[1] The latter clearly prophesied that across the Atlantic would be discovered not only a new world, but a new route to the East.

Political considerations confirmed the traditions kept alive by the bolder geographers and men of science of antiquity, and also of the renaissance. Da Gama's dis-

---

[1] Luigi Pulci, 1431-1487, "sire of the half-serious rhyme":—

"But see, the sun speeds in his western path
To glad the nations with unexpected light."

There was a general looking forward in the thirteenth, fourteenth, and fifteenth centuries, to the discovery of the American and the Australasian continents. The lines of Dante, 1265-1321, in the *Vision of Purgatory*, in which he alludes to the Southern Cross, are well known. I believe that the leading minds of ancient Rome had an equally clear, if not even a clearer conception of the as yet unrevealed lands lying indefinitely beyond the Atlantic and Indian Oceans. Pliny (Bk. II., Chap. 65) positively asserts the existence of the Antipodes; and records (Chap. 67) the tradition of "certain Indians, who sailing from India" for the purpose of commerce had been driven by tempests into Germany. If the story had any foundation in fact, these Indians could only have been North American Indians, such as the Esquimaux. Seneca's hackneyed line: "Nec sit terris ultima Thule" is not so vague a prophecy of the Americas as it appears separated from the context (*Medea*, Act II., lines 370-

covery of the Cape route to the Indies had been to the
benefit of a Portuguese monopoly, not of the commercial interests of Europe at large. For a century
the Portuguese enjoyed as undisturbed a supremacy east
of the Cape as the Spaniards had for three-fourths that
period on the Spanish Main. When the English navy
was in its infancy that of Portugal had reached its prime,
and was, indeed, squandering the magnificent inheritance
of Da Gama and Albuquerque. It seemed to English
navigators and merchants that the only practical way of
coping with the Portuguese in eastern seas was by the
discovery of a new route thither of which England
might claim and possess the sole right of usage. In the
sixteenth century English naval enterprise found its
chief impulse in this consideration, and when the next
century was marked by the beginning of an East India
Company whose programme was to compete with the
Portuguese and Dutch—for the latter had also, and

380): and he really seems to have anticipated the advice of the American humourist in not prophesying before he knew, when his poetical vision of the New World is compared with a prosaic passage, which I believe is now brought to light for the first time in this connexion, from his *Quæstionum Naturalium Libri Septem*. Herein he distinctly states that the distance from the west coast of Spain to "the Indies" was so short, that it could be sailed over, if the wind was favourable, in a few days. His actual words are : " Curiosus spectator contemnit domicilii angustias. Quantum enim est quod ab ultimis litoribus Hispaniæ usque ad Indos jacet? paucissimorum dierum spatium, si navem suam ventus implevit." It was always the quest and invention of the Indies that inspired Columbus and his English successors in the exploration of the New World; and they but picked up the Americas and the greater part of the Aus-tralasias as unconsidered trifles by the way.

before us, embarked on the same undertaking—in a trade by the Cape route, there were many who turned with unconcealed longing to the earlier scheme, as holding forth the promise of easier and more complete success. It was in this hankering feeling after a monopoly and a sway not to be disputed that men like George Waymouth and other advocates of the North-West Passage found their best opportunity and argument.

Such were the prevalent views when Captain Waymouth proposed a fresh search for the North-West Passage, and obtained the sanction of the Court to his design. Although a fleet had sailed only a few months before by the Cape route, then new to Englishmen, the generality of the Company showed every disposition to patronise another attempt to open a route peculiarly dear to the English, and identified with their name. Yet even in this matter, an unexpected obstacle presented itself in the alleged prior rights of the "Muskovia Companie," the parent of the Russia Company of our time. Delays and objections ensued as to the respective privileges of the two Companies, and the deliberations of chosen delegates did not greatly further any practical or definite conclusion. The discussion might have continued indefinitely had not the East India Company taken legal opinion as to their rights, and finding them ample for the purpose in hand sanctioned the scheme as their "Second Voyage" to the Indies. Finding them so firm, the Muskovia Company waived their loftier pretensions, and proceeded to associate themselves in the enterprise. For the purposes of this voyage, a special levy of one shilling for each pound deposited by the adventurers for the Cape experiment was ordered, and special terms, mainly dependent, however, on the result of his voyage, were made with Captain Waymouth. The objects of the journey itself are well expressed on pp. 198-9, whereat are recited some of the chief passages of Elizabeth's patent as well as the reasons which swayed the decision of the Court. The formal agreement between the Company and George Waymouth sets forth that the Governor and Company had deliberated on "the longe and tedious course wch hath benne hetherto houlden by all such as do trade or sayle from these parts of the world in to ye East Indies alonge the coast of Europe and Africa by ye Cape of Bona Esperansa and of the great adventures wch are borne in soe longe a viage by many kinds of daungers offered therin and beinge moved wth great hope that ther is a possibility of discovery of a neerer Passage into ye said East Indies by seas by ye way of the North-west yf the same were vndertaken by a man of knowledge in Navigaçon, &c. &c," and had in consequence entrusted the task to Captain Waymouth. In a subsequent passage further details are supplied as to how it was thought this would be effected, and these constituted what would now be termed Captain Waymouth's sailing orders. He was to "sayle toward the coast of Groynland into that part of the open seas wch is described in sundry generall mapps by ye name of fretum Dauies and shall passe on forward in those seas by ye northwest or as he shall fynd the Passage best to lye towards the parts or kinge-

domes of Cataya or China, or y^e *backside of America.*"
Queen Elizabeth attached sufficient importance to the
undertaking to write a special letter to the Emperor of
China and "Kathia," the use of the double names for
the one country implying rather the excess, or cautious
completeness, of diplomatic courtesy than geographical
ignorance.

Considering the great expense to which the Company
went in the matter, the many hopes that were based on
the enterprise, and the confidence of the commander himself, the speedy, not to say the ignominious return of the
expedition, was extremely disheartening. The Court
Book throws no further light on the causes of the failure
of this well equipped expedition to achieve what was
not then known to be impossible, than to attribute it
to the intrigues of the minister or preacher, Mr. Cartwright. But Captain Waymouth endeavoured, and
not unsuccessfully, to convince the Court to overlook his
failure, and to take up new schemes for the discovery of
another route, not by the North-west, but by the Southwest, or round Cape Horn. There is little doubt that
he would have carried his purpose had he not allowed
himself to be drawn into litigation with the Company
about what he considered his just claims in the matter
of the abortive voyage. These were firmly resisted, with
the consequence that he failed not only to obtain his
damages, but also to induce the Company to employ him
on a fresh voyage, as had been intended.

The opposition of the Court to Captain Waymouth's
demands and propositions was made the more inflexible

by the safe return of the ships that had sailed by way of the Cape of Good Hope. The arrival of the *Assention* showed where the practically useful route to the Indies lay. It had its difficulties, delays, and dangers, but in comparison with a mythical North-West passage it acquired greater substantiality as one prosperous voyage regularly succeeded another. Hudson, Button, and Baffin followed at short intervals, and with more favourable results, in the footsteps of Waymouth; but even their successes went to demonstrate the impracticability of the main purpose of their voyages, the opening of a North-West Passage. The first Court Book, characteristic in every particular and important in most, is historically curious as officially marking the first indication of the waning hopes of the school of Cabot and Frobisher, and the rising expectations, soon to be confirmed by facts, of that of Lancaster and Middleton, of Saris and Marlowe. The North-West Passage was a great idea based on an error of fact. The long and tedious route by the Cape was a magnificent certainty which supplied English naval skill and daring with their most profitable and glorious field of enterprise. The pretensions of the Portuguese to a monopoly being steadfastly repelled, the opulent trade with the Indies became the prize in a fair and open competition of merit and energy. The present volume is evidence, not of the triumph of the English Company, but of the way in which they made up their minds to deserve and win it. The fruits of the victory they ultimately secured over all rivals, after a contest of two centuries, by the open ocean round the Cape of Good Hope, have been retained unimpaired now that the narrow seas from Gibraltar to Aden have become, since the piercing of the Suez Isthmus, the general thoroughfare to the Indies; and if the North-West Canadian Pacific Railway should realise the anticipations of its authors the practical solution of the old North-West Passage problem would leave the English-speaking races victors still in the secular and mortal struggle of the leading countries of the civilised world for commercial ascendancy, and political existence. The states which through degenerate weariness and faint-heartedness in well doing, fail in this implacable competition are foredoomed to forced decay.

Undying then should be our gratitude to the founders of the East India Company, for they were indeed the pioneers of the unparalleled colonial and mercantile supremacy of modern England: and we may be sure that wherever

"The strong hearts of her sons"

are not borne down, as they have been, for well nigh a whole generation among ourselves, by the miserable sense of constantly reiterated public shame, but are kept up by the high hopes on which they are perennially nourished in the invincible Republic of the West, and in the proud dominions of the British Crown in the great South Sea, there the names of these middle class Elizabethan merchant adventurers,—who so well understood, when occasion called, how by transgressing, most truly to keep the moral law,—will be for ever cherished and revered as of " brave men, and worthy patriots, dear to God, and famous to all ages."

Our own destruction, as a beneficent power among the nations, may be as inevitable, as our peril, arising mainly from the weakness of the historical instinct in the English democracy, at this moment seems imminent; but in the worst case we shall have bequeathed the secret of empire, in the New World and the Old, to more resolute inheritors of our common traditions and splendour.

GEORGE BIRDWOOD.

India Office, Westminster,
 " Queen Elizabeth's Day" [17*th November* [1]], 1886.

---

[1] The anniversary of the accession of "the Most Mightie and Magnificent Empresse Elizabeth" continued to be kept as a public holiday in England even within the last century, and it should still be so observed, at least in the India Office, and in British India, and the State of Virginia, in praise perennial of Her imperious Majesty's heroic memory.

"Cynthia prima fuit, Cynthia finis erit."

" Her deeds were like great glusters of ripe grapes
Which load the branches of the fruitfull vine,
Offring to fall into each mouth that gapes,
And fill the same with store of timely wine.

*   *   *   *   *   *

Her thoughts are like the fume of Frankincence,
Which from a golden Censer forth doth rise,
And throwing forth sweet odours mounts fro thence
In rolling globes up to the vauted skies."

THE COURT RECORDS OF THE EAST INDIA COMPANY

The names of suche persones as haue writtin withe there owne 1599 handes, to venter in the pretended voiage to the Easte Indias (the whiche it maie please the Lorde to psper) and the Somes that they will adventure the .xxij. Septembr. 1599. viz

1	Sr Stephin Soame, L^o Mayor London	l. 200	0	0
2	Sr John Harte and George Boales	l. 1000	0	0
3	Sr John Spencer viij^c	l. 800	0	0
4	Mr Nicholas Mosley alderman	l. 300	0	0
5	Mr Paule Baynynge alderman	l. 1000	0	0
6	Mr Leonarde Hallydaie alderman	l. 1000	0	0
7	Mr Richard Goddard aldreman	l. 200	0	0
8	Mr John Moore alderman	l. 300	0	0
9	Sr Stephen Soame. Ric'd Carter, &c^o	l. 400	0	0
10	Mr Edward Holmden alderman	l. 500	0	0
11	Mr Robarte Hampson alderman	l. 300	0	0
12	Mr Richard Staper	l. 500	0	0
13	Mr Thomas Symonds	l. 200	0	0
14	Mr John Eldred	l. 400	0	0
15	Robarte Coxe grocer	l. 250	0	0
16	Nicholas Leatt yremonger	l. 200	0	0
17	Thomas Garwaye drap	l. 200	0	0
18	George Holman grocer	l. 150	0	0
19	Thomas Hiccocke	l. 100	0	0
20	Robarte Sandye grocer	l. 200	0	0
21	Nicholas Pearde cloatheworker	l. 100	0	0

1599	22	Thomas Edwardes	t.	200	0	0
	23	Nicholas Barnesley grocer	t.	150	0	0
	24	William Dale	t.	100	0	0
	25	Nicholas Linge	t.	100	0	0
	26	Nicholas Style groc̒	t.	200	0	0
	27	Lawrence Greene	t.	200	0	0
	28	Edwarde Collins clotheworker	t.	200	0	0
	29	ffraunces Cherie vintener	t.	200	0	0
	30	Oliver Style grocer	t.	300	0	0
	31	Richarde and James Wyche	t.	200	0	0
	32	Thom̅s and Robte Midleton. Robt Bateman	t.	500	0	0
	33	Nicholas ffarrer skynner	t.	200	0	0
	34	ffraunces Terrell	t.	200	0	0
	35	Thom̅s ffarrington vintener	t.	200	0	0
	36	Richard Wragge	t.	200	0	0
	37	Richarde Aldeworthe	t.	200	0	0
	38	William and Ralfe ffreman	t.	300	0	0
	39	William Romney	t.	200	0	0
	40	Willm Paule. George Cañynge	t.	300	0	0
	41	John Newman. Reinold Greene	l.	200	0	0
	42	John Woodwarde yremonger	l.	300	0	0
	43	Baptiste Hick mercer	t.	400	0	0
	44	Richarde Cockain and Comp̄	t.	3000	0	0
	45	Clement Mosley. Jerome Suger	t.	250	0	0
	46	Richarde Stephens	t.	200	0	0
	47	Thom̅s Wheeler. Larance Wethrall	t.	200	0	0
	48	William Chambre. Willm Stoane	t.	500	0	0
	49	Willm Adderley and mr. thom̅s Henshawe	t.	300	0	0
	50	Thom̅s Cambell. Miles Huberd	t.	200	0	0
	51	Mr Willm Garwaye drap	t.	500	0	0
	52	Richard Cock℈ grocer	l.	200	0	0
	53	Ralfe Hamor m̅chn̅ttailor	t.	200	0	0
	54	Walter ffletcher	t.	200	0	0
	55	John Robinson senior m̅chn̅ttailor	t.	200	0	0
	56	Leonarde White	t.	200	0	0
	57	Mr Thomas Cordell mer℈	l.	300	0	0
	58	Mr Richarde Wiseman goldesmithe	l.	200	0	0

59	Richarde Browne &c°	l.	500	0	0	1599
60	Roger Owfield	l.	300	0	0	
61	Willm and Edward Turner	l.	200	0	0	
62	Thomas Cutteler grocer	l.	200	0	0	
63	Edwarde Jaymes	l.	200	0	0	
64	Robarte Bell John Potter	l.	200	0	0	
65	John Highlord and John Marris	l.	200	0	0	
66	Willm Gore, and John Gore	l.	300	0	0	
67	Richarde Howse and Henrye Robinson	l.	200	0	0	
68	Thoñs Bostocke. John Ramridge	l.	200	0	0	
69	Roger Howe	l.	200	0	0	
70	Willm Harrison, and Wm Bonde m̃chñtay	l.	200	0	0	
71	Mr Robarte Lee alderman	l.	300	0	0	
72	John Buzbridge. James Turner	l.	200	0	0	
73	Vrye Babbington	l.	200	0	0	
74	Mr Thoñs Smithe haberdasher	l.	200	0	0	
75	Nicholas Crispe and comp	l.	200	0	0	
76	Richarde Burrell groc̃ &cº	l.	200	0	0	
77	John Hewett	l.	333	6	8	
78	John Cornelis goldesmithe	l.	200	0	0	
79	Willm Hallidaie merc̃. John Duckett	l.	200	0	0	
80	Humfrey Wymers. Richard Edmonds	l.	200	0	0	
81	Augustine skynner. Robte Brooke. tho. Westray	l.	300	0	0	
82	Thoñs Haies. Robte Barley. Mathew Hamond	l.	300	0	0	
83	Rowland Backhouse. barth and edwrd Barnes	l.	400	0	0	
84	Sr Richard Saltonstall and his children	l.	200	0	0	
85	John Coghill Henrye Parkehurste	l.	200	0	0	
86	Thomas Juxon groc̃	l.	200	0	0	
87	Richard Barrett Willm Allen merc̃	l.	200	0	0	
88	Barthilmew Barnes Edw. barnes. Row. backhous	l.	000	0	0	
88	Thoñs Eaton Willm Essington	l.	200	0	0	
89	John Cowp notarye	l.	200	0	0	
90	James Deane drap	l.	300	0	0	

THE COURT RECORDS OF

1599
91	John Coombe	t.	200	0	0
92	John Swynerton Junior	t.	300	0	0
93	Giles Doncomb. Ricd Welbye	t.	200	0	0
94	Edmond Nicholson groc	t.	200	0	0
95	Henrye Bridgeman lethersellēr	t.	200	0	0
96	John Suzan Samewell Garrard	t.	200	0	0
97	Willm Barrell Walter Porter	t.	400	0	0
98	Willm Offeley the elder	t.	200	0	0
99	John Harbie skynner	t.	200	0	0
100	Ralfe Buzbie grocer	t.	200	0	0
101	Henrye Poalstedd george Whitmor	t.	200	0	0
		t.	30133	6	8

An assembly of the psons heervnder named holden the xxiiijth of September 1599.

Sr John Hart knight
Mr Aldⁿ Moseley
Mr Aldⁿ Bannyng
Mr Aldⁿ Hollyday
Mr Aldⁿ Godderd
Richard Stap
Thomas Middleton
Richard Wyseman
John Highelord
Wm Rumney
Thoms Symondes
John Eldred
Robt Cocke
Niclas Leet
George Holman
Thomas Hickock
Robt Sandie
Niclas Pierd
Thomas Edwardes
Niclas Lynge

Niclas Style
Edward Collins
ffrauncis Cherie
Richard Wiche
Robt Midleton
Niclas fferro
Thomas ffarrington
Thoms Haiyes
Austin Skynner
Richard Aldworth
W^m ffreman
Raphe ffreeman
Reynold Greene
Babtist Heckes
Richard Cockein
Wm Cockeyn
Clement Moseley
Richard Steephens
Thomas Wheeler
Wm Chambers

Thomas Henshawe
Thoms Cambell
Ric Cockes
Walter ffletcher
Leonard White
Ric Browne
Wm Turnor
Robt Bell

Ric Howse
Henr Robinson
Thoms Bostock
Roger Howe
Jon Busbridg
Vry Babington
Nicho Cryse
Jon Cornelis
Thoms Backhouse

1599
24 Sept.

HEREAS the severall psons abovenamed together wth divers others whose names ar Regestred in the begynnyng of this booke, by the suffraunce of almightie god after Royall assent of or Soveraigne Lady the Queenes most excellent Maie first therunto had and obteyned, do entend for the honor of our native Cuntrey and for thadvauncement of trade of merchaundize wthin this Realme of England vppon ther severall adventures accordinge to the severall proportions of the sommes of money by them severally sett downe and inregestred vnder ther owne handes, To set forthe a vyage this present yere to ye Est Indies and other the Ilandes and Cuntries therabouts and ther to make trade by the sale of suche commodities as vppon further delibation shalbe resolved to be provided for these parts or otherwyse by buying or barteringe of suche goodes wares jewelles or mchaundize as those Ilandes or Cuntries may yeld or afforthe. And for the better ordering and disposing of the said viage intended and for thencoragemt of all suche as have already determined to adventure in the same or shall before the viage set forthe determine to adventure therin, They have thought it meet to direct them selfes by certen Rules and orders to be holden and observed aswell in the preparing of suche shipping as shalbe thought fitt for this enterprice as of all other provision of wares merchandize bullion and suche other thinges as are to be provided and adventured in the same. And therfore at this assemblie it is agreed ordeyned and resolved as followeth.

1599
24 Sept.

First that noe ship shalbe receavid to be brought in by any adventuro^r in this viage to be imployed in the same as his stock or portion of adventure at any rate whatsoever.

Also that all shipping to be imploied in this viage shalbe bought and provided by suche as shalbe therto appointed for ready money onlie.

That noe commoditie shalbe accepted in the said viag to be brought in as any mans portion of adventure but that all goodes wares and other thinges shalbe bought and prepared by suche as shalbe thervnto appointed as Comitties and directors of the said viage, for the buying and providing of shipping and merchaundize.

And this assemblie do electe nōiate and appoint thes fifteene persons heervnder named Comitties or directo^{rs} of this viage to manage order and direct the affaires belonginge to the same aswell concerning sewte to be made to her ma^{ie} for sole priviledg to be graunted to these adventuro^{rs} for soe manie yeres as can be obteyned and for such ỹmūyties and freedomes of Custome and other tollerations and favors as may be gotten as also for the providing for shippinge wares and merchaundize to be adventured in the said viage, Ratefying and allowing whatsoever the said Comitties or directors of the said viage or the greater nūber of them shall do or agree vppon in the premisses provided nevertheles that no factor or other officer to be imployid in the viage shalbe admitted or appointed therto but by a generall Assemblie of the adventuro^{rs} and ther elected by the consent of the greater nūber of them [elected] assembled.

Comitties or ye Directors of ye Viage.

Mr Aldⁿ Godderd	Mr Tho Symondes
Mr Aldⁿ Moore	Mr Nich Style
Mr Rich : Staper	Mr Nich Lyng
Mr Tho Cordell	Mr Rich Wiche
Mr Wm Garway	Mr Roger Howe
Mr Tho Midleton	Mr Wm Cockin
Mr Tho Cambell	Mr Nich Leet
Mr Rich : Wiseman	

And the said Assemblie have chosen for ther Thre'rs for the receaving and paying of the moneys imploied in the same M`r` John Highlord and m`r` W`m` Romney vnto whose handes the contributions of everie severall adventuro`r` in the viage is to be brought in at two severall payment(ℯ videlt the first payment by the   of November and the seconde paym`t` by the   of December. 1599 24 Sept. Treasurer

It is resolued at this assemblie that from henceforth no adventuro`r` in this viage shalbe re`d` to adventure in the same for a lesse some then 200`li`.

And it is generallie agreed that ther shalbe brought in to the handes of the Thre`r`s w`th`all expedition for the defraying of some present pettie charges that shall be expended in the affaires of the said viage xijd vppon everie C`li` sett downe and to be sett downe vppon every mans portion of adventure to be collected by him that warneth the adventuro`rs` to ther assemblies or otherwyse to be brought in by them selves to the Thre`r`s.

At an assemblie of the Comitties or y`r` directo`rs` of the viage the xxv`th` of Septemb`r` 1599.

M`r` Ald`n` Godderd	M`r` Rich Wiche
M`r` Ald`n` Moore	M`r` Tho Cambell
M`r` Rich: Staper	M`r` Roger Howe
M`r` W`m` Garway	M`r` W`m` Cockin
M`r` Nich Style	M`r` Nich Lyng
M`r` Tho Symondes	M`r` Nich: Leet

1599 25 Sept.

HES Comitties to whom the direction of the affaires of the viage is comitted beinge assembled together doe devide the present busines of the said viage to be followed and solicited by some of them at the Courte for the obteyning of a priviledge and other liberties and freedomes therto belonging and by some of them in surveying and seeking out of suche shipping as is thought

1599
25 Sept.

meet for the viage to w{ch} severall imploym{ts} the said psons by mutuall assent *have agreed* to vse ther travell, viz.

to solicite y{e} ll. of y{e} Councell	to seek for shippes
M{r} Ald{n} Godderd	M{r} Nich: Style
M{r} Ald{n} Moore	M{r} Tho Symondes
M{r} Rich: Staper	M{r} Rich: Wiche
M{r} Tho Cordell	M{r} Roger Howe
M{r} W{m} Garway	M{r} Nich Lyng
M{r} Tho Cambell	M{r} Nich: Leet
M{r} Tho Middleton	M{r} W{m} Cockin
M{r} Rich: Wiseman	

And it is resolued that a petition shalbe exhibited to y{e} LL. of her ma{es} most honorable privy Counsell in the name of the adventuro{r} shewing ther honors that divers merchaunt{es} induced by the successe of the viage pformed by the Duche nation [who] and beinge informed that the duchemen prepare for a newe viage and to that ende have bought divers ships heere in England, were stirred vp w{th} noe lesse affection to advaunce the trade of ther native Cuntrey then the duche merchaunt{es} were to benefite ther Comon wealthe, and vppon that affection have resolved to make a viage to the est Indias yf her ma{ie} wilbe pleased to add to ther entention the better to pforme the enterprise, these severall petitions or Request{es} following viz.

To graunt to the adventures a priviledge in succession and to incorporate them in a Companie for that the trade of the Indias being so farre remote from hence cannot be traded but in a Joint and a vnyted stock.

That the shipping of the adventuro{rs} being prepared for ther viages be not staied vppon anie pretence of [anie] service for y{t} the stay of one moneth loseth the oportunetie of a whole yeres viage.

That it may be lawfull for the adventuro{rs} anie Sta{t} notw{th}standing to sende out forrein Coyne, and yf ther shalbe a want of forrein Coyne to furnishe this present viage that ther may be quyned in her ma{es} mynt so muche forrein quyne as shall supply the want out of suche bullyon or plate as shalbe brought in by the adventuro{rs} or by ther meanes.

THE EAST INDIA COMPANY 9

That freedome of Custome be humblie requirid for all suche goodes as are carried out in 6 viages the rather for that many experimentẽ are to be made before the Cuntrey shalbe fitted wth marchaundize vendible ther, and for that also the Duche ñchauntẽ for ther better encoragem^t are freed for divers yeres bothe of Custome outward and inwarde

1599
25 Sept.

An assembly of Committies holden at m^r Ald^n Goddard the 4 of october 1599.

1599
4 Oct.

Mr Ald^n Goddard
Mr Ald^n Moore
Mr Rich: Staper
Mr Wm Garwey
Mr Thomas Cambell
Mr Tho Middleton

Mr Rich: Wiseman
Mr Tho Symondes
Mr Rich: Wiche
Mr Roger Howe
Mr Nich Lyng
Mr Nich: Leet

A PETITION havinge bene deliuered to y^e Ll of her Ma^es most honorable privie Counsaill accordinge to the agreement of the [said] Comitties in the last conference and the Ll. havinge re^d the same and favoringe thenterprise promysed ther furtheraunce to her Ma^ie for the obteyning of the thinges seet downe in articles mencōned [to] *in* the said Petition This assemblie doe resolve that a present course is to be taken to solicite ther honors againe for her Ma^es *answer* to the said Petition and articles and to that end the psons herevnder named are appointed to goe to ye L. Thrēr and Mr Secretary yf they be in Towne and yf not to goe to the Co^rte to solicite ther honors and the residewe of Ll at the counsaill boarde.

Mr Rcih Staper
Mr Wm Garway
Mr Tho Cambell

Mr Tho Midleton
Mr Rich: Wiseman
M^r frauncis Chery

c

1599
16 Oct.

The 16 of october 1599 an assembly of yᵉ Comitties.

Mʳ Aldⁿ Godderd   Mʳ Roger Howe
Mʳ Rich : Staper   Mʳ Rich : Wiche
Mʳ Wᵐ Garway   Mʳ Wᵐ Cockin
Mʳ Thomas Cambell   Mʳ Nich Leet
Mʳ Tho Symondes   Mʳ fra : Chery
            Mʳ   Hacklett

PPON the reporte of divers Comitties who have bene at yᵉ Court of her Maᵉʳˢ gratious acceptaunce of the viage and vppon like reporte that the Ll. do require that some of the Principall of the adventurors shuld resort to yᵉ Court to morrowe to receave ther honors order for oʳ further proceadinge It is ordered that the p̃sons hereafter named shall repaire to the Court to attend ther honors direction at the Counsell boarde and as they shall finde fitt oportunetie to tender a Petition to ther honors conteyningᵍ theẞ severall requestẽ followingᵍ viz.

That ther Ll. would by ther ho : order of ther assembly at the Counsell boarde geave the Companie a warraunt to proceade in the viage assuringe assuring them that they shall not be impeached in the same.

That they may have Warraunt to carry out in this first viage wᵗʰout charge v mˡ weight of Bullion at the least.

That they may proceade wᵗʰ the drawingᵍ and preparingᵍ in a redines of a graunt of priviledgᵍ vppon suche pointẽ as shalbe reasonable and fyt for suche a trade.

The Comitties above mencõned appointed to Solicite the Ll.
            for these favoʳˢ are
        Mʳ Cordell   Mʳ Chery
        Mʳ Stapers   Mʳ Symondes
        Mʳ Midleton   Mʳ Wᵐ Cockin
            Mʳ Leet

Mᵈ that by reason of a treatye of peace in hand betwene the Queenes Maᵉʳˢ and the kinge of Spaine the Company solicitingᵍ awarraunt from the ll. that they might p̃ceade in ther viage wthout anie impeachem^t; notwthstanding the said treaty and that by reason [of] thereof they shuld not be staied when ther shipping was p̄pared the ll. denied to geave them suche a warraunt as thincking it *more* beneficiall for the generall state of m̄chaundize to enterteyne a peace then that the same shuld be hindred by the standing wth the spanishe Comissioners [to breike the peace to holde the] for the mainteyning of this trade to forgoe the oportunety of the concluding of the peace. Wervppon the adventuro^{rs} fearing lest after they were driwen into a charge they shuld be required to desist ther viage did proceade noe further in the matter for this yere but did enter into the preparation of a viage the next yere following as hereafter may appeare.

1599
16 Oct.

At an assemblie in the ffounders hall the 23 of Septembe^r 1600.

1600
23 Sept.

HEREAS divers merchaunt̄s whose names are regestred in the begyning of this booke for the honor of ther natyve Cuntrey and for thadvauncem^t of the trade of merchaundize wthin this realme of England vppon ther severall adventures apportioned and sett downe of ther voluntarie assent have vndertaken to sett forthe a viage for the discoverye of the trade of the East Indias and to that ende have Solicited the Ll. of her ma^{ts} most honorable privy Councell to move her most Excellent ma^{ie} for her gracious and royall assent to the said enterprise and for to further the same wth a graunt of [a] priviledge and other tollerations and favors [fytt] for the advauncem^t of the said trade. And whereas the said Ll. favoring so honorable an [enterprise] *attempte* have *accordinglie* moved her most excellent ma^{ie} for her gratious assent in this behaulf and having founde her ma^{ie} gratiously inclyned to [further the said viag] the furthering of the same viage and [to graunt] ready to graunt vnto the petition of the said adventuro^{rs} touching the p̄ticler demaundes by them exhibited [in ther petition] did directe ther L̄res to the said

East India
[ship]
Viage

1600
23 Sept.

Adventuro^{rs} [encoraging them to proceade in ther purpose] signefying therby that it was her ma^{es} pleasure that they shuld proceade in ther purpose assuring them that [noe occasion whatsoever shuld] they shuld not be staied or phibited therin [by any pretence of warres] wishing them to accepte of ther Certefycat of her ma^{tes} pleasure as an ernest of a further warraunt wch afterwardes shuld be to them graunted by her ma^{ie}. Whervppon the said adventuro^{rs} in full and ample nūber assembled did geave ther generall Consent by erecting of handes (the [matter] *question* being putte to scruteny) that they would [proceade] *goe forward* in the [said voiage preparation of the] said viage, and to thende that they might the better dispose thereof and of *all* preparations necessarie for the same bothe for shipping merchaundize and money to be imployed therin they did [electe and chuse] *make choice of* the severall psons hereafter named to be Comitties and Directors, of all the [busines] preparations and busines concerning the said viage Reposing them selves wholy vppon ther fydelities [for the pre] and provident handling and ordering thereof wch Comittyes or the greatest number of them, from tyme to tyme assembled are [to] by the gen̄all Consent of the said adventuro^{rs} aucthorysid and warraunted according to ther discretions to *sett forthe and* mannage the whole viage vppon the proportion of stocke and adventure gen̄ally Contributed and sett downe [by all the adventurors], and vppon any occasion [or necessarie service to b] for the furtheraunce of the said viage to vse the helpe of anie adventuro^{r} in any imploym^{t} requiring the same in tyme convenient.

Comitties or directurs of the Viage

Mr Ald^{n} Bannyng	Mr Rich. Wyseman
Mr Ald^{n} Hollyday	M^{r} fra: Chery
Mr Ald^{n} Goddard	Mr Allabaster
Mr Ald^{n} Smyth	Mr Roger Howe
Mr Rich. Staper	Mr Rich: Wyche
Mr Wm Garway	M^{r} Jo Eldred
Mr Tho Cordell	M^{r} Jo: Bate
Mr Lancaster	Mr Wm Chamber
Mr Harryson	

THE EAST INDIA COMPANY

The 25 of Septemb 1600.

Mr Ald^n Bannyng
Mr Ald^n Hollyday
Mr Staper
Mr Wiseman
Capten Lancaster
Mr Howe

Mr Chambers
Mr Wiche
Mr Harryson
Mr Eldred
M^r Jo Bate
[M] Capteyn Davies

1600
25 Sept.

HE [parties] *Comitties* above named *or the most of them* having bene yesterday at Wolw^{ch} [debt] Deptford and Reddereth to viewe the severall shippes called the [Assention] Susan, the Globe the Paragon, the Phenix the Newcastleship the Liones the May flowre the Prousperous the Rowe Buck, and havinge pvsed them severally doe finde of the said shippes in respecte of ther burthens, that the Susan is the most [fittest] strongest and greatest burthen and so consequentlie most fittest for this viage and therfore in this assemblie [proceading] proceaded to bargaine wth m^r Ald^n Bannyng for the same ship wth *her furniture expressed in the Inventory exhibited* and did agree wth him for the same at the rate of 1600^{li} vppon condition that he shall receave her againe vppon her retorne from the viage wth suche furniture as she shall bring wth her at the rate of 800^{li} the wch he vndertaketh to geave for her againe.

The Susan bought

this condicion is discharged and a sale in writing sealed from m^r Ald^n the 24 Januarie 1600

[And it is agreed that m^r Garway m^r Wyseman m^r Chery and m^r Howe shall goe downe this afternone to Deptforde *and* Reddereth to reviewe the Globe the Newcastle ship the may flowre and the prosperous and to make choice of suche of them as they shall thinke fittest for the said vyage and as neare as they can to drive a prise of suche *of them* as they finde to be most fittest for ther vse.]

The L. Admirall being rode into Wilshire *and the messenger retornid from the court wthout delivering the l$\bar{r}$e directed to him* [and] m^r foulke Gryvell *Thrēr of the Navye* being moved by m^r Chery and Richard *Wright* for his furtheraunce in the L Admiralls absence for the vse of the Dockes of Wollw^{ch} and Deptford resorted hether to this assembly and promysed them

lrēs to my l. ō a messenger sent about ye vse of the dockes

1600
25 Sept.

to sende a messenger into wilshire wth all speede to my L. Admirall for his assent and that he in the meane tyme would take order the dockes shuld be prepared and made ready that the shippes may taken in at an instant after retorne of my L. aunswer.

Surveiors for the preparing of the shippes

It is ordered by the said Comitties that to everie ship that shalbe imployid in this viage ther shalbe 4 surveyors that shall take charge of the survey of eche ship in the sheething buildyng and all other provisions and to the shippes already bought [and apointed] these psons are severally appointed viz.

    Surveyors for the Hecto^r
  Mr Wiseman   Mr Leate
  Mr Burrell   M^r [Pierde] Pierd
    Surveyo^{rs} for the Assention
  Mr Garway   Mr Hamersley
  Mr Bostock   M^r [Lyng] Lynge
    Surveyors for ye Susan
  Mr Aldⁿ Bannyng   Captein Middleton
  Mr Tho Richardson   M^r [Lyng] Highlord

And it is ordered that the said [Comitties] *surveyo^{rs}* being apointed to the said shippes shall have aucthority [to] according to ther discretion wth thadvyse of the Carpenters to supply all defectes and [necessarie] repations *and all other necessarie provisions* of suche shipping as they are severally appointed vnto [and all other necessa]

The 26 of Septemb 1600.

1600
26 Sept.

  Mr Aldⁿ Bannyng   Mr Wm Chambers
  Mr Aldⁿ Hollyday   Mr Rich: Wiche
  [M^r] Captein Lancaster   Mr Harryson
  Capteyn Davies   Mr Wysemen

FFER was made to thes Comitties by M^r ferrers and m^r Toppesfelde of a hulke called the Phenixe of the burthen of   Tuns at the prise of 1400^{li} and to take her againe for 700^{li} at her retorne orels at xij^{cli}

ready wthout condition to take her againe wch offer is to be considered of and respited vntill another meeting.

1620
26 Sep^r.

Mr Alderman Bannynge is entreated by the resideu of the Cōmitties nowe assembled to deale wth m^r Alderman Holmeden for the sale of the Cherubim and to make report at the next meeting howe he findeth him disposed for the sale of the same ship and what he demaundeth for her.

It is ordered by thes Comitties assembled that the officer apointed to Warne the adventuro^{rs} of this viage shall Sommon them severallie to bring in their moneis viz the 3 part of ther adventure by the last of this moneth.

Mr Roger Howe is requested by this assemblie to travell in to the West Cuntrie to make provision for Dollers and victtelles for the shippes wherin he geveth no pnte assent but promiseth to advyse thereof and to geave his aunswere this daye.

An Inuentory of the Hector

Hector her inuentory

A mayne maste a mayne tope maste and a tope gallante maste,
A fore maste and a fore tope maste,
A boate spreete and a spirrit saile tope mast &c.
A missen mast and a mizen tope mast,
A tope
A mayne Course bonnet very good
A forecourse and bonnett
A mayne tope saile,
A spirrite saile bonnet,
A topp gallante sayle and a spirrit saile topp saile,
3[1] ankers and a kedger wherof one broake,
4 Cables good and bad,

10 wast clothes and a topp armor of bridgwaters
22 barrelles of powlder,
371 round shott,
400 base barr shott,
13 langerell shott,
13 lincke shott,
61 crosse barreshott,
18 musketts and 3 Callivers,
42 bandaleers musketts & callivers,
10 Swoards,
A sturbowe and a bender,
44 musket arrowes,
20 casses barrshott,
2 steele targetts,
Certen firewoorks,
4 dozen of latten Cases,
10 longe pikes,
11 shorte pikes,

A smale barrell of smale shott
7 demy coulveringes ladles &
  6 sponges,
2 saker ladles and 2 sponges,
3 minion ladles and 2 sponges,
2 wadhook
3 saker 3 demycoulveringᵉ and
  2 mynion formers &c.
Certen rowles of Match,
1 fier peeke,
A greate meltinge ladle and 1
  small.
2 ancyentᶜ and 28 pendauntᶜ

and a smale [stage] *flag* for the
  boat spirrit
A boate skiffe wᵗʰ 6 oars,
24 { 12 demicoulveringᶜ
     10 sakers
     2 mynions
7 Crowes Iron,
All such rigginge as shee
came from the sea wᵗʰ besidᶜ a
newe maynetope mast shrowd a
hawser cut out and made for
mayne *shrowdes* and a smale
rope.

The Inventory of the Asention

5 great ankers
2 Cables she rideth by,
2 Cables spiced together newe,
  one hath bene wett 6 tymes,
  the other never wett,
1 Cable never wett,
1 great warpinge hauser,
mastᶜ and yeardᶜ,

mayne Corse duble,
fowre Corse duble,
maine topsaile,
fore topsaile,
Sprit saile,
missonne
mayne bonnet,
fore bonnet,

2 top gallaunt sailes

All these are good sailes hauinge serued a strightᶜ voiage,
1 duble foresaile,
1 maine topsaile,   } all newe
1 wayne bonnet duble at the Clivers,
30 Shiners of brasse,
All standinge rigginge and runninge ropes, as haue serued for
  a straightᶜ voiage
9 demy Culueringes
13 Sackers   } wᵗʰ their Carriages brechingᶜ and tackels
2 fowlers
25 barrelles of powder,
shott rownd crosbar and langer sufficient for the powder,
10 Crowes of Iron,

40 musketṣ,
14 Calivers,
24 Pikes,
Spunges
Ladles ⎬ sufficient for such ordnaunce.
Ramers

The Inuentory of all such furniture and provision as belongeth to the good shipp called the great Susan.   *Great Susan her inuentory*

In primis 14 Demy Culueringṣ wth their carriages,
10 sakers wth their Carriages
1 hole newe shotte of cable never wett,
2 cables more she doth ryde by newe,
1 Cablett hawser,
3 warpes,
4 great ankers of 17^c 16^c & 14^c,
2 small ankers kedgers,
3 Catt blockes,
6 fidṣ and fid hamm^{rs},
1 newe mayne Course & bonnett,
1 newe mayne topsaile,
1 ould mayne topsaile,
1 newe fore course and bonnett,
1 other fore course bonnett and drabler,
1 fore topsaile,
1 sprit saile course and bonnett,
1 sprit saile topsaile,
1 mayne top gallaunt saile,
1 fore top gallaunt saile,
1 mizen course and bonnett,
  hir owningṣ fore and afte and hir mast clothes,
4 brasse shivers in her mayne knight,
4 brasse shivers in her mayne ramhed,
3 in her fore knight,
2 in her fore ram head,
2 in her cutt head,
2 in the knight of her mayne topsaile sheetṣ,

2 in her fore sheetẽ,
2 in hir boatẽ head and David,
2 in the fore shettẽ,
40 Coakes in blockes, wth all hir rigging well furnished wth mastẽ yeardẽ top mastẽ top gallaunte mastẽ and other hir appurtenaunces,
1 flag Antient, 7 pendauntẽ,
1 bell,
   the mayne shrowd,
   the mayne top mast shrowdẽ, the mayne top gallaunt mastẽ shrowdẽ the fore shrowdẽ fore top gallaunt mast ringinge, her sprit saile spritesaile top saile ringinge her mizen shrowdẽ and mizen topsaile shrowdẽ & rigging
8 barrellẽ of powder,
3 tanned hides and 2 peecẽ,
2 bondge barrells and som powder in one of them,
1 barrell of matche,
1 barrell wth pap Cartrages,
12 Dozen of Canvas Cartrages,
23 pottẽ wth powder,
24 [barrellẽ] *Ballẽ* wth fier woorke,
5 fier pikes wth stauẽs,
6 fier pikes w^{th}out stauẽs,
2 trunkẽ wth fier woo^rke,

18 swordẽ,	16 ladles for ordnaunce,
33 lattin cases,	3 wadhookes,
1 latten budge,	4 furmers,
1 close lanthorne,	28 shorte pikes,
30 musketẽ,	13 longe pikes,
6 hargabush a Crocke,	12 billẽ,
12 mouldẽ for muskettẽ & hargabush a crocke,	9 boare speeres,
	9 roddẽ for musketẽ,
2 meltinge ladles,	1 leather for a budge barrell wth charges in 28 baggẽ for small shott,
41 bandaliers,	
4 dozen of tuchboxes,	
6 steele targetẽ,	1 sheepskin,
26 sponges for ordnaunce,	1 fawkenett ladle and sponge,

1 wadhooke,
320 demy culueringe round shott,
220 saker round shott,
47 Demy culveinge crosbar & saker crosse barr,
27 langrell and Chaine shott,
45 fawkenett shott,
24 breechinge for ordnaunce, part of a small coyle of rope
10 Lashers of ordnaunce,
46 takles of ordnaunce,
1 greate meltinge ladle, muskett shott in a box being full
24 leadℓ for peecℓ
11 crowes of Iron,
6 rope sponges,
1 great kettle of Copp to seeth vittles in for 80 men
1 pease pott. 1 skimer. 2 gridirons,
2 frieinge panns. 2 spittℓ. 1 trivitt,
1 paire of pott hookℓ,
1 mustard querne,
2 axes. 3 trayes. 1 fleshooke,
6 lanthornes, 1 tapborer, 5 gannchookℓ,
1 paire of bellowes,
1 great lanthorne for Admirall,
1 longe boat and a skiffe wth their oares belonginge to the boate,
1 standinge bed wth pillers vallens and curtaynes for the richauntℓ,

7 Running glasses 7 Compasses,
18 newe topsailes sheett blockℓ for store
25 single blockℓ wooden pinnes.
25 duble blockℓ wooden pinnes,
26 Deadman eyes,
1 newe foretopsaile purrell,
1 newe top gallaunt purrell,
10 Iron esses for shrowdℓ,
10 Deadman eyes bound wth Iron hooke for hir Chamwellℓ,
2 pompes. 2. Iron brakes,
1 Iron hooke to hale vp boxes,
6 oares to the pinnesse wth mastℓ and saile
12 oares for the longe boate,
1 Winles ⎫
1 David ⎬ belonginge to the boat wth a [rud]
1 Rudder ⎭ saile
lyne for Rutline,
3 boy ropes. 4 boyes. 2 haunsplugℓ,
2 dipsey leadℓ. 4 soundinge leades,
3 newe boate hookℓ, 4 luffe hookes,
Sennett and spun yarne and Canbins esteemed 1^c w^{tt},
1 dozen of platters 2 steepe tubbs,
6 burrecoes. 2 firkins wth tallowe,
1 great baskett for bread,
1 duble windinge blocke,
1 single windinge blocke,

1 snatche blocke,	& afte,
4 brase shivers to the 3 blockes esteemed 1ᶜ wᵗᵗ	16 newe chaynes and chayne bultℓ for the mayne shrowdℓ @ 3ᶜ 3ᵠʳ 9ˡ
1 grinstone wᵗʰ his Irons and trough	12 newe platℓ of Iron for the mayne takles @ ᶜ wᵗᵗ,
1 windinge hawser newe,	1 settle bedd in the Cabbin,
1 table wᵗʰⁱⁿ the Cabbin, grateningℓ & nettingℓ fore	6 small baskettℓ for bread,

⚜

The 27 Septemb̄ 1600.

Mʳ Aldⁿ Bannyng	Mʳ Wᵐ Chambers
Mʳ Aldⁿ Hollyday	Mʳ Roger Howe
Mʳ Rich: Staper	Mʳ Rich Wiche
Mʳ Wᵐ Garway	Mʳ Harryson
Mʳ Rich. Wiseman	Mʳ Burrell

1000 Dolleɾs of Mʳ highe-lorde

THIS assembly have contracted wᵗʰ mʳ Hilliard for 1000 Dollers at the rate of 4s. 6d. the doller to be taken [also] at that rate for his stocke of 200ˡⁱ, and the overplus beinge [repᵈ] 25ˡⁱ is to be pᵈ vnto him vppon the deliuery of his dollers, and yf the adventurors shall at thende of Two monethes mislyke to [take] hold them at the said valewe of 4s. 6d. then the said mʳ heliard is content and hath agreed to Receave the same againe at the same rate and to repay the xxvˡⁱ to him dd by the said adventuroʳˢ or ther Thr̄er.

The Mare scurge

Wher a motion hath bene made by mʳ Stap for the Buyinge of the Erle of Cumb̄landes ship called the Mare scurge the same ship being offered vnto them after they *have* furnished them selfes of the proportion of shipping agreed vppon by the geñalyty these Comitties cannot by any warraunt to them geaven proceade in the buying of the same ship her burthen being so great, wherby ther Tunage agreed vppon shalbe so greatly exceaded, but are of opinion that yf she were prepared and fyttid for service she would be a meet ship for the next [yeres ship] yeres viage but in any wyse not to doubt wthall for the present action in hand.

Mr Howe having bene moved at the Last meeting to take a iorney for the furthering of this viage into the West Cuntrey for the providing of Ryalls and to Joine wth Capten Davies for the provision biskett and syder, dothe very freindlie and kindly assent to take the same busines in hande and wilbe ready to ryde the next weeke, against wch tyme Remembraunces and instruccõns of the proportion of thinges to be provided are to be considered if, and howe the thinges provided shalbe p^d for together wth ther Charges to be defraied. Mr Howe & captein Davies to go in to the west Cuntrey

Mr Burrell is at this assemblie apointed and is contented to take the *generall* survey from tyme to tyme of all the shippes apointed for this viage, who may informe the Comitties of the wantes of the same shippes and what necessarie supplies belongeth vnto them. Mr Burrell generall surveyor

And it is ordered that Surveyors of the severall shippes wch are apointed to see the Supplies of the same [shalbe] shall before they proceade to enter into the said Supplies present vnto the Comitties in some of ther assemblies the pticlers of the wantes [and to be supp] and then to supply the same by order by the said cõmytties [to them to] be geaven to the said Surveyors. Suruetighers of ships

[The] One of the owners of the Phenix being here before the Comitties who could of him self wthout his partno^r assent to ther offer of 1200^{li} for the same ship, tyme is taken vntill monday for the ferther agreem^t in the bargaine thereof, and wthall that in the said agreement be included certeñ furniture of the ship wch is not mencõed in the inventory exhibited, viz a Cable a cablet 13 coile of rope on coyle of white Ropes 8 barrelles of pitche 5 barī tarre 18 boltes of Ipsw^{ch} Poldavies and x boltes of wormall Poldavies.

It is ordered that m^r Burrell shall provide timber for the wantes of the shipping and what money he shall disburce therin at reasonable rates shall be rep^d him by the Thr̃ers or one of them. Provision of tymber by Mr Burrell

The 29 of September.

Mr Aldⁿ Bannyng
Mr Aldⁿ Hollyday
Mr Rich : Staper
Captein Lancaster
Mr Rich Wyseman
[Captein Davies]

M^r fra^s Chery
Mr Wm Chamber
M^r   Harryson
Mr Allabaster
Captein Davies
Mr Burrell

I^r is resolved that Captein Davies shall drawe out a p^po^rtion *of victualles* for 500 men for that is supposed that so great a nomber of men wilbe imployed in this viage.

It is alsoe agreed that Capten Lancaster Capten Davies Mr Chambers and Mr Harryson shall goe downe to morrowe morning to see what Pynnaces they can finde in the River fytt to be imploied in the viage and to morrowe in the after none to meet at Mr Aldⁿ Bannynges and ther to make report to ye residewe of the Comitties of ther opinions of suche Pynnaces as they have surveid.

An Inventory of such thinges as belonge to the Assention
    28 September 1600.

Assention her Inuentory

A mayne mast fore mast and a mizen mast wth all their top mastes,
A mayne top, mizen top and sprit top saile,
Itm yeardes for all these mastes,
Itm a mayne course buble,
Itm a mayne bonnet double at the at the clewes,
Itm a newe mayne bonnet duble at the clewes,
Itm a mayne top saile,
Itm a newe mayne top saile,
Itm a mayne top gallaunt saile,
Itm a fore Course duble,
Itm a newe fore course duble,
Itm a fore bonnet and a drabler,
Itm a fore top saile,
Itm a fore top gallaunt saile,

Itm a sprit saile,
Itm a sprit saile bonnet,
Itm a sprit saile top saile,
Itm a mizen,
Itm a mizen bonnet,
Itm a flagge and an Antient,
Itm twelue ould pendaunt(,
Itm scrowdes, stakles, pendent(, wth block(&c belonginge to the mast(and saiies,
Itm thirty shivers of brasse,
Itm two Cables wch she rideth by,
Itm a shott of Cables,
Itm a newe Cable,
Itm a great hawser,
Itm a shete anker of eighteene hundreth,
Itm two other Ankers of 1500 p peece,
Itm an other Anker of 1300 p peece,
Itm an other Anker of 800,
Itm a boates Anker,
Itm a skiffes Anker,
Itm two pompes,
Itm two standardes of Iron,
Itm two pompbrakes of Iron,
Itm divers pompbockeses,
Itm two kittles for the fornases,
Itm an other kettle for victualles,
Itm a pitch kettle,
Itm nyne Demyculvering(,
Itm thirteene sakers wth their Carriages, Conies and bedes,
Itm two fowlers wth their fowre Chambers,
Itm a murtherer wth two chambers,
Itm takles and britching(for the ornaunc,
Itm sponges and ladles for the ordnaunce,
Itm round shott crosse barr and langrell, and case shott indifferent store,
Itm 25 barrelles of powder,
Itm six brasse bales,

Itm Thirty cases for carriages,
Itm two tand hides,
Itm ten crowes of Iron,
Itm Thirty five muskettℯ,
Itm Thre hargabushes of croke,
Itm 16 Callivers,
Itm thirty bãdalires,
Itm two lattin bugge barrelles,
Itm three Carriages of iron for shott,
Itm two dozen of pikes,
Itm five billes,
Itm muskett and caliver shott,
Itm a longe boate,
Itm a skiffe,
Itm ten oares,
Itm two paier of Canhookes,
Itm a bell,
Itm mast clothes of redd Cotten,
Itm a greate lanthorne for the poop wth six others.

The 30 September 1600.

Mr Aldⁿ Hollyday   Mr Rich. Wiche
Mr Rich : Staper   Captein Lancaster
Mr Wm Garway.   Mr Wm Chambers
Mr Rich Wiseman   M^r   Harrison
M^r Jo : Eldred   Mr John Bate
Captein Davies

The thrers warraunt for y^e payment of [moneys] moneys

T is orderid that the Thrers of this felowship shall dysburce for the provision and furniture of the shippes and other necessarie occasions belonging̃ to the viage suche somẽs of money as shalbe warraunted by order of [three] *fowre* of the Comitties at the least vnder ther handes and they shall not otherwyse wthout suche warraunt disburce vppon anie one occasion at anie tyme above the valewe of x^{li} vppon ther owne pill.

It is ordered that m̃ Allabaster shalbe entreated to take the charge of keapinḡ of the Accomptes of this felowship yf his leasure will p̱mitt him, and yf otherwyse then Julinus Beamishe to be requirid to take the same charge. _{M^r Allabaster}

At this assemblie m̃ Altham was present and did reade over and penne the booke of priviledges of this Soscietie havinḡ spent all the forenone in the p̱vsinḡ thereof for the wch thes Comitties appointed m^r Aldⁿ Bannynḡ on of the Thr̄ers to [pay him] geave him for his paines therein the somme of fowre poundes. _{The reading of the drawght of the pattent}

A warraunt signed to one of the thr̄ers to pay m̃ *Wyseman* [Staper] a hundred poundes for the provisyon of thinḡs necessarie for the hecto^r. _{Hecto^r 100^{li}}

A coppy of a l̃re written in the behalfe of Capten Davis to the
right ho: the Erle of Essex.

Right honorable o^r dewties most humbly remembred vnto yor good L: wheras wee and divers other m̃chaunts of London were heertofore desirous to sett forth a viage to the East Indians in trade of m̃chaundize and for want of meanes to further o^r intention haue bene hetherto staied, wee haue nowe at length obteined not onely her ma^{ies} roiall assent to procead therin but are promised such tollerations and favo^{rs} otherwise both for the transportation of manyes the better to make o^r trade and other ỹmũyties and priviledges to pas vnder the greate seale as that wee are incorrraged therby wth all expedition to enter into the preparation of shippinge and furniture fitt for such an attempte and beinge thus farre entred into o^r provision wee nowe rest vppõ thassent of this bearo^r Capten Davies yor L: servant to be imploied in the viage as a principall Director of the same whoe havinge ben moved to that ende seemeth soe farr willinge to deale in the action as yor L. shall give likinge therto, wheruppon we humbly presuminge vppon yor L: redines to further anie enterprise wch may bringe hono^r to o^r country or benefit to the com̃on wealth do herby humbly intreat yor L^s: favo^{rs} to be [to be] added to this busines and to give your L: Consent for his imployment in the same, in wch behalf wee shall accompte yor L: an honorable patron therof and so humbly take o^r leave of yor good L: London the last of Sept:

1600.
The [2] *first* of october 1600.

Mr Aldⁿ Bannyng   Mr Rich: Wiseman
Mr Aldⁿ Hollyday   Mr John Eldred
Mr Aldⁿ Smithe   Mr Wm Chambers
Mr Rich. Staper   Mr   Harryson
Mr Wm Garway   Mr Rich Witche
Mr Captein Lancaster   Captein Davies
Mr Burrell

A proportion of Victualles.

T this assemblie Captein Davies presented [a proportion] in wryting a proportion of vittell both bread meale beare [beavere] ceyder wyne Beefe Porke &c as appereth by the pticlers thereof sett downe [after other thinges in this meeting sett downe and agreed vppon] and redd at this assemblie.

Proportion of victualles comitted to Ald Bannyng Cap Lancaster Cap davies Mr Allabaster

But the same *proportion* being pvsed and exaīed in this assemblie it was thought fytt the same shuld be cōmitted over againe to be further considered of by m̄ Aldⁿ Bannyng Captein Lancaster and Capteñ Davies together [at] wth mr Allabaster at mr Allabasters house [shuld] *wher they may* meet to morrowe morning and ther [to] sett downe an exact proportion of the said vittell and other thing^s [and] *in w^h conference* what soever proportion of vittell they shall agree vppon *this assemblie do agree* shall stand for a Resolution of the whole provysion of vittell for the viage.

Peas to be prouided

Mr Garway acquainting this assemblie that he hath bene solicited for the accepting of a certeñ proportion of peas for the said viag is requirid to talke wth the partie and to gett his lowest prise for the same.

a proportion of merchaundize

It is alsoe orderid that the said m̄ Aldⁿ Bannyng Captein Lancaster m̄ Allabaster together wth m̄ Eldred and mr ffitche shall in ther meeting to morrowe morning at m̄ Allabasters house *conferre* of the merchaundize fitt to be pvided for the viage and to [make] sett downe ther opinions of the said marchaundize that the same may be presentid to these Comitties at ther next meeting to be further resolved vppon.

Mʳ Waldo resorted to this assemblie and solicited them for the imployment of one frauncis Wilson to be imployed in the viage as a Purser of one of the shippes, to whom this assemblie made aunswer that they would consider of his motion. *frauncis Wilson his sute to be a Purser.*

John Johnson dwellinge at lymehouse doeth offer him self to [them] this assemblie to be imploied as a m̃ in the viage.

The 3 of [Septemb] *October* 1600.

Mʳ Aldⁿ Bannyng   Mʳ Wᵐ Garway
Mʳ Aldⁿ [Smythe] Hollyday   Mʳ Wᵐ Chambers
Mʳ Aldⁿ Smyth   Mʳ Wᵐ Harryson
Captein Lancaster   Mʳ Rich: Wiche
Mʳ Jo Eldred   Mʳ Allabaster
Mʳ Roger Howe   Capten Davies
                Mʳ Burrell.

THE adventure of the viage rysin͡g so farre above the proportion first expectid [Requiring] Requireth a larger proportion of shippin͡g then was formerlie agreed vppon and therfore this assemblie thinke it fytt the mare scurge wᶜʰ is nowe taken in to the docke at wolwᶜʰ shallbe surveyd and exaīed whether in state as she is she may be made fytt for this viag̃ in convenient tyme and yf she be founde in suche state as she may be made fytt then my L of Cumberland to be [further] delt wᵗʰall touchin͡g the pryse of his ship wᵗʰ suche as shalbe hereafter agreed vppon And for the Survey of the state of the said ship thes persons herevnder named are appointed [who hav] to go downe to morrowe and to serche into all her defectes and sett downe anote of the same in wrytinge wᶜʰ done to present the same at the next meetin͡g of the Comitties. *Mare scurge*

    Capteñ Lancaster   Mʳ Chambers
    Mʳ Burrell   Capteñ Mydleton
    Mʳ Wyseman   Mʳ Harryson
      wᵗʰ suche Carpenters as they thing meet to vse.

My l. thrers lre touching S Tho Michelborne knight

A lre written from the L Thrẽrer to thes Comitties in the behaulf of Sr Edward Michelborne to be imployed in the viage as a principall Cõmaunder was reade wherin his L. vseth muche pswasion to the Companie to accept of his imployment yet soe as he is lothe to vrge them against ther liking wch motion [because] this assemblie have [not] noe lyking of for that they purpose not to imploy anie gent in any place of charg or cõmaundem^t in the said viage for that besides ther owne [conceipte] *mislike* of the imploym^t of suche they knowe the genʃalyty will not indure to hear of such a motion [but] *and* yf they shuld be ernestlie prest therin they would wthdrawe ther adveutures, therfore this [Companie] *assembly* do intreat m^r Garway to [entreat] *move* his L : [not to expecte] to be pleased [that] noe further to vrge the imploym^t of this gent to the Companie, and to geave them leave to sort ther busines wth men of ther owne qualety and not to expecte that they shuld make any further motion of this matter to the genʃalyty lest the suspition of the imploym^t of gents being taken hold vppon [will] do dryve a great nũber of the adventurers to wthdrawe ther Contributions.

[It is resolved at this assemblie that ther shalbe no pynnaces imployed in the viage but *onlie* suche *small* Lancher pynnaces as shalbe carried in the shippes to be putt out as occasion shall serve and to be taken in againe]

A Comission for the provision of thinges in the West Cuntrey

Captein Lancaster m̃ Allabaster and m̃ howe are required to sytt together to morrowe morning and to wryte a Comission to Captein Davies and suche other as shalbe imployed in the west Cuntrey for the provision of suche vittelles and other thinges as [that] those partes to yelde.

The iiijth of October, 1600.

My Lorde of Comberland.

M^r alderman Baynynge
M^r alderman Hallidaie
Mr Willm Garwaye
Mr John Eldred

Mr Willm Harrison
Mr Middleton
Mr Richard Wiseman
Mr Richard Stap

Mr Willm Chamber   Mr Roger Howe
Mr Richard Wyche   Captein Lancaster
         Mr Burrell

Y Lord of Combrland makinge an offer of his shippe called the Mallescourge, to the Companie to Sve in this voiage to the Easte Indias, and the Comytties abouenamed havinge pvsed the Invetorye of the said said and made some estymate of her valewe, they did offer vnto his honor, ffor the said shippe and all her ordenance Sailes Cabls Anckers and all her fourniture as she is nowe, the sōme of three thowsand pound℮, the whiche *his* honor will not Accept, But did tell them yf they could thinke well of yt he would sell her vnto them for ffower thowsand pound℮ As she nowe is wth all her ffornyture, affyrmynge that he would not take five hondreth pound℮ more, of enie other, and after muche dispute his honor and the Comitties abouenamed are agreed that fower Marchant℮ and [twooe] *fower* carpenters shall vewe and survey the said shippe, and vpon there Report℮ they will consider againe of the matter, and geue his honor a full answer.

    Speche had wth ye Erle touchinge the Mall escourge

    These Comytties haue agreed that M^r alderman Baynynge shall deliu vnto M^r howe five hondreth pound℮, to be sent into the west contrey, there to be Imployed in suche busynes as apptayneth to the voiage, ffor whiche also divers of them haue subscribed a warraunte ffor his further discharge accordinge to the Comp̄ order, and for the pvidinge of the said breade or enie other necessaries there is appointed to goe to Dartmowthe and Plymowthe, Thomas Baker and Robarte Pope to Joyne wth capteine John Davies ffor pvidinge all thing℮ there.

    500^li to be deliuered Mr Howe to be sent to the West Cuntrey

    Mr Harrison is Requested to write to some of his ffrind℮ at Hull ffor the pvision of Peason, and that he will vndertake the fournishinge of them, and that they shall need one hondreth quarters of peason and fiftie quarters of Beanes, he saithe he will doe his beste therein but saithe it weare there best to send one downe expresse and so they should be assured to haue it well done, but he saithe he will write and geue order ffor it, and they haue agreed that *if* he will send downe *one* of purpose for pvision

    Prouision of peas & Beanes

of the same pease and beanes he shalbe allowed ffor his paines and traveile.

Prouision for Caske

Capteine Lancaster, Capteine Middleton, Mr chambers, and Mr harrison are Requested to take care for p̃vidinge of all the caske that maie be needefull for the voiage wch is as follow^th.

The proportion of Caske.

caske ffor biere, 170 tõnes, to be of pipes bound wth ashen hoopes
The Wine to be in good caske, and to be Iron bound
30 Tonnes of caske ffor beeffe in newe hogeshedẽ Iron bound
40 Tonnes of hogeshedẽ ffor Porke
30 Tonne of drie caske ffor peason and beanes
12 Tonne of drie caske for Oatemeale
30 Tonne of caske for veniger, to Iron bound
3½ tonne of Iron bounde caske for aquavita
6 barrells ffor honie bound wth Iron
one Tonne of drie caske ffor mustard seed
one Tonne of drie caske ffor Rice
2½ Tonne in smale caske for Rape Oile Ironbound
Water Caske hooped wth Iron 150 Tonnes whereof 40 Tonnes of hogeshedẽ
8 Dozen of baricoes hooped wth Iron.

   in the Afternoone Did meete more
  Mr Staper   Mr Cordell
  Mr Wiseman   Mr Stephins
  Mr Burrell   Mr Burde
    nic° Symons

The said *Comitties* beinge desyered to talke and conferre aboute the price of the Mall escourge, had long conference aboute the same and in the end my lorde came againe him sellffe tellinge them he p̃ceaved what paines they had taken about this busynes, but he said he would take no lesse then .iiij. m. l̃ whiche seeinge they would not geue, he would lose no tyme more aboute the same, but since they would not buye her he would p̃ceede about his owne busynes, and so prayed them to doe thers and so dep̃ted, but they offred him 3500ˡ—&c.

The 6 of october 1600.

Mr Aldⁿ Bannyng	Mr Roger Howe
Mr Aldⁿ Hollyday	Mr Wm Chamber
Mr Rich: Staper	Mr Rich. Wyche
Mr Lancaster	Mr John Bate
Mr Rich: Wiseman	Captein Dovies
Mr John Eldred	Mr Burrell

MR Richard Stap and Mr John Eldred are required bothe by them selfes and by ther best meanes that they shall thinke meet [fitt] to vse, in the provision of all Clothes and kersies that shall be thought fitt to be sent in this viage. *Comitties for ye Prouision of clothe & Kersey*

Mr *George* Smythes and Mr *Richard* Yonson being admitted this day to adventure in the viage CC^{li} a peece they do promise to bring in ther said adventures in Spanishe money [at the rate] Ryalles of 8 at xviij^d the li proffite and yf the Companie do buy them at a lesse rate then they will accepte of lesse as other men do sell them. *Smythes & Yonson Goldsmithes to bring in 400^{li} in Royalles of 8.*

It is ordered that m̃ wiche and Richard Wright shall compounde wth m̃ Covell for the prouision of 60 or 70 quarters of peas white kylne dried, and to geave [som] him suche consideration for his travell therin as they can drawe him to accepte of *Prouision of Peas*

⁕

The 7 of october 1600.

Mr Aldⁿ Bannyng	Mr Allabaster
Mr Aldⁿ Hollyday	Mr Roger Howe
Mr Rich: Staper	Mr John Eldred
Mr Wm Garway	Mr Wm Chambers
Captein Lancaster	Mr Rich: Wyche
Mr Rich: Wyseman	Captein Davies

THES Comitties entringe into Conference to drawe the [resolution] bargaine of the Malyce Scurge to a resolution [or ende] to the ende the preparation of the viage be not hindred by restinge in an vncertentie of o^r shipping they did in thende growe to this *The Malyce Scurge bought for 3700^{li}*

Conclusion that Mr Ald^n Bannynge and Mr Ald^n Holliday for the Companie, shuld Joine wth m^r Garway and m^r Allabaster who have Comission from my L of Cumberland to agree vppon the prise of the same ship, who departinge aside after some [offer] Loovinge and biddinge [thervppon] betwene them did agree vppon the price of three thousand seven hundred poundes to be p^d for the same ship wth all her ordnaunce Carriages tackle mastes sayles and all furniture whatsoever as well expressed in the inventorie as not therin mencōned wch anie way doeth belonge to the said ship, and the said parties havinge made this agreem^t amonge them selfes presented the same to the residewe of this Assemblie who did well allowe of ther said bargaine and accepted thereof accordinglie and afterwardes my L. of Cumberland him self cōminge hether and beinge made acquainted what had past touchinge the bargaine of the said ship by the said Mr Garway and Mr Albaster did *for his part* assent to the said bargaine, and in like sort these Comitties for ther part. Soe as an absolute agreem^t was made by both parties to take the ship in the Companies charge wth all worke to her belonginge from this day.

Bargaines & sales of the 4 shippes to be made to feoffees in trust.

It was at this assemblie agreed that 4 severall bargaines and sales by writinge indented shuld be made betwene the severall owners of the 4 shippes and fowre of thes Comitties to take the bargaines and sales of the same shippes to ye vse of the generall adventuro^{rs} wherbie the propertie of the same shippes may be transferred out of the owners in dewe forme of Lawe and the parties to whom the *sale of the* said shippes shalbe conveied [vnto] are the persons heervnder named videlt

feoffees in trust for the shippes bought } Mr Roger Howe
Mr John Eldred
Mr Wm Chambers
Mr Rich: Wyche
Mr Governor

This Comitties have also appointed for the surveyinge of the worke and prepation of the saide ship called the Malice Scurge, and for the providing of all thinges necessarie for the same ship the psons heervnder named viz.

 Mr Thomas Cordall   Mr Robert Bell   *Surveyors of*
 Mr Rich: [Wytche] Wyche   Mr Greenewell   *ye Malice Scurge*

 Mr Aldn Bannynge doeth geave his worde to this assemblie   *Josephe Salamon Purser of the Susan*
to be aunswerable for *Joseph Salamon* the Purser of the [susan]
Susan, that he shall faithfully pforme anie trust that the Companie shall imploy him in the preparing of thingℓ necessarie for
the same ship and in disposing of the same.

 Mr [Aldn] Rich. Stap doeth in like manner geave his worde   *Georg Parsons Purser of the Hector*
for the like fidelitie and trew service of George Parsons, the
Purser of the Hector.

 Mr Wm Garway doeth alsoe vndertake for the like fidelitie   *Wm Leake Purser of the Assention.*
of the service of Wm Leake Purser of the Assention.

 Wm Burrage Boatesoñ of the Malice Scurge to whose handes   *The Boateson of the Malice scurge*
the Custodie of muche of the rigging of the same ship was
cōmitted by my L. Cumberland came before thes Comitties [as]
and was by them enterteyned to loke to the furniture [and] of
the same ship and to the worke to be done vppon her in furnishing her for viage, the wch he is Content to do.

    The viijth of October 1600.

 Aldn Bannyng   Mr Wm Chambers
 Aldn Hollyday   Mr Rich Wyche
 Aldn Smythe   Mr Harryson
 Mr Staper   Capteñ Davies
 Captein Lancaster   Capteñ Myddleton

T is agreed at this assemblie that ther shalbe pd to   *100li for provision of Caske*
Mr Wm Chambers the somme of one hundred
poundes for the provision of Caske and yron
hoopes, and a warraunt geaven to the Threr
vnder 4 of the Comitties handes for the paiment thereof.

 It is also ordered that mr Richard Wiche and Richard Wright   *Beanes & Musterd seed*
shall contract wth mr Covell for the buying and provyding of
xxtie quarters of Beanes and 30 Bushelles of Musterd seed to

F

be bought at the best rates he can [and] for the provision of the viage.

A Computation agreed vppon the 8 of octobo⟨r⟩ 1600 for the victualling of the shippes following in a viage to y⟨e⟩ Est Indies rated in Tonnage and men as hereafter followeth viz.

The Scourge allowed men	200	rated tuñz 600
The Hector allowed men	100	rated tuñs 300
Thassention allowed men	80	rated toñs 260
The Susan allowed men	80	rates toñz 240
The Pynnace allowed men	40	rated toñs 100
	Men 500	toñz 1500

Bread for 20 monethes	Bread for 16 monethes of 30 daies p moneth					
this propor-tion altered 15 octobre by the Comittyes then assembled.		c	lb		li s d	
	at 24ˡⁱ p man	1714 1 4	toñz 150		1028 08 0	
	Meale for 4 monethes at 30ˡⁱ p man p moneth					
			li			
		535 2 24	toñs 30		267 17 4	
Beare for 20 monethes Syder Wyne	Beare for 4 monethes at a pottle p man p day the hoggeshed accoumpted cleare of leakeage 80 gallons	gℓ 30000	toñs 170		510 00 00	
	Syder for 8 monethes at a quart p day at the former rate	gℓ 30000	toñs 170		680 00 00	
	Wine for 8 monethes at a pint p day at the former allowaunce	gℓ 15000	toñs 80		960 00 00	
	Beef for 4 monethes at [a] 1ˡⁱ p man p day					
		c q li				
		538 2 14	toñz 30		428 10 00	
	Porke for 10 monethes at ½ˡⁱ p man p day					
Meate for 17 monethes		c				
		669 2 16	toñz 40		669 12 6	
	Peace and beanes for porke adioyning for 10 monethes at ⅛ pint for day p man is bushellℓ					
	1172		toñs 88		293 00 00	
	ffyshe for 3 whole monethes at a bacaliaw p man p day	45000 fishes	toñs 25		225 00 00	

Otemeale for 3 monethes adioyning to fishe at
½ p day for a man makes bishelles 351   lt   s   d
                                        tons 12   105   06   00
Steele wheate extraordinarie and w^{th}out pro-   No proui-
portion for 3 monethes at ½ pinte p man p   sion for
day is bushell 351   tons 9   87   00   00 meate for 3
                                                                      monethes in
Cheese being olde holland cheese at discretion   the Cuntrey
                                                                      wch the
the whole fleet winds 20   tons 2½   60   00   00 Cuntrey
                                                                      shall finde
Butter reparted vppon all the shippes fir-   this proui-
kins 80   tons 2   72   00   00 sion altered
                                                                      the 15 of
Oyle for 16 monethes at a quart p man p   october and
moneth gallons 2000   tons 10   500   00   00 reduced to
                                                                      250 bushells
Vineger for all the shipps to be repted 30 tons
                                         tons 30   270   00   00

Aquavite for all 14 hogsh^{ds} viz

    The Scourge   6 ⎫
    The Hector   3 ⎪   lt   s   d
    Thassention   2 ⎬ hh 14   tons 3½   175   00   00
    The Susan   2 ⎪
    The Pinnace   1 ⎭

Honny for all the shippes together
                        barr^{ells} 6   tonz 1   56   00   0
Suger
Spices   sinamn 30^{ll}   nutmegges 15^{ll}
Cloves 6^{ll}   suger 50^{ll}   pepper 12^{ll}   16   05   00
Musterd seede for all the fleet
                        bushell 32   tons 1   12   16   0
Rice for all the shippes   20   tons 1   20   00   00
Rape oile for lampes for all the shippes
            hogshedd 10   10   tons 2½   60   00   00
Candelles 250^{ll} for 4 shippes couered in wax
                                     tons [16] 2   16   13   4
Lampes for all the shippes 5 dossen 60 t   00   15   0
Candelles 100^{ll} eche shipp ordinarie Candells
                                     tons ½   8   6   8
Cookes prouision at discretion

A saine hookes fizgigꝭ harping iron
Salt for all the whole 5 shippes 2 waigh toñs 2   7 00 00
Water Caske for all the fleete   toñs 150   150 00 00
                                       ─────────   ─────────
                          To all toñs 1011   6600 4 10
                                       ─────────   ─────────

    The merchaundiz to be sent in the said shippes viz.

                                                                                     ₶   s   d
Yron   toñs 30 at   270 00 00
Tynn wrought   toñs 5   330 00 00
Tynn vnwrought in barres   toñs 5   420 00 00
Leade   toñs 100   1700 00 00
        Clothes 80 of thes sortes vizt
2 skarlettꝭ in 4 halfes
4 Stammettꝭ
8 blewes
8 Azures
8 Plunkettꝭ
8 popingoies
4 grasse greenes
8 sadd greenes
8 venice greenes
4 olive Collers
8 Reading Clothes mingled 2 of eche colo'
2 heare Collers
4 violettꝭ
4 primerose Collers
───   ₶   s   d
80   at 16ˡⁱ p cloᵗʰ p esteme   1280 00 00
───
Deuonshire kersies of like Collers 80 peeceꝭ
             s
        at 50 p kꝭ   200 00 00
hamshires of all collers   20 peceꝭ at 3ˡⁱ 10ˢ   65 00 00
Norwᶜʰ stuffe 100 at discretion   250 00 00
    The present to be geaven to the kinge
A Belt or girdell
A Case of Pistolles   ₶i
Some [Plumes] Plewmes   present 30

Looking glasses
Platters spones and toyes of glasse
Spectakell[es] and Drinking glasses of all sort[es]
An Ewer of plaine Silver

	li	s	d
To all 4545 oo oo	6600	4	10
	4545	0	0
	11145	4	10

Order is geaven [by] *in* this assemblie of the Comitties before menconed that Mr Ald^n Bannynge Mr Ald^n holliday Mr Ald^n Smithe Mr Stap & Capteiñ Lancaster shall agree and Compounde wth Captein Davies for his enterteynment in this viage and to geave him therin all reasonable contentment and having compounded wth him to report what they have done therin at the next assemblie of the Comitties.

Captein Davies his enterteynment.

Mr Ald^n Bannyng Mr Wm Chamber
Mr Tho Cordell   Mr Rich Wiche
Mr Wm Garway   Mr Wm Harryson
Mr Roger Howe   M^r Jo Bate
Mr John Eldred   Capteiñ Middleton

At this assemblie the Comitties appointed to Compounde wth Capteiñ Davies for his enterteynment in the viage have deliuered in wrytinge ther said Composition wherto the said Captein Davies hath Subscribed his name wch agreem^t is to this effect, first they have agreed to geave him for his Charges expended and to be expended in attending the preparation of the viage the somme of C^{li}, and to Lende him the somme of CC^{li} to be rep^d againe to ye Companie vppon his retorne out of suche allowaunce of proffit as is allowed him for his viage W^{ch} they do agree to allowe him in this manner viz. That yf the retorne of the viage do bringe forth and yeld for one, two, then he to have of that profite five hundred poundes, and yf the proffite of the viage doe bringe forth [out] Three for one then he to have out of the said proffite one thousand poundes And yf it bringe forth fowre for one then he to have out of [that] *the said* proffite fifteene hundred poundes, and yf the proffit of the viage to yeld for one five then he to have of [that] *the* proffit the somme of two thowsand poundes for his full

The full agreement wth Captein Davies

recompence of the said viage. W^th wch enterteynment the said Capteín Davies is verie well pleased and hath promised to pforme his indevo^r faithfullie in the said viage accordinge to his best knowledge and skill, and hath sett his hand to a note of this Composition wch remaineth in the Custodie of Richard Wright the Secretorie of the busines of this viage.

<small>The copie of a L^re written by my L. Th^rer for credite of muneis to be dd in the West Cuntrey</small>

After my hartie comendacõns I am desired by divers of the merchaunt(es) of the East Indian trade that suche money as yo^u have in yor handes of her ma^es might be p^d unto them or suche as they shall depute in that behaulf for the receipte thereof They having great occasion to imploy the same money ther for the setting forth of the same viage to the East Indies and they will pay here into her ma^es receipt presentlie so muche money againe as they shall receave of yo^u This offer of thers seemeth to me to be verie good for yo^u and as I make no doubte of ther sufficiency being sundry aldermen and m̃chaunt(es) of great wealth that are to repay the same So nevertheles I do leave it to yor self to doe therin that wch yo^u shall thinke best for her Ma^ts service and yor owne safetie and so I Commende yo^u to god this 8 of october 1600

Y^r verie Loving frend
T: Buckhurst

To my verie Loving frendes her Ma^es receivors of the Counties of Devon and Cornewell and to all the officers of the Portes w^thin the same Counties.

<small>Syder</small>

Mr Chambers is intreated to deale wth one M^r fletcher for the puision of suche sider as he can procure to be deliuered here in London at the best rate he can drawe him vnto.

<small>Capteín Baker. A Comission for ye pruision in the West Cuntrey
Peter fraunccis a Portugall enterteyned.</small>

A Comission for Capteñ baker to goe downe in to the west Cuntrey for provision of victuall drawen by m̃ howe was read and he intreated to write it out againe that it may be signed by the Comitties.

Mr Ald^n Bannyng m^r Ald^n hollyday m^r Ald^n Smyth and m^r Richard Stap being also aucthorised by the residewe of the Comitties to compounde and agree wth one Peter ffrauncis of Bridgewater in the Countie of Somersett a Portugall borne for his enterteynment in this viage in to the Est Indies Doe present vnto this assemble a Contract made wth the said Peter ffrauncis vnder his hand to this effect, That the said Peter is to have for his said viage x^{li} in hande to beare his charges vntill the shipps do enter into ye viage, and in the viage to have v^{li} p moneth to goe in the shipp wher Captein Davies doeth goe, and to have 2 monethes wages p^d him before hande, and 4 monethes wages more to goe in stocke of proffite or losse of the viage and for this enterteyment he promiseth to pforme all his best endevo^r and skill for ye forthering the viage, And he is also enterteynid the meane tyme before the viage beginne, to loke to the workyng and repayring of the shipping and to be allowed vj^s viij^d p weeke for his diett.

The 10th of october 1600.

Mr Aldⁿ Bannyng
Mr Allabaster
Captē Lancaster
Mr Rich. Wyche
Mr Roger Howe
Mr Wm Chambers

Mr Wm Harryson
[Captein Middleton]
Mr Rich : Wyseman
M^r Jo Bate
Captē Midleton
Mr Burrell

T this assemblie were directed hether severall tres of commending to the imployment of the Est Indie viage thes severall psons hereafter namid to be vsed as pursers videlt from Mr Thoms Midleton one—Robt Creswell from m^r Stap one—Richard Babington— and from Captein Midleton—[one] Henry Midleton his brother wch severall sewters being seene appeare psonall and fitt men for imploym^t Yet notwthstanding this assembly Consisting but of a small niiber and for that the busines of the viage is not come so farre as to make election of men of Charge they thought it fytt to take a further tyme for thes matters.

Lres Commending of severall men to be imployed

Robt Creswell, Rich: Babington, Henry Middleton

ther is apointed by this assemblie to goe downe to see [the] howe the worke of the [shipping] *Mallice scurge* goeth forward and to attend the same from day to day vntill the ships be ready thes persons following [viz] who shall lye at Wolw^{ch} all the

surveyo^r of the workes of the malyce scurge

weeke at the Companies Charge.   Henr Mydleton
                                 Edward Hylliard

The smith at Wolw^ch

It is agreed that the Smythe wch dwelleth at Wolw^ch whose name is Justice mullett shalbe imployed in the yron worke ther soe as he vse Spanishe iron.

a warraunt to take vp shipwright

Ther was dd at this assemblie to m̃r Burrell a Warraunt signed by my L. Thr̃er for the taking vp of Carpenters and shipwright℈ to be presentlie sett on worke in the shippes paying them suche wages as they can be agreed wth all.

Beare allowed to the workemen in the Malice Scurge

Order is geaven to the said henry Mydleton and Edward hylliard according as they shall see cause for the better holding together of the workemen from runing from ther worke to drinke, to allowe them of the Companies charge a barrell of beare everie day, and to have a speciall care they leave not ther worke to Runne to the Alehouse.

the boat belonging to the Malice Scurge

It is ordered that a note be inserted in captein Bakers Comission who goeth into the west Cuntrey that he geave order to sende vp the shipe boate belonging to the Malice scurge wch lieth at Plymouth or els wher in the west Cuntrey.

Robt Hughes Bolton Saylemakers

It is agreed at the request of m̃r Burrell that one Robt hughes and   Bolton shalbe vsed in the making of the sayles of the Mallyce scurge.

Comitties to ppare the genall busines.

It is thought meet and a *meane of* speciall expedition and furtheraunce of the busines of this viage that some psons be selected out of the number of the Comitties who shall dailie meet together and conferre of pointes and Remembraunces meet to be propounded when the generall Comitties do assemble and in some sorte to prepare the businesses readie for the same Assemblie, to ye ende to avoide the Long dispute of [thing] questions wch we finde be experience doeth growe when matters are propounded to *the* whole [Companie] Comitties before they be in some sort prepared before hande.

      Mr Ald^n Bannyng   Mr Allabaster
      Mr Staper Mr Cordell   Mr Roger Howe
      Capten Lancaster   Mr Wyche
          to meet at m^r Ald^n Bannynges

M{r} Allabaster being moved to take the Charge of the ordering the Accoumptes of this viage, [doeth] ether by him self or his servaunt doeth excuse him self by the multytude of his owne busines to attende the same him self, but is contented that his man shall attende the same busines and he will nowe and then oversee what his man doeth w{th} w{ch} this assemblie holde them selfes satysfied, and in regard of this service wilbe thankfull to m̃ Allabaster. <small>M{r} Allabister touching the Accoumptes</small>

Order is geaven to m̃ Ald{n} Bannyng Thr̃er to deliver to Capteiñ Lancaster and m{r} Chambers 200{li} to be imployed in yron worke and Caske. <small>yron worke & caske 200{li}</small>

Lyke order is geaven to y{e} said m̃ Ald{n} to deliver to Josephe Salamon Purser of the Susan to be imployed in the preparation of thinges necessarie for the same ship the som̃e of one hundred poundes. <small>100{li} for y{e} susan</small>

Order is geaven to m̃ Allabaster to sende Comission to his servaunt at Callis to take vp all the Royalles of plate he can at the best rate he can gett although it come to [two or] three thowsand poundes and to sende the same over for England. <small>Moneis to be pvided at Callys</small>

Prouision to be made by Comission in the west Cuntrey geaven to Captein Baker.

<small>Syder   100 {tons}
breade   1200 {antalles}
Bockallrowe *fishe* 37500 great tale
wheate   351 bushelles Winchester
Meale   538{c}
Sanies, *nettℯ*, hookes, fysgiggℯ and harpe Irons</small>

A Commission drawen by m̃ howe for Capteiñ Baker and M{r} Pope being reade at this assembly was signed vnder the handes and deliuered to m̃ howe for the dispatche of the said Capteiñ Baker to goe away this after noone. <small>A Comission in to the West Cuntrey</small>

John Busbridge Lynnen Drap dwelling vppon London Bridge was [compounded w{th}] *compounded [moved] w{th}* by m̃ Ald{n} Bannyng and m̃ Staper for 10 toñs of the best sort of English iron *ordinary barrs* at xj{li} p tonñ to be deliuered [bet] at Lo{n} by the first of December and for x toñ of small barres of like iron about C [or] barres or theraboutℯ in a toñ [for w{ch}] he asketh <small>Prouision of iron</small>

xx ḿke p toñ but promiseth it shalbe better cheape yf can.

Malice Scurge

An Inuentorie of the thinges nowe remayning wth the Malice Scurge.

A fore course, bonnett and drabler little vsed
A maine co^rse bonnett and drabler litle vsed
A maine Topsaile litle vsed
a missen and a missen bonnett litle vsed
a newe spritt saile little vsed
an olde maine co^rse bonnett and drabler
more another maine co^rse
more an olde foreco^rse
more a Top gallont saile
a spritt saile Topsaill
x Iron scantions
2 Iron Cheines   4 nettinges
3 Cables by wch the shipp rides broken
2 ankers of 30^c weight or therabout℔ a peece
1 anker of 16 weight
1 anker of 12ᶜ weight
3 olde muck℔
  a whole sute of rigging as the ship cam̃ from Chatham saving that the most part of the small rūning ropes is spent and hath bene otherwise vsed
  A sewt of winding tackle blockes wth 4 shevers of brasse
  Brasse shevers more 50
x Iron pompe staves
3 Iron pompe brakes
3 Crowes of Iron
2 paire of Cañ hookes
1 paire of billowes
5 esses of maine cheines of iron
3 dead mens eies wth cheines of iron
6 tackell hookes
5 port hinges
4 boat hookes
2 fidd hammers

2 fidde
4 capsquares for carriage
a Loose hooke
2 dipsy leades
1 harping iron
1 fisgig
1 hawser of 7 inches
2 hawsers one of 7 inches ¼ thother of 7 inches
40 guñers tackles
120 roles of matche decaied
4 dossen of plate Cartringes wch are in 2 cheste
14 exceltries
17 plates of leade to lay over the peeces
5 great brasse bolles
3 old brasse ladles
36 sprigges and runners
4 ladles
2 wadhookes
300 weight of square shott
16 breechinges
1 table in the great Cabin wth 4 stooles and one chaire
2 earthen great potte for water
1 pompehooke
  A Bell of brasse
  A Longe boate lying at Plimoth verie litle vsed
2 fornaces in the Cookerome wth iron worke to binde the Cookerome
  The top mastes and yerd serviceable
  Demi Cannott shott 49
  Culvering shott 162
  Demi Culvering Crosse barre 49
  Demi Culvering rounde 34
  Sacre Crosse barre 14
  Sacre round 12

	c	qr	℔		
1	60	0	0		Demy Can-
2	60	0	0	} 6 toñs	nons.

THE COURT RECORDS OF

		c	q	℔		c	q	℔	
	1	42	0	0	9	36	2	0	
	2	42	0	0	10	36	2	0	
	3	42	0	0	11	36	2	0	
Culverin-	4	42	0	0	12	36	2	0	31 toñz 8ᶜ
ges 16	5	42	0	0	13	36	2	0	
	6	42	0	0	14	36	2	0	
	7	42	0	0	15	36	2	0	
	8	42	0	0	16	36	2	0	
		c	q	℔		c	q	℔	
	1	29	0	0	7	29	0	0	
	2	29	0	0	8	29	0	0	
Demy Cul-	3	29	0	0	9	29	0	0	17 toñs 8ᶜ
vering	4	29	0	0	10	29	0	0	
12 pece	5	29	0	0	11	29	2	0	
	6	29	0	0	12	29	2	0	
		c	q	℔		c	q	℔	
	1	20	2	0	5	20	2	0	
Sacres 8	2	20	2	0	6	20	2	0	8 toñs 4ᶜ
	3	20	2	0	7	20	2	0	
	4	20	2	0	8	20	2	0	

Sm Toᵗᵃˡˡ of the toñz of ordnaunce, 62 toñz 27ᶜ

The 11ᵗʰ of october 1600.

Mʳ Aldⁿ Bannyng   John Eldred
Mʳ Rich: Staper   Rich: Wyseman
Mʳ Thomas Cordell   Erle of Cumbland
Capteñ Lancaster   Capteñ Middleton

Wᵐ Broadebent

THES Comitties thinke that Wᵐ Brodebent of Graveshend is a verie fitt man to take charge in this viage and to that ende resolve to sende for him and to see how he is affected to the said viage.

A Cheine pumpe for Scourge

The Erle of Cumberland adviseth that a Chaine Pumpe is verie necessarie to be vsed in the malice Scurge.

Mr Wyche informeth this assemblie that Capteiñ baker told him that m̃ Sergeaunt heale would be content to deliuer vnto the Companie as ther assignes in the west Cuntrey to be pd him here in London the somme of 400ˡⁱ It is therfore thought good he be talkd wth all and to that ende m̃² howe is intreatid to talke wth srgeaunt heale.   *Srgeaunt heale to be talked wth for money*

The Eare of Cumbsland sealed a bargaine and sale of the malice scurge to m̃ howe m̃ Eldred m̃ wych and m̃ Chamb9 and had 2 warraunts for 1700ˡⁱ the one to m̃ Aldn Bannyngs for 1000ˡⁱ the other to Aldn Hollyday for 700ˡⁱ to be pd this day and his Lp hath putt downe him self an adventuror of 1500ˡⁱ, [in the] and apointed m̃ Cordell an adventuror of 500ˡⁱ, wch two somes of adventure together wth the 1700ˡⁱ pd him by the 2 Thiers make vp the whole somme of 3700ˡⁱ being the price of the malice scurge bought of his Lp.   *Malice Scourge 1700ˡⁱ pd for the Scourge and the rest of the ships valewe sett downe by the Erle and by Mr Cordell.*

A warraunt signed by 4 of the Comitties for the paiment of 600ˡⁱ to m̃ fra: Elington for the provision of Cloth wch warraunt is directed to Aldn Bannyng.   *600ˡⁱ for prouision of Clothe*

Another Warraunt to Aldn hollyday for the Purser of the Scurge for the paiment of 100ˡⁱ   *100ˡⁱ to ye purser of the Scourge.*

The 13 of october 1600.

Aldn Bannyng
Mr Rich: Staper

Mr Eldred
Capteiñ Lancaster

T is thought meet by thes Comitties that ther shalbe noe adventuror refused that will adventure 200ˡⁱ vntill the whole adventure do ryse above 55000ˡⁱ for that it is supposed that somme [suche] wch have sett downe [that] ther contributions will drawe backe againe.   *howe farre aduentures shalbe red hereafter.*

The 15 of october 1600.

Aldⁿ Bannyng
Aldⁿ Hollyday
Mr Tho. Cordell
Mr Wm Garway
Captein Lancaster
Mr Rich: Wyseman
Mr Wm Chamber

Mr Roger Howe
Mr John Eldred
Mr Wm Harryson
Mr Rich: Staper
Mr Rich: Wyche
Capteiñ Davies
Phi͞p Grove

Mr Burrell

Proportion. THES Committies [have] do resolve to alter the proportion of breade from the proportion sett downe in ther note of the generall provision, and do alter it from 16 monethes to xx^{tie} monethes provision so as by ther **Biskett** present resolution ther is to be provided in byskett [2000^c 0^q 0^{ll} 280] 180^{mt}.

Meale And they do agree that ther shalbe provided in meale over and besides the provision in breade, 535 bushelles of Winchester measure being 8 gallons to the Bushell.

Wheate Wheate 250 Bushelles kill dried of like measure.

Syder 60 Toñs of Syder.

fishe 20 m^l newe [found] land fishe great tale.

Comission in to ye West Cuntrey to be altered Comission having bene geaven to Capteiñ Baker and m͞^r Pope for the provision of thes severall victualles above mencõed at the rates and proportions formerlie sett downe in the generall note of Proportion newe advyse is to be geaven them to make ther provision according to these rates above mencõned.

Mr Burrell Whereas Mr Atye semethe discontented and doeth not apply him self to furnishe suche provisions as belongeth to the preparing of the shippes [at Wolwiche] in suche sorte as the necessytie thereof requireth order is geaveñ to Mr Burrell to furnishe all suche provision of Tymber as the shippes stande neede of wthout depending vppon m͞^r Atye or enduring of any further delaies in this busines.

A newe boate for ye Malice Scurge Ordered that there shalbe made a [newe] longe boate Carvell fashion for the malice scourge to be sett up in the Cuntry.

Order is geaven that ther shalbe p^d to Mr Burrell the somme of C^{li} for provisions [and] of tymber to be used in the shippes by m^r Ald^r Bannyng Thier and a warraunt to that ende signed.

100^{li} to be p^d to Mr Burrell.

The 16 of October 1600.

Ald Bannyng   Mr Wyseman
Ald Hollyday   Mr Howe
Mr Cordell   Capten Lancaster
        Erle of Cumberland

RDER is geaven by thes Comitties to Mr Ald^r Bannyng to pay to Capten Davies to beare his charges in to the next Cuntrey the some of 20^{li} vppon an accompte of the pticlers of his charges in the said jorney.

20^{li} to Capten Davies.

A Bill from Sergeaunt Hele to Warwicke Heale in the West Cuntrey wherby he is Required by the said sergeaunt to pay CC^{li} to Mr Roger Howe or his assigns at x daies sight is delivered to Capten [to receive the leave wch the said] [*Davies to leave wth*] Mr Ellicott Baker or Pope to Receave the money accordinglie. W^{ch} bill doeth mencon that the money is already p^d to m^r Heale here in London althoughe he hath not yet re^d it. W^{ch} bill beareth date the 15 of October 1600.

Sergeaunt Heale.

Composition is made wth Phillip Grove Pylote for to goe in this viage as he shalbe apointed. And he is contented to be imploied in the [*same*] viage according to the direction of the Comitties as Pilot to any ship apointed for the consideration of the somme of one hundred poundes to be p^d him to furnishe him self and to geave him the proffite of five hundred poundes as God shall blesse the viage. And vppon thes considerations he promyse to pforme all fidelytie and good service that Layeth in his power.

Phillip Grove Pylott.

Laus deo   London the 10th of October.

Lovinge frends etc As wee have Intreated you to take some

A Comis-

sion to Capten Baker and Mr Pope to goe in the West Cuntrey for Provisions &c.

paines for vs in the West Country Where now by Gods grace you are to take yor Jornie for the procuringe and providinge of such victualls and other provision as wee in those parts are to be furnished of for our pretended viage wth god prosper. The pticulers wherof herafter shalbe expressed soe wee hope that by your good and discreete meanes you will not onely take that good dilligent and provident Care in the providinge of that wch is very good well handled and in all respects soe orderly as the necessetie of so longe a viage importeth The first and most especiall things that wee recomend vnto your care is for your bisket to see that the same be twice well dryed and that extraordinaryly for it is an extraordinary viage as you knowe and procure as neare as you may to have five Cakes to a pound and that they be whole and sound as neare as you may and for such Cakes as ffalle oute to be rather hollowe or broken that you appte them from the rest and keepe them be them selves that they may be first spent wee thinke it your best place to pvide the same in wilbe lañe Apsome Darmouth, Plimouth and the places to them adjoyninge for yor meale yon may provide the same When yon can gett the best driest and hardest corne and fittest for yor purpose and old corne is best yf yon can gett it and being conv'ted into meale yon are to take the branne out of it and soe packe it into good drie and sweet caske and to packe it verie hard and Closse and to see the same well hooped and packed cold. Nowe for the Syder yon are to be carefull to provide that wch is good and beinge provided to wracke and for that it is newly made it wilbe good that that when you buy it to condicõn wth them to recs the same some 6 weekes after or sooner yf you please to your Choise the reason is for that in the meane tyme it may be settled and growe to be fine alsoe some it will excuse, it were not amisse you bringe yor owne Caske for yf you should remove it from hence it wilbe longe before it be fine againe. Alsoe you are to condicõn wth them of whome you buy it that they at their charge deliver it at the water side I meane at the next convenient porte for ladinge of it Nowe the sider beinge bought doth accompte very much to have very good Caske and wel houped and three

Iron Hoopes vppon ech end of ech Cask for What prevaileth it to haue good suder and the cask be not good sweet and well hooped and this beinge effected to sent the same to Dartmouth wch must be the place of the assembly of all your prouisions the fittest place for the pvidinge of your suder is Colletton Seaton Axmouthe Newton Bushea and aboute Apson̄ and Dartmouth.

As for o^r Newland fishe if you are to pvide you are alsoe to be carefull to see yf the same not onely be good fish and well handled but also very Dry and that you take take not anie that ether head or tale be anie thinge moist as often tymes that fishe falleth out to be but yf you be forced to take anie in your ptide you may keepe them by them selues to be first spent And this beinge donne you are to lay the same in a good Close and dry Laughte and pvide good store of ffurre to lay vnder vppon and aboute the same to keepe the moist aire from yt and herafter you shall receaue further order from vs ether for the packinge of the same Cask or to bunndell it vpp 200 fishes in a bundell old corne wilbe best yf you can gett yt whether old or newe it must be keild dried and after packed in good cask(e) and as for saynes Hookes and Linnes you are to pvide them at the discretion of Capten Davis such and soe many as you shall thinke fitt and needefull further at your cominge into the Country you are presently to enquire and lerne what quantetie of wine and vinegre ther is tobe had and at what price and also the price of beanes and pease both white and gray also what store of Iron hoopes ther are to be had and at what price but not to buy anie untill you heare further from vs for that wee are ptly mynded to send you some from hence Likewise you are to write vs forthw^{th} whether ther wilbe cask had ther sufficient and good to serue what you shall neade there or not for y^t yf you cannot fitt your selues thear wth such and as much there as you shall neede that then vppon notice therof from you wee may supply o^r want(e) from hence Alsoe you are to certefie vs of the state and price of all those pvisions that wee
 you in charge to pvide and therw^{th} all yor opin̄ions howe you shalbe able to effect and accomplish the same as neare as

you may wee are Informed as you knowe of a prize brought to Plimouth wch some 40 tt(^n of Cassalla wines wch o^r desire is that one of you wth as much speade convenient as you may for to taste them and to knowe the lowest price of them and findinge them good of that sorte of wines and such as will serue o^r tornes to buy them yf you may haue them at a reasonable rate to say not passing 10 or 11^{li} p tt(^n at the most but for lesse what you may it is a kinde of wine not vendible here in o^r Country and they haue benn sold here in London at 7^{li} p tt(^n very good wines but yf you cannott gett them as aforüs^d then may you pcure the loest price of them and take the pties pmise for some 12 daies respect in that tyme at your choise ether to take or leaue them and so forthwth to certefie vs thereof yo^u may shew them that yf yo^u buy them they shall have their present   for them wch wilbe some cause to see them the better cheape and yf at your cominge hether they be not landed out of the ship wee would you could agree wth them to deliver them heere at his charges and adventure though they cost vs the more as of necessetie they will what further directions to give you presently wee knowe not for the pvidinge of these thing(^s and doe referre vs to your good discretion and care for the managinge and well orderinge of these businesses. By this you perceaue what o^r desire is to haue donn wch yf you cannot accomplishe as you would yet as well and as neare as you may.

    Nowe resteth order and meanes to be taken for the furnishinge of you wth monies for the paiment of the pvisions aforesaid

not exceedinge 1000^{li} or two at the most.

wch o^r desire ys that you take vpp in the country soe much monie as you may and to give yor bills in Alde^r Banning(^e Alde^r Hollidaies for the repayment of it heer wch bill(^s wee will see well p^d and for the better obteininge of monie ther wee haue pcured my Lo: Treasurers l^{re} to the receivers and customers of Dovor and Cornewall to helpe you vnto such moneis as they

you are to leaue this lre wth Mr Ellerot at Exet^r

haue in their custodie of her ma^{ies} as the said l^{re} doth import wch wee delivered unto yor   you may show as occasion may serue to such as it is directed and what you doe receive of them you may give them bill(^s in the Alderman aforesaid for the repaym^t of yt heere wch shalbe well p^d and wth what by these

meanes you shall not be able to furnishe yo\` want\[\] wee will
vppon intellegence from you furnish you from hence from tyme
to tyme in the best order wee may and for an earnest pennye
wee will give order that you shall receive presently this next
weeke in the country 5 o 600^(li) but the more you cann pcure in
the country the lesse charge and adventure wee shalbe at in
sendinge downe of yt from hence ffurther for Royall\[\] of plate
wee pray you that you wilby all good meanes possible procure
as many as yo^u may of 8 &c 2 at the least Rate you may and
for maym^t of them ether to pay them ther yf you cañ get monies
or else to give yor bill\[\] as afores^d or to take some short tyme
yf wee may send the same downe yf they will not take their
monies heer for such as you can gett to bagg them vp and
seale the bagg\[\] and make them and   them in some sure
and trustye mennes hand\[\] some in one mannes hand\[\] and some   viz in the
in another vntill o^r further order also you are to pcure some   hands of
                                                                   Mr Ellicot
out of Brittaine from Mort and St Mallowes both by your owne   Mr Williā
                                                                   Martin at
meanes of yor frend\[\] although you deliuer monies ther in their Exeto^r or
Country to such m̃chaunt\[\] as trade for them plac\[\] before hand   Mr Simes
                                                                   in Charde,
beinge two sure men to some 200^li and some 300^li some more   you must
some lesse as you shall thinke the men to be of honesty and   take bonds
                                                                   for such
abilitie to performe such bargaine as they shall make wth you   monies as
wch must be for so much English monies as they binde them   yo^u graue
                                                                   out to be
selues to deliuer you so many Royalls of plate of 8. 4. and 2. by repd by a
such a tyme wch tyme must be at furthest the midle or end of   day.
novem^r herof you are to certefye vs what you thinke you
shalbe able to help vs vnto by that tyme and that as soone as
you may for that wee cannot furnish o^r selues ther wee may
take some other order heere for o^r bisket wee hold it very necessary that the bakers that bake it stand bund for the same
shall continew good and sweet for 2 yeares at Plimouth ther is
the m̃alice skourges boate wch ship we have brought and therfore are to have the boate wch we pray you may be trim̃ed and
sent vp hether by the first convenient meanes you may and
to se whether she may be worth trim̃inge or no and to advise
vs therof forthw^th at Captin Davis his com̃inge downe wee will
write you further whose opinion order and direction for the

providinge and orderinge of o' said victualls wee pray you to
followe for that he is not onely well experienced herin but also
is to spend and to take his pte herof in the viage.

The provisions as followeth

Bread 1200ᶜ Syder 100 tt(ᵒ⁰ Meale 835ᶜ Wheat 251 busshell(
Newland ffishe 3785 Saynes Hookes Lynes &c. at Cap: Davies direction

Yoʳ loving frend(

Paull Bannyng   Ric Staper   Roger Howe   Jo Bate
Leonerd Hollyday   Ric Wyseman   Wᵐ Harryson
James Lancaster   Wᵐ Chambʳ   Ric Wyche

Captein Davies Comission going into the West Cuntrey for provisions &c.

Lovinge freind Mʳ Davis since the makinge & geavinge of
oʳ former order & comission to Mʳ Backer and Mʳ Pope wᵗʰ
the wᶜʰ you are acquainted notwᵗʰstandinge for yoʳ better remembrannce herewᶜʰ wee geve youᵘ the Coppie wᶜʰ is at lardge
concerninge the providing of Victuals & Roials of plate in the
West Cuntrie as to the said comission wee referre vs wee say
since that tyme wee have had further conference & consideracõn touchinge our said Commission for the proporcõn of suche
victualls etc as wee gave order ꝑ the same to provide & now
havinge dulie considered there of wee have thought good to
alter our former pretence & to lessen the proporcõn in some
and encrease it in other some as hereafter shall appeare wᵗʰ
wᶜʰ alteracõn and now our determincõn youᵘ are at yoʳ comige
downe pʳsentlie to accquainte Mʳ Backer and Mʳ Pope
ether by conference wᵗʰ them or ꝑ yoʳ lŕes and so to appointe
a place of meetinge that youᵘ may not onlie know what is done
but also to take order for the accomplishinge of the rest and at
yoʳ meetinge wee hope you will so exactlie consider of all
matters that you will lay your plate in that good order that our
said Busines may be effected for our good & yoʳ creditt(&
espetiallie for you Mʳ Davies vppon whom wee do so muche
rely & whom it doth so nere touche bothe in credit and for your
owne vse to see that wᶜʰ is or shalbe provided to be good and
well ordered eche provicõn accordinge to his qualetye As therof
wee hold it needlesse to vse any further direcõn for that wee know
your experience & discrecõn to be suche that in these matters

you may rather directe vs but onlie hereafter to note somethingℓ vnto you wch are as followethe.

First at yor cominge to the   wee pray you to conferr wth Mr Thomas Syms and to know of him what Royalls of plate he hath provided and what quantety he thincketh shalbe able to provide and in what tyme and of him yo^u shall know wher Mr Backe^r and Mr Pope are and at your cominge to Exceter you are to make the like enquirie of Mr Ellecote and Mr Martin concerninge Royalls of plate & to request them all to procure vs as many as possible by any meanes they may and for the payment of such as they shall provide to chardge us by exchaunge accordinge to our former comission whose Bills shalbe well paide   Also that Mr Ellecote & Mr Martin p̄cure to take vpp as much moneys as they cann gett not passinge and to charge us for paym^t thereof p their Billes as aforesaid wch may serve for paym^t of our pvic̄on and Roials of plate as occasion servethe and for such Roials as they provide of 8. 4. & 2. that they make them vpp in canvas Baggℓ made of new canvas   in eche Bagg & so seale them & lett them remaine in yor custody untill o^r further order & for their paines & labour in theise Busines they shalbe considered & for suche Bondes or Billes as you shall have ther in the cuntrie made vnto you ether for the accomplishinge of provic̄on or moneis wee pray you that they may be all lefte wth the said Ellecote & Martin takinge a note of their handes for all suche thinges as yo^u shall leave in truste wth them and for such thinges I meane Billes or Bondes that are for the pformaunce of matters ther in the cuntrye you may leave the notes wth Mr Backer & Mr Pope & for the rest you may bringe alonge wth you at yor Retourne wch wee would willinglie should be as soone as you may for that wee shall have nede of you here for sundrie cawses But duringe your beinge ther wee once againe pray you to geve furtheraunce to all our Busines as well for provic̄on as for Roialls of Plate as muche as possible you may.

If anie of yor freindes ther in the cuntrie are desirous to adventure in this our viadge you may accepte of them in such order as wee here doe that noe one be les then 200^li and that the moneis be provided in Roials of plate and paid to Mr Ellecote or Mr Martin p the fyne of November next at the furthest accomptinge their Roialls of plate at vj^d p pece and to make them suche further allowaunce(as wee allowe vnto other men of whom wee ther buy them & for suche as do adventure lett them sett downe their names in a shete of pap vnder their owne handes as wee do here & so you may bringe the same alonge wth you that they may be admitted   But wee would not have you to take adventures not above 2 att most.

Wee vnderstand by one Mr Lecheland who dwelleth at Culleton that ther are some 100 Bushells of white pease to be had at some 2^s 8^d or 2^s 10^d wch yf you find them at that price wee pray you to buy them and althoughe you pay 3^s for them yf you like them & so thincke good   Wee understand that Porcke is also ther good cheape at your cominge downe lett not to write to vs presentlye how you find matters ther and what you thincke concerninge the effectinge of our Busynesses that accordinglie wee may go forward wth our Busines here   And thus wee leave you and all your endeavours to the direccon of Thalmightie.

O^r proporcon of Victuals is as followethe

200 Newland fishe great toele

60t(sider & no more all to be sent to London in their caske

1800 of Biskett

535 Bushells of Meale Winchester measure of 8 gallens

250 : Bushells of Wheate of the same measure

Wee deliver yo^u herew^th Mr Sergent Heale his Bill of exchaunge & a l̃re to Mr Warwicke for the receivinge of 200^li, at 10 daies sighte

      Yo^r lovinge freindes
        Pawl Baninge
        Leonard Holliday
        Richard Wiseman
        Thomas Cordell
        Roger Howe

A second comission to Captein Baker and

O^r Lovinge Freindes o^r former Comission directed to you bothe and delivered to Capten Baker wee have related to Captein Davies and to the end he may be accquainted wth all provisions touchinge

the said viage wherin wee have appointed you to deale wee have Mr Pope
geaven him a coppy of your said Commission But vppon further altering the first pro-
consideracon of our said provisions and the revewe of the pticlers portion of victualles.
thereof wee are induced vppon good respect(' to alter the said
proporc̃ons enlarginge some of them and abridginge othersome
of them accordinge to the rates herevnder pticlerlie menc̃oed
wch pticlers wee do resolve shall stand for our provision wthout
alterac̃on and therfore wee pray you to directe your proporc̃on
of all the said victuall accordinge to these quanteties
wch wee have delivered to Captein Davies Whervppon our
desire is that you do all conferr together and dyspose of the
provic̃on thereof as you may best sorte the same every one of
you endeavoringe the good of the voyage as wee hope yo^u will
wth good agreem^t and consent together.

    The proportion of Victualles
20 thowsand newland ffishe great tale
60 Tons of Syder
180 thowsand Biskett
535 bushelles meale Winchester measure
250 bushelles Wheat of the same measure.
      Yo^r lovinge frendes
        Paull Bannyng
        Leo Hollyday
        Ric Wyseman
        Thomas Cordell
        Roge^r Howe.

    21 October 1600.

ARRAUNT geven to Mr Ald^r Hollyday Threr̃ to 200^{li} to
pay to Mr Roger Howe to pay over to Sergeaunt S^rgeaunt Heale
Heele vppon a bill of exchaung to be p^d in Plymouth
the some of 200^{li}.

 Warraunt geaven to Ald^r Bannyng threr̃ to pay Mr Howe 50^{li} to Laur Waldo.
to pay over to Laurence Waldo for the like valewe vppon his
bill of exchaung to be rep^d at Exceto^r the somme of 50^{li}

100ˡⁱ for Caske & iron hoopes.	Warraunt for the paym^t of 100ˡⁱ to Mr Chambers to provide Caske and iron hoopes.

22 October 1600

Ald^r Bannyng   Mr Wyseman
Ald^r Hollyday   Mr Harryson
Mr Staper   Mr Wyche
         Mr Cordall.

30ˡⁱ Php Grove.	ARRAUNT geaven to Mr Ald^r Hollyday to pay to Phip. Grove vppon accompte of his wages the some of thirtie poundes.
100ˡⁱ Purser of the Scourge.	Warraunt is geaven to Ald^r Bannyng to pay to Henr Mydleton Purser of the Scourge for the defraying of charges aboute the same ship 100ˡⁱ.

the 23 octob^r 1600.

Ald^r Bayning   Mr How
Ald^r Holliday   Mr Cordell
Mr Stapers   Mr Harrison
Mr Lancaster   Mr Chambres

1100ˡⁱ to Robert Steuens by letter off Mr Joh elacott.	WARRANT given to Mr Ald Bayning to pay ye 1100. to Robert Stephns; by vertew of a letter fr̄ō Mr John Ellacott of Exceter of the 18 present, that hee hath in a more some made Imployment of In Ryalls of plate.
120ˡⁱ to fir evington by bil of Robt Pope.	Warrant given to Mr Ald Holliday for payment of ye 120. to ff^r Evington; ffor a bill of ex^c frō Robt Pope; that hee R^{sd} towards pvyding of pvisions in the West countrey.
A leter to Joseph Sabbanck	Written a letter to Robt Salbanck purser of the Susann to will him to suffer Mr Burrell to take such men as it shall please him out of his shipp towards the more speedy execution of the work of the malice scourge.
Thomas Wasse desyrous to bee Imployed.	By the motion of Mr Richard Candler it was ordred to sett down one Mr Thomas Wasse, who was desyrous to bee Imployed in this voyadg as a factor.

Yt is at this Assembly accorded that M[r] Sandy should con- *prouyding* tynew his wryting into the west countrey for pvyding of Ryalls *of Ryalls of plate in y[e]* of plate, warranting him that his bills should bee well payd. *west countrey.*

The 25 october 1600.

Ald[r] Bannyng   M[r] John Eldred
M[r] W[m] Garway   M[r] Roger Howe
         M[r] W[m] Harryson.

ORDER is geaven by thes Comitties to Ald[r] Bannyng Threr for the paiment of the somme of 200[li] to M[r] Coles for soe muche by him p[d] to Rob[t] Pope in the West Cuntrey. *200[li] to be p[d] to M[r] Coles by exchaung.*

The like order is geaven for the paiment of one hundred markes to M[r] Garwey for to be imploied in the necessarie repacons of the Assension vppon accompte. *100 markes vppon repacons of the Assension.*

Also order is geaven to the said Ald[r] Bannyng Threr to disburce vppon the necessarie repacons of the Susan vppon accompte the somme of fyfty poundes. *50[li] vppon repacons of the Susan.*

The 27 Octob[r] 1600.

Ald[r] Bayning   M[r] Lancaster
Ald[r] Holliday   M[r] Harrison
M[r] Garway   M[r] Wyche
M[r] Wyseman   Capt: Middleton
         M[r] Cordell

T this Assembly it was ordred and determyned and a warrant given to Thomas Evesett to warne all the adventurers in this voyadg to bee at a court at ffounders hall on thursday the 30 of this moneth there to take notyce of hir Ma[ties] pleasure signifyede by a letter fro the lords of her ma[ties] Counsayle. *Warraunt for a generall Court.*

Yt is also appoynted that *M[r] Ald[r] bayning Ald[r] Wattes* M[r] Cordell, M[r] Lancaster & Capteyne Middleton shall take *Chusing of M[rs] & mariners*

I

order in the choosing & appoynting of maysters ffor the shipps in this voyadg—

<small>Captein Lancaster</small>

Also that Mr Ald Bayning *Ald^r Hollyday*, *Ald^r Moore* Mr Cordell, Mr Garway & Thomas Alabaster *or any 4 of them* to deale wth capt. Lancaster ffor the taking of the government of this voyadg as the cheiff [generall] *commander* thereof.

Octob^r the 27th 1600.

<small>50^{li} Nichas Holway</small>

EVEN a warrant to [capt] M^r ald^r Holliday ffor payment of y 50li to Mr Nycholas Holway, by a bill of exc̃ frõ Rob't Pope of the 19 hereof.

<small>Comission for Royalles to Calleis & Roun.</small>

Alsoe this day it is accorded that Mr Alabaster shall contynew his cõmission ffor Callais & Roane for the pvyding of Ryals of plate to the vallew of ffyve thousand pownds wth pmyse that his bills of exc̃ shalbee payd & contented.

The 28 octob^r 1600.

| Mr Ald^r Bayning | Mr Eldred |
| Mr Harrison | Mr Howe. |

<small>1000^{li} to Rob^{rt} Stephens by bil frõ J^{no} Ellacott</small>

EVEN a warrant to Ald Holliday ffor paym^t of y 1000li to Mr Rob^{rt} Stephins in full of a bill of exc̃ frõ Mr John Ellacott of Exceter ffor the vallew there Rs̃d to bee Imployed in Ryalls of plate.

<small>44^{li} to peter sampson.</small>

Geven a warrant to Mr Ald Holliday ffor paym^t of y 44li to peeter sampson by bill of exc̃ frõ Mr John Sandy of Exceter; for the vallew there Rs̃d by him to the companyes vse.

A Gen^rall Courte.   The [last] 30 of Octob^r 1600 in the presence of the Comitties and Generalytie hereafter named viz :

<small>Comitties.</small>

Sr Johñ Hart knight	Mr Wm Garwey
Ald^r Bannyng	Mr Thomas Cordall
Ald^r Moore	Mr Richard Wysemañ
Ald^r Hollyday	Mr Wm Chamber
Ald^r Smyth	Mr Johñ Eldred
Mr Ric: Staper	Mr Roger Howe.

M̃ʳ Johñ Eldred }
M̃ʳ Wᵐ Harrysoñ }
   Genʳalyty
James Deane
Edward Leanyng
Nicħas Leat
Nicħas Piece
Olyuer Style
Humfrey Smythe
Robᵗ Sandy
Richard Pomtell
John Highelord
Humfrey Style
Nicħas Farrar
Thomas Farringtoñ
John Combe
Robt Offeley
James Turnor
Maurice Abbott
Leonard Whyte
Georg Chambleyn
John Cornelys
Raph Busby
Wᵐ Jennyns
Robt Bell
Thomas Whyte
Nicħas Lyng
Wᵐ Palmer
Nicħas Cryspe
Robᵗ Cockes
Wᵐ Wastall
Johñ Bate
Hugh Hamersley
Nathaniel Martiñ
Barthew Holland
[Richar Cockes]
Wᵐ Stone

John Frier
Frauncis Dent
Richard Ball
Roger Hemmyng
Frauncis Evingtoñ
Thomas Westweawe
Daniel Marshe
John Midletoñ
Robt Gore
Raph Gore
Wᵐ Cater
John Buzbridg
Thomas Horton
Wᵐ Bond Mc̃hantailer
Augustin Skinner
Rich: Taileby
Robᵗ Middletoñ
Robt Batemañ
Robt Waldo
Wᵐ Dale
Lau: Waldo
Henry Bridgemañ
Samuel Armitage
Edward Harrysoñ
Edward Nicholsoñ
Clement Moseley
Humfrey Walcott
Reynold Greene
Robᵗ Mildmay
Georg Chaundeler
Wᵐ Burrell
Thomas Henshaw
Wᵐ Ferries
Wᵐ Hewett
Wᵐ Fisher
Nicħas Salter
Wᵐ Angell

Nicłias Barnesley
Henry Polsted
Andrew Bannyng
Barthew Haggett
Robt Buck
Johñ Hodgesoñ
Richard Piott
Georg Coles
Raphe Hamor

Henry Archer
John Casoñ
Richard Beale
Richard Washer
George Holmañ
Frauncis Barker
Richard Deane
Richard Ironsyde
James Dunkiñ.

THIS generall Assemblie being called together as well to acquaint them of the proceading of the busines hetherto pformed in the preparatioñ of the voyage as to informe them of the slacknes of many of the Contributo[rs] who had sett downe ther names and ther sommes pretended to be adventured and had hetherto brought in noe moneys to furnishe the provision, first the said Assemblie were putt in mynde of ther geñall Petition and projecte of the viage wch was offered in all ther names to the ll: of her Ma[ts] most honorable privy Councell, wherby ther Lordships were humbly intreated by them to Solicite her ma[e] in ther names, for her gratious Licence and assent that they might vndertake a voyage to the East Indies for the hon[r] of o[r] Cuntrey and for the advancem[t] of the trade of merchaundize of this Realme conteyning in ther said Petition divers Clawses for the furtheraunce of the said viage. It was alsoe remembred vnto them that the Lordes having acquainted her ma[e] wth ther said Petition did retorne them her ma[es] gratious aunswer and free assent therunto geaving them incoragem[t] to goe forward wth assuraunce that ther shuld noe staye be made of ther vyage wch was certyfyed vnder the handes of the Lord Threr̃ Lord Admirall L Chambleyn S[r] [Robt] Wm Knowles Sr Robt Cycill and Secretery Herbert by a lr̃e bearing date the 16 day of Septëber last. And they were further putt in mynde that vppon this Warraunt Certefyed by the lordes of her ma[es] Assent and assuraunce to proceade the Companie had since mett together and at ther Gen'all assemblie holden the 23. of Septemb [last following] they, or the most of them having vnder ther owne handes sett downe ther adventures [had] did make choice of Seventeene of the said Contributors whom they appointed to be comitties to dispose and manage the whole busines and preparatioñ for the said viage. According to wch Comission geaven the said Cōmitties had hetherto proceaded and had defraied in the [said] preparation of the said viage and stoode ingaged to be aunswerd by exchaung and otherwyse for the soñie of xx m^l poundes at the least; The busines being thus farr proceaded in they were further geaveñ to vnderstand That many of the companie who had sett downe ther adventures begaune to wthdrawe ther purpose of proceading and wthheld ther paym^t of ther moneys vppon some Rumo^{rs} or doubtes geaveñ out that the viage was lyke to receave soñie stay for the removing and clearing of wch doubt that meanes had bene made by soñie of the Comitties to the lordes of the Councell for ther certifycat to the adventurers that they might wth full assuraunce proceade wthout any just cause of doubte, Who theruppon wrote ther lrës to Generalyty confirming ther former lrës of certificat that the said viage shuld receave noe stay or interruptioñ wch lrës being vnder the handes of the Lord keeper the L Thrër the L Admirall Sr Robt Cicell Sr John ffortescue, the L Chief Justice, and Mr Secretary Herbert were openlie read and beare date the 26 day of this instant october [and wthall it was delivered unto theñ]. In wch last recyted Lrës besides the warraunt of incoragem^t geaveñ to the Companie to proceade It was notid unto theñ that the actioñ vndertakeñ by theñ was a publike action and not to be dallied wthall [and to that the] and therfore did require that the names of such as did ether wthdrawe them selfes or practise to wthdrawe others from proceading thein shuld be certefyed to ther Lorshipes that they might examine the reasoñ of ther discoragem^t. After the discourse of all wch severall matters and proceadinges all the said Assemblie by generall consent did agree to bring in ther moneys wch was by former [assent] order payable the most of them being behinde but for the second paym^t wch was payable this present day and some of them being behinde both for the first and seconde payment, [saving some] *amongest wch only* two or three of contributors, ther present denied to adventure at all viz John Bate Robt Osseley *Nathaniell Martyn* and Hughe Hamersley the said John Bate geaving his aunswer that he was disapointed by some that shuld have ioyned wth him in the adventure of CC^li and did fall from him, so that he could not adventure for his owne adventure above C^li, and the said Robt Osseley *Nathaniell Martyn* and Hughe Hamersley alledging that they held them selfes discharged by a clawse that was sett downe in the last gen'all assemblie, wch was that he that brought not in his adventure by the last of September shuld not be pmitted to adventure at all.

The generalytie having thus agreed to bring in ther monies to further the expedition of the viage they required that order might be taken for all others wch w^thheld ther contributions and came not at this assembly to geave ther assentes, that they might be called vppon to bring in ther money or to geave ther reason of wth holding it to thende, that according to the Councelles l^res they might called before ther Ll: to aunswer the cause yf they did deny to adventure or would not bring ther moneys as by ther owne agreem^t they are to doe.

And forasmuch as the Pattent is already drawen and in the handes of Mr Attorney ready to be pfytted by the course of wch Pattent the Companie is to consist of a governo^r 24 Comitties and the gen'alyty this Court have by a most free Election, noiated for ther governo^r Mr Thomas Smyth Ald^r whose name they do desire may be sett downe in the Pattent to be offred to her Ma^ie, and allowed for ther first Governo^r.

And whereas hetherto ther hath beene appointed by the gen'alyty but 17 Comittyes to dispose and manage the affaires and busines of the trade, nowe forasmuch as by the Pattent ther is to be apointed 24 Comitties for that purpose   Ther is choice made at this Assemblie of the full number of fowr and twenty whereof some part are of the former Comitties heretofore imployed in the said busines and the residewe are supplied out of the Geñalyty. Soe as the names of all the said Comitties as they are nowe agreed vppon be as hereafter followeth videlt:

Ald{r} Bannyng	M{r} Richard Wyche
Ald{r} Hollyday	M{r} John Eldred
Ald{r} Moore	M{r} W{m} Chamber
Ald{r} Holmedeñ	M{r} W{m} Harrysoñ
M{r} Rich: Staper	M{r} Olyver Style
M{r} W{m} Garway	M{r} Rob̃t Sandy
M{r} Thomas Cordell	M{r} John Highelord
Capteñ Lancaster	M{r} W{m} Rumney
M{r} Rich: Wysemañ	M{r} John Middletoñ
M{r} Fra: Chery	M{r} Nicħas Lynge
M{r} Allabaster	M{r} Johñ Combe
M{r} Roger Howe	M{r} Rob̃t Bell

This Co{r}te havinge thus apointed ther Governo{r} and Comitties they doe referre and Comitte to ther Governm{t} *preparatioñ* and directioñ all matters whatsoever concerning the viage. Be it concerning shipping victualling merchaundizes moneys or appointing of officers to be imployed in the same. Allowing and holding for good all and whatsoever they or the most of theñ w{th} the Consent of the Governo{r} shall direct or agree vppon.

The severall psons heervnder named do promyse to bring in ther adventures in this manner videlt:

Johñ Wastall will bring in his money in dollers at xviij{d} the ".

Daniell Marche offereth to bring in his money yf he may be imployed.

Augustine Skynner will bring in his money at xx{d} the doller or els pay in Englishe money.

W{m} Addersley his adventure shalbe brought in by M{r} Henshawe

Nicħas Salter will bring in his money

Thomas Ironsyde will bring in his money

Morice Abbott will bringe in his money the next weeke.

The 31 October 1600.

Ald^r Bannyng	M^r
Ald^r Hollyday	Mr Wm Chamber
Mr Olyver Style	Mr John Midleton
Mr Wm Garway	Mr Niclias Lynge
Capteñ Lancaster	Mr Robt Bell
Mr Rumney	Mr John Combe
Mr Roger Howe	Mr Rich Wyche
Mr John Highlord	Mr Wm Harrysoñ
Mr Robt Sandy	Mr John Eldred

50^{li} to John Purnell

RDER is geaveñ to Ald^r Bannyng Threr to pay to Johñ Purnell the somme of fyfty poundes for so much by him dd, in Spanishe Ryalles to Thomas Baker in Plymmothe.

24 to Wm Turner

The lyke Warraunt is geaveñ to him to pay to Wm Turno^r the somme of twentie and four poundes for soe much dd by Richard Moone to Thomas Baker in Plymouth.

Robt Popes lres of advyse.

Lres from Robt Pope the one of 22 the other the 25 of this present froñ Plymouthe were reade wheriñ he geaveth the Companie divers advyses of his severall proceadinges in the Companies busines both for provysions and moneys. W^{ch} lres Mr Roger Howe is required to aunswer in the Companies name and having made aunswer thereof the same is to passe the handes of some of the Comitties to be sent him for his further Comissioñ.

Capten Baker's lres of advyse.

The lyke order is geaveñ to Mr Howe to aunswer another lre of advyse writteñ to the Companie by Captein Baker touching provision of money and other thing^s menĉoned in his lre.

Mr Ellycot of Exeto^r

Lres of advyse froñ Mr Ellycot to Mr Sandy were read wherby it appeareth that he hath made provysion of Ryalles of plate for the Company but not in suche sort as the Companie entended for they Required his travell as an agent for them to pvyde them moneys at the best rate he could and they would recompence his travell thankefully, but ment not that he shuld make a trade of theñ to buy theñ for his owne vse and to sell them to the Companie at the rates as the prise goeth in london as *it semeth by his lre* he ſposeth to putt them uppon the said Company Therefore it agreed that his lrēs shalbe aunswered and a plaine course taken wᵗʰ him ether to pvyde them as other that are putt in trust in those partes do buy them or els to desyst and provyde noe more.

Warraunt is geaven to Mʳ Aldʳ Banyng to pay to the Purser of the Scourge to be imployed in the repayring of the same ship the some of one thowsand poundes. 1000ˡⁱ to the Purser of the Scourge.

Warraunt is geaven to the said Mʳ Aldʳ Bañig ther to pay to Robt Stevens by a bill of exchange from Mʳ Ellicott of Execetoʳ the some of one thowsand poundes. 1000ˡⁱ by exe from Mʳ Ellycot.

Roger and Persevall Style are Sawtres to be imployed in this vioge. Style.

[Warraunt is geaven to Aldʳ Banyng ther to pay to the Purser of the Scourge]

A Warraunt to Mʳ Aldʳ Banyng to pay to Mʳ Richard Wysemañ to be imployed in reparacons and provisions for the hectoʳ the somme of one hundred pound(?). 100ˡⁱ for yᵉ Hectoʳ.

Order is geaven and renewed to Richard Wyche and Ric Wright to deale wᵗʰ Mʳ Covell in Tower Street for the provision of the full of 70 quarters of peas and 30 quarters of beanes. according to former order. provision of peas & beanes.

Order is geaven to Mʳ Aldʳ Bannyng to pay to Wᵐ Burrell Surveyoʳ of the generall pvysion of shipping to be imployed in Timber the some of Two hundred poundes. 200ˡⁱ to Mʳ Burrell.

Order is geaven to Aldʳ Bannyng to pay to Joseph Salbancke Purser of the Susañ to be imployed in repacons and other necessaries of the same ship the some of 100 merkes. 100 merkes to the Susan.

First Nouembʳ 1600.

Mʳ Aldʳ Smyth goʳ
Aldʳ Bannyng
Aldʳ Hollyday
Mʳ Olyuer Style
Mʳ Thomas Cordell

Mʳ Rich : Staper
[Mʳ Robt Sandy]
[Mʳ Aldʳ Smythe] Mʳ Aldʳ Moore.
Mʳ John Combe

66   THE COURT RECORDS OF

   Mr Rob̃t Bell.   Mr John Highelord
   Mr Wm Harrysoñ   Mr Rob̃t Sandy
   Mr Thomas Allabaster   [Mr Rob̃t S———]
   Mr Wm Chambers   Mr Roger Howe.

200^{li} to Mr Specke taken up by ex^e

WARRAUNT is geaveñ to Mr Ald^r Hollyday threr to pay vnto Mr George Speake Esquier the soñe of two hundred poundes for soe muche takeñ vp in the West Cuntrey by Rob̃t Pope.

Ires unto the West Cuntrey per the Post.

Lres *were* written in to the West Cuntrey *severally* to Capteñ Davies Capteñ Baker and Rob̃t Pope in aunswer of ther lres of advyse of ther proceeding written vp hether wch lres were signed by the Comitties being devysed by Mr Howe and were presentlie delivered to the Post of Exet^{or}.

Ire to John Ellicot at Excetor.

Another lre was read writteñ by Mr Rob̃t Sandy to Mr Ellycott of Exeto^r in aunswer of his lre whereiñ Mr Sandy writethe his myslyke of Ellicott^s dryfte to be allowed xviij^d the ℔ for Ryalles seing the Company entended only to vse him for añ agent. to pvyde theñ Spanishe money and not buy Ryalles of theñ.

A Warraunt from ye L. Threr. for the provysion & passing of pease & beanes.

It is agreed that a warraunt shall be made and offered to the L Threr to obteyne his hande to ye same directed to the Justices of peace in Camb^rshire and Norff. for the Licencyng of Covell to provide and to bring out of those Counties wthout stay or impediment of 100 quarters of pease and 40 quarters of Beanes for the provysioñ of the voyage.

Ires to Mr Sandy of Excetor

Another lrẽ read writteñ to Mr Sandy of Exceto^r and sent away by the Post in aunswere of a lrẽ by him directed to Ald^r Bannyng and Mr Stap touching the provysioñ of Royalles of plate wherin he is advysed not to exceade xij^d the ℔.

Captein Lancaster.

The Comitties formerly apointed to conferre wth Capteñ Lancaster touching his imploym^t in the voyage as the Chief Comaunder thereof are required to pceade therin as sone as they cañ, to thende his aunswer being hadd they may proceade to the electioñ of others. wch are to be imployed in speciall places in the viage ether as marchaunt^s m^{rs} and other officers.

It is agreed by this Assemblie, in respecte of the great experience of Mr Ald^r Wattes in shipping and other directions in viages ther may be great vse of the opinoñ of the said Mr Ald^r Wattes in the further proceading of this viage That according to the warraunt giveñ by the geñalyty to the said Comitties in that behaulf That the said Mr Ald^r shalbe warned to all meetinges and to be vsed as a Comitty in all thingẽ concerning the busines. — Mr Ald^r Wattes.

The 3 of Novemb 1600.

Mr Ald^r Bannyng	Mr Robt Sandy
Mr Ald^r Hollyday	M^r Jo. Eldred
Mr Olyver Style	Mr John Middletoñ
Mr Rich: Staper	Mr Richard Wyche
Mr Rich. Wysemañ	Mr Robt Bell
Mr Thomas Cordell	Mr Wm Chambers
Mr Roger Howe	Mr Wm Harrysoñ

ROBT COBBE beinge one of them that is behinde wth his moneys was called hether. did for the securytie of his paym^t deliver vnto the handes of Mr Ald^r Bannyng bondes dated the 8 of the next moneth wch this company thought fyt to reteyne in ther handes de bene esse not accepting theiñ as his adventure. — Robt Cobbe

Ordered that ther *be* provysioñ made of 130^c byskett to carry the shippes into the West Cuntrey the care of wch provysioñ is comitted to Mr Stap and Mr Cordell. — Biskett.

One thowsand of holland lynge to be provided for the victualling of the shippes vntill they came downe into the West Cuntrey wch provysioñ is comitted to Ald^r Bannyng and Mr Robt Bell. — Holland lyng

Order is geaveñ for the provysioñ of 240 Tuns of beare of severall brewingẽ for the whole voiage to be apointed to be brewed by the order of Mr Cordell and Mr Lancaster. — Beare.

40 Tuñ of Syder is provided by Mr Chamber and Mr Harry- — Syder.

soñ and bought of one M⁽ʳ⁾ Fletcher and Company and 60 Tuns more is to be provided in the West Cuntrey by Capteñ Davies Capteñ Baker and Robt Pope.

500ˡⁱ to Mʳ Allabaster for provision of Royalles.

Order is geaveñ to Mʳ Aldʳ Hollyday Threr to pay to Mʳ Allabaster the somme of fyve hundred poundes to be exposed by him before hand to Calleis or other partes for the provysioñ of Ryalles for the voyage.

400ˡⁱ to Sʳ Hughe Portman p exᵉᵉ.

Lyke order is geaveñ to the said Mʳ Aldʳ Hollyday to pay to Sʳ Hewghe Portmañ or to assignes the somme of fowre pounds for so muche by him dd in exchange to Robt Pope in the West Cuntrey Taking vp the Bill.

Beef Porke.

The provysioñ of beefe and *porke and* the Survey of the ordering thereof is comitted to Aldʳ Bannyng and Mʳ Wysemañ who are content to vndertake the same.

The 5 of Novemb. 1600.

Mʳ Aldʳ Smythe Goʳ
Mʳ Aldʳ Bannyng
Mʳ Aldʳ Hollyday
Mʳ Aldʳ Wattes
Mʳ Aldʳ Moore
Mʳ Rich. Staper
Mʳ Tho Cordell
Mʳ Rich. Wysemañ
Mʳ Fra Chery

Mʳ Olyver Style
Mʳ Wᵐ Garway
Mʳ Jo: Highelord
Mʳ Wᵐ Rumney
Mʳ Wᵐ Chambers
Mʳ Robt Sandy
Mʳ Nich Lyng
Mʳ Jo: Middletoñ
Mʳ Robt Bell.

Mʳ Wᵐ Harrysoñ

200ˡⁱ to be pᵈ by Exchaung to Ellis Crysp for Thoˢ Jones.

RDER is geaveñ to Aldʳ Hollyday Threr to pay vnto Ellys Cryspe for soe much reᵈ by Capteñ Baker of Thomas Jones of Plymouth by Exchaunge to be pᵈ in Londoñ, the soñe of two hundred poundes vppon paiment whereof he is to take vp the Bill.

Wᵐ Tavernoʳ mariner.

Mʳ Staper maketh report to this Assemblie that he and Mʳ Wysemañ hath compounded wᵗʰ Wᵐ Tavernoʳ to be imployed in this viage by the Companie in what ship or place they wyll assigne him for the enterteynm^t of sixe pounde sterling p moneth geving him the somme of fourtie poundes before hand vppon his wages for wch enterteynm^t he promiseth his vttermost endeavo^r to be pformed wth all fidelyty.

Warraunt is geaveñ to Ald^r Bannyng Thre^r to pay vnto Robt Stephens the somme of Nyne hundred pounds for soe muche re^d of him by Exchaung p^d to Mr John Ellicott at Exceto^r vppon Two severall Billes the one of fowre hundred poundes the other of five hundred poundes. vppon the payment whereof he is to take vp the Two severall Billes

900^li to be p^d to Robt Stephens p exchaung.

Mr Ald^r Wattes Capteñ Lancaster Mr Cherie and Mr Chamber *are required to make* [have made] Composition wth Roger Hankiñ marino^r to goe in this viage for a m^r in one of the shippes for this enterteynment [viz] in the best sort they can for the good of the Company and what Composition they shall make the Company will accept thereof.

Roger Hankyn marino^r.

Warraunt is geaveñ to Ald^r Bannyng to pay to Mr Thomas Bowles of Tavestock the somē of thirtie poundes sterling for so muche by him p^d to Capteñ Baker in the West Cuntrey by a bill of exchaung wch bill is to be takeñ vp vppon the paiment thereof.

30^li to be p^d to Tho. Bowles by exchaunge.

It is resolved that all the shippes shalbe Symented vppoñ ther sheething before they come out of the dockes and to that ende order is geaveñ to Mr Burrell to see the same prepared.

Symonding of the shippes.

The 6. of Novemb 1600.

Ald^r Smyth Go^r
Ald^r Bannyng
Ald^r Hollyday
Mr Staper
Mr Richard Wysemañ
Mr Wm Rumney
Mr Wm Chamber

Mr Rich: Wyche.
Ald^r Wattes
Mr Tho Cordell
Mr Wm Garway
Mr John Highelord
Mr Robt Sandy
Mr Roger Howe.

The Erle of Cumbland

110ˡⁱ to John Stanfield for John Painter by exᶜᵉ.

RDER is geaveñ to Aldʳ Bannyng Threr̃ to pay vnto Johñ Stanfeld or his assignee the somme of one hundred and tenn poundes sterling for so muche takeñ vp̄ by Mʳ Sandy of Dertmouthe of Johñ Painter of the same Towne to be pᵈ by Bill of exchaung to the said Stanfeld vppoñ the payment whereof he is to take vp̄ the Bill of exᶜ.

That the marinerˢ shall have 2 monethes pay & 2 monethes wages in adventure.

It is ordered by the generall consent of this assemblie that for the commoñ and ordinarie mariners that are to be enterteyned for the voyage they shalbe severally allowed for the better provysioñ of every severall mariner to see he shall have Two monethes wages before hande. And for the better advauncemᵗ of his sallarie, that everie the said mariners shall have two monethes wages in adventure as his stocke provided that for his wages takeñ before hand every one geave such cawtioñ to the Threr̃s of the viage or the Purser of the ship wherin they serve that the said Marinoʳ shall not depart from the voyage to the disapointing therof but be ready when the shippes shalbe sett forward.

The proportion of victualles

It is ordered that Mʳ Aldʳ Wattes shalbe joined wᵗʰ the other Comitties apointed for the proportioñ of victualles and to exañe what provisioñ hath bene made according to the proportioñ sett downe, to thende that to see howe the preparation of the viage doeth presentlie stande.

100ˡⁱ to the Purser of the Malice Scurg

Order is geaveñ to Mʳ Aldʳ Bannyng Threr̃ to pay to the Purser of the Malice Scurge the soñe of one hundred poundes to be imployed in the building preparatioñ and provisioñ of the same ship.

Roger Hankyn.

Warraunt is geaveñ to Mʳ Aldʳ Wattes *Mʳ Chery & Mʳ Chambers or 2 of them* to proceade in the concluding [by agreemᵗ] wᵗʰ Roger Hankiñ for his imployment in this viage And yf they cañ not bring him to *consent to be holden an* adventurer in the voyage for the soñe of one hundred poundes or vnder wᵗʰout wages theñ to agree wᵗʰ him for 50ˡⁱ to be geaveñ him freely and teñ poundes p̄ moneth for his wages. as was yesterday agreed vnto.

It is ordered that Ald^r Bannyng Ald^r Hollyday [Mr Cordell] Ald^r Wattes, Ald^r More Mr Cordell Mr Gorwey Mr Allabaster or anie 3 of theiñ shall compound wth Capteñ Lancaster and to offer him the offer agreed vppoñ yesterday as the geñall offer of the Company wch will not be encreased and to take his aunswer directly *to* accept or refuse the same offer that the Compañie may resolve what course they may rest vppoñ. Capten Lancaster. the offer is knowen but not sett downe.

It is ordered that Mr Wysemañ *and Mr Burrell* shall take and vse the mast that lyeth on the key at Savages wch was Ald^r Bannynges mast and the Compañ will save him harmeles therin and satisfie the proprietors thereof. A mast for the Hecto^r

It is ordered that ther shalbe p^d *by Mr Ald^r Hollyday* to Peter Grove according to the composition made wth him the some of seventy poundes in full paym^t of the Agreem^t of the money to be dd him. 70^{li} to Peter Grove.

The 7. of Novemb 1600.

Mr Ald. Bannyng	Mr Tho. Cordell
Mr Ald^r Hollyday	Mr John Highelord
Mr Ald^r Wattes	Mr John Eldred
Mr Ald^r Moore	Mr Robt Sandy
Capteñ Lancaster	M^r Jo. Combe
Mr Rich : Staper	Mr Riche Wyche
Mr Olyver Style	Mr Wm Chambers
Mr Wm Rumney	Mr John Middletoñ

T this Assemblie was signed a Bill of the Receipte of the severall peeces of Tymber herevnder men- coed wch was borrowed of her Ma^e out of the Storehouse at Wolw^{ch} for the repairing of the Scourge

N^o.	Feet	N^o.	Feet	
1	33	5	24	peeces of timber marked wth
2	49	6	45	
3	28	7	64	
4	24	8	39	

```
           9  ——— 45            14 ——— 61
                                15 ——— 26
                   350          16 ——— 60
          10 ——— 46             17 ——— 33
          11 ——— 61             18 ——— 32
          12 ——— 15             19 ——— 60
          13 ——— 44                    ———
                                       440
```

of feet in all ——— 791
In tons of 40 ⎫ tons   feet.
foote p tuñ ⎭ 19 — 31

At this Assemblie Consideration was had of the number of meñ that shuld be shipped in the severall shippes of the viage bothe of factors and mariners and have resolved that they shall be manned severally wth thes numbers following viz.

```
          In the Scourge    ——— 180 ⎫
          In the Hecto^r    ——— 100 ⎬ meñ.
          In the Ascentioñ  ——— 080 ⎪
          In the Susañ      ——— 080 ⎭

                                440
```

A reviewe of the proportion of victuall.

It is also agreed that Mr Ald^r Wattes and Capteñ Midletoñ shalbe ioyned wth Mr Ald^r Bannyng Capteñ Lancaster Capteñ Davies and Mr Allabaster who formerlie sett downe the proportioñ of victualles. and they altogether to enter into the reviewe of the same proportioñ; and to consider what is prepared thereof *and* what is further to be done in enlarging or abridging thereof and whatsoever they shall doe therein the Companie will allowe thereof.

Tho. Eldred of Ipesw^rh

Mr Johñ Eldred acquainteth this Assemblie that one Thomas Eldred of Ipesw^ch a mañ of good report who hath bene imployed wth Capteñ Candishe is willing to be imployed in the voyage and would go as Capteñ or M^r of one of the shippes, to whoñ aunswer is made that the Companie will enterteyñ none vntill they see him and speake wth him, and have willed that M^r

Eldred shall wryte vnto him that he thinketh yf he come vp the Company are likelie to enterteyn him.

Order is geaven to Ald' Hollyday Threr to pay vnto M' W'" Harvy of Bridgewater the somme of fyfty poundes sterlinge for so muche re^d of him by Robt Pope to the use of the voyage by a bill of exchange vppon the payment whereof he is to take vp the bill.   *50^li to W Harvy*

The like order is geaven to the said Ald' Hollyday threr to pay vnto James Prockter of London the somme of one hundred poundes sterling for so muche re^d by Robt Pope of Thoms Trowbridge in the West Cuntrey to the vse of the voyage by a bill of exchaung vppon the paym' whereof the bill is to be taken vp.   *100^li to James Prockter*

[M^r] *Capten* Lancaster having bene alreadie talkd wth all by some of the Comitties wch were yesterday apointed to that ende, and noe agreement fully made wth him he beinge present at this Assemblie and the matter havinge bene something debated amongest them he yeldeth in the ende to comitt the absolute agreement of his enterteynment to the consideration and finall ende of Mr Ald Smythe Governo^r Ald^r Bannynge Ald^r Wattes Ald^r Hollyday Ald^r Moore Mr Cordell and Mr Allabaster or any 6 of them. And this Assemblie in the behauf of the Company do lykewyse referre them selfes to ther Censure, shewing ther assent by erecting of handes.   *Captn Lancaster*

The viij^th Novemb' 1600.

Ald^r Bannyng	Mr John Highelord
	Mr Wm Chambers
Mr Garway	Mr Roger Howe
Captein Lancaster	Mr John Eldred
Mr Rich: Wyseman	Mr Wm Harryson
M^r. John Combe	

lres out of the West Cuntrey.	IVERS lres out of the West Countrey, brought by the Post of Exetor the one a generall lre from Capten Davies Capten Baker Mr Pope, and Mr John Sandy were read menconing ther severall proceading in the Busines wch lres are delivered over to Mr Howe to be noted and aunswered, and the aunsweres reterned by the Post.
40li to Wm Harvey p exc	Warraunt is geaven to Aldr Bannyng Threr to pay vnto Mr Wm Harvy of Bridgewater or his Assigne the somme of fowrtie poundes sterlinge for soe muche red of him by p exchaunge delivered to Robt Pope, wch bill is to be taken vp vppon the paiment made.
100li to Wm Lacy p exc	The like Warraunt is geaven to the said Threr to pay vnto Wm Lacy of Hertrowe or his assignes the somme of one hundred and tenne poundes sterling for soe muche by him delivered p exchaung to Robt Pope vppon the paiment whereof the bill is to be taken vp.
100li Malyce Scurg	Warraunt is geaven to Mr Aldr Hollyday to pay to the handes of Edward Stephens Carpenter the somme of one hundred poundes sterlinge vppon accompt of Tymber for the Malice Scurge.
80li the Susan.	Warraunt is geaven to Aldr Bannyng to pay to Joseph Sulman Purser of the Susan to be imployed in the pparation of the same ship vppon an accompt the somme of four score poundes.
200li to Mr Burrell.	Warraunt is geaven to Aldr Hollyday Ther to pay to Mr Burrell Surveyor of the shipping to be imploied in preparing therof vppon accompt the somme of Two hundred poundes.

November the 10th.

Mr Aldr Halmden	Mr Harrison
Mr Style	Mr Sandy
Mr Lancaster	Mr Middleton
Mr Wych	Mr Combe
Mr Wyseman	Mr Howe

Mr Ald: Bayning:

AT this assembly it was ordred & appoynted ffor the provyding of all the pvisions to these men there seuerall pvisions aff° viz.

To Mr How & Mr Sandy Mr Combe ffor these pvisions
   ffor 13 Hogesheads aquavitæ   Aquavitæ: 13 hh^{ds}
   ffor Spyces viz 112℔ sūgar   Spyces: 225^{lb}
             30℔ synamon
             15℔ nūtmeggs
             6℔ clowes
             50℔ ginger
             12℔ pepper
   ffor Ryce 20c   ryce 20c
   ffor sault 16 tonns   sault 16 tonns
To Mr Cordell and Stapers
   ffor 240c of bread at london   bread 240c
To Mr Cordell and Mr Wych { 75 tonns smale   beere 150 tonns
   ffor 150 tonns of beere— { 75 tonns of 50^{ss} p tonn
  To Mr Harrisson, Combe & Sandy, & Mr Howe & Mr Bell & Mr Lancast^r
   ffor 66 tonns of wyne.   Wyne 66 tons

           November 1600 the 10th
To Mr Ald bayning and Mr Wyseman
   ffor C 707. —. 16 ,, beeff   Porck C883. 3. 20.
   ffor C 883. 3. 20 ,, porcke   Beefe
To Mr Wych and Mr Wryte
   ffor pease & beanes 1031¼ bushells   Peas beanes
To Mr Ald bayning:
   ffor 1000: of ling great tale   lynge
To Mr Ald Holliday
   ffor 10000 stock fish great tale   stock fishe
To Mr Ald Bayning
   ffor 30 quarters oatmeale is 240 bushells   Otemeale
To Mr Wych to speake to Mr Covell
   ffor 70 bushells oatmeale   Otemeale
To Mr Sandy, Mr Harrisson & 2 pursers
   ffor 20 way of cheese   Cheese
   ffor 70 ffirkens butter   Butter

Sweete oyle	To Mr Ald bayning, Mr How, Mr Garway, & Mr Eldred ffor 2000 gallons sweete oyle
Vineger	To Mr Combe, Mr Howe, & Mr Sandy ffor 24 tonns of vineger
Hony.	To Mr Sandy; Mr Howe & 2 pursers ffor 6 barrells of honey
Musterd-seed	To Mr Wych ffor 30 bushells musterd seed
Candells	To Mr Wyseman, Mr Bell, Ald Holliday & Mr Chambres ffor 1200 lb candles covered wth wax ffor 400 lb Ordynary candles
rape oyle	ffor 10 hh^{ds} rape oyle ffor lamps
Caske	To Mr Chambres & Mr Harrisson ffor 8 dozzen barrycods
	ffor 150 tonns water caske
	ffor 150 tonns ffor beere wth ash hoopes
	ffor 44 tonns ffor beeff

    50 tonns ffor porck
 150 tonns syder & strong beere
  24 tonns ffor vineger
  13 tonns ffor oyle & aquavitæ in barrells
   2 tonns ffor honey & Rape oyle
   6 tonns ffor tarr in yron hoopes
  10 tonns ffor oat meale
   2 tonns ffor musterd seed & ryce
  26 tonns ffor beanes & pease

Novemb^r 1600 the 11th.

Ald^r Smith governour	Mr Eldred
Mr Ald^r bayning	Mr Style
Mr Ald^r Holliday	Mr Chambres
Mr Wyseman	Mr Cordell
Mr Lancaster	Mr Sandy
Mr Wyche	Mr Chambres

Mʳ Harrison   Mʳ Linge
Mʳ Combe   Mʳ Middleton
Mʳ Highlord   Mʳ Rumney
                  Mʳ Alabaster

THIS Assembly gave cōmissions to every of the   Comissions
cōmissioners ffor the pvyding of their severall   for victuals:
coīnissiers as are before written on the 10ᵗʰ
hereof as appeareth.

Mʳ Ald Bayning, Mʳ Ald Watts, Mʳ Alabaster, Mʳ Ald   to agree wᵗʰ
Holliday, Mʳ Ald More, Mʳ Cordell, Mʳ Style, Mʳ Combe   Capt: Middleton
Mʳ Rumney appoynted to agree wᵗʰ Capt Middleton about
going on this voyadg

    The names of such as are sett down & mencioned to goe   factors
       factors on this voyadg.   nominated.

Capteyn Jnᵒ Middleton	Henry Annis
John Haiward	Daniel Marsh
ffrancis barnes	Robert Chamberlayne
Robert Pope	Thomas Tudd
William Brend	William Rutton
Elkana Cole	John Taylor. will vent 200ˡⁱ Elkana Cole
William Wilford	Tho: Morgan
Thomas Dassell	Hollywell
Roger Style	Phillip Winchecombe
William finchcomber	Robt Greene
Edward lokar	Edm. Scott
Danyel Tucker	Giles Georg
Thomas Salter	Tho Hickes
Richard Collimore	Hugh Wryte
William russell	Tho Hurlestoñ
William Starkey	Tho. Hickes
Robert Cressell	Henry Midletoñ

               John Wray

At this Assembley it was ordred that Mʳ Smith governour   ₅₀₀ˡⁱ to
Mʳ Ald Holliday, Mʳ Ald Watts, Mʳ Ald More, Mʳ Cordell,   bee coyned
Mʳ Garway and Stapers, should bee suyters to the lord treasurer

ffor a warrant ffor the pvyding & coyning of y 5000ˡⁱ in the towar; & ffor pvyding of bulleyne for the same & for the finishing the Pattent

A Warraunt for yᵉ transportation of Victualles from the Portes.

The sayd cōmittyes appoynted to make suyte to the Lord treasurer for a lycence to transport pvisions in the west countrey according to a letter of Mʳ Jnᵒ Sandy

November 1600 the 11ᵗʰ.

Mʳ Ald bayning	Mʳ Chambres
Mʳ Ald Holliday	Mʳ Lancaster
Mʳ Garway	Mʳ Alabaster
Mʳ Wyseman	Mʳ Middleton

Maisters & Officers

T this Assembly it was agreed and concluded that the committyes *and the maisters* ffor euery shipp shall take the charge of provyding [maisters &] other officers in the same shipps: wᵗʰ maryners, & what they shall doe herein shalbee well done.

The 12 Novemb 1600.

Aldʳ Bannyng	Mʳ Wᵐ Rumney
[Aldʳ Holmedeñ]	Mʳ Robt Sandy
Aldʳ Hollyday	Mʳ Johñ Combe
Aldʳ Wattes	Mʳ Rich Wyche
Mʳ Aldʳ Holmedeñ	Mʳ John Middletoñ
Mʳ Rich: Staper	Mʳ Robt Bell
Mʳ Wᵐ Garway	Mʳ Nich: Lynge

100ˡⁱ to yᵉ Purser of the Malice Scurdge

RDER is geaveñ to Aldʳ Bannyng to pay vnto Henr Mydletoñ Purser of the Scurge to imploy in the provysioñ and preparatioñ of the same ship vppoñ accoumpt the somē of one hundred poundₑ

40ˡⁱ per exᶜ to Jo: Wyndeham

Order is geaveñ to the said Aldʳ Bannyng to pay vnto Mʳ Johñ Wyndhañ. vppoñ a Bill of exchaung the somme of *fowrtie* poundes for soe much paid by the said Bill to Robt Pope, in the West Cuntrey to the vse of the voyage.

It is agreed that a Warraunt for the transportation of all provysions made in the West Cuntrey for this voyage vnder the L Three hande to the officers of the Portes and other officers shalbe solicyted, and to be sent downe in to the West Cuntrey wth all convenient speede.   *Warraunt to be procured for the shipping of all pvision in the West Cuntrey.*

It is ordered that Mr Hilliard Mr Sandy Mr Chambers and Mr Grove, shall consyder of the small and extraordinary merchaundize of glasses knyves and Norrom boroughe ware fytt for the voyage and to bespeake suche thing^{es} as are newlie to be made   *Glasses knyves Norromborow ware &c.*

Mr Sandy Mr Bell are appointed for the provysion of Leade and Tynn who together wth Mr Grove shall consider of the Quantety and of the kindes of the same comodyty.   *lead & tynn*

❦

Novemb^r the 14th 1600

Mr Ald Bayning	Mr Roger Howe
Mr Ald Watts	Mr Olyver Style
Mr Ald Holmenden	Mr Linge
Mr Ric̃ Wyseman	Mr Robert bell

T this Assembly given severall warrants in Mr Ald Bayng for payment of these severall somes ffollowing to say.

Off y 50   to Nyc^n Symons for timb^r for y^e Susann   £50: to Nyc^n Symonds.

y 66 ,, 13 ,, 4   to Joseph Salbanck for necessaryes & wages for the same shipp   £66. 13. 4 to Salbanck

y 39 ,, — ,, —   to Roger Gibbons by a bill of exc^r for Mr Robert pope.   £39 : by bill for pope.

y 100 ,, — ,, —   to Mr Richard Wyseman for the hecto^r provision.   £100: to Mr Wyseman for the Hecto^r

The 15 November 1600

Mr Ald^r Bayning	Mr Combe.
Mr Ald^r Watts	Mr Rumney
Mr Tho: Cordell	Mr Highlord
Mr Fra: Lancaster	Mr John Middleton
Mr John Eldred	Mr Nicholas Ling
Mr William Chambres	Mr Richard Stapers
Mr Wm Harrisson	Mr William Garway

g 30^{li} to Wm Kemp for Capt. baker

EVEN a warrant at this assembly ffor paym^t of y 30. to William Kempe by bill of exc^r for Thomas Bakar frõ Plymouth;

Order for carrying the shipps into docke for payment of the charg ffor provyding of 5000^{li} of bulleyne.

Also it is agreed that Mr Wyseman shall see the bills of chargs ffor bringing in of the shipps into the docks dischardged & payd.

Also it is ordeyned that *Mr Ald Bayning* Mr Ald Holliday together wth Mr Wyseman shall take the charge for the pvyding of 5000^{li} of bulleyne ffor the coyning of the lyke vallew & also Mr Stapers to assist thereunto.

The 18. Novemb^r 1600.

Ald^r Smythe Go^r.	Mr Wm Chamber
Mr Ald Bannyng.	Mr Nich: Lyng
Mr Ald Hollyday.	Mr Wm Rumney
Mr Ald^r Wattes	M^r [Robt] *John* Comber
Mr Rich: Staper	M^r
Mr Wm Garway	Mr Rich: Wysemañ
Mr Robt Sandy	Mr Thomas Allabaster
Ald^r Holmeden	Mr Rich: Wyche
Mr Olyuer Style	Mr Robt Bell
Mr Wm Harrysoñ	

40^{li} to Thomas Northeover

RDER is geaveñ to Mr Ald^r Bannyng ther to pay to Mr Thomas Northeove^r the somme of fowrtie poundes for so muche by him dd in exchange to

Robt Pope in the West Cuntrey vppoñ paiment whereof the bill is to be takeñ vp.

Lyke order is geaveñ to the said Threr to pay vnto Johñ Lant of Excetor the somme of one hundred and fyfty poundes sterling for so much by him dd in exchange to Robt Pope in the West Cuntrey vppoñ payment whereof the bill is to be taken vp. 150ˡⁱ to Jo: Lant of Excetoʳ

This [Companie] *Assemblie* falling into Delibatioñ of some generall Course to be takeñ in the enterteymt of [the] *three* principall factoʳˢ for three of the shippes and of the other sortes of factoʳˢ vnder the principall in ther severall Degrees and places. They do resolve of ther severall rates of allowaunce and enterteynment(?) following viz. that the 3 principall factoʳˢ shall have every of theñi one hundred poundes geaveñ theñi to provide theñi to sea and every of theñi the gaine of 200ˡⁱ adventure [as thowghe they had severally had putt in] and for the the 4. severall seconde sorte of factors they will allowe theñi severally fyfty poundes apeece to provide them to sea, and the [adventure] gaine of the adventure of one hundred pound a peece, and and for the 3 sorte of factors ther is allowed to theñi 30ˡⁱ a peece to be geaveñ theñi for ther provysion and the gaine of 50ˡⁱ adventure and for the fowrth and Last sorte of factors they will allowe theñi twenty poundes apeece and the gaine of *the adventure of* fowrtie poundes a peece. The enterteymnᵗ of all thes factoʳˢ

The allowaunce and enterteynmt of the said factoʳˢ beinge resolved vppoñ the said Comittees proceaded to the Election of the 3 principall factoʳˢ of the said voyag whervppoñ electioñ being made by Scruteny vppoñ seaveñ of the Chieffest Sewtors to the Companie to be imployed as factors in the said viage. Choice was made of Capteñ Mydletoñ. Johñ Havard and Frauncis Barme. for the said 3 principall factors [to be imployed in the said shippes] to be sorted and placed in the shippes as hereafter it shalbe considered by the said Comitties. Of wᶜʰ severall factoʳˢ only Johñ Havard beinge present was called in and acquainted wᵗʰ the Electioñ and wᵗʰ the enterteynmᵗ is well contented therwᵗʰ and doeth willingly accept thereof. The election of 3. principall factoʳˢ

Capten Midleton
Jo: Havard
[Fra.Barme]
Wᵐ fisher

THE COURT RECORDS OF

The 19 Nouemb 1600.

Mr Ald^r Smyth Go^r	Mr Wm Chamber
Mr Ald^r Bannyng	Mr John Eldred
Mr Ald^r Moore	Mr Robert Bell
Capteiñ Lancaster	Mr John Combe
Mr Wm Rumney	Mr Frauncis Chery
Mr Roger Howe.	Ald^r Hollyday
Mr Richard Wyche	Mr Nichñs Lynge
Mr Wm Harrysoñ	Mr Rich: Stapers
Mr Ald^r Wattℓ	Mr Tho. Cordell
Mr Rich: Wysemañ	Mr Robt Sandy
Mr Olyuer Style	Mr Wm Garway

M^r Jo: Highelord.

40^{li} to M^r joⁿ God per ex^{te}

RDER is geaveñ to Mr Ald Bannyng Threr to pay vnto Mr Johñ God the somme of fowrtie poundes sterling for soe muche by him p^d and delivered in exchaunge to Robt Pope in the West Cuntrey vppoñ the payment whereof the bill is to be takeñ vp

100^{li} p^d to ffrauncis Covell for provision of peas and Beanes

Order is geaveñ to ye said Threr to pay vnto ffrauncℓ Covell towardes the providing of Peas and Beanes for the voyage the somme of one hundred poundes sterling vppoñ accompte of that provisioñ vppoñ payment whereof take his receipte.

The Election of the 4. second sort of factors, Robt Pope Wm Brand Tho. Saltern Wm Starky

The seconde sorte of factors being putt in Election at this assembly and eight sewtors for the fowre places being sorted out and putt to Scruteny the Comitties ṗceded to the Electioñ of 4 of them. *In wch election* ther was choseñ for the places ofthe seconde sort of factors thes psons following viz. Robt: Pope Wm Brand Thom^s Salterne and Wm Starky to be sorted and placed in the severall shippes according to the Discretioñ of the said Comitties.

500^{li} to Mr Allabaster for provision of Royalles.

Order is geaveñ to Mr Ald^r Bannyng Threr to deliver vnto Mr Thom^s. Allabaster the somme of five hundred poundes sterling to be imployed by exchaung in provisioñ of Royalles of plate.

THE EAST INDIA COMPANY

The said Assemblie proceading to the Election of the third sort of factors to be imployed in this voyage ther were propounded eight severall sewters for the said places vppon wch the Comitties proceaded to scruteny and did elect these severall psons following for the supplying of the places of the third *sort* of facto^{rs} videlt. Thomas Hickes Henr Mydleton Wm Wilford nathaniell [Gumbrell] Gamrym to be sorted and placed in the shippes by the discretion of the Comitties.

(margin: The Election of the third sort of factors. Thomas Hickes Henry Midleton Wm Wilford Natha: Gamrym)

The Election of the fourth sort of facto^{rs} being pceaded in by the said Comitties ther were also propounded the names of Eight sewters. out of wch by scruteny were chosen. these severall psons whose names are subscribed to be sorted and placed in the shippes at the disposition of the said Comitties viz Percivall Stragling Thom's Morgan Phillip Winchcomb and Thom's Tudd.

(margin: The 4 sort of factors. Percivall Stradling Tho Morgan Phillip Wynchecomb. Thomas Tudd.)

The 21 November 1600

Mr Ald^r Smythe Go^l	Mr Wm Chambers
Mr Ald^r Hollyday	Mr Rob't Sandy
Mr Ald^r Wattes	Mr Rich: Wyche
Mr Staper	M^r Jo: Eldred
Mr Olyuer Style	M^r Jo: Midleton
Mr Rich: Wyseman	Mr Nichas Lyng
M^r Jo: Highelord	Mr Wm Harryson
Capten Lancaster	M^r Jo: Combe

Mr Rob't Bell.

ARRAUNT is geaven to Ald^r [Bannyng] *Hollyday* Thre^r to pay vnto Richard Stratford by a Bill of exchaunge from John Sandy for so muche by him taken and re^d of John Eydes *at Excet^r* the somme of fyfty poundes.

(margin: 50^{li} per ex^c to Ric Stratford for Jo Eydes.)

Lyke warraunt is geaven to the said Thre^r to pay to Mr John Ellecott the somme of five hundred poundes sterling vppon his bill of exchaunge. to be rep^d at Exceto^r to the vse

(margin: 500^{li} to be p^d to Jo: Ellecott to be rep^d)

<small>at exceto^r to ye vse of ye Company.</small>
of the Companie vppoñ the paym^t whereof he is to receave his billes.

<small>100^{li} p^d to Edw: Highlord purser of the Scourge.</small>
Order is geaveñ to Mr Ald^r Hollyday Threr to pay to ye Purser of the Scourge the somme of one hundred poundes vppoñ accoumpte to be imployed in the preparing of the same ship

<small>40^{li} p^d to Rich: Walton p ex^e.</small>
Order is geaveñ to the said Ald^r Hollyday Threr to pay vnto Richard Waltoñ the somme of fowrtie poundes sterlinge for soe much by him p^d and delivered in ex^{ce} to Mr Johñ Sandy at Exceto^r vppoñ paiment whereof the bill is to be takeñ vp

<small>60 to be p^d to Rich: Rudd by ex^e.</small>
Lyke order is geaveñ to the said Ald^r Hollyday Threr to pay vnto Richard Rudd the somme of sixtie poundes sterling for so muche re^d of the said Rudd at Exceto^r by Mr Johñ Sandy to the vse of the voyage vppoñ payment whereof the bill is to be takeñ vp

<small>50^{li} to be p^d to Nichas Rantoñ by ex^{ce}.</small>
Lyke order is geaveñ to the said Ald^r Hollyday Threr to pay vnto Nicħas Rantoñ the somme of fyftie poundes sterling for so muche re^d of him, by the handes of Johñ Sandy to the vse of the voyage vppoñ a bill of ex^{ce} vppoñ paiment whereof the bill is to be takeñ vp

<small>Mr. Allabaster.</small>
Comissioñ is geaveñ to Mr Thom͠s Allabaster to take suche Course as he shall thinke meet for the conveyaunce of suche Bulleiñ or Royalles froñ Callyce as shall be sent froñ thence by exchaunge to the vse of the voyage.

<small>300^{li} to Mr Sandy to be rep^d by him at Exceto^r.</small>
Order is geaveñ to Mr Ald^r Bannyng Threr to pay vnto Mr Robt Sandy the somme of three hundred poundes sterling to be rep^d by him at Exceto^r to the handes of Mr Johñ Sandy to the vse of the voyage.

<small>40^{li} to be p^d to Rich: Gregory by ex^{ce}.</small>
Order is geaveñ to Mr Ald^r Hollyday Threr to pay vnto Richard Gregorie or his Assignes the somme of fowrtie poundes sterling for soe much re^d by Robt Pope at the handes of the said Gregorie in the West partes *by exchaunge* to the vse of the Companie. vppoñ paiment whereof the bill is to be takeñ vp.

<small>Order for suche as refuse to</small>
At this Assemblie order is [geaveñ] takeñ that the names of as many of these as have sett downe ther [names] handes and

sommes of adventure and have since denied to pforme the same, shalbe called vppoñ to geave ther resolutioñ what they will do, to thende some course may be takeñ wth theiñ before the Pattent be putt to ingrossing. bring in ther adventure.

A lře from the L. Threř in the behaulf of one Henry Aneys. to bee imployed in the said voyage was read vppoñ the reading whereof. aunswere was geaveñ to the beare^r wch was Mr Suckley my L. secreterie, that the Companie were sorie that they had not notice of his L^ps pleasure before the Election of ther factors [were] *was* past, yet notw^thstanding they will endevo^r vppoñ anie occasioñ of the Refusall of anie of them that are choseñ. or vppoñ anie other occasioñ to [pleasure] imploy the said Anys yf they cañ finde fytt vse of his service Henry Anys comended by the l. Thrers lres.

The 22 of the Novemb^r 1600.

Mr Ald^r Smyth Go^r	Mr Wm Chamb.
Mr Ald^r Hollyday	Mr Robt Sandy
Mr Ald^r Wattes	Mr John Combe
Mr Wm Garway	Mr Rich: Wyche
Mr Olyuer Style	Mr Wm Harrysoñ
M^r Jo: Highelord.	Mr Robt Bell.

Mr Roger Howe

ORDER is geaveñ to Ald^r Hollyday Threř. to pay vnto Wm Mallett gent. or to his Assignes the some of threescore and teñ poundes sterlinge for so muche by him paid by exchaunge to the handes of Robt Pope in the west Cuntrey vppoñ the paiment whereof the bill is to be takeñ vp. 70^li to be p^d to Wm Mallett by exchaunge

Order is geaveñ to the said Threř to pay to the handes of Mr Wm Garwey the somme of two hundred poundes sterling vppoñ accoumpte to be imploied in the repairing and preparing of the Assentioñ. 200^li to be dd M Garway for the Assention.

The like order is geaveñ to the said Threř to pay vnto Wm Burrell Generall Surveyo^r of the repairing and preparing of 100^li to be p^d to Mr Burrell.

86   THE COURT RECORDS OF

the shippes the somme of one hundred poundes sterlinge vppoñ accoumpte for the provisioñ of Timb^r and other necessaries for the shippes.

Poll Davies for bagges. It is ordered that Mr Roger Howe shall buy Poll Davies for the making of bagges and to putt theiñ out to making that they may be sent into the west Cuntrey

All factors to putt in sewrties. It is ordered by the generall Consent of this Assemblie that all factors. imployed in this voyage shall geave securytie to the lykinge of the Comitties before he be putt in to anie charge. that he shall pforme all faithefull service to the generalitie and shall abstaine froiñ all private trade

Roger Style. Roger Style one that hath bene brought vp vnder Mr Olyver Style doeth make this humble sewte to the Companie that wher in the Electioñ of the 16 factors his name was putt in choyce and failed he is content to be imployed wthout Salary. so as he may be imployed as a facto^r yf anie of the rest shuld dye in the voyage, and is also content to be Left in the Cuntrey of the East Indies vntill the retorne of a seconde voyage in wch residence he is content to apply him self to lerne the language wch motioñ is well lyked of and shalbe further delt in hereafter

The 25 of Novemb 1600.

Mr Ald^r Hollyday	Mr Wyche
Mr Tho. Cordell	Mr Wm Harrysoñ
Mr Wm Garway	Mr John Combe.
Mr Wysemañ	Mr Roger Howe
M^r fra: Chery	Mr John Highelord
Capteñ Lancaster	Mr Robt Sandy
Capteñ Middletoñ	Mr Wm Chambers

Meale brought in the prize. 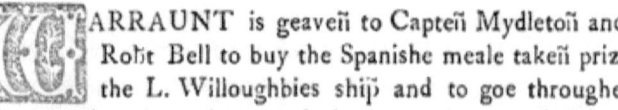 ARRAUNT is geaveñ to Capteñ Mydletoñ and Mr Robt Bell to buy the Spanishe meale takeñ prize by the L. Willoughbies ship and to goe throughe wth the bargaine thereof as good cheape as they cañ leaving the sume to ther discretioñ.

50^{li} to Order is geaveñ to Mr Ald^r Holliday Threr to pay to Edward

Stephens principall [tymber] *Carpenter* in the Scourge the somme of fyftie poundes sterling to be imployed by him in the repayring of the same shipp. And to geave an accoumpte thereof. for wch his receipte is to be taken <small>Edward Stephen for ye Scourge.</small>

It is agreed that the enterteynment of a fourth M^r wch is not yet done shalbe referred to Mr Staper Mr Cordell Mr Garway and Captein Lancaster. and that they also may proceade to Compound wth anie other officer of the shippes at the best rate they can <small>Order for the hyring of a M^r & other officers.</small>

It is also ordered that Mr Garway Mr Cordell Mr Stap and Richard Wright shall attende and solicyte my L. Threr for suche bullyon as is in the tower being about the valewe of 3000^li and to procure as much respite and Libertie of tyme as they can gett for the bringing in of the Like quantety of bullein againe into the Tower <small>Bullyon to be had out of y^e tower.</small>

27 Novemb. 1600.

RDER is geaven to Ald^r Hollyday Threr *by advyse from Robt Pope* to pay vnto John Portman Esquier or his Assignes the somme of two hundred poundes sterlinge for so muche to him delyvered by *the said Threr* in exchaunge to be p^d to the vse of the voyage. to the handes of Robert Pope in the West Cuntrey vppon payment whereof a Receipte is to be taken at the handes of Mr Porteman or of him that receaveth the money as his Assignee: to make paym^t accordinglie <small>200 dd p cx^re to Mr John Portman</small>

Order is geaven to Ald^r [Hollyday] *Bannyng* Threr to pay vnto the handes of Edward Highlord Purser of the Scourge the somme of one hundred poundes sterling to be imployed in the repayringe of the shipp scourge vppon accoumpt vppon payment whereof yo^u are to take his receipte <small>100^li to the Scourge.</small>

The 28 Nouemb 1600.

The Erle of Cumbland	Mr Ald. Wattes
Mr Ald^r Smythe Go^r	Mr Ald Moore

88   *THE COURT RECORDS OF*

  Mr Olyver Style   Mr Wm Chambers
  Mr Rob̃t Sandy   Mr Rich: Wyche
  Mr Tho. Allabaster   M^r fra: Chery
  Mr Johñ Highelord.   Mr Wm Harrysoñ
  Mr Ald^r Hollyday   Capteñ Lancaster
      Capteñ Myddletoñ

y 112^{li}: to Wm Dale by exc frõ robt Pope

WARRANT is given to Ald Bayning ffor payment of y 112^{li} to Wm Dale by a bill of exc^e of the 15 hereof in tantonn frõ Robert Pope ffor the lyke vallew by him Receyved of Wm Macy

Pattent read.

At this Assemblie the Pattent of the previledges for the East Indie voyage was read and order geaveñ to the Secretorie to solicite the Queenes Attorney to make an end of the same.

100^{li} to y^e Hector.

Order is geaveñ to Mr Ald^r Hollyday threr̃. to delyver and pay vnto the Purser of the Hecto^r the somme of one hundred poundes sterling to be imployed in the repayring and preparing of the same ship vppoñ accoumpte.

    The 29 Nouemb̃ 1600

  Mr Ald^r Hollyday   Mr John Highelord
  Mr Tho Cordell   Capteñ Midletoñ
  Capteñ Lancaster   Mr Wm Chambers
  Mr Olyuer Style   Mr John Combe
  Mr Rich: Wysemañ   Mr Niclias Lynge
  Mr Roger Howe   Mr Wm Garway

4^{li} p^d in recompence to a poore man for boulging his Crane wth the Scourges Anker. Advyse in to the West Cuntrey.

ORDER is geaveñ to Ald^r Hollyday *Threr̃* to pay vnto a pore mañ in recompence of the boulging of his Crane by an Anker of the Scourge the somme of fowre poundes sterling.

Order is geaveñ to Mr Howe to write to Mr Pope, Mr Baker and Mr Sandye that they provide noe more biskett or meale for that vppoñ the viewe of the perticlers̃ of provysion of breade and meale the full quantety is accomplyshed

100^{li} to M Cole dd in ex^{ce}.

Warraunt is geaveñ to Mr Ald^r Hollyday Threr̃ to pay to Mr Johñ Colles Esquier the somme of one hundred poundes sterlinge by exchaunge to be rep{ed} againe by him or his Assignee in the West Cuntrey to the handes of Robt Pope to the vse of the voyage vppon the delivery of w{ch} money the bill of ex{c} is to be re{d}.

The like Warraunt is geaven to the said Ald{r} to pay to the handes of Capten Lancaster the somme of one hundred poundes sterlinge vppon the Reckoning of his enterteynment for the voyage. 100{li} to Capten Lancaster.

The p{r} December 1600.

M{r} Ald{r} Holliday	M{r} Rich: Wych
M{r} Ald{r} Watt{e}	M{r} W{m} Harrison
M{r} Ald{r} More	M{r} Rob: Sandy
M{r} Tho: Cordell	M{r} Jn{o} Combe
M{r} Rich: Stapers	M{r} Rob: bell
M{r} Richard Wyseman	M{r} Jn{o} Meddleton
M{r} Capt. Lancaster	M{r} Hihlord
M{r} W{m} Chambers	M{r} Style—

AT this assembly written a letter to m{r} Denman & m{r} Hale of the bridghouse to delyver to m{r} w{m} burrell 2 peecs of tymber, eyther taking his receipt w{th} promyse to redelyver the lyke, or to take money of him ffor the same. M{r} Denman & M{r} Hale for 2 peecs timber to be dd m{r} burrell.

Also it was at this tyme agreed & appoynted that the officers of the shipps [are to] *should* bee *hyred & placed* in the order ffollowing & their wages to bee agreed as also ffolloweth—

Carpenters	ffor the scourge	4	to bee hyred by m{r} Bŭrrell & their wages to bee allowed & agreed vpon, vpon his report of what he hath done at the table	Carpenters
	ffor the hecto{r}	3		
	ffor th'assension	2		
	ffor the susann	2		
Cawkers	ffor the scourg	4		Cawkers
	ffor the hecto{r}	3		
	ffor the assension	2		
	ffor the susann	2		

Gonners.	Gonners	ffor the scourge 10;	the cōmittyes & m^r Lancaster to agree wth them
		ffor the hecto^r 6	the own^{rs} that were, to agree wth them
		ffor the süsann 5	
		ffor th'assension 5	

Stewards — Stwewards ffor ech shipp himself and his mate
Cookes — Cookes ffor ech shipp one and his mate
Surgeons — Surgeons ffor ech shipp twoe & a barber

Generall, pilot major & m^r Bradbanck. To deale wth m^r Beare.

Also it was ordeyned that the generall the pilot major & m^r bradbanck maister should goe in the Scourge.

Also it was ordeyned that m^r ald Watts m^r Cordell & m^r Stapers should take in hand to deale & conferr wth m^r Beare to bee one of the 4 chief maisters.

The prim° December 1600.

£172.7.9 d vpō ald Holliday to pay to m^r ffor 95 quarters 6 bushels & 10^{lb} meale.

Geven a Warrant vppon ald Holliday to pay y 172^{li}. 7^s. 9^d to . . . . in full ffor 95 qwarters 6 bushells & 10^{lb} of meale bought by m^r Bell of one m^r gawldsmith being taken a pryze at xxxvj^s the qwarter amounting to the sayd some—.

The 4 of Decemb 1600.

Ald^r Moore:
Capten Lancaster
Mr Rich: Staper
Mr Wm Garway
Mr Tho Cordell.

Mr Olyuer Style
Mr Rich. Wysemañ
Mr Wm Chambers
Mr Wm Harrysoñ
Mr Johñ Midletoñ.

IT is ordered by these Cōmitties that the psons heer vnder named shall conferre wth Capteñ mydletoñ touching his enterteynment in this voyage. and whatsoever they shall agree vppoñ to be geaveñ him shall be pformed by the generalyty and the said Capteñ mydletoñ for his part submytteth him self to ther agreem^t.

THE EAST INDIA COMPANY

The Erle of Cumbland
Mr Aldr Moore
Mr Tho Cordell } or any 3. of them.
Mr Wm Garway
Mr Rich Wysemañ

It is also ordered that mr Stap Capteñ Lancaster mr Tho. Allabaster and Richard Wright shall conferre together touching *suche* lres as shalbe solicited from her maie to suche princes and Potentates as are in the places of the Este [whether] wher trade shalbe sought

Touching lres to be writt from the Queene to the East Indies.

And it is ordered that Aldr Hollyday and Richard Wright shall sett downe the names of [such] all those that shalbe mencoñed in the Pattent and Carry them to Mr Attorney that the booke may be ingrossed.

And lastly it is ordered that vppoñ munday next a generall Cort shalbe called to enforme the generalyte of the proceadinges of the Comitties and how farre the busines is in a redines.

The 5 of Decembr 1600.

Aldr Bannyng	Capteñ Lancaster
Aldr Hollyday	Mr Wm Chambers
Aldr Wattes	Mr Ry Wysemañ
Mr Olyuer Style	Mr Wm Harrysoñ
Mr Nich. Lynge.	

T this Assemblie it was resolved that mr Thomas Allabaster his Comissioñ for prouisioñ of Ryalles shalbe contynued the same to be provided froṁ suche partes as formerlie it was ordeyned

Warrauntes were geaveñ to mr Aldr Hollyday for the paiment of these Sommes followinge viz.

five hundred poundes to mr Thomas Allabaster for provisioñ of Ryalles   500ˡⁱ . 0 . 0

one hundred poundes to mr Wm Garway for the provysioñ of thassension.   100 . 0 . 0

100ˡⁱ . o . o	One hundred poundes to Mʳ Wᵐ Chambers for the provision of Caske.
120ˡⁱ . o . o	Warraunt is geaveñ to Aldʳ Bannyng to pay one hundred [poundes] and twentie poundes. to Josephe Salbanck

The 6 of December 1600.

Mʳ Aldʳ Smythe Goveʳ   Mʳ Jo : Highelord
Mʳ Aldʳ Hollyday   Mʳ John Eldred.
Mʳ Thomas Cordell.   Mʳ Wᵐ Chambers
Mʳ Olyuer Style.   Mʳ John Midletoñ
Capten Lancaster   Mʳ Nicĥas. Lynge
       Mʳ Robt Bell.

80ˡⁱ to Mʳ Wᵐ Burrell

WARRAUNT is geaveñ to Aldʳ Hollyday to pay to mʳ Wᵐ Burrell for the provisioñ of Tymber and other necessaries for the shippes the soñe of fowrscore poundes sterling to be dd him vppoñ accoumptes.

80. to Mʳ Nich: Symondson

The Like Warraunt is geaveñ to Aldʳ Bannyng to pay to nicĥas. Symondsoñ for provisioñ of Tymber and paiment for ware the somme of fowrscore poundes sterling

50ˡⁱ to Wᵐ Angell, fishemongʳ

Another warraunt is geaveñ to *the said mʳ Aldʳ Bannyng to pay to* Wᵐ Angell fishemonger vppoñ accoumpt of fishe the soñe of fyfty pounds sterling

Order is geaveñ for the warning of a generall Court vppoñ munday next to informe the geñalyty of the present state of the voyage for the better proceading wherein thes pticler [pointes are to] thinges [touching] are to be notyfyed vnto theñ touching the handling of the busines hetherto. viz.

The Choice of factoʳˢ in ther severall places.
The Choice of the severall Mʳˢ
The redines of the shippes to come out of ther Dockes.
The present necessitie of the bringing in of money to pay wages because the officers and mariners are to [come] appointed to ther shippes.—&c

A Gen{{r}}all Court the 8. Decemb{{r}} 1600
in the presence of

M{{r}} Ald{{r}} Smyth Go{{r}} M{{r}} Roger Howe
M{{r}} Ald{{r}} Hollyday M{{r}} Rych: Wyseman
M{{r}} Ald{{r}} Moore: M{{r}} W{{m}} Chambers
M{{r}} Tho. Cordell M{{r}} Jo: Combe
M{{r}} W{{m}} Garway M{{r}} W{{m}} Harryson
M{{r}} olyuer Style. M{{r}} Nich: Lynge
M{{r}} Jo Middleton: M{{r}} Robt Bell.

And of a great nüber of the gen{{r}}alyty whose names are forborne to be noted for the shortenes of the tyme.

 IT is agreed by the generall assemblie for the better advauncem{{t}} of the voyage that whosoever is behinde w{{th}} his whole adventure by him sett downe and shall not wholie bring in the same by the 13 of this moneth beinge Satherday next that whatsoever damage shalbe susteyned by the deteyning of the shippes heare soe long w{{ch}} are only deteyned by the not bringing in of the adventures shalbe laid vppon those that by the want of bringing in of ther moneis have bene the occasion of so great a damage.

for the bringing in of the adventures.

The said Generalitie beinge made acquainted *by m{{r}} governo{{r}}* w{{th}} the redines of the preparation of the shippes victualles and all other furniture belonging to the same and also w{{th}} the Choice of the principall facto{{rs}} who are to be imployed in the said viage (the placing and sortinge of w{{ch}} facto{{rs}} being pticlerly noted and declared vnto them) the said generalyty were of opinion that in the disposing of some of the principall places and sorting of the facto{{rs}} in the same, the said cömitties had neade better to informe them selfes, then they have done for that in the seconde sort of factors ther is *placed* one M{{r}} Brund a grave and discreet mchaunt and one w{{ch}} hath the arabyan Spanishe and Portugall Languages w{{ch}} may better deserve [a principall] *the* place of a principall facto{{r}} then some of those w{{ch}} are placed in the first place and therfore the generalyty do wyshe the Comitties in ther next assemblie to

The eleccon of one of the principall factors.

advyse better of the same election and that they would consider thereof when they are mett in most ample number assuring them that m^r Brunde will not accept of a Second place especially the first being supplied by younger men and of *lesse* experience and desert then him self

The 10th of Decemb̄ 1600

Mr Tho: Smythe Go^r	Mr Capten̄ Lancaster
Mr Ald^r Hollyday	Mr John Eldred.
Mr Ald. Moore	Mr Rob̄t Sandy
M^r olyuer Style	Mr Rich: Wyseman̄
Mr Tho Cordell	Mr Wm Chambers
M^r fra: Chery	M^r Jo: Middleton̄.
Mr John Highelord	Mr Niclīas Lynge
Mr Wm Chambers	Mr Wm Harryson̄.
Mr Rich: Staper	Rob̄^t Bell.

Henry Napper.

IT is ordered that Capten̄ Lancaster and Capten̄ Midleton̄ shall conferre wth Henry Napper touching his imployment in the voyage to goe therin as they and he can̄ agree the former Composition̄ made wth him by Mr Staper notwthstanding. and as they proceade in the same conference. to acquainte the Comitties therwth at ther next meeting.

This assembly proceading to the reviewe and reexaīation̄ of the former election of the .4. first principall factors places. according to the order of the last generall Court did in this meeting vppon̄ good delībation enter into consideration̄ of the matter and did wth a generall Consent by Scrouteny make choice of Mr Wm Brunde to be one of the fowre principall factors in this voyage *and* to be [sorted placed] sorted as heerafter followeth [viz] And it ys *also* agreed that the Generall and [principall] other the said principall factors shalbe sorted and placed as hereafter followeth viz

    Capten̄ Lancaster in the Scourge.
    Capten̄ Midleton̄ in the Hecto^r.
    Wm Brund in the Assention̄
    John̄ Havard in the Susan̄.

Order is geaveñ to Ald^r Bannyng ther̃. to pay to henry mydletoñ purser of the scourge the some of 300^{li} vppoñ accoumpt for the provisioñ of the Scourge vppoñ paym^t whereof he is to take his receipte. *(300^{li} to ye Scourge.)*

Lyke order is geaveñ to the said *m^r Ald^r* Bannyng to pay to Wm Walthall 224^{li} 2^s 0 for 29 fodder 4^C 1^q 16^{lb} of Peate Lead bought at vij^{li} xiij^s iiij^d the ffodder. *(224^{li} 2^s 0^d for lead bought of Wm Walthall.)*

Further order is geaveñ to the said Mr Ald^r Bannyng to pay vnto Edwyñ Babingtoñ the som̃e of 100^{li} sterlinge in part of payment for Canary Wynes provided for the voyage. *(100^{li} to Edwin Babington for wynes.)*

Order is geaveñ to m^r [Thom͠s. Allabas] Ald^r. Hollyday to [pay] deliver to m^r Thom͠s Allabaster vppoñ accoumpte the somme of five hundred poundes sterling to be imployed by him for thexchaunge of Royalles. for the vse of the voyage. *(500^{li} to Mr Allabaster for Royalles)*

The like order is geaveñ to the said m^r Ald^r to pay vnto Edward Stepheñs Carpenter of the Scourge the somme of fyfty poundes sterling vppoñ accoumpte to be imploied in the Repairing and preparing of the same ship *(50^{li} to y^e Carpenter of the Scourge.)*

The 11th of Decemb^r 1600.

Mr Ald^r Hollyday	Capteñ Lancaster
Mr Wm Garway	Capteñ Middletoñ
Mr Rich: Wysemañ	M^r Jo: Combe
Mr Wm Chamber	Mr Robt Bell
Mr John Eldred.	Mr Rich: Wyche
M^r olyuer Style	Mr Nich: Lyng
Mr Wm Harrysoñ.	

ORDER is geaveñ to Ald^r Hollyday *ther^r* to pay vnto Raphe Salter Surgeoñ enterteyned for this voiage the somme of thertie and two poundes sterlinge being allowed vnto him by Composition for the furnishing of his Chest wth all kinde of necessaries and remedies belonging to a Chirurgioñ to be vsed in this viage vppoñ paiment of wch money [you are] he is to take his acquittaunce. *(32^{li} to Raphe Salter Chirurgion.)*

Ther is also order geaveñ to Ald^r Bannynge to pay vnto M^r *(100^{li} to)* frauncis Covell for peas & beanes.

frauncis Covell the somme of one hundred poundes sterling vppoñ Accoumpte for the provysioñ of peas and beanes. vppoñ paiment whereof he is to take his receipte

100ˡⁱ to the Hectoʳ

The like order is geaveñ to the said Aldʳ Bannynge to pay to mʳ Richard Wysemañ the somme of one hundred poundes sterlinge to be delivered to the Purser of the Hectoʳ for the Charges of provisioñ and p̃paratioñ of the same ship vppoñ accoumpte.

The Scourge is hearafter to be called. by the name of the Red Dragoñ.

It is ordered that the great ship called the Scourge wᶜʰ is to be lanched this after none. shall be called heerafter by the name of the Redd Dragoñ. and noe more to be knoweñ by the former name of the Scourge.

The 12ᵗʰ of Decemb̃. 1600.

Mʳ Tho. Cordell   Mʳ Robt Sandy.
Mʳ Rich: Staper   Capteñ Lancaster
Mʳ olyuer Style.   Capteñ Middletoñ
Mʳ Rich: Wyseman   Mʳ Wᵐ Harryson
          Mʳ Nicħas. Lyng.

71ˡⁱ. 13. 4ᵈ to Mʳ Attorney and his Clerkes.

RDER is geaveñ to Mʳ Aldʳ Bannyng threr̄ to pay vnto mʳ Robt Sandy the somme of seventie *one* poundes *xiijˢ iiijᵈ* sterling for somuche by him dysbursed for the Charges of oʳ Pattent and the Warraunt for coyning dewe to Mʳ Attorney and his Clerkes for the drawing and ingrossing of the same pattent and Warraunt. I say seventie one poundes thirteene shillingſ and foure pence.

The 13 of Decemb̃ 1600.

Mʳ Aldʳ Wattes   Mʳ W: Rumney
Mʳ Aldʳ More   Mʳ Robt Sandy.
Captein Lancaster   Mʳ Wᵐ Chamber
Mʳ Tho. Cordell.   Mʳ Nicħas Lyng
Mʳ olyuer Style   Mʳ

THE EAST INDIA COMPANY

RDER is geaven to Ald[r] [Hollyday th] Bannyng ther̃ to pay vnto John Busbridge *lynnen*drap[r] the somme of one hundred twentie and five poundes tenn̄ shillinge[s] sterling for Lynnen Clothe of him bought by M[r] Stap and M[r] Lyng for the vse of the voyage. whose pticlers appeare. and are to be dd wth the warraunt for the paiment of the money.   125[li] 10[s] for lynnen Clothe.

Order is geaven to Ald[r] Hollyday ther̃ to pay vnto W[m] Cater. and George Cater. the somme of twentie eight poundes fourteene shillinge[s] for 24 peeces of Roan̄ Cloth viz 475 elnes at xiiij[d] ob̄ p elne bought of them by m[r] Niclas Lyng. vppon̄ payment whereof he is to take his receipt in full.   28[li] 14 0 for Roan̄ Canves.

Order is geaven to m[r] Ald[r] Hollyday to pay vnto M[r] Roger Hankin M[r] of the Assention̄ the somme of thertie sixe poundes [three shillinges] and fowre pence for the fraight ballast and other Charges dewe thervppon̄ of two hoyes. to goe to the severall shippes of this voyage vppon̄ paiment whereof he is to take his receipte.   36[li]. 0. 4[d] for ballast for the shippes and for the fraight of 2 hoyes to go to the shippes.

It is ordered that all the Pursers of the severall shippes shall be warned to appeare vppon̄ twesday before the Comitties and to bringe in ther accoumptes of the disbursem[ts] of moneys delivered then̄ to be imployed aboute the shippes and other occasions of the Companie.   Pursers to bring in ther Accoumptes.

M[r] W[m] Chambers made a motion̄ to this Assemblie in the behaulf of one Walter Poyner to be imployed in the voyag: as a facto[r] at large w[th]out salarie w[th] this hope that if anie facto[r] faile, that he may supplie his place or the place of some other of the facto[rs] that shalbe removed to the place of the decessed or to be left in the Indies as a resident facto[r] whose motion̄ is well lyked of and the matter to be further considered of at some other meetinge when the Companie shall [consider] assemble them selfes to take a Survey of the facto[rs].   Walter Poyner.

The like motion̄ is made by m[r] Sandie in the behaulf of m[r] w[m] martens sonne of Exceter for to be imployed in the voyage. for whose fidelyty his father wyll geave good security to the Companie. and is content to be imployed as the [said] Companie shalbe pleased or left in the Indies for a facto[r] resident ther.   W[m] Martin

o

The 15 Decemb^r a^o. 1600.

Mr Tho: Cordell   m^r Alderman more
Mr Ryc^r Stapers   captaine lancaster
Mr Rob^te Saundye   m^r ollyver style.
Mr W^ms Chamb^rs   m^r wiche.
Mr Jno Highlord.   m^r fraunces Cherry
    m^r Ryc: Wyseman.

26^li. 13^s.
James Lovering [Daniel Lee] Chirirgeon of y^e hecto^r.

RDER is geven to m^r Ald^rman Baninge to pay vnto [Daniel Lee] *James Lovering* surgeon of the hecto^r entertained for this viadge the some of twenty fyve pounds ster^l beinge alowed him by Composicion for the furnisshinge of his chest wth all kinds of remedyes and necessaryes belonnginge to a chirurgeon to be vsed vpon this viadge. vponn paim^t of wch monney yo^u are to take his acquyttance.

20^li. to Xpofer newchurch surgeon of the Assencon

There is also order geven to m^r Alderm̄ Banning to pay vnto chrystopher newchurche surgeon of the Assencōn for twentye pounds str^l Allowed him by Composicion for the furnishinge of his chest wth all kind of remedyes and necessaryes belonnginge to a chirurgeon to be vsed vpon this viadge. vpon paym^tt of his monney yo^u are to take his acquyttance.

20^li. to Jno. gamond surgeon of the susann

There is also order geven to m^r Aldermann baninge to pay vnto Jno gamond twentye pound str^l allowed him by composyc̄on for the furnishinge of his chest wth all kind of remedyes and necessaryes belonnginge to a chirurgeon to be vsed vpon this viadge; vpon paym^tt of this monney yo^u are to take his acquyttance.

The 16 of Decemb 1600.

Mr Staper   Captēn Midletoñ
Mr Garway   Mr Harrysoñ
Mr Cordell   Mr Eldred
Capten Lancaster   Mr Chamber.
Mr Wysemañ   Mr Highelord.
Mr Howe.   Mr Sandy
    Mr Chery

R Ald^r Wattes Mr Cordell Mr Wysemañ Mr Howe and Mr Harrysoñ *or any*. 3. *of them* are appointed Auditers to receve the Accoumptes of the Pursers and to examine the same and as they finde the said accoumptes to stande to Certefie ther opinions to the residewe of the Comitties to thende yf anie thinge fall out in the same accoumptes worthie the consideratioñ of the said Comitties [the] order may be takeñ therin by them. *Auditors*

Order is geaveñ to m^r Ald^r Bannynge to pay vnto the Purser of the Hercules the somme of one hundred poundes sterlinge. vppon accoumpte to be imployed in the preparatioñ and repayring of the same ship *100^{li} to the Hect^{r}.*

The like order is geaveñ to m^r Ald^r Holliday to pay vnto ye Purser of the Assentioñ the somme of one hundred poundes sterling vppoñ accoumpte to be imployed in the preparatioñ and repairinge of the same ship *100^{li} to ye Assentioñ.*

It is agreed that whereas the proportioñ for the provisioñ of iroñ was formerlie agreed to be but 30 tuñz it is nowe resolved that ther shalbe provided 20 tuñz more so that the whole quantetie of iroñ shalbe 50 tuñs. and that ther shalbe provided furthe some convenient quantety of faggot iroñ being in small barres fitt to be converted in to nayles. *yron to be provided 50 tuñs in the whole.*

The same day in the after none.

Mr Ald^r Smyth Go^r	Capteñ Lancaster
Mr Ald^r Hollyday	Mr Highlord.
Mr Ald^r Wattes	Mr Chambers
Mr Ald^r Moore.	M^r Jo Combe.
Capteñ Lancaster	Mr Nich : Lyng
Mr Thomas Cordell.	Mr Rich : Wyche.
M^r olyuer Style.	Mr Wm Harrysoñ
Mr Rich : Wysemañ	Mr Robt Sandy
Mr Wm Rumney	Mr Wm Burrell

Mr Wm Garway.

HIS assemblie beinge [be] mett in conference for the placing and sorting of the Principall officers to be imployed in the voyage, they have agreed that they shalbe severallie sorted in the said shippes in manner and forme followinge viz.

The sorting of the principall factors & other officers

In the red [Lyon] *Dragon*. Admirall.

Capteñ Lancaster generall.
Capten Davies   Pylott Maio^r of the fleet
Wm Broadbent   M^r of the same ship

In the Hector.   Vice Admirall.

Capteñ Midletoñ. principall facto^r in that ship
Henry Napper. M^r of the same ship.
Phillip Grove [Pylott] second Pilott of the fleet.

In the Assention.

William Brunde. principall factor in that ship.
Roger Hankin M^r of the same ship

In the Susan.

John Havard principall factor in that ship.
Samuel Spencer M^r of the same ship.

The 17th of Decemb 1600.

Mr Ald^r Smithe Go^r Mr Wm Rumney.
Mr Ald^r Hollyday   Mr Rich. Wyche
Mr Ald^r Wattes   Mr Robt Sandy
Mr Ald^r Moore   Mr Nich: Lynge
Mr Rich: Staper   Capteñ Middletoñ
Mr Thomas Cordell   Mr John Combe
Mr Rich: Wysemañ   Mr Fra: Chery
Capteñ Lancaster   Mr Wm Chambers
M^r olyuer Style   Mr John Highelord
           Mr Roger Howe.

THE EAST INDIA COMPANY

HE choice of the factors formerlie made being interrupted by reasoñ of the [refusall] *falling of* of some of theiñ ther was a newe proceeding in the election of [someñ] *divers* of the said factors wch geaveth occasioñ to make someñ alterationñ of the sorting and placing of the second, third and fourth sorte of *them*. [factors the the same factors] wheruppoñ at this Assemblie the said severall factors are sorted and disposed in manner and forme [following viz.] mencõed on thother syde.

A newe placing and disposing of the 2. 3. and 4 sort of factors.

Robert Pope who hath bene imployed in the West Cuntrey in the provysioñ of victualles moneys and other necessaries for the voyage. being come vp̃ and present at this assemblie forasmuche as he hath takeñ paines in the said preparations and is one of the second sort of factors. appointed for the voyage : this assemblie have added to the ordinarye allowaunce geaveñ to the rest of the said seconde sort of factors to be [geaven] *paied*, to the said Rob̃t Pope the someñ of fyftie poundes sterling^g over and besides his Charges hetherto expended wch money shalbe p^d him before his going forthe.

*50^{ll} to Rob:
Pope factor.*

The names of the seconde third and fowrth sort of factors. and ther places as they are appointed to be shipped

Robert Pope	in the Red Dragoñ	2 sort of factors
Wm Starkey	in the Hector	
Tho Salterne	in Assentioñ	
Henry Middletoñ	in the Susan.	
Nathaniel Gamram	in the Dragoñ	3. sort of factors
Thomas Dassell	in the Hecto^r.	
[Rich: Collymer] *Roger Style*	in the Assentioñ	
Wm Wilford	in the Susañ.	
Xpofer Stradling	in the Dragon.	4. sort of factors
Tho. Tudd	in the Hecto^r.	
Phillip Winchecomb	in the Assentioñ	
Tho Morgañ	in the Susañ	

The names of suche facto^{rs} as are admitted to goe wthout Salarie to [be] take place yf anie of the former enterteyned factors do dye. or to be left in the Cuntrey as residentſ ther to lerne the Language. and to looke in to yͤ trade of those Cuntreis at the discretioñ of the Generall and other principall facto[rs]

D. John Smythe.
H Walter Poyner.
   [Roger Style]
S. George Allyñ.
A Roger Martiñ.
A Thomas Warde.
D. Thomas Webbe.
H. Hughe Hule.

} to be placed in the shippes at the dispositioñ of the Chief Generall and principall factors.

The 19 December 1600.

  Mr Ald[r] Holliday   Capt. Lancaster
  Ald[r] Watts   M[r] Wyseman
  Ald[r] Moore   Mr Style
  Thomas Cordell   Mr Chambers
  Wm Garway   Mr Howe
  John Eldred   Mr Sandy.

EVEN a warrant vppõ ald[r] Bayning ffor paym[t] of y 800. to Robt Stevens in full of a bill of y 1400. frõ m[r] John ellacott of exceter.

y 800. vppõ ald bayning to robt stevens

Geven a warrant vppõ ald Holliday ffor paym[t] of y 600. to Robt Stevens & *Roger Howe* in full of a bill of y 1400. frõ m[r] John ellacott of exceter

y 600. vppõ ald: holliday to Robt stevens.

Geven a warrant vppõ ald holliday ffor paym[t] of y 241. to m[r] ffrancis west by a bill of exc̄ frõ John Sandy frõ exceter

y 241. vppõ ald. holliday

Geven a warrant vppõ ald [holliday] Bayning for paym[t] of y 105. 12:4[d] to walter clarck ffor lyke vallew Receyved in exceter by John sandy in Ryall of plate as p the bill.

y 105. 12. 4 vppõ ald holliday to walter clarck.

Yt was at this assembly ordeyned that m[r] thomas Alabaster should not proceed any ffarther in provision of Ryalls frõ callais.

m[r] alabaster not to proceed in ryalls.

THE EAST INDIA COMPANY

Order is given to mʳ Roger How to take the charge in answering of certayne letters Rh̍d frō the factors in the west countrey & to give a Remembrance to mʳ Robᵗ pope bound thither ffor the manadging of the busynesse there concerning [all] as well Ryalls of plate as all other provisions their made & to take an accōpt of euery of the rest of the factoʳˢ there wᵗʰ such other directions as hee shal thinck meete for these busynesses.

Given a warrant vppō al̍d Bayning for paymᵗ of y 30. to Wᵐ Wilford for his salary in this voyadg

30ˡⁱ to wᵐ wilford one of the factors·

The 20 december 1600.

Mʳ Goũernoũr   Mʳ richard stapers
Mʳ Aldʳ Moore   Mʳ Harrison
Mʳ Richard Wyseman   Mʳ Chambres
Mʳ olyver Style   Mʳ Combe
           Mʳ Lancaster.

GEVEN a Warrant vppō al̍d Bayning ffor payment of y 231 . 10 . — . to george hangar ffor 22 pypes of canaria wyne at 10£ . 10ˢ — ᵈ p pype.

231ˡⁱ.10ˢ.—ᵈ to mʳ hangar.

The 20 december 1600.

Geven a warrant vppō al̍d Bayning ffor paymᵗ of y 378. to mʳ wᵐ harrisson ffor 36 pypes of canarya wyne at y 10 . 10 . — p pype.

378 ˡⁱ to mʳ harrisson

Geven a warrant vppō al̍d Bayning ffor paymᵗ of y 160. to mʳ Edwin babington in full for 26 pypes of canary wynes at y 10 p pype.

160ˡⁱ to mʳ Babington

The 22 december 1600.

Mʳ Gouernour   Mʳ
Mʳ Cordell   Mʳ Eldred
Mʳ Wyseman   Mʳ Lancaster
Mʳ Style.   Mʳ Middleton
Mʳ Rumney   Mʳ Stapers
           Mʳ highlord

EVEN warrants vppõ ald^r Bayning ffor paym^t of these somes ffollowing to say—

100^{li} to Lewes Tate smith ffor smithery by him delyvered

100^{li} to henry middleton purser of the Redd dragoñ.

50. to Roger hanckey m^r of the assension vppõ accõpt of his wages.

100^{li} to william Burrell ffor $p$vision for the shipps

40^{li} to John coles by exc^e for Lewes pope in absence of Robert pope to the hands of gyles Barrey.

200^{li} to m^r wyseman to pay ffor wax candles & provision for the hecto^r.

Geven a warrant vppon ald^r Holliday ffor paym^t of y 100. to Richard Hart smith ffor smithery ffor the assension.

The 24 Decemb^r: 1600.

Mr Ald^r Watts	Mr Sandy
Mr Cordell	Mr Harrison
Mr Cherrey	Mr Howe :
Mr Style	Mr Lancaster
Mr Wyche.	Mr Ald^r Hollyday
Mr Wyseman	Mr Middleton
Mr Eldred	Mr Highlord.

EVEN at this assembly warrants vppõ ald^r Bayning ffor these somes ffollowing viz

y 30 : to thomas dassell ffor his wages in this voyadg

y 100 : to william Bradbanck maister of the dragon vppõ accõpt

y 150 : to John Buzbridg vppõ accõpt of yron by order of mr. sandy

y 100 : to Robt warner vppõ accõpt of 35 tonns of yron

y 210 : to m^r Robt savadg ffor 20 [tuns] pypes of canaria wyne

y 100 : to m^r william Chambres towards provision of caske &c :

The 24 December 1600.

1600
24 Dec.

Geven warrants vppõ ald^n Bayning ffor payment of these somes ffollowinge—

₺ 10. 5. 8, to henry lambard ffor 89 black iacks

₺ 50.—.—, to xpofer [Smith] thomson smith vppõ accõpt of yron wark for the hecto^r

₺ 17. 4. 11, to ffrancis covell in ffull of provisions made by him as by accõpt

₺ 50.—.—, to william Dixson purser of the Redd dragon for the vse of that shipp

Geven warrants vppõ ald^n Holliday ffor payment of these somes ffollowing viz

₺ 100. to m^r w^m Garway for the assention

₺ 150. to w^m Candish vppõ accõpt of lead by order of m^r Sandy.

At this assembly it was determyned that Roger Style should take the place of Richard Collymore ffor one of the third sort of ffacto^{rs} & to have the same allowance & salary as the other of that sort are allowed, and vppõ this agreem^t m^r olyver style hath in his behalf pmysed to adventure ₺ 200.—.—

Roger Style.

Also it was ordered that every sort of ffacto^{rs} before elected to take chardge in this voyadg [vnder] *in* the number of the sixteene should give in bonds ffor their truth & good behavio^r as followeth—

Bondes of the factors.

The ffirst ffower to give bonds of ₺ 500.—.—

The second fower to give bonds of 500 marcks

The third sort to give bonds of 200^{li} p peece

The fforth sort to give bonds of 100^{li}

The 27 of Decemb^r 1600.

1600
27 Dec.

ARRAUNT is geaven to Ald^n Bannyng *thẽr* to pay vnto Robt Stephens for the vse of John Ellicott the some of [one h] five hundred poundes sterling in part of paiment of seven hundred poundes. taken vp by him in Ryalles of plate.

500^{li} to Mr Ellicott for royalles.

106   THE COURT RECORDS OF

1600
27 Dec.

25ˡⁱ 1ᵈ to
John Sheir
for money
by ex-
chaunge.

The like warraunt is geaven *to Aldⁿ Hollyday* ther to pay vnto Laurence Waldo the somme of Twentie and five poundes sterling and is for somuch taken vp by exchaunge of John Sheer of Exeter and pᵈ to the handes of John Sandy to the vse of the Company.

200ˡⁱ to y
Purser of
the Scourge

Another Warraunt is geaven to the said Aldⁿ Bannyng to pay to Edward highlord Purser of the Read Dragon vppon accoumpte for provision and preparatioñ of the same ship the somme of Two hundred poundes sterling.

50ˡⁱ for
timber for
the read
Dragon

There is also another Warraunt made to the said Aldⁿ Bannyng to pay the soñie of fyfty poundes to Edward Stephens vppon the accoumpt of Tymber for the red dragon

1600
29 Dec.

The 29 December 1600.

Mʳ Tho Smythe Goʳ	Mʳ John Highelord
Mʳ Aldⁿ [Wattes] Hollyday	Mʳ John Eldred.
Mʳ Aldⁿ Wattes	Mʳ Robt Sandy
Mʳ Wᵐ Garway	Mʳ Wᵐ Chamber.
Mʳ Rich: Staper	Mʳ Wᵐ Harryson.
Mʳ Tho Cordell.	Capteñ Lancaster
Mʳ Rich: Wyseman	Capteñ Midleton:

700ˡⁱ to Mʳ
Allabaster
for royalles.

ARRAUNT is geaven to Aldⁿ Bannyng to pay vnto Mʳ Thomṡ Allabaster towardes the payment of certen billes of exchaunge. the soñie of seven hundred poundes sterling in part of payment of the said billes wᶜʰ do come to 880ˡⁱ being for the provision of royalles.

50ˡⁱ to Wᵐ
Starky.

Another warraunt is geaven to Aldⁿ Hollyday to pay vnto Wᵐ Starky one of the factors the somme of fyftie poundes sterling for so muche allowed him [vppon] *for* his enterteyn- ment for his preparation [of] *in* the voyage.

100ˡⁱ in gold
to be geaven
in gratuity.

It is ordered that ther shalbe geaven according to this con- ference the somme of [one h] Two hundred angelles in gratuyty from the Companie to suche psons as mʳ Garwey and Richard Wright by this assembly are directed to attende for that pur- pose. And it is ordered that

It is alsoe ordered and Warraunt is geaven to m^r Ald^r holly- day to pay to the handes of Richard Wright for the providing of the said 100^li in gold and for 50^li more in silver to pay other Charges for the passing of the Pattent and the Warraunt for Coyning the Signet the privy seale and great seale.

1600 29 Dec. 50^li for the charges of the bookes.

The 31 December 1600

1600 31 Dec.

Mr Ald^n Smithe Go^r	Mr Wm Chambers
Capten Lancaster	Capten Midleton
Mr Tho. Cordell.	Mr Nich : Lynge.
M^r olyuer Style	*Mr Staper.*
Mr Robt Sandy	Mr Wm Garway
M^r Jo : Combe.	Mr Robt Bell.

ARRAUNT is geaven to m^r Ald^n Bannyng to pay vnto to pay vnto John Gover. for viij hh. of Aquavite cñ^te 482 gallons. [of Aquavitæ] the somme of nynty six poundes viij^s at iiij^s the gallon / in full payment.

96^li. 8^s. for aquavite

It is ordered that the Thrër̄s accoumptes shalbe pvsed wth all expedition and to see what moneis hath bene p^d in by the adventuro^rs and what remaineth in ther handes . to thend that yf ther appeare a want of money wch cannot be other- wyse supplied then by the encrease of the geñ'all adventure, that then the geñ'ality may be called together and ther is apointed for Auditors. Mr Cordell m^r Style. Mr Wyseman. Mr Harrison.

Auditors for the Thrër̄s accomptes.

It is agreed that the goodes shipped by the Companie and the Caske shalbe m̃ked wth this geñ'all marke in the mergent and that an Iron be prepared wch shall make the said marke

Order is geaven to Mr Sandy to provide CCCC ½ of Castle Soape.

The 2 of January 1600.

1600 2 Jan.

Mr Ald^n Smithe Go^r	Mr Ald^n Hollyday
Mr Ald^n Bannyng	Capten Lancaster

1600 2 Jan.	Mr Tho Cordell. Capten Middleton
	Mr Garway Mr Niclias Lyng
	M^r oliuer Style Mr Robt Bell
	Mr Rich: Wyche. Mr Wm Harryson
	Mr John Combe. Mr Rich: Staper
	Mr John Eldred Mr Robt Sandy.

100^{li} to y^e Purser of the Read Dragon.

RDER is geaveñ to m^r Aldⁿ holliday *thr̃er* to pay vnto Wm Dyckes Purser of the Read Dragon the somme of one hundred poundes sterling to be imployed vppon necessary provision of the same ship vppon Accoumpte.

250^{li} to the Purser of the Susan.

Order is geaven to Mr Aldⁿ Bannyng thr̃er to pay vnto Joseph Salbanck Purser of the Susañ. to be imploied in the necessarie provision of the same ship the soñe of Two hundred *and fyftie* poundes sterling vppon accoumpte.

100^{li} to Robt Stephens by bill of exchaunge from Jo: Ellicott

The lyke order is geaven to m^r Aldⁿ holliday thr̃er to pay vnto Robt Stephens the soñe of one hundred poundes sterling by a bill of exchaung of John Ellicott directed to Robt Sandie written in the West Cuntrey vppon paiment whereof [yo^u are] *he is* to take his acquittaunce together wth the Bill.

Streamers Flagges & Auncients.

It is ordered that ther shalbe provided for eche of the shippes 12 Streemers. 2 fflagges and one Auncient wth all convenient speede, and that the same shalbe provided by the severall Comitties formerlie appointed to the said severall shippes for the provision of thinges necessarie for the same.

30^{li} to Roger Style factor

Ther is order geaven to Ald^r [Hollyday] *Bannynge* to pay to Roger Style one of the third sort of factors. the somme of thirtie poundes sterlinge. being the allowaunce graunted by the Companie for his provision.

The 8 of Januarie 1600

1600 8 Jan. Edm: Scott admitted to go in the voyage

DMUND SCOTT is admitted to goe in the voyage putting in Two hundred poundes venture: whereof C^{li} is to be p^d in hand and the other C^{li} at 14 daies next following . and where he was willinge rather then not to be imploied in the voyage to have geaven X^{li} to the Company for his diett aboard they are content to remitt the said X^{li} in hope of his good service in the choice of Drugſ and spices wherin he pretendeth to have knowledge.

1600
8 Jan.

A generall Court holdeñ the 9 of Januarie 1600. in the presence of

1600
9 Jan.

Mr Ald Smithe go^r	Mr Robt Sandy
Sr John Spencer	Mr John Eldred.
Mr Ald^n Bannyng	Mr Johñ Middleton
Mr Hollyday	M^r fra Chery
Mr Ald^n Wattes	Mr Roger Howe
Mr Tho Cordell.	Mr Rich: Wyche
M^r olyver Style	M^r Jo: highelord
Captein Lancaster	M^r Jo: Rumney :
Mr Rich: Wyseman.	And the greater part of the geñ'alyty.

WARRAUNT is geaven to Ald^n holliday thrēr to pay vnto Robert Stephens the somme of one hundred poundes sterling vppon a bill of Exchaunge from Johñ Ellicott out of the west Cuntrey Directed to Mr Robt Sandie vppon the East Indie accoumpte.

100^{li} per exc^e from Jo: Ellacot.

At this Courte the Pattent [it is ordered th] vnder the great seale was read [and] to the generalitie wherby it appeareth that ther is power geaven to the generalyty to admitt in to the priviledges. of the Company suche as [shal] they shall thinke good from tyme to tyme according to wch power forasmuche as divers have of late contributed to the voyage 200^{li} a peece whose names are not conteyned in the said Pattent therfore according to the warraunt geaven the Companie by the said Lres Pattentſ this Court have ordered that the same Contributors shalbe holden to all ententſ and purposes as free as [all] anie other [the] whose names are expresselie mencōned in the said graunt—the names of wch Contributors [are heervnder written viz] are

Admitting of freemen.

1600
9 Jan.

The want of the necessarie supplie of the adventure howe it is to be raised.

hereafter to be presented [at the next geñ'all Court and] then to be confirmed as free brothers of this felowship.

This Court was informed that the comon adventure sett downe for the voyage falleth out too short by the some of fowre or five thousand poundes. of that wch shall be necessarie to be sett forth considering the great preparation of the Ductche wch are ready to goe to the same places of the East Indies to wch o^r voyage is directed, and that also some of the adventure^rs wch have sett downe ther contributions have brought in noe part thereof and other some *do* defaulte of that wch they sett downe alledging that will not adventure so muche as they sett downe *at the first*. by wch meanes the adventure will fall short of that wch is necessarie *to be* [still further] *adventured to make a good voyage* by the some of eight or nyne thowsand poundes in the whole vppoñ wch information this Court falling into the delibation howe in best sort they may supply this present want. It was agreed [that] therfore by this geñ'all Court for the advancem^t of this voyage and for the avoyding of the preiudice that may happen by the want of a convenient proportion of adventure [for this present voyag^e enterprise], *and that* by the generall assent of this assemblie and establyshed as a Lawe Warraunted by the said lres Pattentes that for the present dispatche away of the shippes and the full augmentation of the Stocke and adventure to be sett forthe ther shalbe enlarged by every contributo^r according^e to the proportion of his adventure ij^s vppon the pounde wth this Cawtion notw^thstanding that yf the full adventure can be otherwyse supplied by any voluntary [supply] *enlargement* of mens voluntary encrease of ther adventures and by the vrging of those that are behinde wth all or part of the adventures to bring them in according to that wch they have sett downe that then all the overplus wch shalbe brought in by the enlargem^t of ij^s the pound. shalbe proportionally restored backe againe to the Contributors and be vsed the meane tyme as money lent. And it is also ordered that a present information and Complaint *shalbe* made to the Ll of the Councell of suche as have disapointed the preparation of the voyag^e [shalbe] *that they may be* called before ther Lord-

shippes to receave suche order as to ther honors shalbe 1600
thought meet. And to thende that this order and decree 9 Jan.
agreed vppon may be executed wth all spede the said rate of
ij^s the li shalbe brought in by everie adventuro^r according to
his proportion by the. 15. of this moneth vppon payne of forfeyture of Double the valewe to be Levied vppon them according to the aucthoritie of the [said] graunt of priviledges. before
mencōned provided all waies and it is agreed that yf any man
shalbe willing voluntaryly to encrease his adventure already
sett downe above the rate of ij^s the li that then he shall not be
w^thin the Compas of this acte of enlargem^t of ij^s the li by way
of Lone.

At this Court according to the warraunt geaven to the
Companie for the election of the . deputie to the Governo^r of
the same. they have proceaded to the election of the said deputie
and by geñ'all consent have nōiated and chosen m^r [John]
William Rumney to execute the same office.

And for the better expedition of the setting forthe of the
shippes on ther voyage. and for the redresse of the wronge
wch suche as have not brought in ther moneis *have offered to
the voyage* order is geaven that m^r governo^r and Comitties
shall apoint suche as they thinke meete to goe to the Co^rt to
[offer] *exhibite* ther information and Complaint to the Lordes.

   10 &. 12. 13. January severall Warraunt^s entred
   Mr Allabaster's booke viz.

300^li to John Busbridge for yron.
100^li to Wm Dixon purser of y^e dragon.
60^li to xpofer Thompson Smythe for the Hector
100^li to Mr Wyseman for the Hector
20^li to Nich: Lynge for charges.
213^li 6. 8. to Andrew Bannyng for oyle
100^li   to Wm Dixon for the hecto^r.

  A Geñ'all Court holden the 14 January 1600. 1600
      Present 14 Jan.
Mr Ald^n Go^r   Sr John Hart

1600
14 Jan.

M' Ald'' Hollyday
M' Jo : Wattes
M' Cordell
M' Wyseman
M' fra Chery
M' Jo: Highelord

M' W'" Chambers
M' Rob̃t Sandy
M' Rich: Wyche
M' Nich: Lynge
M' W'" Chambers
M' Olyuer Style.

And the geñalyty or the greatest part of this Court was called vppon occasion of the [vrgent] order takeñ by the Lordes of the Councell touching those that have sett downe ther Contributions. and have not brought in the same. ether in part or all and the assemblie being gathered together *the said* order taken by ther Lordships was published and read to the geñalyty wch order being vnder the hande of [the] one of the Clerkes of the councell and enregestred in the Councell booke doeth followe in thes wordes. viz.

1600
11 Jan.

At the Whytehall the xjth of January 1600.

Present.

L. Keaper
L. Threasurer
M' Comptroller

M' Secretory Cycill
S' Jo : Fortescue
L. Chief Justice

M' Secretory Herbert

Vppon complaint made to ther Ll̃p by the newe aucthorised Companie of merchaunt℘ preparing to trade to the East Indies that certen persons wch had heertofore promised and assured by ther subscriptions when the said voyage was first proiected to advaunce certen sommes of money for the proceading in the same vppon confidence [had] and Assurance Whereof the preparation for the said voyage hath bene vndertaken and advaunced to a full redines and yet nevertheles that the said psons would since vppon some vndue pretences retract ther former promyses in that behaulf whereof would ensue that by the want of ther promised contributions the voyage must breake Ther Ll̃p vppon due consideration howe greatlie it doeth import the hono' of the Realme and the state of the present affaires thereof that the said voyage shuld not be hindred or overthrowne by any such default [or accident] and indirect meanes and considering $^\text{g}$ also howe weake allegations of excuse have bene made by the persons refusers It hath bene therfore this day ordered by ther LL$^\text{p}$ that notw$^\text{th}$standinge the pretences of the foresaid psons they shall w$^\text{th}$out further delay and namelie by satherday next furnishe ther promysed contributions or otherwyse that order shalbe taken by the LL$^\text{p}$ w$^\text{th}$ suche as shall refuse the same to Comitt them to prison vntill they Conforme them selfes and make satisfaction according to their subscriptions

<small>1600 14 Jan.</small>

   This is a true copie of ther LL$^\text{p}$ order w$^\text{ch}$ by ther LL$^\text{p}$ cōmaundem$^\text{t}$ is entred into the Regester of the Councell.

         Thomas Edmondes.

Vppon the hearing of w$^\text{ch}$ order it was conceaved by divers of the generalytie that yf the moneis dewe by the said refusers were brought in according to the said order that then ther shuld be no neade of the supplying of ij$^\text{s}$ in the ℔ vppon everie adventuro$^\text{r}$ as was intended by the last geñ'all Court but when it was related vnto them that notw$^\text{th}$standing all the contribution w$^\text{ch}$ was sett downe would fall too short to supplie [the] a convenient adventure by 4 or 5 thousand poundes . and that of [necessitie we] necessitie the ij$^\text{s}$ in the ℔ was to be brought in the geñ'alytie did w$^\text{th}$ one assent confirme ther former order and were content to bring in the said supplie accordinglie.

It was also ordered that a Common scale shuld be made for the vse of the Companie and the rather that the same beinge made everie contributo$^\text{r}$ might have a bill of adventure of his Contribution vnder the Comōn scale of the Companie.

<small>A comūn scale.</small>

      the 15 January 1600.

<small>1600 15 Jan.</small>

Ald$^\text{n}$ Bayning :	William Harrison
Tho : Cordell.	Robert Sandy
Rich : Wyseman.	Rich : Wyche
Olyver : Style :	Jeames Lancaster
John Eldred	William Chambers.

Q

1600
15 Jan.

l 100 : to John Ady.

GEVEN a warrant to Aldⁿ: Bayning: for paym^t of t 100 : to John Ady carpenter vppō accōpt of Timber hee delyvered to the vse of the hecto^r & Assention.

l 80: to W^m ffisher.

Geven a warrant to Aldⁿ Bayninge : ffor paym^t of t 80 : to W ffisher ffor 24 barrells of candy oyle at 3^{li}. 6^s. 8^d p barrell

l 194 : 5 : 6 to W^m garway.

Geven a warrant to Aldⁿ Halleday : ffor paym^t of t 194 . 5 . 6 // to w^m garway ; ffor 58 barrells 4 gallons 3½ tt at t 3 . 6 . 8 p barrell.

The 15 January 1600.

l 150 : to Wm Garway for the assention.

Geven a Warrant to Aldⁿ Halleday ffor paym^t of t 150. to w^m garway ffor the vse of the Assention towards repayracion of hir.

l 70 : to Wm Harrisson ffor 7 tonns vineger :

Geven a warrant to Aldⁿ Bayning ffor paym^t of t 70 : to william [garway] Harrisson in ffull ffor 7 tonns vineger at l 10. p tonn.

120 oxen for victualling the shippes.

It is ordered that m^r Aldⁿ Bannyng and m^r Wyseman shall provide 120 oxen. for the provision of the voyage for that vppon Computacōn made of the beef Cutt out and salted for the victuallinḡ of the shippes ther appeareth a want of so muche as the said number of oxen doeth come vnto.

150^{li} to Wm Dixsy for the redd dragon.

Geven a warrant to aldⁿ halleday ffor paym^t of t 150. to w^m Dixsy purser of the Redd dragon ffor the repayration & vse of that shipp.

20^{li} to bee coyned.

At this assembly it was ordeyned & determyned that there should bee coyned in the towar over & above the t 6000. already appoynted the vallew of twenty pownds st^rling money to bee delyvered vnto m^r wryte to bee distributed vnto the lords & other as vnto him shall seeme good.

l 200 : to Thomas Barbar.

Geven a warrant to aldⁿ Bayng ffor paym^t of t 200. to thomas Babar ffor & on accōpt of canvas ffor the shipps.

The 17 January 1600.

1600
17 Jan.

M^r deputy rumney :	Mr Eldred :
Mr Stapers :	Mr Lancaster :
Mr Garway :	Mr Harrison

Mr Highlord   Mr Style   1600
Mr Sandy   Aldn Halliday   17 Jan.
Mr Combe   Aldn Watts
            Aldn Moore

EVEN a warrant vppõ aldn [Halleday] bayning ffor   133. 6. 8.
paymt of [℔] 133ˡⁱ 6ˢ 8ᵈ in ffull of his ⅙ pte of the   to Robt
assension I say to Robert Rickman pte owner of   Rickman.
the sayd shipp.

Geven a warrant vppõ aldn Bayning ffor payment ℔ 128 .   ℔ 128. 1. 8.
1 . 8 *to mr robert sandy* in ffull ffor sondrey disburcements made   to Robert
by him as p the warrant pticularly appeareth.   Sandy.

Geven a warrant vppõ aldn Bayng ffor paymt of ℔ 200. to   ℔ 200 : to
Robert stevens ℔ 100. by a bill of exc̃ & ℔ 100 by order of the   Robt Ste-
sayd ellacott ffor the vallew, in himself.   vens.

Geven a warrant vppõ aldn Bayng ffor paymt of ℔ 500. to⎫
Sr hugh portman by a bill of exc̃ for Robt Pope of the 2 ⎪
January   ⎬ ℔ 1000 : to
Geven a warrant vppõ aldn Halleday ffor paymt of ℔ 500 to⎪ Sr Hugh
Sr hugh portman by a bill of exc̃ for Robert Pope of the⎪ Portman.
10 January   ⎭

It is ordered that Mr Aldn watts mr Aldn Moore mr *Wyseman* mr Chery and Richard Wright Secretorie shall goe to the
Court to morrowe morning and ther to exhibite the names
to the LLp of suche that have not brought in ther moneis according to ther LLp order and to aunswer the peticõns of suche
as detract ther paiments by some colorable pretences.

Order is geaven to Aldn Hollyday Threr to pay to ye handes   100ˡⁱ to Mr
of mr Wm Burrell the somme of one hundred poundes sterling   Burrell.
vppon accoumpte to be imployed in the provision of boats
and other necessaries.

Warraunt is geaven to aldn Hollyday to pay vnto Anthony   25ˡⁱ 10. 0
moseley the somme of 25ˡⁱ 10ˢ 0 for 4 tuñs and 1 hoggʰᵈ of   to Anth:
vineger bought by Mr Combe and mr Howe.   Moseley for
                                                           vineger.

The Like warraunt is geaven to the said threr to pay to   20ˡⁱ to
Humfrey Phipps [for] the somme of 20ˡⁱ sterling for tuñs of   Humfrey
wyne vineger bought by him of mr Combe and mr Sandy.   Phips fo
                                                        wine
                                                        vineger.

THE COURT RECORDS OF

1600
17 Jan.
14ˡⁱ 12ˢ: to Mʳ Combe for wine vinegar.
69ˡⁱ 8. 2 to Mʳ Wasse.

The like warraunt is geaven vnto the same thr̃ to pay vnto mʳ John Combe the somme of xiiijˡⁱ xijˢ for so muche pᵈ by him to a mariner for 2. Tuñs of wyne vineger at 7 6 p tuñ.

Another Warraunt is made to the said Thr̃ to pay vnto Mʳ Cristopher Wasse by order of mʳ Cherie for a silver fountaine and a *Case* [silver Bowle or basen] the somme of [fourscore] 69ˡⁱ poundes eight shillinges and 2ᵈ sterling in full paiment.

Looking glasses.

It is ordered that 2 faire *Costlie* Looking glasses shalbe prouided to be geaven a way as present̃ yf cause do require.

Pursers wages.

It is agreed that the Generall Wages of all Pursers imploied in the voyage. shalbe xlˢ the monethe to be accoumpted from the tyme of the setting sayle to the shippes and for ther imploym̃ in harborowe. they are to be allowed xxˢ the moneth besides ther borde wages wᶜʰ is already allowed. And it is ordered that the Scourge shall have 2 Pursers.

26. 13. 4 to a Preacher.

Warraunt is geaven to Aldⁿ Hollyday to pay to Thomas Pulleyñ preacher apointed to goe in the voyage the somme twentie six poundes 13ˢ 4ᵈ for his provision to Sea.

1600
19 Jan.

The 19ᵗʰ January 1600.

Thomas Cordell   Jnᵒ Combes
Wᵐ garroway   Roḃte Sandy
Ryc̃ Staper   Ryc̃ Wytche

30ˡⁱ to Mʳ Spencer mʳ of the Susann

RDER is geven to Aldermann banninge to pay to samuell spencer mʳ of Susann the some of thirtie pounds sterlinge and is for his advauncemᵗ aforehaund accordinge to agremᵗ

1600
21 Jan.

The 21 January 1600.

Mʳ deputy rumney   Mʳ Style :
Mʳ Stapers :   Mʳ Sandy :

Mr Harrison   Mr Middleton   1600
Mr Lancaster   Mr Combe   21 Jan.
                    Mr Bell.

T this assembly it was appoynted and concluded that
peeter ffrancis a portugall who goeth on this voyadg peter francis
should goe in the susann wth mr John havard and   a portugall.
ffor his wages to have ffyve pounds p month so long as hee
serveth in that voyadg

Given a warrant vppō aldn Bayning ffor payment of ł 333.   333ˡˡ 6ˢ 8ᵈ
6. 8 // st'ling money on the last of ffebruary next to wm skid- to wm
more in ffull of his ˡ pt of the assention.   skidmore
                                                           ffor ⅓ of th'
                                                           assention.

Order is given at this assembly ffor the provyding of a
bason and an ewer of playne whyte silver poīz 100 ounces by
mr wyseman & mr style   3 peecs of
Also order is given to the sayd mr wyseman & mr style   plate.
ffor the provyding of 2 standing cupps & 2 other peecs of
other whyte plate that should way about 30 ounces p peece.

Order is given to these ffollowing committyes ffor to take
the care of provyding of necessaryes ffor the shipps ffor the
Gunners stewards cookes and boatswaynes *and Carpenters* stores
viz   necessaryes
                                                           ffor the
    To capteyn middleton ffor the hector   ships.
    To mr Jnº Havard ; ffor the Susann
    To mr Ric Wych ; ffor the Dragon
    To mr William Harrisson ffor the Assention.

Geven a warrant vppō aldn Bayning ffor payment of ł 200.   ł 200: to
st'ling money to Joseph salbanck purser of the Susann ffor the Joseph sal-
provision of that shipp to bee Imployed vppō hir   banck

Geven warrants vppō aldn Halleday ffor payment of these
sommes ffollowing—
    ł 250 : to wm Dixson purser of the Redd dragon.
    ł   6. 13. 4 // to thomas Symonds.
    ł 250.—.— to Ric wyseman ffor the purser of the
             hector.
    ł 150.—.— to [wm garway ffor] wm leake the purser of th'
             assention *for men's wage.*

1600
21 Jan.

    ₤ 250.—.— to Jn⁰ havard ffor the Susann ffor mens wages.
    ₤ 19. 6. 3 to george Davyes ffor chests ffor cloth

le 21 January 1600.

Order is taken that m^r [Ald^n] Richard stapers & m^r sandy should enter all the goods and pay the custom of them and to make a cargazon ffor the whole.

Also order is given to m^r Sandy ffor provyding ffor ech shipp these pcells ffollowing viz :

        1 hhd of prunes
        1 barrell of currents
        1 barrell of Reysons solis

1600
22 Jan.

The 22 of Januarie 1600

Mr Wm Rumney deputie	Mr Nich : Lynge
Mr Ald^n Moore	Mr Wm Harryson
Mr Rich : Staper	Mr Wm Garway
M^r [Rich] Tho Cordell	Mr Roger Howe
M^r olyuer Style	Mr Robt Bell
Mr Robt Sandy	Cap̃te Lancaster

Cap̃te Middleton.

Plate for presents

IT is agreed that ther shalbe prepared for presentes or otherwyse disposed 4 standing Cuppes of bigger and lesser sizes to be carried in the voyage the same to be chased white vnguilt. the 2 greatest at 30 oż. the 2 lesser at 15 oż. the wch are agreed for at 5^s. 6^d the oż.

Mariners shares of reprisalles

Wheras this assemblie were acquainted that ther hath bene some question made by some of the mariners [for] what allowaunce they should have vppon suche reprisalles as may happen in the voyage. It is vppon that question aunswered that ther is noe intention to [enterteyn anie] make anie attempte for reprisalles but onlie to pursue the voyaǵ [wth] in a m̃chauntlike course. Yet notwthstanding yf anie oportunety be offered wthout preiudice or hassard of the said voyaǵ [the] Captein Lancaster is to take suche co'se therin as he shall thinke meet and thervppon to [so] make suche agrement w{th} the mariners for shares as he thinketh good. vppon suche oportunety yf anie suche happen.

Vppon advyse required out of the West Cuntrey for the conveyinge of suche Spanishe moneis as is in the West Cuntrey to be brought on ship boarde order is geaven to m{r} Sandy to write to m{r} Ellicott and m{r} Robt Pope to conferre together and to take the best co'se therin that they can proceading therin according to ther discretion at the Companyes adventures.

Warraunt is geaven to [the Widowe Bennett] Ald{n} Hollyday th{er} to pay vnto Widowe Bennett vppon accoumpte for iron for the shippes and the voyage the some of one hundred poundes sterling.

The Like warraunt is geaven to the said Th{er} to pay to Percevall Stradling one of the fourth sort of factors the some of xx{li} agreed to be geaven him for his enterteynm{t} to provide him self before his going forth

A warrante ys granted to Alder{n} Holledaye to paye vnto S{r}geant helle, the some of fyve hundred pound{es} for so moche he cawsed to be payd at Exeter to m{r} John Ellecote, for the vse of the Companye the 23. Jañ 1600.

A warn{t} vpon m{r} Allderman bannyng to pay to Henry plvmpton threeskor & *seven* [nyne] pounds nyne shillyng{es} & was ffo{r} 7 peec{es} of Rape oyle bought of him by w{m} Chamber ffo{r} the vse of the Company this 23{th} January 1600.

The 24 of January 1600.

M{r} Ald{n} Smythe Go{r}	M{r} frauncis Chery
M{r} Ald{n} Bannyng	M{r} John Eldred
M{r} Ald{n} Halmeden	M{r} Robt Sandy
M{r} Rich : Staper	M{r} Rich : Wyche
M{r} Lancaster	M{r} W{m} Chambers
M{r} olyuer Style	M{r} W{m} Harryson
M{r} Ald{n} Hollyday	M{r} Robt Sandy.

1600
24 Jan.

T is resolued that ther shalbe sent from hence in to the West Cuntrey Two of the Comitties to see the shippinḡ of oʳ moneys and victualles when the shippes shall come thether to thende [they] vppon ther returne the Companie may be satysfied howe [ther] ther busines is [disch] dispatched and cleared vppon the departinḡ of the said shippes from the coast. And it is thought [meet] that mʳ howe and mʳ Sandy in respecte that they have had the dealing and directinḡ of the West Cuntrey busines, that they are the meetest men to be imployed in the said busines.

It is resolved that especiall care be taken and mʳ Aldⁿ Hollyday conferred wᵗʰ all that the full valewe of vj mł łi. in money be coyned in the Tower. rather wᵗʰ [an] *a large* overpluſ then *ther shuld appeare* any want of the said somme . to thende all quarrelles or questions of breache of Coveñnte may be avoyded. that might geave impediment or damage to the voyage.

50ˡⁱ to Tho. Salterne one of the 2 sort of factors.

Warraunt is geaven to Aldⁿ Hollyday to pay to Thoms Salterne the somme of fyftie poundes sterlinḡ for his enterteynmᵗ to be pᵈ him in money by agremᵗ made wᵗʰ him as one of the Second sort of factoʳˢ.

30ˡⁱ to Roger Style oñ of the 4 sort of factors.

Warraunt is also geaven to mʳ Aldⁿ Bannynge Thrēr to pay vnto Roger Style one of the 3 [4] sort of factors imployed in this voyage the somme of thirtie poundes sterlinge for so muche agreed wᵗʰ him *for his* enterteynmᵗ in the voyage.

250ˡⁱ to Joː Dixon Purser of the Dragon.

Order is geaven to mʳ Aldⁿ [Holliday] *Bannyng* to pay vnto [the] Wᵐ Dixon Purser of the Read dragon the somme of twoo hundred and fyftie poundes sterlinḡ vppon accoumpte for the provision [of the] and preparation of the same shiṗ.

The sale of the Susan sealed.

Wheras the 26. of September Last mʳ Ald Bannyng solde to the Comitties the ship called the Susan at the rate of 1600ˡⁱ vppon condition to take her againe at her Retorne wᵗʰ her furnyture and to geave for her 800ˡⁱ. It is nowe agreed that the bargaine and sale of the said ship shalbe absolute . and the condition discharged, and thervpṗ. an absolute sale in wryting was sealed this day to mʳ howe to mʳ Eldred mʳ Chambers and mʳ Wyche by mʳ Aldⁿ Bannyng.

Warraunt is geaven to m^r Aldⁿ holliday ther to pay vnto phillip winchecombe one of the fowrth sort of factors the somme of Twentie poundes sterling for so muche allowed him for his provision and preparation to sea according to [his] agreament.

1600 24 Jan. 20 to phillipp wynchecombe one of the 4 sort of factors

Order is geaven to m^r Aldⁿ Bannyng to pay vnto one Bradley for Ballast. the some of Twentie Nobles. in full demaunde . who by vertue of a pattent claymed the ballasting of all the 4 shippes or to be p^d therfore whether he found ballast or not.

6 13 4 to one Bradley for Ballast.

The 26 of Januarie. 1600.

1600 26 Jan.

Mr Wm Rumey deputy
Mr Aldⁿ Bannyng
Capten Lancaster
Mr Wm Garway
Mr Midleton

Mr John Eldred
M^r [Jo] Robt Sandy
Mr Rich. Wyche
Mr Wm Chambers
Mr Wm Harryson.

IT is ordered that the provision of suche cordage pitche tarre and other thinges of that kinde that the Company shall have occasion to vse shalbe re^d and provided wth one Browne and Companie yf they shalbe well vsed ther yf otherwyse to take it wher they may have it at the best hand.

provision of cordage pitche tarre &c;

Warraunt is geaven to m^r Aldⁿ hollyday to pay to George Persons Purser of the Hecto^r the somme of one hundred poundes. for provisions by the motion of Capten Lancaster.

100^{li} to the purser of the Hecto^r.

The like warraunt is geaven to the the said Aldⁿ to pay to Patrick Johnson for 12 way of Salt the somme of xxxviij^{li}.

38^{li} for 12 way of salte

Complaint beinge made to this Assemblie that some abuse hath bene offered to the Companie in provysion of thinges for the voyage by requiring and putting to accoumpte more then is paid for thinges provided and the matter being exāied It was confessed by Peter fenton that the Carpenter of the Susan had re^d of the Company 3^{li} 6^s for a mast more then he p^d for the same. and for another smale mast that cost but 20^s he re^d of the Company 25^s.

Deceipt vsed by the Carpenter of the Susan

The 27 of Januarie 1600.

Mr Ald Smyth Go^r	Mr Aldⁿ Bannyng
Mr Wm Rumney deputy	Capten̄ Midleton
Mr Tho Cordell	Mr Roger Howe.
Capten Lancaster	Mr Nich: Lynge.
M^r Jo: Eldred.	Mr John Combe
Mr Wm Chambers	Mr Wm Harryson
Mr Rich: Wyche.	Aldⁿ Wattes.

326. 13 4 to Simon furner for powder.

ARRAUNT is geaven to m^r Aldⁿ hollyday to pay vnto m^r Symon furner the 10th of marche next the somme of three hundred twenty six poundes 13^s 4 for 98 ba^{lrs} of ordinarie powder cn̄^{ts} [100^{li}] five score^{li} neat in eche barrell at viij^d p ti

20^{li} to Tho: Tudd on of the 4 sort of facto^{rs}.

Warraunt is geaven vnto Ald^r holliday Thr̃er to pay vnto Thomas Tudd on of the fowrth sort of facto^{rs} enterteyned for the voyage the somme of twentie pound℮ sterling for soe muche agreed to be geaven him for his enterteynm^t and to make his provision.

Moneis reported to be shipped in the shippes.

Ald^r Hollyday propoundeth to this assembly a forme of reptition of the moneis in his Custody provided to be shipped for the voyage wch being considered of at this assembly is well lyked and allowed of and is as followeth

Newe moneys.

In the read Dragon 3 chests cn̄^{ts} 8 bagges a pece cn̄^{ts} ech bag 500 pec℮ of 4^{ss} ster̄ wth the proffit amounteth to aboute	2600	. ^s	. ^d
In the Hecto^r 2 chest℮ cn̄^{ts} ech chest 8 bagg℮ and 500 pec℮ of 4^{ss} in ech bag and amounteth wth the proffit	1733	. 6	. 8
In the assention 1 chest cn̄^{ts} 8 bagges of 500 pec℮ of 4 p bagg amounteth	866	. 13	. 4
In the Susan—1 chest cn̄^{ts} 8 bagg℮ of 500 pec℮ of 4^{ss} p bag amounteth	866	. 13	. 4

Spanishe money.

In the read Dragon 2 chest℮ cn̄^{ts} 8 bagg℮ p chest and in ech bag 500 peic℮ of 8 Riolles amounteth	1733	. 6	. 8

In the Hecto^r—2 chestes cñ^ts 8 bagg̃ p
chest and in ech bag 500 peecc̃ of 8 Royalles
amounteth   1733 . 6 . 8

In the Assensioñ 1 chest cñ^ts 8 bagg̃ and
500 p̃c̃ of 8 Ryalles in the bag   866 . 13 . 4

In the Susañ 1 chest cñ^ts 8 bagg̃ and 500
pec̃ of 8 Ryalles in ech bag   866 . 13 . 4

<small>1600
27 Jan.</small>

Whereas ther are shipped in the shippes severally certeñ peec̃ of vnwatered Chamlettc̃ cñ^tg 60 peec̃ in alle. wch are shipped w^thout any geñall order of the Comitties it is ordered that the same Chamlettc̃ shalbe taken vp againe [and] by him that entred and shipped them vppon payne of suche forfeiture as shalbe assessed vppon him for an offence of privat trade being mchaundize not allowed to be shipped by the Company.

<small>Chamlettes shipped w^thout warr̃unt.</small>

It is ordered that ther shalbe allowed and deliuered to Samuell Spencer m^r of the Susan a barrell of oyle for his provision to sea for that he eateth in ordinarie salte victualles that is provided for the Companie.

<small>Samuel Spencer.</small>

Order is geaven to Ald^r hollyday to pay vnto John Havard one of the 4 principall factors the somme of one hundred poundes sterling̃ for soe much allowed for his enterteynm^t to be imployed in the voyage

<small>100^li to Jo: Havard one of the 4 principall factors.</small>

The 29 of Januarie 1600.

Mr Wm Rumey deputy	Mr Robt Sandy
Mr Ald^n Bannyng	Mr Robt Bell
Mr Ald^n Moore	Mr Wm Harryson
Mr Rich : Staper	Mr Rich: Wyche.
M^r Jo. Highelord	Capteñ Lancaster
Mr Rich : Wyseman	M^r Jo : Midleton.

<small>1600
29 Jan.</small>

RDER is geven to Ald^r Bannynge thẽr to pay vnto m^r [Ald^r] Wattes in full paiment [of] for 22 shirtes of mayle the somme of 36 . 10 . 10. to be p^d the 28 of Marche next.

<small>36 . 10 . 10 to Mr Wattes for shirtes of Maile.</small>

Mr Hacklett the historiographer of the viages of the East

<small>Mr Hacklett.</small>

1600
29 Jan.

Indies, beinge here before the Comitties and having read vnto them out of his notes and bookes divers instruccõns for provisions of Jewelles. was required to sett downe in wryting a note of the principall places in the East Indies wher Trade [was] is to be had to thend the same may be vsed for the better instruccõn of o' factors in the said voyage.

prises of tymber.

It is ordered that M' Wyseman m' harryson and M' wyche shall agree wth the Carpenters for the prises of Tymber dd for the shippes wheruppoñ some difference resteth for the said prises.

1600
31 Jan.

The 31 Januarie 1600.

M' Ald^n Smithe Go'	M' Ald^n Hollyday
M' Wm Rumney deputy	M' Ald^n Wattes.
M' Rich: Stapers	M' Wm Chamber.
M' Rich: Wyseman	M' Nich: Lynge
M' Roger Howe	M' Jo Combes.
M' John Eldred	M' Rich: Wyche
M' Robt Sandy	M' Wm Harryson.

Augustine Skinner.

T is ordered that m' Augustine Skinner his adventure of 200^li shalbe re^cd in the West Cuntrey in Ryalles according to his lres directed to M' Ellecot dated the 30 jnte. wch lre is [directed] delivered to M' Sandy. to be sent to M' Ellecott.

Private trade.

It is ordered that the psons herevnder named together wth the Secretorie shall devyse and sett downe certen ordenaunces for the avoiding of private and pticler trade in this voyage. And the same ordenaunces to be Considered of by the Comitties and afterwardes psented to the generalitie to be Confirmed as Lawes to be holden and observed for the Common good of the voyage.

Comitties for to devise orders against private trade.
{ M' olyuer style
  M' Thomas Cordell
  M' Tho: Allabaster
  M' Rich: Wyche
  Rich: Wrighte.

60. Tho: Shere.

Warraunt is geaven to Ald^n holliday thrēr to pay vnto

Thomas Shere of Exceto' threescore poundes sterling for so muche re^d of him by M^r Jo: Sandy to be imploied in Ryalles in the West Cuntrey. ⟶ 1600 31 Jan.

Warraunt was geaven to Ald^n Bannynge to pay vnto Thomas Parkins for 32 Jarres of honny. twentie poundes one shilling sterling. ⟶ 20^li 1^s for honny to Tho Parkins.

It is ordered that Ald^n Wattes shall conferre wth of Colchester touchinge the dammag^e required for the [amo^t of] hurt done to his ship by the Anco^r of the Scourge. ⟶ Damage for the hurt done by the Anco^r of the Scourge.

It is ordered that Mr Governo^r shall gratifie [m] one Wm Walter who dedicated to the Companie the book of the flemynge voyage. wth the some of xx^s and to be rep^d the same by one of the thr̃s. ⟶ xx^li to Wm Walter.

It is apointed that the Comitties apointed for the shippes wth suche as Were owners of the same before they were bought shall go to the severall shippes and take an Inuentorie of all the furniture as well formerlie sold wth the shippes as bought since for the said shippes for the preparation of the voyage. ⟶ Comitties for the shippes.

Warraunt is geaven to Ald^n Bannyng ther to pay vnto Leonard Shawe thirtie seven poundes [sterling] xv^s vj^d sterling for Chese bought by m^r Sandy and 14^li v^s fo^r butter being in the whole 52^li. ⟶ 52^li to Mr Shawe for butter and chese.

The 3. of february 1600.

Mr Wm Rumey deputy   Mr Wm Harryson.
Mr Rich: Wyseman   Mr Ald. Bannyng
Mr John Eldred.   Mr Rich: Staper
Mr Wm Chambers   Mr Robt Bell.

1600 3 Feb.

RDER is geaven to Ald^r Holliday ther to pay vnto Mr Wm Brunde on of the Principall factors of the shippes the somme of one hundred poundes sterling for somuch [by] to him allowed for his enterteynm^t to be p^d him for his provision to sea: ⟶ 100^li to Mr Brund one of the principall factors.

Whereas Thomas Johnson servaunt to the Earle of Oxford is secretlie departed from his [said] service being imploied in office of trust w^thout geving vp anie accompt intending to goe ⟶ The erle of Oxfordes man Run away.

1600
3 Feb.

to sea. Therfore it is ordered that inquisition shalbe made in the severall shippes for the said John and suche order taken that he shall not be pmitted to go in anie of the shippes.

The Comitties of the shipps to call the officers of the shippes to accoumpt.

It is ordered that the Comitties of the severall shippes shall have aucthoritie to call before them all officers of the said shippes and to take an accompte of them. what provisions of anie of the said shippes hathe bene re^d or brought into anie of the said shippes by them or anie of them and wher the same hath bene had and *at* what prises.

20^{li} to Thomas Morgan.

Order is geaven to Mr Ald^n Bannyng̃ thēr to pay vnto Thomas Morgan on of the fowrth sorte of the facto^{rs} of this p̃nte voyag^e: the somme of twentie pound€ sterling for so muche agreed to be p^d him for his enterteynm^t to provide him to sea.

180^{li} to M^r Jo: Lacy by assignm^t of the Moskovia Company.

Order is geaven to m^r Ald^n *Bannyng* [holliday thrēr] to pay vnto m^r John lacy by the Assignm^t of [m^r] the Company of the Moscovia the somme of one hundred fowrscore and eight poundes sterlinge vppon accoumpte of cordag̃ wch hath bene had of the said Companie for the provision of cordage for the [sai] voyage: [vppon] the money to be p^d the Last of Marche next.

100 to the Purser of the Assention.

Order is geaven to m^r Ald^n Holliday to pay vnto *Mr Garway* *or* the Purser of the Assention the somme of one hundred poundes sterling vppon accoumpt for the provision of thing€ necessarie for the same ship.

It is ordered that m^r Andrewe Bannyng shalbe required to pay the 200^{li} sett downe for Jeffrey kirby for that the 200^{li} sett downe for Bartliew Haggett thes comitties are content to forbeare and to suspend his admission for a further tyme vntill they shall be aunswered ether that he will bring in money or els to exclude him from the p̃viledges.

90^{li}. 10^s. to Mr Robt Bell for Paper.

Warraunt is geaven to Mr Ald^n Holliday to pay vnto m^r Robt Bell the somme of fourscore and tenn poundes [sterling] and tenñ shilling€ sterling for paper bought of him for the vse of voyage.

Mr Gouernour	Mr Stapers
Mr Deputy	Mr Wyseman

Mʳ Aldⁿ Holleday   Mʳ Highlord   1600
Mʳ Sandy   Mʳ Bell   3 Feb.
              Mʳ Linge.

Order is appoynted that mʳ lancaster & mʳ middleton should end and agree wᵗʰ him ffor his charges & enterteynmᵗ in this voyadg.

Geven a warrant vppŏ aldⁿ Bayning ffor paymᵗ of ł 300 : to Mʳ John davyes pylott maior ffor his salary to goe this voyadg.

Geven a warrant vppŏ aldⁿ halleday ffor paymᵗ of 188 . 16 . 3. to mʳ george smithyes ffor plate bought of him.

              The 5. February 1600.   1600
Mʳ Rumney deputy   Mʳ Lynge   5 Feb.
Mʳ Tho : Cordell   Mʳ Roger Howe
Mʳ Ric Stapers   Mʳ Ricᵈ: Wych
Mʳ Ric : Wyseman   Mʳ Highlord
Mʳ John Eldred   Mʳ Sandy
              Mʳ Bell.

It is ordred that mʳ chambres & mʳ harrisson shall agree wᵗʰ mʳ ffletcher & his company to reckon wᵗʰ them and so make an end and cleere accŏpt wᵗʰ them. *Cleering of accōpts wᵗʰ mʳ fletcher.*

Also that mʳ Richard wyseman should cleere accŏpt wᵗʰ mʳ william Burrell. *wᵐ burrell*

Also that mʳ aldⁿ Halleday should cleere accŏpt wᵗʰ william Angell. *wᵐ Angell*

Also mʳ Sandy to cleere accompt with mʳ peard. *mʳ peard*

Also to cleere accŏpt wᵗʰ Mʳ Howe. *mʳ Howe*

To make maurice Abbott credditoʳ by Mʳ Rickman ffor 100ˡⁱ.

Also mʳ aldⁿ halleday to cleere accŏpt wᵗʰ Mʳ Gosson.

Order is geaven to mʳ Aldʳ Bannyng to pay vnto Wᵐ Dixon Purser of the [hector] *redd Dragon* the some of two hundred poundes sterling vppon accompt for the provision of the same ship. *200 to the dragon.*

It is ordered that the psons heervnder named shalbe conferred wᵗʰ all for the going in to West Cuntrey to see the *West Cuntrey.*

1600
5 Feb.

discharge of the shippes there to thende that two of them at the least may appointed to that imployment.

    M{r} Robt Sandy   M{r} Jo: Combe
    M{r} Roger Howe   M{r} Nich: lyng
    M{r} W{m} Chamber

Damage required for hurt done by the Anker of the read dragon.

It is ordered that m{r} Cordell and m{r} highlord shall attend my l. of Cumberland concerning the demaunde [of] made by the shippes for the damag̃ susteyned by the Anker of the read dragon and to pray his lordship to take some co'se w{th} the Judge of the Admiralty therin signifying vnto him that it seemeth that one of the officers of the Court followeth the cause as a solicito{r} being interested by [Comission] Composition for that w{ch} may be recovered therein.

1600
7 Feb.

The [6] 7. of February 1600.

    M{r} W{m} Rumney deputy   *M{r} Ald{n} Hollyday.*
    M{r} Ald{n} Bannyng   M{r} Rich: Wyche.
    M{r} Ald{n} Wattes   M{r} Nichũs Lyng
    M{r} Tho: Cordell   M{r} W{m} Chamber
    M{r} Robt Sandy   M{r} W{m} Harryson
    M{r} Jo Combe   M{r} frauncis Chery.

W{m} Brodebent M{r} of the Dragon 100{li} lent vppon Land morgaged

PPON the ernest request of [the Co] W{m} Brodebent to deliver him of a preiudize w{ch} he is like to vndergoe vppon the morgage of certen landes in the handes of m{r} Hughe Beeston [ther is] it is agreed that ther shall be lent vnto him the somẽ of one hundred poundes vppon the like assuraunce made of the same land to m{r} Cordell and m{r} wyche to the vse of the Company for the repayment of the money at 6 monethes and to that ende warraunt is geauen to Ald{n} Hollyday thẽr to pay the same money to the said m{r} Brodebent.

M{r} flemyng

It is ordered that ther shalbe stay made of [an iron] a Smithes Bill of wares made for the voyage who hath re{d} his iron of m{r} fflemyng̃ and paieth him not for it And the Smyth is content that m{r} fflemynges money shalbe p{d} viz the 17. of feb: 1600 he agreed therto.

THE EAST INDIA COMPANY   129

Order is geaven to Aldⁿ Bannyng ther to pay vnto Josephe Salbanck Purser of the Susan the some of one hundred poundes sterling vppon accoumpte of the Charges imployed for the provision of the voiage.

1600
7 Feb.
100^{li} to the purser of the Susan.

Order is geaven to Aldⁿ Holliday to pay vnto the Assignee of Thoms Billett Costemer of Poole the some of two hundred poundes sterling for soe much taken vp by ex^{ce} in the West Cuntrey by Robt Pope for the vse of the voyage.

200. to Tho: Billett by exⁿ.

Lyke order is geaven to the said ther to pay vnto Thomas Lieth Pewtero^r the some of sixtie eight poundes xviij^s vppon a bill of pcelles of Pewter bought of him by m^r Sandy and m^r Bell.

68 18 for pewter.

Another warraunt is geaven [to the] to Aldⁿ Bannyng ther to pay vnto m^r Ald^r Wattes the some of thirtie and six poundes sterling for iron hoopes bought of him for the vse of the Companie.

36^{li} to Ald Wattes for iron hoopes.

Warraunt is also geaven to m^r Aldⁿ Holliday ther to pay vnto Robt Warner the some of ffowrtie three poundes 16 . 6 sterling vppon a bill of pcelles of glasses rc^d to the vse of the Companie amounting to 143 16 6 whereof 100^{li} is already p^d.

43 . 16 . 6 for Glasses.

A Gen^rall Court the xth of february 1600.
Present.

1600
10 Feb.

Mr Thomas Smythe, Aldⁿ Go^r   Mr Rich: Staper
Mr Wm Rumney
Mr Rich: Wyche   & a verie great nuber of
Mr Nich: Lynge   the gen^ralyty.

T this Co^{rt} the companie accordinge to ther priviledg pceading to establish and enacte certen Decrees and lawes fitt for the present occasion. and to be vsed as directions. for the guiding of the trade and traffique belonging to ye present voyage. nowe to be sett forth Do at this assemblie ordeine and Decree thes severall ordinaunces to be holden and kept as standing ordinaunces [for] to be vsed in [ther] the

s

1600
10 Feb.

That all thinges be mannaged as a iointe stocke, & noe priuate Trade to be vsed.

The preuencon of priuate traffique

Againste fraude in the genall venture & the penaltie.

voyages wthout alteration or chaunging the teno^r whereof hereafter ensue videlt.

It is ordayened and decred that all the preparation of moneis merchandizes and other provision for [the saide] *this present* voiadge and all Coṁodityes moneis Jewells and other merchandize retourned in the saide voiadge shalbe holden reputed and accompted and be carried mannaged ordered and handled as one entyre Joynte and Coṁon Stocke of adventure wherein no private traffique barter exchaunge or merchaundizinge shalbe vsed practized or admytted by any pticuler Governo^r Capten merchaunte Agent facto^r m^r marriner officer or other pson whatsoever imployed in the saide voiadge or permitted to goe in the same vppon payne of the losse & forfeiture to thuse of the Generall Companie and Adventures in this voiadge of all soṁes of money Jewells warres goodes or ṁchandizes wch shalbe founde in the saide shippes or els where, carried forthe or retourned home by any private or pticuler man and not contayned and brought in to geñall and coṁon accompte & ioynte adventure of the saide voiadge And to thend this prejudice of private traffique may the better be avoyded It is alsoe ordeyned & appointed y^t due inquisicõn be made in all and euerie the seũall shipps of the saide voiadge and els where by serche of all such Chestes boxes Packes Packetts bookes wrytingẽ and other meanes whereby discoverie may be made of the breache of this present ordinaunce.

And yt is in like manner ordayned and decred for the avoidinge of all vnfaithfullnes and deceipte to be vsed in the saide voiadge in the defraudinge of the geñall adventure wch is prepared and sett forth that the greate Costẽ and Chardgẽ of such as repose there trust and confidence in the officers and mynisters imployed in the saide voiadge that what pson soever shalbe found vnfaithfull or vniust in the saide voiadge by ymbesselinge or wthdrawinge of any the goodes wares merchaundizes Jewells or other coṁodityes Whatsoever ether belonginge to the adventure sent out or beinge pcell of the retourne of the same wch was is or shalbe ether prepared bought or belonginge to the coṁon or generall Stocke or adventure that such pson shalbe barred and concluded to demaunde of the Governo' & Companie of the saide merchaunt(e of London tradinge into the East Indies any accompte rekoninge or paym' of any wages salary contract or entertainm' for his imployment in this voiadge wherevnto he was or otherwise might have binne interessed yf such offence had not binne comytted And further *that* everie such pson soe offendinge shalbe [p̄sented] *prosecuted* by the saide Governor & Companie of the saide m̄chaunt(e of london tradinge into the East Indies accordinge to the qualetie of his offence in that behalfe by the lawes and Statut(e of this Realme.

<small>1600 10 Feb.</small>

And further more yt is ordeyned that yf vppon the deliūie of her Matie lres to the prinnces of those places where our shipps shall arrive [yō] *the generall and* [*merchaunt(e*] *factors* shalbe peaceablie received & entertayned as m̄chaunt(e to commerce and traffique wth the people of those Cuntries or places and be secured & warranted hereafter to frequente and visite those ptes Then yt is ordayned and agreed that *ther* shalbe selected out of the yongest sorte of *the* facto^{rs} *or others* entertayned or voluntarily suffred to goe in the voiadge such and soe manye of the aptest and towardest of them as [yō] o' *principall merchaunt* shall thincke meete and *w^{ch}* shall have best approved them selfes fitt for [such our] *the* imploym' *of the Companie* to resyde & abide in the saide places where [yō] *they* shalbe soe peaceablie received yf [yō] *they* may be p̄mitted therevnto takinge sufficient and carefull order for the [dischardginge] *defrayinge.* and supplyinge of there Chardge vntyll those places shalbe hereafter visited by another fleete sent frō hence And leavinge wth them such advyse and direction for ther better informac̄ōn howe to carrie them selves in those places as by *the* [yo'] good direction *of o' principall merchaunt* wth thadvyse of suche as [yō] *he* shall consulte *wth all* thereof shalbe thought meete and as tyme and experience of those places shall directe [you] them whilest the shippes Do lye in thes partes.

<small>Leavinge of factors in the East Indies.</small>

At this court was read a Com̄ission conceaved by the Comitties to be Delivered vnto the generall *or principal merchaunt(e & others in succession* vnder the Com̄on seale of

<small>A Comisyon for the Gen'all & in succes-</small>

1600
10 Feb.

sion vnder the Comon Seale.

the Companie concerning the managing of the trade by avoyding of private traffique & vnfaithfull Dealing and *to geave order for the* Leaving of fitt factors to reside in the East Indies vntil the retorne of [the next] *a seconde* fleet *thether* wch Comission was well lykd of and agreed to be written in fowre severall ptes and vnto everie part the Comon seale of the Companie to be [annexed] added to thende that *in* everie ship one of the said Comissions may be kepte in the handes of the principall m^rchaunt^{es} of [the] everie ship wch Comission doeth followe in thes wordes. viz :—

The Commission to the Generall or principall marchant.

Whereas wee the governo^r and Companie of the m^rchaunts of London. trading into the East Indies have chosen yo͡ Mr James Lancaster for the chief governo^r or gen'all to governe or Rule all suche merchaunt^{es} marrine^{rs} office^{rs} and other her Ma^{ies} Subiet^{es} wch are ymployed by vs or are or shalbe shipped in anie of the fowre shippes by vs prepared and sett forthe for this p͡nte intended voiage towardes the East Indies And whereas the Queens most excelent Ma^{ie} approvinge and allowinge of our Choice of yo^u to the said government and favouringe the said enterprise hath by her gratious Lres pattent^{es} vnder the great Seale of England the better to enable you to keepe yor whole Companie in good agreement one towardes another and in obedience and dew respect towardes you geaven you aucthoritie to chastice and correct such offences as shall arrise in the said voyadge accordinge as in the said Lres Pattent^{es} at large appearethe wch Lres Pattent^{es} extendinge onlye to the generall governm^t of yor whole Companie shipped in the said shippes for their Croill behaviour whilest they are abroad in the said viage and not vnto the mannaginge and orderinge of the trade of merchaundize for wch the said voyadge is principallie appointed and sett forthe wee therfore by these our pnte Lres [Pattent^{es}] or Comission vnder our Common Seale for the orderinge and disposinge of all such merchaundize gold pearle Jewells and other Commodities wch are to be bought bartered procured, exchaunged or otherwyse obteyned in this pnte voyage do for yor remembraunce and direcc͡on in that behaulfe sett downe

theise Clawses ordeñnc℮ and decrees hereafter followinge de- 1600
claringe hereby our purpose and entenčōn how wee appointe 10 Feb.
and ordeyne that the traffique of this p͠nte voyadge shalbe ordered
and carryed wch ordeñnces and decrees wee will and require you
to observe and keape and do geave you power and aucthoritie
to see the same executed and putt in vse accordingly vidett wee
do ordeyne and decree that all the preparacōns of moneis
m͠chaundizes and other provision for the said voyage and all
Commodities moneis Jewells and other merchaundize retourned
in the said viage shalbe holden reputed & accompted and be carred
mannaged ordered and handeled *as* one entire Joint and
Common Stocke of adventure wherein no private traffique
barter exchaunge or merchaundizinge shalbe vsed practized or
admitted by any pticler Governo^r Captein m͠chaunt Agent
facto^r Mr Marrine^r officer or other pson whatsoever imploied
in the said viage or pmitted to go in the same vppon paine of
the losse and forfeiture to thuse of the generall companie and
adventurers in this viage of all somes of moneis Jewells wares
goodes or merchaundizes wch shalbe found in the said shippes
or els were carried forthe or retourned home by any private or
pticler man and not Conteyned and brought into the generall
and common accompte and ioynte adventure of the said viage
And to thend this preiudice of private traffique may the better
be avoyded wee do ordeyne and appoint that due inquisicōn be
made in all and everye the severall shippes of the said viage
and els refer by searche of all such chest℮ boxes pack℮ packett℮
book℮ writing℮ and other meanes whereby discovery may be
made of the breache of this present ordeñnce And wee do in
like manner ordeyne and decree for the avoydinge of all vn-
faythfullnes and deceite to be vsed in the said voyage in the
defraudinge of the generall adventure wch is prepared and sett
forthe att the great cost℮ and charges of such as repose their
trust and confidence in the office^{rs} and mynisters imploied in
the said viage that what pson soever shalbe found vnfaithfull
or vniust in the said voyadge by embesselinge or wthdrawinge
of anie the good℮ wares merchaundizes Jewells or other com-
mdoties whatsoever other belonginge to the adventure sente

out or beinge pcell of the retourne of the same wch was is or shalbe ether prepared bought or belonginge to the common or generall stocke or adventure that such pson shalbe barred and concluded to demaund of the Governo^r and Companie of the said merchaunt{ of London tradinge into the Est Indies any accompt reckonige or payment of anie wages salary contract or entertaynm^t for his imployment in this viage wherevnto he was or otherwyse might have bene enteressed yf such offence had bene comitted. And ffurther that every such pson so offendinge shalbe prosecuted by the said Governor and Companie of merchaunt{ of London tradinge into the East Indies accordinge to the qualety of his offence in that behaulfe by the lawes and Statut{ of this Realme.

And furthermore wee do ordeyne that yf vppon the delivery of of her Ma^rs Lr̃es to the prinnces of those places wher our shippes shall arrive yet shalbe peacably received and entertayned as merchaunt{ to Commerce and traffique wth the people of those Cuntries or plac{ and be secured and warraunted hereafter to frequent and visitt those ptes then wee do ordeyne and agree that you shall select out of the yongest sort of our facto^rs *and others* entertayned by vs or voluntarily suffered to go in the voyage such and so many of the most aptest and towardest of them as you shall thincke meet and as shall have have best approved them selves fitt for such our employment to reside and abide in the said places wher yo^u shalbe so peaceably received yf you may be pmitted therevnto takinge sufficient [order] and Carefull order for the defrayinge and suppliinge of their charges vntill those places shalbe hereafter visited by another fleet sent from hence and Leavinge wth them such advise and direc̃on for their better enformac̃on how to carry them selves in those plac{ as by y^r good discrec̃on wth thadvise of such as you you shall conferre thereof shalbe thought meet and as tyme and experience of those places shall direct you.

And forasmuche as the daies of manns liefe are lym̃ited and the certeintie thereof for their continuance and end onlie knowen vnto God Wee the said Governour and Companie of merchaunt℮ of London tradinge into the East Indies do hereby ordeine and provide that yf it shall happen you the said James Lancaster to depte this mortall liefe before the retourne of the said shippes then from and after the decease of yo^u the said James Lancaster wee do by this o^r p̄nte Comission vnder our Com̄on Seale constitute and appointe y^o^u Mr John Middleton to be the cheife Governo^r or generall of the said merchaunt℮ marrine^{rs} officers [and other officers] and other her Maties subject℮ by vs ymployed or otherwise shipped in the said viage willinge and requiringe you and gevinge you like power and aucthoritie to putt in execuc̄on the said ordennc℮ and decrees concerninge the orderinge and disposinge of the traffique and merchaundizinge of the said viage as wee have done to the said James Lancaster and yf it shall happen by god℮ appointment that both you the said James Lancaster and John Middleton shall decease in the said viage then wee ordeyne and appointe the principall and generall government of the whole Companie therein imploied or shipped in this p̄nte viage vnto you Mr William Brund beinge also one of o^r fowre principall merchaunt℮ whom we have chosen and entertayned for the orderinge and disposinge of the merchaundizes and traffique of the said viage Requiringe you yf you shall fortune to survive the said James Lancaster and John Middleton to observe and keape the same o^r ordeīinc℮ and decrees before menc̄oed ordeyned and appointed by vs for the traffique and merchaundizinge of the said voyadge geavinge you the like aucthoritie to execute the same as is formerlie herein geaven to the said James Lancaster and John Middleton or ether of them and yf you the said William Brund shall fortune to decease in the said viage then wee do appointe the ymediate succession and execuc̄on of the said charge and governm^t aforesaid vnto you Mr John Havard one other of our said principall merchaunt℮ requiringe you to see our said ordeīinc℮ and decrees to be kept and pformed geavinge vnto you the same power and aucthoritie as wee have hereby geven to the said James Lancaster Jo: Middleton and William Brund *or any of them* And yf it should fortune that all the said severall psons imploied by vs as our principall merchaunt℮

1600
10 Feb.

1600
10 Feb.

in this p̄nte viage to decease then wee ordeyne and appointe the whole governm^t and Charge before men͠coed to be vndertaken by one of you fowre wth are of the second sort of merchaunt(s or facto^rs by vs imployed in the said viage the same to be taken and executed successively [by] one after another as anie of you shall happen to decease after the said Charge by the trew meannge hereof shalbe cast vppon you wch Charge wee do ordeyne shall succeade in this manner videlt *first* to our second merchaunt shipped in the Redd dragon next to our second merchaunt or facto^r shipped in the Hecto^r thirdly to our second merchaunt or facto^r shipped in the assention and lastlie to our second merchaunt or factor shipped in the Suzan [Reposinge in you our severall m̄chaunt(s and all you our severall officers appointed and entertayned in this viage espetiall hope trust and confidence that you will accorde and agree together and ioyne in freind shipp and amyty to do and execute yor vttermost endeavo^rs for the benefitt of the voyadge w^thout contenc̄on discord or emulac̄on to be vsed amongst you guidinge yor selves therein by that generall Reigment and Sea government wch our Englishe fleet(s do vse when they sorte themselves togeather And so wee commend you and yor travilles to god & providence who guide you wth his feare and defend yo^u from all daungers.]

And wee do further Ordeine that as wee have appointed a Succession of o^r Principall merchaunt and governor of the Whole Companie imploied or shipped in this viage so wee do order and decree that vppon soever the said governm^t in succession shall fall by the decease of anie the psons before named that he shall or may shipp or imbarke him selfe in the Admirall of o^r fleete and enioye and receive such place Cabbin easement and commandm^t therein as o^r said generall and principall governo^r formerlie did.

And Lastlie whereas her Ma^ie by her Commission vnder the great Seale haith onlie appointed the generall governm^t of all her Subiect(s imploied in the said viage vnto the said James Lancaster w^thout anie appointinge of Succession by like Warraunt to any that is imploied in the said viage and that it lieth not in vs to geave anie warraunt for the Correcŏn of offencᵉ by pennall lawes to be executed vppon the bodies of anie her Maⁱᵉˢ Subiectᵉ wee do in that behaulfe as to menn haveing reason and discreŏn and to men that feare god offer vnto youʳ good Consideraŏns the benefitt of order and peaceable agreement in matters and enterprises vndertaken for a Common good Reposing in yoᵘ oʳ seũall ṁchauntᵉ and all yõ oʳ seũall officers appointed and entertayned in this voiadge a specyall hope trust and confidence yᵗ yõ will accorde and agree together and Joyne in freindshipp and amytie To doe and execute yoʳ vnttermost endeavoʳˢ for the benefitt of the voiadge wᵗʰout Contenŏn discorde or emulaŏn to be vsed amongest yõ guidinge yoʳselves there in by that genʳall Reigemᵗ and Sea govermet wᶜʰ oʳ Englishe fleetᵉ doe vse when they sorte themselves haveinge a specyall and due respect to him that is yoʳ princypall or cape merchant And soe we comende yoᵘ and yoʳ travailes to gods providence who guide yõ wᵗʰ his feare and defende yõ frõ all Daungers.

1600
10 Feb.

Whereas by an order of Court of the 9 of Januarie last It was agreed that he *that* [shall] *did* not bring in by the way of supply *to be added* to his adventure formerlie sett downe ijˢ vppon everie pound [of his adventure by him so sett downe] *of his stock or contribution* by the 15. of the same moneth should forfeit xˡⁱ vppon *everie* the Cˡʰ *of the said adventure* notwᵗʰstanding wᶜʰ [lawe] order ther are divers that have not brought in ther said supplies by wᶜʰ meanes ther resteth forfeited out of ther said stockes the said ijˢ in the pound wᶜʰ cometh to [xxˡⁱ] xˡⁱ vppon everie cˡⁱ [sett downe *and whereas* notwᵗʰstanding wᶜʰ penaltie divers of the Companie were still behinde and have not yet brought in ther said Supplie by meanes Whereof] the voyage is *still* [for no] in a great afterdeale and want of moneis to supplie present and necessarie paimtᵉ [by the want whereof] *by meanes whereof* the shippes are deteyned here *at the companies great charge.* It is therfore ordered for the avoyding of the daunger [that] *wᶜʰ* thes delaies of bringing in of moneys may bread [that] and for the encoragemᵗ of suche as wilbe forward to supply the wantᵉ thereof that [whosoever] *as many* of the Com-

An act touching the bringing in of the supplie of 2ˢ in the li.

1600
10 Feb.

pany *as* will bring in to the handes of the Thrēr the sōme of xx^{li} to be added to his *or ther* owne adventure formerly sett downe having brought in his full principall and his supply *of ij^s the li* by the said recited act agreed vppon, shall for the said xx^{li} by him or *them* voluntaryly brought in have not only the benyfyte of the gaine thereof but the [benefytt or] *principall and* gaine of the sōme of xx^{li} by the said act forfyted by sōme one that hath not brought in his supply of ij^s the li. And to that ende thursday next is geaven to all those wch are behind wth ther said supplies ether to bring them in or els to lose xx^{li} [vppon or] out of [ther] every cc^{li} of ther stocke to be added to the stockes of them wch will supply it for them [&] in ther default, the same to be sett over at the next gen'all Courte wch is intended to be on fryday next [And is]

1600
11 Feb.

The xjth of february 1600.

Mr Ald. Wattes	M^r Jo: Highelord
Mr Rich: Staper	Mr Rob̃t Sandy
Mr Rich: Wyseman	Mr Wm Chambers
Mr Wm Garway	Mr Wm Harryson.

207 to fraunces Parrott for Norromborghe ware.

ORDER is geaven to m^r Ald^n Bannyng̃ to pay vnto fraunc̃ Parrett for Norromborowgh ware bought of him the somme of Two hundred and seven poundes sterling pcell of 407^{li} arysing to that some by the pcelles delivered to the handes of m^r Allabaster wherof the said 207^{li} is presentlie to be p^d and the resideue the last of Aprill.

Order is geaven to Ald^n Bannyng to pay vnto George Davyes for chestc̃ filled wth showes shirtes Cassockc̃ and breeches the sōme of Eleven poundes [sterling] one shilling sterling.

Order is geaven to Ald^n Holliday to pay vnto m^r Derick Lypson for steele bought [by] *of* him by m^r Wm Garway the somme of fowrtie fowre poundes sterling as apereth by a bill of pticlers of the same.

Order is geaven to the said Mr Ald^n Hollyday to pay vnto Phillip Grove the somme of Eleven poundes sterling for his Charges of diet and boat hire expended in the travelling of the Companies busines.

THE EAST INDIA COMPANY.

The xij^th : of Febr : 1600.

Mr Wm Rumney deputy	Mr Rich : Wyche
Mr Rich : Stapers	Mr Wm Chambers
Mr Wm Garway	Mr Wm Harryson
Mr Rich : Staper	Mr Robt Bell
M^r Jo : Eldred	M^r Jo : Midleton
Mr Robt Sandy	Mr Tho : Cordell.

1600
12 Feb.

[Motion is made]

T is ordered that Phillip Grove shall have a bill of adventure for the Composition wch is made wth him for his enterteynm^t in the voyage.

    Warraunt is geaven to m^r Ald^r Holliday to pay to Nathaniell Jamryn one of the 3 sort of factors appointed for the voyage according to the agreem^t made wth him for his enterteynm^t the some of xxx^li sterling.

    Warraunt is geaven to Ald^r Hollyday ther to pay to Mr Wyseman to be dd over to the Purser of the [hercules] Hecto^r the somme of one hundred poundes sterling for the paym^t of mens wages in that ship.

    Warraunt is geaven to Ald^r Holliday ther to pay to Wm Done Cowper for worke done for the voyag vppon the rest of a genrall Reckoning of 53^li. 7^s. 7^d in full paym^t the some of xxxviij^li vij^s vij^d.

    Warraunt is geaven to Ald^r Hollyday threr to pay vnto Mr Wm Segar one of the herrault^e for the wryting of her ma^ts L^res. to the kinges of the East Indies the some of xiij^li vj^s viij^d and xij^d for a boxe bought by him to putt in the same l^res.

    Warraunt is geaven to Ald^r Bannyng ther to pay vnto Capten Lancaster vppon the Companies Agreem^t w^h him vppon his enterteynm^t the somme of two hundred poundes.

    The like warraunt is geaven to the said threr to pay to the said Capten Lancaster. for soe much by him [deliuered] laied out vppon the Companies occasions the somme of Eleven poundes vij^s viij^d.

    Another Warraunt is geaven to the said threr to pay to the [Purser] Wm Dickson Purser of the Read Dragon for the

Phillip Grove.

Nath : Jamryn 30^li.

100^li to the Purser of the Hecto^r.

38^li. 7^s. 7^d to Wm Done Cowper.

13^li. 7^s. 8^d to Wm Segar for the Q^us lres.

200^li to Capten Lancaster.

11^li. 7^s. 8^d to Capten Lancaster.

200^li to the Purser of the Dragon.

140   *THE COURT RECORDS OF*

1600
12 Feb.

provysion of the said ship vppon accoumpte the somme of two hundred poundes.

[Order is geaven to Ald^r Hollyday thr̃r of the to pay vnto m^r Richard Wyseman.]

100^{li} to Capten Midleton.

Order is geaven to Ald^r Holliday *thẽr* to pay vnto Mr John Mydleton for his enterteynm^t in the voyage the somẽ of one hundred poundes sterlinge for soe much allowed him by Composition.

100^{li} to ye Assention.

Order is geaven to Ald^r Hollyday thr̃r to pay vnto Mr Wm Garway vppon accoumpte for the provisyon of the Assention, the somme of one hundred pound℈.

8^{li}. 3^s. 7^d

Order is geaven to Ald^r Hollyday thr̃r to pay vnto Capten Mydleton vppon a Bill of pticlers of charges by him disbursed in the Companies occasions the somme of viij^{li}. iij^s. vij^d.

※

1600
13 Feb.

The 13th of february 1600.

Mr Wm Rumney deputy	Mr Wm Chamber
Mr Aldⁿ Wattes	M^r Jo Combe
Mr Wm Garway	Mr Rich Wyche
Mr Tho Cordell	Mr Wm Harryson
Mr Rich : Wyseman	Mr John Middleton
Mr Roger Howe	*Mr Aldⁿ Moore*
Mr Aldⁿ Hollyday	Mr Nich. lynge

M^r Jo : Highelord

Mr Roger Howe M^r Jo Combe xx^{li} a peece.

R. Roger Howe and Mr John Combe having bene delt wthall to travell into y^e west Cuntrey [for] to see the discharge of the shippes having otherwyse as they constantly affirme ernest busines of ther owne doe notwthstanding assent to be imployed to doe anie good office for the voyage [and] vppon whose assent it is resolved by this assemblie to gratyfye them wth the consideration and gratification of xx^{li}. a pece to bestowe vppon them in plate or otherwyse at ther pleasure and to beare all ther Charges for them and ther servaunt℈.

400^{li} to M^r

Order is geaven to m^r Aldⁿ Hollyday thr̃r to pay vnto one

Mr William Harvy or his Assignes the some of fowre hundred poundes sterling for soe muche re^d of him in the West Cuntrey by the handes of Robt Pope by bill of exchaung dated the 18 of Januarie. 1600 13 Feb. W Harvy per ex^h.

It is informed this Assemblie that o^r shippes are too deeply Laden and therfore moved that some smale ship shalbe hired to stowe the spending victualles and to followe the shippes some part of the voyage and to retorne againe, but it is resolved that the shippes shall all fall downe to Gravesend and then they shalbe surveyed what necessitie ther wilbe of the provision of suche a smale ship and then accordinglie order to be taken. a small ship for the spendinge victualles.

Order is geaven to Ald^r Hollyday to pay vnto m^r Pope sergeaunt of thadmiraltie vppon a bill of charges for the buriall of those wch were slaine in the Hecto^r the some of Liij^s. 2^{li}. 13^s. 0^d to Mr Pope sgeaunt of the Admiralty.

Warraunt is geaven to Ald^r Holliday to pay vnto Henry Mydleton one of the seconde sort of factors vppon the Composition made wth him for his enterteynment in the voyage the somme of fyftie poundes sterling. 50^{li} to Henry Midleton, vpon his enterteynmn^t.

It is ordered that Mr Garroeway and Richard Wright shall resorte to the l. thre^r and m^r Secretorie and to entreat ther honors warraunt to deliver out of m^r Governo^{rs} howse the plate and other presentes wch are prepared for the voyage. Whose pticlers hereafter followe viz.

A founteyne wth a bassen white of 205 oż.	
A standing Cup wth a Cover	63 oż.
2 standing Cuppes wth Covers	64 oż.
2 standing Cuppes wth Covers	32 oż.
A Bason & ewer.	102 oż.
A ship basen & ewre.	30 oż.
2 fans of fethers.	
2 plumes of fethers.	
3 Looking glasses	

A Target and headpece belonging to ye Muskovia company
A Comon Seale of the Companyes.—

Order is geaven to Ald^n [Bannyng] Hollyday and Mr Eldred to

1600
13 Feb.

see the moneis provided to be shipped out of the Port of London and reported by a repertition made at an assemblie of the Comitties the 27. of Januarie last and the same [being entred] *to enter* in the Custome howse *and to see it* to be waterborne and carried downe to the shippes at Gravesend and ther to be delivered a board eche ship that the same may be safely shipped and stowed accordinglie.

1600
14 Feb.

The 14. of february 1600.

Mr Wm Rumney deputy	Capten Middleton.
Mr Rich : Staper	Mr Roger Howe
Mr. Thomas Cordell	Mr. John Combe
Mr Wm Garway	Mr Robt Sandy
Mr Rich. Wyseman	Mr Nich : Lynge
Capten Lancaster	Mr Wm Chamber.

361^{li}. 15^s. 0^d
to Mr Simon
furno^r for
powder.

RDER is geaven to Mr Ald^n Hollyday to pay vnto Mr Simon furno^r 371^{li} . 15^s . 0^d rest of of 698 . 8 . 4. dewe to him for powder Brimston and Saltepeter delivered for the shippes whereof *for* 326^{li} . 13 . 4 Warraunt is formerlie geaven and the said 371^{li} . 15^s . 0^d is to be p^d at three monethes after the date hereof.

61^{li}. 5^s. 9^d
to Simon
Yomans for
butter &
cheese

Lyke warraunt is geaven to the said Thrër to pay vnto Simon Yomans Chaundeler for 52 fkß of butter at 19^s the fß and for x^c ℔ xij^{li} of chese at xxiij^s the Cth; the somme of sixtie and [two] *one* poundes [nyne] *fyve* shillinges [three] *ix* pence.

86 . 0 . 0
to W^m
Vffington
for wax
candelles.

Lyke warraunt is geaven to the said Thrër to pay vnto Wm Vffington waxe Chaundeler for 1310^{li} of wax Candells *at* xv^d ob the li and for viij Chestß and 4 boxes. the somme of fowrscore and six poundes sterlingß.

34^s. 3^d.

Geven by warraunt vpon [Ald^n Hallydaye] *Mr Chambers* to pay vnto Capten Mydleton . as by a bill of pticulers.

100^l to m^r
Wisman for
the Purser
of ye Hector

A warrant geven vpon Ald^n Hallyday to paye to m^r Wiseman [for] to be geven to the purser of the hector. for defrayeinge of charges the some of one hundrethe poundß by direction of Capten Mydleton.

Munday 16. february 1600.

Wm Romenij Depute	Capt mydleton
Mr Aldⁿ Watt℮.	M^r wiche.
Mr Cordell	Capt. Davis.
Mr Style	Mr Linge
Capt. Lanckester	Mr Combes.

OMPLAYNT beinge made of the overchargenge and pesteringe bothe of the Susan and the rest of the Shippes. but espetially of the Susan. it was ordered that that a hoygh or some other ship of one hundred Tuns or more should be bought to goe a longe wth the shippes as farre they shuld it fytt and then to take suche co^rse wth the ship so bought as they shuld thinke meet ; and Mr Cordell and   were intreated to seeke out for suche a ship.

Order is geaven to Mr Aldⁿ Bannyng to pay vnto Thoñs Parkins Cowper in full paym^t of Caske as by his accoumpte audited by Mr Chambers and m^r Harryson appeareth the somme of threescore and eighteene poundes sixtene shillinges and fowre pence sterling.

78 . 16 . 4 to Tho: Perkins for Caske.

Order is geaven to Ald^r Holliday to pay vnto m^r Wm Candyshe in full paym^t and Clearing of his accompt for leade the somē of fowrtie and Nyne poundes sterling.

49^{li} to Wm Candishe

Order is geaven to Ald^r Holliday to pay vnto James Emerson *for the just and* in full paym^t of Fyve hogg^{hdds} of aquavitæ the somme of [three] thirtie poundes sterling for wch ther hath bene p^d him already the somme of xxx^{li}:

30^{li} to James Emerson for Aquavitæ.

Ther is geaven to M^r [Ald^r] Hackett by thassent of this assemblie for his travelles taken in instrucc̃ons and advyses touching the preparing of the voyage and for his former advyses in setting the voyage in hand the Last yere the somme of tenn poundes and xxx^s for 3 mappes by him provided and did to the Companie the same money to be p^d him by Mr Ald. Hollyday.

11^{li} . 10^s. to be geaven to Mr Hacklett.

Ther is geaven to Mr Henrie Napper m^r of the Hecto^r in consideration of his extraordinarie travell and paines taken in the preparation of the shippes and for his expences [taken]

20^{li} to Henry Napper for his paines & expences

1600
16 Feb.

expended in attending the same the somme of Twentie poundes to be p^d him by m^r Ald^n Bannyng.

1600
17 Feb.

The 17th of febr 1600.

Mr Wm Rumney deputy   Capten Midleton
Capten Lancaster   Mr Rob̃t Sandy
Mr. John Combe.

100^li to the Purser of the dragon

RDER is geaven vnto Mr Ald. Holliday to pay vnto Wm Dixon Purser of the Read Dragon vppon accoumpte the one hundred poundes sterling to be imploied in the p̃paration and clearing away of the same ship.

50^li to the purser of the Hector.

The like warraunt is geaven to the said Threr to pay vnto Mr Wm Garway or to the Purser of the Assention vppon accoumpte the somme of fyftie poundes sterling to be imploied in the preparation and clearing away of the same ship.

The 17th of feb 1600.

Mr Wm Rumney deputy	Capten Middleton
Mr Ald^n Hollyday	Mr Rich : Wyche
Mr Tho Cordell	Mr John Combe
Mr Rich : Wyseman	Mr Rich : Staper
Mr John Eldred	Mr Wm Harryson
Mr Wm Garway	Mr Rob̃t Sandy
M^r olyuer Style	Mr Ald^n Wattes
Mr John Highelord	Mr Ald^n Moore
M^r frauncis Chery	Mr Rob̃t Bell.

T this Courte was reade two severall formes of Billes of adventure to be geaven to every adventuro^r in the voyage and to everie facto^r enterteyned in the same to be passed vnder the Comon seale of the Company. for the better satisfaction both of the adventuro^rs and of the said factors and to geave testimony of ther moneys brought in [and] *by the adventures* and of the Contractes made wth the said factors. the teno^r of wch billes do followe in thes wordes viz:

Whereas A. B.   is entertayned by vs the Governo[r] and Companie of merchaunt[s] of London tradinge into the East Indies to go as one of our   facto[rs] in this p̃ñte voiage nowe by vs prepared towardes the said Indies and is allowed for his imployment in the said viage the somme of   for his preparacon to Sea the wch he hath received before his goinge forthe Nowe know yee that wee the said Governor and Companie for the further allowaunce wch the said A. B. is to have and receive accordinge to o[r] agreement wth him do acknowledge and testifie and do promise and agree by these p̃nt[s] that the said A. B.   shall have and enioy for his further allowaunce and entertaynment in the said Voiage vppon the gaine and proffitt w[ch] god shall send by the retourne of the same voiage (the principall adventure thereof and all Charges of the voiage . first deducted suche rate and proporc̃on of proffitt as [if] he had bene an adventurer of the somme of   and as yf he had putt in so muche readie money in stocke in the said voiage the said rate and proporc̃on of proffitt to be paied vnto him after his retourne into England in suche manner and forme as the gaine and proffitt of the said viage is paied to other the Adventur[rs] generallie vppon the Somme of   by them adventured So as he procead in the said viage and do not retourne before the viage be ended. And yf he happen to dye before the retourne of the said shippes from the said East Indies havinge lived and Contynued in the said voiage vntill the shippes shalbe laden or vntill he *or* [and] other facto[rs] shall have Contracted and made provision for their Ladinge. then the said gaine proportioned the said rate of   adventure to be paid to his Executo[rs] administrato[rs] or Assignes as it should have bene paied to him yf he had retourned wth the shippes Provided alwaies that yf he decease before the shippes shall arrive in the east Indies that then the money imprested and delivered him before his goinge to Sea shalbe vnto him a full recompence of his entertaynment agreed vppon for the voiage And vppon theise condic̃ons and proviso before menc̃oed Wee the Governo[r] and Companie under o[r] Common Seale have geaven vnto the said A. B.   this

Side notes: 1600 17 Feb. — The forme of the Bills to be giuen to euy adventurer. — And to euy ffacto[r] in the voiadge

1600
17 Feb.

p̄ñte bill of Contract and adventure dated the   day of february Anno regni R̄ᵉ Eliz. xliij⁽ᵉᵗᵒ⁾.

Whereas A. B.   one of the adventurers and one of the Brethren of the Governo⁽ʳ⁾ and Companie of Merchaunt⁽ˢ⁾ of London tradinge into the East Indies havinge sett downe for his adventure w⁽ᵗʰ⁾ the said Companie for their first voyage into the east Indies the Somme of   sterlinge hathe not onlye paied the said somme of   to   Thrēr of the said Companie but haithe supplied accordinge to the ordeīnce of the said Companie The Somme of   sterlinge more w⁽ᶜʰ⁾ is after the rate of ij⁽ˢ⁾ the pound of his said adventure Wee therefore the said Governor and Companie do by this our p̄ñte Bill of Adventure promise and agree to and w⁽ᵗʰ⁾ the said   That wee the said Governo⁽ʳ⁾ and Companie and our Successo⁽ʳˢ⁾ shall and will vppon the retourne of the shippes or anie of them sett-out by vs in this p̄ñte voiage or w⁽ᵗʰ⁾in Convenient tyme after their said retourne in the same deliver vnto the said   his Executo⁽ʳˢ⁾ and administrat⁽ʳˢ⁾ a[nd] trew and iust accompte and payment of suche Stocke benefitt and proffitt of Stocke as god shall send vppon the said voiage accordinge to the generall distribuc͠on proporc͠on and alotment w⁽ᶜʰ⁾ shalbe alotted disposed and geaven to all and everye the severall adventurers in the said voiage proportionall to their severall adventurs In Wittnes whereof the said Governo⁽ʳ⁾ and Companie have heervnto annexed ther Common Seale the   day of Febr. 1600.

It is ordered that m⁽ʳ⁾ Ald⁽ⁿ⁾ Hollyday shall carry downe to Graveshend some convenient som̄e of money to the valewe of 4. or 5 or 6 hundred poundes for the payment of Harboroughe wages and other Reckoning⁽ˢ⁾ for the clearing of the shippes.

1500⁽ˡⁱ⁾ to be taken at interest by the Thrers.

It is ordered that M⁽ʳ⁾ Ald [hollyd] Bannyng and M⁽ʳ⁾ Ald⁽ʳ⁾ Holliday shalbe entreated to geave ther Credites for the Companies vse forthe taking vp of fyfteene hundred poundes sterling for three monethes and the Companie shall save them harmeles.

61⁽ˡⁱ⁾ for Caske.

Order is geaven to Ald⁽ⁿ⁾ Hollyday to pay vnto Henry Ryvell⁽ˢ⁾ Coop for Caske in full paym⁽ᵗ⁾ of his accoumpte audited by m⁽ʳ⁾

Chambers and Mr Harryson the some of threescore and one poundes. *1600 17 Feb.*

The lyke order is geaven him to pay vnto John Hardway Coop for Caske in full payment of his accoumpte audited and allowed by Mr Wm Chambers and Mr Wm Harryson the some of ffyftie and seven poundes fyfteene shillingℓ. *57^li. 15^s. 0^d for Caske.*

At this Court Richard Hart a Smythe to whom the Company are to pay money for yron worke is content that the rest of money dew to him vppon his reckoning shalbe staied in the thr̃ers handes and p^d to m^r Flemyng in part of payment of the said Hartes debt dewe to him for yron. *Hartes debt for yron to be p^d to Mr Flemyng.*

Order is geaven to Ald^n hollyday to pay

It is agreed that m^r Cordell m^r Wyche and m^r Bell shall proceade in the auditing of the Pursers accompte and all other accoumptes appteyning to the read dragon. *The accompte of the read dragon to be audited*

At this Co^rt is read the Copie of a Comission geaven to m^r Howe and m^r Combe and allowed and liked of and they required that it might be written over againe wth some of the pointes altered according as Direction was geaven them and the Comitties at ther next meeting will signe it. *A Comission to Mr Howe & M^r Jo. Combe to go in to the West Cuntrey.*

It is ordered that the psons heervnder named shall goe downe to Gravesend to see the discharge of the shippes and to take order in suche thinges as shalbe necessarie to be dispatched ther and order is geaven them to dispose of all accedentℓ and occasions that shall be fytt to be determined ther according to ther discretions and whatsoever they shall doe therin the Companie will ratefie and allowe thereof *Comitties apointed to go to Graueshend*

    Mr Wm Rumney deputy   Mr Wm Garway
    Mr Ald^n Hollyday   Mr Rich: Wyche
    Mr Ald^a Wattes   Mr Wm Harryson
    Mr Ald^n Moore.   Mr Rob̃t Sandy.
    Mt Tho Cordell   M^r olyuer style.

At this Co^rte m^r Cordell maketh report that he Captein Lancaster and others have bought of M^r fraunceℓ Chery and of Ratclyff a ship called the guift of the burthen of 6 score tun for the somme of three hundred pounds sterlinge to be p^d one hundred poundes the Last of this moneth *The guyft bought for 300^li.*

THE COURT RECORDS OF

1600
17 Feb.

another C[th] li. the last of m̃che and the third C[th] li. the last of May following w[ch] bargaine the Companie do well allowe of, and do imploy the said ship in following of the fleete wth victualles.

1600
18 Feb.

The xviij[th] of february 1600.

M[r] W[m] Rumney deputy   M[r] Ald[n] Moore
M[r] Ald[n] [Moore] Wattes   M[r] Rich : Wyche.
M[r] Ald[n] Hollyday.

Phillip Grove.

 BILL of adventure sealed vnder the Common Seale to Phillip Grove Pylott for [*the gaine of*] five hundred poundes adventure vppon the gaine of the voyage allowed him.

100[li] to y[e] Purser of ye Susan.

Warraunt is geaven to Ald[r] Bannyng *ther* to pay to [the] Joseph Salbanck Purser of the Susañ vppon accoumpte for the provision of the ship and the Clearing of her away the somme of one hundred poundes sterling.

40[li]. 12[s] to leonard Onnyslowe Coop.

Warraunt is geaven to Ald[r] Hollyday thēr to pay vnto Leonard Onnyslowe Coop for Caske the some of fowrtie poundes twelve shillinĝs sterlinĝ in full paym[t] his accoumpt being audited and allowed by m[r] W[m] Harryson.

19. 16. 0 to John Spencer Cooper.

Warraunt is geaven to Ald[r] Bannyng to pay to John Spencer Coop for worke done in Caske wrought for the Companie as apereth by his Accoumpt allowed by the said Ald[r] the somme of xix[li] xvj[s] iiij[d].

36[li]. 19. 0 to Georg Chapman Cowper.

Lyke warraunt is geaven to [the said] Ald[r] Hollyday theï [the some] to pay vnto George Chapman Cowper the somē of thirtie sixe poundes xix[s] sterlinĝ for Caske wrought for the Company being rest of a former accoumpt [allowed] audited by m[r] Harrison.

1600
20 Feb.

The 20th february 1600.

M[r] Wm Rumey deputy   M[r] Wm Garway.
Mr Ald[n] Hollyday   M[r] Rob[t] Sandy
M[r] Tho. Cordell   M[r] Rich. Wyche
M[r] Rich: Staper   M[r] Jo : Combes.

 BILL of adventure sealed vnder the Common seale to Mʳ John Ellecott for 220ˡⁱ adventure put in stocke.

1600 20 Feb. John Ellecot his bill of aduenture of 220ˡⁱ.

Geven a warrant vppõ Aldᵣ Holleday ffor paymᵗ of ł 29. to Thomas Duck ffor anchients & streamers to the dragon as p bill.

The 20ᵗʰ February 1600.

 BILL of adventure sealed vnder the Comon Seale vnto Wᵐ Allen of London Esquier for 200ˡⁱ adventure putt in stock.

Wᵐ Allen esqr.

A Bill of Adventure sealed vnder the Comon seale vnto [Wᵐ Starky and] Raphe Allen mᵉcer and Wᵐ Starky Skynner for 400ˡⁱ of adventure put in stock.

Raphe [Starkey] Allen Wᵐ [Allen]Starky

Geiven a warraunt vppon Alderman Hollidaye for paymᵗ of fower score poundꝭ to Josephe Page Baker for an accompte of breade.

Joseph Page Baker 80ˡⁱ

A bill of adventure sealed vnder oʳ Coīnon Seale to Wᵐ Starkie one of oʳ seconde sorte of factoʳˢ of a 100ˡⁱ [venture] adventure vppon the gaine of the voyage.

Wᵐ Starkie

Geiven a Warrante vppon Alderman Bannynge for paymᵗ of 27ˡⁱ. 6ˢ. 6ˡⁱ to Robte Myddleton in full for sugar deliued to the Shippes.

Robte Middleton 27ˡⁱ. 6ˢ. 6ᵈ

Geiven a warrante vppon Alderman [Bannynge] *Hollidaye* for payment of 7ˡⁱ 10ˢ to John Pywell for head peces and morrens.

7ˡⁱ. 10ˢ to John Pywell.

A Bill of adventure sealed vnder oʳ comon Seale to Roger Style grocer one of oʳ Third sorte of factors of fiftie poundes adventure vppon the gaine of the voyage.

Roger Style

A Bill of adventure sealed vnder oʳ Coīnon Seale to Phillipe Wynchcombe one of oʳ fourth sorte of factoʳˢ of ffowrtie poundꝭ adventure vppon the gaine of the voyage.

Phillipe Wynchcombe.

A Bill of adventure sealed vnder oʳ Comon Seale to Thoīns Salterne of the Cytie of Bristowe one of oʳ seconde sorte of factoʳˢ for a hundred poundꝭ adventure vppon the gaine of the voyage.

Thomas Salterne.

Geiven a warrant vppon Alderman Hollidaye for payment of a hundred poundꝭ to Christopher Thomson Smithe vppon an accompte of yron.

Christopher Thomson Smithe 100ˡⁱ

1600
20 Feb.
Wᵐ Brunde.

A Bill of adventure sealed vnder oʳ Comon Seale to William Brunde of London one of oʳ princypall factors for two hundred poundẹ adventure vppon yᵉ gaine of yᵉ voyage.

John Hauarde

A Bill of Adventure sealed vnder oʳ Comon seale to John Havard Grocer one of oʳ princypall [merchantẹ] factoʳˢ for two hundred poundes adventure vppon the gaine of yᵉ voyage.

Captaine Lancaster.

A Bill of Adventure sealed vnder oʳ Common seale to Captaine Lancaster The Genʳall of oʳ ffleete for fiftene Hundred poundes adventure or three hundred poundes sterling accordinge to the condition of the said Bill. vppon the gaine of the voyage.

The xxjᵗʰ of february 1600.

1600
21 Feb.

Mʳ Wᵐ Rumney deputy   Mʳ Robt Sandy
Mʳ Aldⁿ Moore   Mʳ Rych: Wyche
Mʳ Thomas Cordell   Mʳ Wᵐ Harryson
Mʳ Rich: Staper   Mʳ Aldⁿ Hollyday.

Wᵐ Wilforde

BILL of adventure vnder the Common seale was sealed to Wᵐ Wilforde one of the 3. sorte of factoʳˢ for 50ˡⁱ adventure vppon the gaine of the voyage.

Nathaniel Jamryn.

A Bill of adventure vnder the comon seale was sealed to Nathanyell Jamryn one of the 3. sorte of factoʳˢ for 50ˡⁱ adventure vppon the gaine of the voiadge.

John Myddleton a princypall factor.

A Bill of adventure vnder oʳ comon Seale was sealed to John Myddleton gent one of the princypall sortes of factoʳˢ for ffowre hundred poundẹ of adventure vppon the gaine of the viage.

John Myddleton an adventurer

A Bill of adventure under oʳ comon Seale was sealed to John Myddleton Gent for 220ˡⁱ adventure put in Stocke.

Thomas Pulleyñ. Precher.

A Bill of adventure vnder oʳ comon Seale was sealed to Thomas Pulleyñ preacher for the some of 50ˡⁱ adventure vppon the gaine of the viage.

50ˡⁱ. 10ˢ. to

A warrante is Geiven to Alderman Hollidaye for the pay-

THE EAST INDIA COMPANY 151

ment of thirtie poundes tenn shilling℥ to Richarde Hall Smithe for two Ankers for the Hector his Bill beinge allowed by Mr Wiseman.

1600 21 Feb. Richarde Hall Smithe.

At Graueshende. the xxiiij^th;
[A distribution of the present℥· by the Comitties.]

Mr Wm Rumey Deputy   Mr Wm Garway
Mr Ald^n Hollyday   Mr Olyuer Style
Mr Ald^n Wattes   Mr Robt Sandy.
Mr Ald^n Moore   Mr Rich: Wyche
Mr. Tho Cordell   Mr Wm Harryson.

1600 24 Feb.

DISTRIBUTION of the presentes prepared for [the] to be presented to y^e Princes of the East Indies wher trade is to be sought devided in *to* the severall shippes by the order of the Comitties above named as followeth viz in

The read dragon.
{ A siluer fountaine & basen of 205 o℥.
1 standing Cup wth a Cover 63 o℥.
2 looking glasses of the greatest.
2 Helmeet℥
2 Plumes of fethers
2 lr̃es.

Hecto^r
{ A basen & ewre of   102 o℥.
1 standing Cup of   32 o℥.
1 lesser Cup of   16 o℥.
[1 Plume of fethers]
1 looking glasse smalest
2 lr̃es.

Assention
{ 1 standing Cup of   32 o℥.
1 lesser Cup of   16 oz.
1 fann of fethers
1 smale looking glasse.
1 Case of dagges.
1 lr̃e.

1600
24 Feb.

Susan
{
1 ship basen & ewre of   50 oz.
1 fanne fethers
2 beltes imbrothered
[2 helmeets]
1 looking glasse.
1 lre͡.
1 head pece & targett of the Moskovy Company.
}

1600
25 Feb.

The xxvth of februarie 1600.

Mr Cordell   Mr Wyche
Mr Garway   Ry Wright } left at Graveshend

John Dauyes his bill of aduenture as Pylott maior.

Bill of adventure was sealed vnder o^r Comon seale to John Davyes gent. Pylott maior of this viage for his [One hundred poundes] adventure vppon the gaine of the viage as yet shall arryse viz yf the viage yeeld two for one then he to have out of the clere pfitt all chardges deducted 500^{li} yf three for one 1000^{li} yf fowre for one 1500^{li} yf five for one 2000^{li} out of wch paym^t w^{ch}soever shall fall *due* to him by the value of the retourne of the saide viage there is to be deducted 200^{li} lent vnto him by the Companie before his goeing forth over and above 100^{li} geiven him for his pvision.

John Dauyes his bill of adventure for a 100^{li} put in Stocke.

A Bill of adventure vnder o^r comon Seale to John Davyes gent Pylott maior of this viage 100^{li} adventure put in Stocke.

Thomas Morgann.

A Bill of adventure vnder o^r common Seale to Thomas Margann one of o^r fourth sorte of factors for fortie poundes adventure vppon the gaine of the viage.

Henrie Myddleton.

A Bill of adventure vnder our Com̃on seale to Henrie Myddleton gent one of our seconde sorte of factors for 100^{li} adventure vppon the gaine of the viage.

Rob͞te Pope.

A Bill of adventure vnder o^r Com̃on seale to Rob͞te Pope one of o^r seconde sorte of factors for 100^{li} adventure vppon the gaine of the viage.

Christopher Stradlinge.

A Bill of adventure for Christopher Stradlinge sealed vnder o^r Comon Seale and one of o^r fourth sorte of factors for fortie poundes adventure vppon the gaine of the viage.

Thomas Dassell.

A Bill of adventure vnder o^r comon seale to Thomas Dassell

THE EAST INDIA COMPANY 153

one of o^r Third sorte of factors for fyftie poundes adventure   1600
vppon the gaine of the viage.   25 Feb.

The xxvjth of februarie 1600/   1600
   26 Feb.

OWRE seuerall comissiones to the generallie and other the factors in succession beinge all of one tenor was sealed vnder the comon seale of the Companie and sen̄allie deliūed to the princypall factor of everie shippe.   Comissions sealed vnder ye Comon seale.

    A Bill of adventure sealed vnder o^r comon seale to Wm Brodebent M^r of the Reade Dragon for One hundred pound€ adventur vppon the gaine of the viage and for twentie marke a monethe for his wag€ contracted wth him And whereas there was geiven him by the Companie One hundred pound€ sterling for his provision to Sea And the warraunte geiven to ye Thr̄er for the payment thereof made mencon that [same] the saide hundred poundes was a paymente vppon his wag€ be it remembred that the saide warrant was mys taken and should have binne a warraunt of a One hundred pound€ ymprested & absolutlie geiven him for his provision to Sea and not in pte of paym^t of any his wages.   Wm Brodebentes byll of aduenture

    A Bill of adventure *sealed* vnder o^r comon Seale to Thomas Tudd one of o^r fourth sorte of factors for fourtie poundes adventure vppon the gaine of the viage.   Tho: Tud his bill of aduenture.

    A Bill of adventure was sealed vnder o^r comon Seale to Roger Style on of o^r thirde sorte of factors for fourtie poundes adventure put in Stocke.   Roger Style his byll of aduenture.

    Whereas the Companie did lende m^r William Brodebent the somē of One hundred poundes for sixe monethes for w^{ch}[yt] was entended y^t certen howses should be morgaged for the companies securitie the saide william Brodebent before his depture from Gravesende beinge vppon an accompte to have received as dewe to him from the Companie the somē of xxviij^{li} (as by the accompte of william dixon purser of the Reade Dragon appeareth) he the said Wm Brodebente hath lefte in the handes   Wm Brodebent.

154   THE COURT RECORDS OF

1600
26 Feb.
of the saide Dixon to thuse of *the* Companie the saide xxviij^{li} in pte of paym^t of the saide 100^{li} And hath assigned m^r Thomas Cordell and m^r William Garwaye to paie to the Companie seventie & two poundes residue of the saide 100^{li} vppon the xxvjth of August next by wch payment and assignaĉon satisfacĉon is made to the saide Companie of the saide 100^{li} by them lent and the saide Mr Brodebent dischardged thereof.

100^{li} to the Purser of the Assention.
Order is geaven to Mr Aldⁿ Hollyday to pay vnto [m^r] Wm Leake Purser of the Assention for the paiment of half wages to mariners and for the clearing of the ship from hence the somme of one hundred poundes sterling whereof he is to geave an accoumpte.

100^{li} to ye Purser of the Hecto^r
The lyke order is geaven to the said Thrēr to pay to *Georg psons* the Purser of the Hecto^r the lyke some of one hundred poundes to the lyke vse.

100^{li} to the Purser of the Susana.
A nother warraunt is geaven him to pay *to Josephe Salbanck* the Purser of the Susan the lyke some of one hundred poundes to the like vse.

180^{li} to the Purser of the read dragon.
A warraunt is also geaven to Mr Aldⁿ Bannyng to pay vnto *Wm Dixson or Edward Highlord* the Purser of the Read Dragon the some of one hundred and fowrscore poundes to the like vse.

1600
28 Feb.
The xxviijth of februarie 1600.

Mr Wm Rumney Depu: Mr Robte Sandye
Mr Thomas Cordell   Mr John Hyghlorde.
Mr Oliuer Style.   Mr Richarde wiche.

15. 7. 0 to Mr Duffield Bruer.
RDER is geaven to Ald^r Hollydaye Thrēr to paie to Mr Anthonie Duffeilde Berebreuer for. 59. barrells of bere deliv̄ed to the Scourge when she laye in docke whereof tenn barrells at iiij^s and the residue at v^s the barrell some xv^{li} vij^s sterlinge.

300^{li} to Mr Chery & Mr Golding for the guift.
Order is geaven to the said Thrēr to pay to Robt Golding of Radcliff mariner for the ship called the guifte bought of him and M^r fraunc̄ Chery the some of three hundred poundes sterlinge whereof by Agreem^t one hundred poundes is deue this

pnte day and another hundred poundes the Last of marche and the other hundred poundes the Last of aprill.   1600 28 Feb.

Lyke warraunt is geaven to the said Thrēr to pay vnto James Bover and Richard Vale for spectacles and Boxes for spectacles wth ther cases the somme of xxiiij^{li} xix^s.   24^{li} 19 0 to James Bover for spectacles.

The seconde of Marche 1600.   1600 2 Mar.

Mr Wm Rumney deputy
Mr Aldⁿ Wattes
Mr Rich: Staper
Mr Rich: Wyseman
M^r Jo: Highelord

M^r Jo: Eldred.
Mr Robt Sandy
M^r Ry: Wyche
Mr Wm Harryson
Mr Nich: Lynge.

'T is agreed that the persons heervnder named shall viewe & *determyne* the reckoning betwene Mr Ady and the Company for tymber deliuered for the building and the repayring of the shippes and *to* agree vppon an indifferent rate of the pticler prices. Whervppon ther is some variaunce. depending betweene the Companie and him.   Mr Ady for Tymber.

To morrowe in the afternone at Mr Aldⁿ Wattes hys house.
{
Mr Aldⁿ Wattes
Mr Staper
Mr Cordell
Mr Burrell
Mr Garway
Mr Wyseman
M^r Jo: Eldred.
or any 4. of them.

And the same psons are required on the behaulf of the Companie [shall] to viewe and determyne the Reckoning of the other shippewrightes for other tymbers dd to the vse of the Companie.   Ship wrightes reckoninges.

[Warraunt is geaven to m^r Aldⁿ Hollyday to pay vnto m^r Abraham Campion vppon accoumpte of 646. 15. [4] 2. dewe to him for beare deliuered to the shippes the some of two hundred poundes sterlinge.]   [200^{li} to Mr Campion for beare.]

1600 2 Mar. 2ˡⁱ to the searcher.	It is ordered that ther shalbe geaven by way of gratifycation to Mʳ Worsenham the Searcher for the clearing of the shippes the some of xlˢ.
Thaccoumpte of the state of the Aduenture bothe for ther debt & Credyte.	It is ordered that mʳ Aldⁿ [Hollyday shalbe intreated to] Bannyng and mʳ Aldⁿ Hollyday shalbe sent vnto to geave order that to morrowe morning ther bookes of Accoumptes may be brought hether and Mʳ Allabasters man be warned hether to meete together to arme an accoumpte of the state of the busines and that the same accoumpte may be pvsed and audited by the psons heervnder named to thende some present order may be taken for the clearing of the Companies debtes. by calling in suche moneys as are vnpᵈ or some other course taken to avoyde the clamoʳ of suche as are vnpaid the billes and Reckoninge dew to them by the Company.

Mʳ Staper   Mʳ Harryson
Mʳ Wyseman   Mʳ Lynge.
Mʳ Wyche   or any three of them.

The 6ᵗʰ of Marche. 1600.

1600
6 Mar.

Mʳ Wᵐ Rumney deputy   Mʳ Wᵐ Harryson
Mʳ Rich: Wiseman   Mʳ John Eldred
Mʳ Oliuer Style   Mʳ Wᵐ Burrell
Mʳ John Highlorde   Mʳ Thomas Cordell.

The state of the aduenture in debt and Credyte.	PPON conference had wᵗʰ the Thrers and an estimate made of the moneys in ther handes. and of the debte owing by the Company and of suche moneys as is dewe to the adventure not yet brought in to the Thrers handes.
9000ˡⁱ owing at this day.	It appereth by the said estimat as the state of the Adventure as it standeth at this day that ther is owing by the Company aboute the somme of ix m̃ˡⁱ, towardes the paiment Wherof ther resteth onlie in ready money in the handes of mʳ Aldⁿ Hollyday Threr̃. 814ˡⁱ or therabouts, that ther is owing by divers wᶜʰ have sett downe ther adventures, and have brought in no part thereof about 5000ˡⁱ that ther is also owing by such

as have brought in part of ther adventures and not the whole and for the Supplies of ijˢ the li. aboute 2000ˡⁱ. So as the state of the Busines standing in this case appeareth. *[1600 6 Mar.]*

Order is geaven to Ald^r Hollyday thrēr to pay to [Josephe] Lewys Tyght Blacksmythe vppon Accoumpte of yron worke wrought to the Read dragon the somme of *[100ˡⁱ to Lewys Tyght, smythe for yron worke to the Read dragon.]*

The like warraunt is geaven to the said Thrēr to pay to Joseph Page Baker vppon Accoumpte of Biskett the somme of fyfty poundes sterling. *[50ˡⁱ to Joseph Page Baker]*

Another Warraunt is geaven to the said Thrēr to pay to frauncis Candell Painter vppon accoumpte for the paintinge of the read Dragon. the somme of thirtie poundes sterlinge. *[30ˡⁱ to frauncis Candell Painter of the Read Dragon.]*

Another Warraunt is geaven to the said Thrēr to pay vnto Richard Hart Smythe for Nayles and iron worke deliuered to the Assention the somme of one hundred sixtie one poundes thirtene shillinges and a pennye in full paym^t of all yron Worke by him dd to the Company. *[161ˡⁱ 13ˢ 1ᵈ to Rych: Harte Smythe.]*

Another Warraunt is geaven to the said Thrēr to pay vnto Edmond Saunderson Turno^r for Launterns Platters and other Turno^{rs} ware dd to the Reade Dragon. *[18ˡⁱ to Edm: Saunderson for Turnurs worke to yᵉ Read dragon]*

Another Warraunt is geaven to the said Mr Aldⁿ Hollyday to pay to Mr Wm Burrell vppon accoumpt for paym^t of moneys owing to divers men the somme of one hundred poundes sterling. *[100ˡⁱ to Mr Wm Burrell vpon Accompt.]*

Another Warraunt is geaven vppon the said Thrēr to pay vnto Wm Bacon for smale mastes and other store for the shippes the somme of sixten poundes tenn pence in full paym^t of a bill of pcelles of xix^{ˡⁱ} vj^s x^{ˡⁱ} whereof iij^{ˡⁱ} vj^s is bated as soe muche wherin the Company were deceaved by the Carpenter of the Susan. *[16ˡⁱ o 10ᵈ to Wm Bacon for Mastes.]*

Another Warraunt is geaven vppon the said thrēr to pay vnto James Waters Iremonger vppon a bill of pcells for the gonners provision *for the Susan* the some of xxx^{ˡⁱ} xij^s iiij^ᵈ in full paym^t. *[30. 12. 4ᵈ to James Waters for gonners pvision for yᵉ Susan.]*

Another Warrante is geiven vppon Aldⁿ Bannynge Thrēr to pay to Nicłias Symondson the soi̅e of One hundred poundes sterlinge in pte of paym^t of tymber and Planke and othe neccessaries for ye Susann. *[100ˡⁱ to Nicłas [Harrison] Symondson for tymber & Plank for yᵉ Susan.]*

1600
13 Mar.

The xiijth of Marche 1600.

M^r W^m: Rumney Deputie   Mr Rob̃t Sandy
Mr Rich: Staper   Mr Wm Chambers
Mr Wm Garway   Mr Wm Harryson.

34. 16. 8
for lighter-
age & port-
age to W^m
Kimber at
Gully key.

RDER is geaven to Ald^r Hollyday Thr̃er to pay m^r Wm Kymber Wharfeinger of Gully Key for Lighterage and portage of goodes to the shippes from the same kay the somme of xxxiiij^{li} xvj^s viij^d [as] being dewe to him vppon his bill of p̃celles. audited and allowed by Mr Highlord m^r Harryson and Mr Lynge.

34. 13. 8
for portage

The lyke order is geaven to the said Thrẽr to pay to the Porters of the Grocers haberdashers Salters and Skynners for Portage and Lading of the fowre severall shippes thes severall sommes following amounting in all to the somme of [xiij] xxxiiij^{li} xiij^s viij^d sterling. as appereth by ther severall billes audited and allowed by the Comitties of the shippes videlt for the read dragon xiij^{li} ij^s xj^d for the hecto^r viij^{li} iiij^s for the Assention six poundes tenn shilling j^d and for the Susan vj^{li} xvj^s viij^d.

11^{li} 6. 8
for wharf-
age to Robt
wood at
wooll key.

Another warraunt is geaven to the said Thrẽr to pay to Rob̃t Wood Wharfeinger of wooll key the somme of xj^{li} vj^s viij^d for wharfage and lighteringe of goodes shipped from the same kay.

42^{li} 8^s 11^d
to M^r
Rumney
for money
disbursed.

Another warraunt is geaven vppon the said Thrẽr to pay to m^r Wm Rumney deputy [for] the somme of fowrtie and two poundes viij^s xj^d whereof [40] 38^{li} 10^s 3 was by him p^d and deliuered at his going downe to gravesend to Capten Mydleton for payment of mariners and the rest being ij^{li} xij^s was disbursed in Charges by him and M^r wyche wth ther servaunt.

1600
21 Mar.

The 21 Marche 1600.

Mr Wm Rum̃ey deputy   Mr John Highclord
Mr Aldⁿ Hollyday   Mr Wm Harryson
Mr Rich: Staper   Mr Nic̃las Lynge
Mr Wm Garway   Mr Wm Burrell
Mr John Eldred   Mr Thomas Cordell
           Mr Rich: Wyseman.

RDER is geaven to Mr Wm Burrell to take vp the boate of thassention that lyeth at Blackwall and to make sale of the sale of the same for the most that can be gotten who hath vndertaken *to* do his best therin.

1600 21 Mar, The Assention's longe boate.

Order is geaven to Mr Harryson and Mr Burrell to gather together all suche provysions and thinges belonging to the shippes that are left behinde as 2 demi Cannons iron stanchions Anker caske and other thinges and putt them in some storehouse to be provided for that purpose to thende they may be solde for the most that can be made thereof.

A storehouse to be provided for the gatheringe together of thinges left behinde.

A Bill of Adventure sealed vnder the comon seale to Stephen Hodgeson for his adventure and supply of 220^{li}.

Stephen Hodgeson the bill stayed.

Order is geaven that all suche as depend in accoumpte wth the Company shalbe called vppon to bring in ther billes that ther accoumptes may be made vp and brought in to a certen state, of wch accoumptaunt^{es} thes persons following are to be called vppon—viz :

Mr Pointell & Rewler &c.   [Jo: More] Nichas Pierd
[M^r fletcher] Ald^r Bannyng   Mr Roger Howe
W^m [Rutter] Burrell.   Rich: Gossen
Wm Angell   Mr Staper.

Order is geaven to m^r Ald^n Hollyday thr$\bar{e}$r to pay vnto Thomas Hewys Clothworker for worke done to the Companie 12^{li} . 8 . 6 in full for his said worke.

12^{li} . 8 . 6 to Tho. Hewys Clotheworker

2^s p lb further supply vppon the like pound in the former act.

xv^l at interest to be p^d Mr. Beareblock.

A Gen^{all} Court holden the first of Aprill 1601.
Present of the Comitties

Mr Wm Rumey deputy   Mr Ald^n More
Sr John Harte   Mr Rich : Staper
Mr Ald^n Wattes   M^r olyuer Style

1601 1 Apr.

1601
1 Apr.

M.r Rich. Wyseman
M.r Robt Sandy
M.r John Eldred
M.r John Highelord
M.r Rich : Wyche

M.r W.m Harryson
M.r Ald.n Hollyday.

w.th the greatest part of the Generality.

A newe supply of ij.s the lb to pay Companies debtes.

HIS Co.rt being called vppon occation of the great debt and afterdett that hangeth vppon the voyage by reason of the severall sommes sett downe by [divers of] the adventuro.rs and not brought in ether in the whole or in part and by divers other somes behinde by some of them as pte of ther adventures *sett downe and not brought in wholy* and also by other sommes behinde for the supplies *over and above the sommes sett downe and brought in* All w.ch do amounte [very neare] to the some of Nyne thowsand poundes and above the w.ch must of necessitie be p.d the same being dewe to a nuber of poore men who importune the Comitties every day for payment vppon consideration of w.ch great arrerages and surplusage of provysion and charge that lieth vppon the voyage this Court resolving that every adventuro.r [was] is for his rate and proportion of his adventure a debto.r for and towardes the whole Credite geaven to the voyage, Did therefore order and decree that a further supply of ij.s the lt vppon every mans adventure shalbe brought in to the Thre.rs of this fellowship towardes the satysfaction of this debt depending vppon them [betwene] by the x.th of this moneth And to thend the paym.t thereof may be the better pformed It is agreed that as many of the brethren of this Company as shall faile in the bringinge in of ther moneis *at that day* [contrary this acte]. ether vppon the former supply of ij.s the lt. w.ch by order of this Company was apointed and ordred to be brought in by a decree of a general Co.rt holden the 9. of Januarye *Last* or contrary to this present act for the further supplie of ij.s the lt. more now presentlie decreed to be brought in shall forfeite *to the vse of the comon stocke* to be defalked out of his *privat* stocke bothe by the one decree and the other [in] wherein he shall [be found to] faile to make payment the severall somes of ij.s vppon every lt of his adventure and it is alsoe ordered for the making good of this penaltie to the vse of the [Comon]

Gen°alyty and the coffion adventure that the Bookeap shall vppon the severall accoumptes of every adventuro' that shall faile in the bringing in of ether of thes supplyes contrary to the trew meaning of both this and the former acte or ether of them defalte from the private stocke of every *suche* contributo' the said penaltie of ij° the ℔. soe forfeyted and make his stocke [credito'] *lesse* by so muche as the said penaltie soe forfeited cometh vnto thend. that the same forfeitures [beinge] may be putt to the coffion accoumpte of profit and losse [may goe to the advauncem' of ther stockes wch have [brou] or shall [supply] bringe in ther supplyes. And it is also ordered that in the Billes of adventure that shalbe geaven out to every of them wch do not bring in their said supplies the valewe thereof shalbe defalked out of his said bill of adventure [and he holden credito' for soe muche lesse as the penatie].

1601
1 Apr.

It is alsoe ordered that wher for the supply of necessarie paiment° and provisions of the voyage before the going of the shippes out of the River Mr Ald^n Bannyng and m^r Ald^n Hollyday the thre͞rs of this felowship did take vp at interest the somme of xv^cli that the ge͞nalyty shall and will save the said thre͞rs harmeles and stande chargeable for ther indempnitie both of the principall and the interest of the said somme of xv^cli.

xv^c li. at interest by the Thers taken up to be discharged by the Company.

At this Co^rte the right honorable the Erle of Cumbland wrote his letter to the generalitie entreating them that he might assigne out of his stocke of adventure of xv^cli the somme of 200^li to m^r Wm Beerblock goldsmithe and therw^th that the Companie would admitt the said Mr Beerblocke not onlie an adventuro^r of so muche but to accepte *and admitt* him as a free brother of this Companie wch motion albeit both in the example [or] *and* president [it seemeth] and alsoe in the [admittaunce of 2 psons] admittaunce in to the freedome of the Companie of 2 psons vnder one adventure once entirely sett downe it may seeme *to be* and is prejudiciall *to order* yet at the request of so honorable a pson [they] *this Court* could not denye to yeld to the said motion and did agree both to the assignation of 200^li adventure to be sett over vnto him and to

Wm Beerblock admitted an adventuro^r of 200^li of the erle of Cumbland his stock of xv^c by way of assignation & also made free.

Y

1601
1 Apr.

admitt him also in to the previledges of the said Companie and he the said Mʳ Beareblocke did agree [to add] by way of increase of the said adventure of 200ˡⁱ and for the supplies thereof according to the ordinaunces of this felowship to add therunto the somme of 50ˡⁱ more and soe to stand an adventurʳ in principall and supplies of the somme of 250ˡⁱ wᶜʰ is by the booke keap to be sett vppon the said mʳ Beerblock and therwᵗʰ 200ˡⁱ to be taken from the Erle of Cumberland his adventure.

1601
3 Apr.

The 3. of Aprill 1601.

Mʳ Wᵐ Rumey deputy   Mʳ John Highelord
Mʳ Rich: Wyseman   Mʳ Wᵐ Harryson
Mʳ John Eldred   Mʳ Thomas Cordell
        Mʳ Robt Sandy.

Mʳ Wᵐ
Megges
140ˡⁱ for
rest of stock
& supplies.

MR Megges being warned before the Comitties for the bringing in of the rest of his adventure of 200ˡⁱ and his severall supplies *havinge brought in* 100ˡⁱ did insist a while vppon a discharge promised him by the bringing in of one Mʳ Clenche to sett down CCˡⁱ was not wᵗʰstanding overruled and in thend brought to assent to pay [in his CCˡⁱ] Cˡⁱ for the rest of his adventure and to pay his supplies when others had pᵈ thers: or els he would procure a discharge to the Company for the valewe of Cˡⁱ wᶜʰ they are to pay to the Muskovia Company for cordage.

1601
7 Apr.

The 7. of Aprill 1601.

Mʳ Wᵐ Rumey deputy   Mʳ Robt Sandy
Mʳ Thomas Cordell   Mʳ Jo: Highlord
Mʳ Rich: Staper   Mʳ Niclas lyng
Mʳ John Eldred   Mʳ Wᵐ Harryson.

li s. d
14. 7. 2
to Mʳ John
Highlord.

ORDER is geaven to Aldⁿ Bannyng to pay to Mʳ Highlord vppon a Bill of pcelles of moneis by him Laid out for the Companies vse the somme of xiiijˡⁱ. vijˢ. iiijᵈ. [vppon present vse].

The 9. of Aprill 1601.

Mr Wm Rumney Mr Rich: Wyseman
Mr Thomas Cordell Mr Wm Harryson

RDER is geaven to m^r Aldⁿ Hollyday thr͞er that whereas he hath p^d to Arnold Mabanck Pullymaker for worke done to the shipps the somme of 30^{li} wthout Warraunt that he shall pay vnto him in full payment of his whole whole worke done the somme of 24^{li}. 7^s. 9^d more and take his acquittaunce for the whole 56. 7. 9.

30^{li} Arnold Mabanck Pullymaker

The Like order is geaven to the said Thr͞er to pay vnto Xpofer Thomson *Smyth* the somme of 34^{li}. 4. 2 being rest of peelles [of] amounting to 274. 4. 2. Whereof all the residue is already *paid* as by a note of the accoumpte from the bookeap appeareth So that this 34 4 2^{li} is in full paym^t.

34^{li} 4^s 2^d xpofer Thompson Smythe.

Warraunt is geaven to Aldⁿ *Holliday* [Bannynge] thr͞er to pay vnto M^r [Robt.] *Mr* [Thomas] John Hedland the somme of sixten poundes one shillinges viij^d for making of cariages for ye shippes as appeareth by his bill of pticlers therof for wch he is to take his acquittaunce in full paym^t, or to abate soe much to Mr Thom͞s Symond͞es vppon his second supply because he hath p^d the same 16. 1. 8. to ye said Jo: Hedland.

16. 1. 8. Jo: Hedland for Carriages.

Warraunt is geaven to Aldⁿ Bannyng Ther to pay vnto Thomas Duck for streamers by him served to the shippes in full paiment thereof the somme of Twelve poundes.

12^{li} to Tho: Duck for streamers.

Warraunt is geaven to Aldⁿ Holliday Ther to pay vnto Lewys Tayte Smythe in part of paym^t of iron worke done for the shippes the somme of one hundred poundes.

100^{li}. 0. 0. to Lewis Tayte Smythe.

Warraunt is geaven to m^r Aldⁿ Bannyng ther to pay to Edward Stephens Shipwright for worke by him done vppon the read Dragon the somme of fyftie poundes in part of paiment.

50^{li} to Edw: Stephens Shipwright.

Warraunt is geaven to Aldⁿ Holliday ther to pay vnto Mr Thom͞s Barbor for Canvas for sailes the somme of one hundred poundes sterling in part of paiment of a mere somme.

100^{li} to Tho: Barbor for Canvas.

Warraunt is geaven to Aldⁿ Bannyng ther to pay vnto Adam

50^{li} to

1601
9 Apr.
Adam Wood for deales & mastes &c. 11ˡⁱ. 0. 0. to Jo: Maxfield Brasier

Wood in part of paiment of deales mastes and timber served to the shippes the some of fyfty poundes sterling.

Warraunt is geaven to Aldⁿ Holliday thēr to pay vnto John Maxfield Brasyer for Copp vesselles by him served to the shippes in full payment thereof the some of Eleven poundes sterling.

42. 15. 0 to Robt Highoo for Canves.

Warraunt is geaven to Aldⁿ Holliday thēr to pay vnto Robert Heighoo for 30 peeces of Ipswᶜʰ Canves at 28ˢ. 6ᵈ the peece the somme of fowrtie two [pence] poundes xvˢ in full payment of the said Canves.

22ˡⁱ. 4ˢ. 0ᵈ to fra: Covell Chaundeler.

Warraunt is geaven to Mʳ Aldⁿ Holliday to pay vnto frauncˢ Covell Chaundelerʳ for provision by him served to the shippes the somme of Twentie two poundes fowre shillinges in full paiment of the same provision.

1601
11 Apr.

A Genʳall Court holden the 11ᵗʰ of Aprill 1601.
                Present

Mʳ Wᵐ Rumey deputy	Mʳ Nich : Lynge.
Sʳ John Hart. knight	Mʳ Rich : Wyseman
Mʳ Aldⁿ Wattes	Mʳ Wᵐ Harryson
Mʳ Rich : Staper	Mʳ Wᵐ Garwey
Mʳ Robt Sandy	Mʳ Jo : Eldred

            Mʳ Jo : Highelord.
wᵗʰ the greatest pt of the genßalyty.

AT this Court was read an order from the LL of her Maᶜˢ most honorable privie Councell taking knowledge of the remissnes of the Companie in payinge ther debtes dewe by the voyage wᶜʰ importeth the honoʳ of the state being a publique action the tenoʳ of wᶜʰ acte doeth followe in thes Wordes.

At the Courte at Whitehall the xᵗʰ of Aprill 1601.
            Present.

L : Archb : of Cant :	Mʳ Comptroller
L : Keeper.	Mʳ Secr : Cecyll.
L : Treasurer.	Sʳ John Fortescue
L : Admirall.	Mʳ Secr : Herberte

PON complaynte made this daye to their ll͠p : by the
Comyttyes of the Easte India Companie, that y^e
debt͠ꝭ of the p͠nte viage now by them sett forthe
amountinge to Seaven Thowsande poundes above the contri-
buc͠ons sett downe by the adventure^rs are not paide, the same
growinge by reason of the backewardenes and frowarde dis-
posic͠ons of di͠vse psons that shewe themselves remisse and vnwillinge to furnyshe there promyssed contribuc͠ons and alsoe
their porc͠ons of the supplyes wch since at there generall meet-
ing͠ꝭ at severall tymes have been agreed on to yeelde above
there adventures a rate of fowre Shilling͠ꝭ in the pounde for
the cleeringe of the saide debte, Their ll͠p: vppon due conside-
rac͠on how muche yt ymporteth the honnor of the state, that
so publique an acc͠on should not receive scandall or shamefull
imputac͠on Have this daye ordered that forasmuche as the saide
debt in all or in pte is proporc͠onablye due to be satysfied by
everie contributo^r of the viage That therefore the saide Companie and everie adventurer thereof shall w^thout further delaye
not only pforme and satysfie there full contribuc͠ons agreed
vppon, promysed and sett downe vnder there handes, But alsoe
there proporc͠onable supplyes accordinge to there agreem^ts at
there gen͠all Court͠ꝭ, Or otherwyse yf any pson or psons shall
refuse to conforme themselves therevnto ; that then the
Governo^r deputye and comyttyes of the saide companye or
any fower of them shall by vertue of this there ll͠p: order
straightlye Injoyne and comande the saide psons to make there
ymediate appearance before their ll͠p: to the end there ll͠p: may
proceed to ye punyshinge of there contempte, by refusinge to
accomplishe there one agreem^t and promyse, so muche import-
inge the publique, as their obstinacye and pversenes shall deserve, And to that end direction is geiven to a Messenger of her
Maties Chamber to attend the saide Governo^r and Companie to
bringe the saide ptye͠ꝭ before there ll͠p:

      Concordat cum Registro.
         Tho: Edmondes.

1601
11 Apr.
The long order for betterpaymt of the Companies debts dew by the voiadge. By bringing in Adventures and supplies.

Vppon the readin͠ꝰ of wch act it was resolved that especiall

1601
11 Apr.

care and travell shuld be taken by the whole Company to free the viage from all imputation and discredit and y' the same might the better be effected forasmuche as Mr Rumney the deputie of the Governo^r to the Company is necessarielie for his health shortlie to take his iorney *to the Bathes* in whose absence the teno^r of ther Lordships order cannot be executed vnlesse the present governo^r of the Company were discharged of his imprisonm^t and at Libertie to travell in the Companies occasions. Therfore for the better ordering of the affaires of this felowship and the gathering in of Contributions and supplies wherby ther debt{{ may be presentlie discharged wch cannot endure the delay and expectation of Mr Thoms Smythe the Late and present governo^r his enlargem^t This Assemblie did proceade to the Election of a nother Governo^r to stande for the government of thaffaires of this felowship vntill the next day of election apointed by o^r priviledges and divers being put in election for the supplying of the same place the said Election by Scruteny is fallen vppon Mr Aldⁿ Wattes who beinge present was placed in the office accordinglie.

At this Courte the generalytie did Noiate and chuse the psons heervnder named to be generall auditors of the Threr̃s Accoumptes and of all other the charges of the voyage to ioine wth the former Auditors apointed by the Comitties and vsed by them in the auditing of the said Threr̃s accoumptes and other the expences and disbursem^{tes} of the voyage all W^{ch} ioining together or anie six of them may audite the accoumptes of the state of the voyage and report the same to the generalyty when all the said accoumptes are disgested and agreed vppon.

Auditors

Auditors form^rly apointed by ye Comitties.	Auditors apointed by the Gen^ralyty.	
Mr Thomas Cordell.	Mr Rich : Bowdeler	
M^r olyver Style	M^r Jo : Harvy	
Mr Rich : Wyseman	Mr Greenewell.	Auditors.
Mr Wm Harryson	Mr Tho Symondes	
	Mr John fletcher	
	Mr Nich : Leat	

After the rysinge of the generall Co^rte warraunt was geaven by the Comitties to m^r Ald^n Holliday th̃r to pay vnto Joseph Page Baker for Biskett made and deliuered [by] to the shippes the somme of fourtie five pound℔ [sterling] tenn shillinge xj^d sterling in full paym^t. 1601 11 Apr. 45^li, 10, 11^d to Joseph Page baker

Lyke warraunt was geaven to Ald^n Bannyng th̃r to pay vnto George Barbo^r the somme of twentie seven poundes five shilling℔ sterlinge [in full] for rest and in full paym^t for [Pulleis] Sailes to the Susan having p^d him xx^li before w^thout warraunt in part. 27. 5. 0 to Georg Barbo for sayles.

Another Warraunt to the said Ald^n Bannyng th̃r to pay John Crane fower poundes Nyne shilling℔ viij^d. for rest and in full paym^t for Pullies having p^d him xvij^li before w^thout warraunt in part. 4. 9. 8. to Jo: Crane for Pullies.

The xx^th of Aprill 1601. 1601 20 Apr.

Mr Ald^n Watt℔ Gouer : Mr Rich : wyseman.
Mr Ald^n Banninge } Mr John Hyghlorde.
Mr Ald^n Hollydaye } Thũrs Mr Robte Sandye.
Mr Rich : Stapers. M^r w^m Harrysoñ.
M^r w^m Garwaye. Mr Niclius Lynge
M^r w^m Burrell.

PON conference had wth the Thr̃es there desire was to see the Accompt℔ and an estemate to be made of the moneys in there hands to paye suche debt℔ as farre as there moneys will extende.

Order was geiven to Ald^n Hollydaye for payment of 200^li to Thomas Barber vppon an accompte of canvas delliuered to the shipps. 200^li to Thomas Barber for Canvas.

The like order is geiven to the same Ald^n to paye to William Hedger in full for building. of a pinnace for the Hecto^r and diũse other thing℔ belongein to the rest of the shipps the some of sixe poundes. 6^li to William Hedger.

Order is geiven to Ald^n Hollidaye to paye to Robte Huse saylemaker in full paym^t of his Bill for makinge of sayles the some of fortye nyne poundes. 49^li to Robte Huse for sayles.

1601
20 Apr.

49ˡⁱ to John Bowden for sayles.

The like order is geiven to the same Aldⁿ to paye to John Bowden sayle maker the some of fortye poundes in full for sayles for the shipps.

42ˡⁱ. 5ˢ. 4ᵈ to Adam Wood Carpenter.

Order is geiven to Aldⁿ Hollydaye to paye to Adam Wood Carpenter in full paymᵗ of his accompte the some of Fowrty & two poundꝭ five shillingꝭ fowre pence.

1601
22 Apr.

The 22ᵗʰ of Aprill 1601.

Mʳ Aldⁿ Wattes Goʳ
Mʳ Aldⁿ Bannyng
Mʳ Rich : Wyseman
Mʳ Robt Sandy.

Mʳ John Highclord
Mʳ Nich : Lynge.
Mʳ Rich : Wyche
Mʳ frauncys Chery

Mʳ Robt Bell.

86. 15. 4 to Robt Bradbery Saylemaker

ARRAUNT is geaven to Aldⁿ Hollyday Thrēr to pay vnto Robt Bradbury Sailemaker in full paiment of his billes for making of sailes for the dragon and the hectoʳ the somme of fowrscore and six poundꝭ fyfteene shillingꝭ and fowre pence.

42. 15. 0 to Robt Highhoe for Canuas.

Order is also geaven to Mʳ Aldⁿ Hollyday thrēr to pay vnto Robt Highoe in full for Canvas he dd to the vse of the Assention as p bill the somme of fowrtie and two poundꝭ fyfteene shillinges sterling [the same being paid]

46. 17. 0. to Mʳ George Bowles for Curraunce.

The like order is geaven to [the] Mʳ Aldⁿ Bannyng thēr to pay vnto Mʳ George Bowles grocer in full payment for curraunce bought of him by Mʳ Robt Sandy for the vse of the shippes the somme of fowrtie and six poundes seventeene shillinges sterlingꝭ.

27ˡⁱ — — to James Waters for iron.

The Like order is geaven to Mʳ Aldⁿ Hollyday thrēr to pay vnto James Waters Iremonger in full paiment of his bill for iron Worke, deliuered to the vse of the shippes the somme of twentie and seven poundes   shillingꝭ sterlingꝭ.

13 0 0 to Hildebrand Spruson saylemaker.

The like order is geaven to Mʳ Aldⁿ Hollyday thrēr to pay vnto Mʳ Hildebrand Sprusen Sailemaker in full of his bill the somme of thirteene poundes sterlingꝭ money.

The like order is given to Mʳ. Aldⁿ hollyday threr to pay vnto Mʳ Peter Pett shipwright in full payment of his bill for worke and charges the somme of seventeene poundes [twelve shillingȩ and six pence] sterlinġ money.

<small>1601 22 April. 17.[12.6¹ to Peter Pett shipwright.</small>

The like order is geaven to Mʳ Aldⁿ Bannynge threr to pay vnto Wᵐ Denham shipwright in full payment of his bill the some of six poundes sterlinġ.

<small>6—0—0 to Wᵐ Denham shipwright</small>

The like order is geaven to Mʳ Aldⁿ Bannynġ ther to pay vnto James Marshe in full payment of his bill the somme of nyne poundes fyfteene shillinges sterlinge. for deales and planckes.

<small>9—15—0 to James Marshe for deales & plankes.</small>

The like order is geaven to Mʳ Aldⁿ Bannynge threr to pay vnto Ffrauncis Covell in full paiment of his bill for provisions dd to yᵉ assention. the somme of twentie and two poundȩ fowre shillingȩ sterlinge.

<small>22—4—0 to francis Cobell Chaundeler for provysion.</small>

Warraunt is geaven to Mʳ Aldⁿ hollyday to pay vnto Mʳ Crosse vintenoʳ the somme of [x] fourteene poundes tenn shillingȩ for a [Butt] Pyke of malliga Wyne geven to the L. Admirall in leiw of the deodand claimed for the hectoʳ.

<small>14—0—0 to Mʳ Crosse for sack geaven to yᵉ l: admirall.</small>

The Like warraunt is geaven to [yᵉ said] *Mʳ Aldⁿ Bannynge* to pay vnto ffrauncis Tailoʳ [Vintenoʳ] *Girdeler* for a Tun of Clarett wyne the somme of Eighteene poundes wᵗʰ wyne was geaven to the L. Admirall in Lieu of the deodand claimed for the hectoʳ.

<small>18—0—0 to</small>

It is ordered at this Assemblie that a Warraunt shalbe sent to the persons heervnder named that have hetherto denyed to bringe in ther Contributions, *subscribed* vnder the hand of the Governoʳ and 4. of the Comitties wᶜʰ warraunt shalbe shewed vnto them by a Pursevant to thend that vppon ther refusall to pay they may be carried before the LL: or els vppon ther assent to pay they may be appointed to come to Mʳ Governoʳ to geave ther Wordes to pay the same to the Threr the tenoʳ of wᶜʰ warraunt doeth followe in these words videlt:

<small>A warraunt for the sōmoning of the Contributors denying to bring in ther Payments.</small>

Whereas yoᵘ the seuall psons herevnder named have binne diuerse tymes required to bringe in yoʳ promysed Contribucõn towardes the sett inge forthe of the Easte Indie viage and have not [done] yet done the same Wee doe eftesones require yõ to geive yoʳ

1601
22 April.

directe answer whether yō will bringe in to one of the Thřers of the Companie yor said contribuc̃ōns or not (yf not) then accordinge to yor warrante of the LL. of her Maties privie counsell to vs in that behaulfe geiven Wee require yo^u to repaire to the Courte & yeald to there lordshipps a reason of yor refusall & yf yo^u will assent to paye yor contribuc̃ōns then to repaire to me the Governo^r of the Companie & to geive yor word for the present paym^t of the same dated the 22th of Aprill 1601.

Richard Champion	Rob̃t Pennyton
Hughe Hamersley.	Ric Hearne
Wm Kellett	Wm Palme^r
Wm Barrett	Rob̃t Myldmay.
Bartliew Haggett.	John Bates
Peter Helinge	Rob̃t Bowyer.

1601
27 April.

The 27. of Aprill 1601.

Mr Aldⁿ Wattes Go^r	Mr Wm Harryson
Mr. Alldⁿ Bannyng	Mr Rob̃t Bell
Mr Rich : Wyseman	Mr Nich: lynge
M^r Jo: Highelord	Mr Rob̃t Sandy
Mr Roger Howe	Mr Rich. Wyche
Mr Wm Chambers	M^r Jo: Combe.

Hughe
Hamsley

HUGHE Hamersley being on of the persons that was convented before the LL : and by their honors comitted [vnto the chain] vntill he had geaven satisfaction to the Company to charg his Contribution sett downe. Did at this assembly appeare and praied the favo^r of the Company towardes him in respecte [whereof in thende] of wch submission and ptly vppon his owne offer to take vppon *him* to satysfie and discharge the Companie of the valewe of 240^{li} to any [the] to whom the Company were indebted This assembly did agree that yf he brought a discharge wthin thes 3 daies from the Agent of the Muskovia Company of the payment of 240^{li} wherby this Company may be discharged of so much for cordage owing them then he the said hughe hamersley shuld be admitted

THE EAST INDIA COMPANY

into the priviledge of this felowship and be discharged of his Cōmittement.   1601 27 April.

John Bate and Robert Bowyer [being] ther names having bene presented to the LL : as those that deny to bring in ther Contributions and supplies and ther LL : having geaven a warraunt for the Comitting of them yf they bringe not in the money before thursday next. Are required to geave ther aunsweres whether they will bringe in ther money accordingly or not who have severally taken tyme betwene this and thursday to advyse of that matter and to geave ther aunswer what they will doe.

The first of Maye 1601.   1601 1 May.

Mr Aldⁿ Wattes Go: Mr Eldred
Mr Rumney Depu :   Mr Sandy
Mr Stapers   Mr Highlorde.

WARRAUNT is geiven to Aldⁿ Hollyday Thr̃er to paye to the kynge of Heraldes the some of Twentie merkes for assigninge a Armes to the Companie by the vertue of his office.   Twentye mkes to the kinge of Heraldes for assigning the companyes Armes.

The 8th of May 1601.   1601 8 May.

Mr Aldⁿ Wattes Go: Mr Aldⁿ Bannynge.
Mr Richard Wyseman   Mr John Highlorde
Mr John Eldred.   Mr Wᵐ Harryson
    Mr Niclias Lynge.

RDER is geiven to Ald" Bannynge to paye to Jeames Skelton in full for Tallowe deliued to the vse of the shippes the some of nyne poundes Sterlinge.   9li to James Skelton in full for Tallowe.

The like order is geiven to the same Ald" to paye to Abraham Campion berebrewar the some of five hundred poundes vppon an accompte of bere deliued to the shippes.   500li to Abraham Campion Brewar.

The like order is geiven to Aldⁿ Hollydaye to paye to Roberte Savadge in full for wastẽ & deales One hundred & Two poundes sterlinge.   102li to Roberte Sauadge for wastes & sayles.

1601
8 May.
29ˡⁱ 1ˢ 4ᵈ
to Justice
Mallett
Smythe for
yron
worcke.
300ˡⁱ to
Thomas
Barbar
for canvas.
90ˡⁱ to
Elizabeth
Bennett in
full for
Nayles.
71ˡⁱ 15ˢ
to Nicholas
Symonson
carpenter
in full for
tymber.

The like order is geiven to the same Aldⁿ to *paie* Justice Mallett Smythe p the handꝭ of Gyles ffleminge in full for yron worcke to the Dragon twentye nine poundꝭ one shillinge fowre pence.

The like order is geiven to the same Aldeⁿ to paye to Thomas Barbar the some of Three hundred poundes stʳlinge vppon an accompte of canvas delivered to the Shippes.

The like order is geiven to the same Aldeⁿ to paie to Elizabeth Bennett in full for nayles &c delified to the Shipps as by her billes appeareth the some of ffowrscore & Tenn poundes stʳlinge.

The like order is geiven to Aldⁿ Bannynge to paye to Nicholas Symonson carpenter in full for tymber delivered to the Susann threescore & eleven poundes ffyfteene shillinges.

1601
15 May.

The 15 of May 1601.

Mʳ Aldⁿ Wattes Goʳ   Mʳ Wᵐ Harryson
Mʳ Wᵐ *Rumey Deputy*   *Mʳ Aldⁿ Bannyng*
Mʳ Rich: Wyseman   Mʳ Thomas Cordell
Mʳ Wᵐ Chambers   Mʳ John Highelord
Mʳ John Combe   Mʳ Roger Howe.

Accomptes
in the west
Cuntrey.

T is ordered that mʳ howe and mʳ Combe shalbe warned to bring in ther accomptes of the Reckoningꝭ and disbursemtꝭ of the west Cuntry to be audited at the next meeting of the Comitties to thende that those accomptes being audited the Companie may proceade to the auditing and pfecting of the geñ'all Accomptes.

3ˡⁱ 15 0
to Peter
Hilles
for Caske.

Order is geiven to Aldʳ Hollidaye to paie to Peter Hilles the some of three poundes fiftene shillinges in full for Caske delified to the Hector.

48ˡⁱ to
ffraunces
Caudell
Painter

Order is geiven to the said Alderman holliday threʳ to pay vnto ffrancis Caudell Painter [for] in full of paintinge worke done by him vppon the Redd dragon the somme of fowrtie eight poundes sterling. vppon paiment Whereof his acquittaunce is to be taken in full paiment.

It is ordered by agreem^t betwene thes Comitties and m^r John Adye for a reckoning of tymber betwene the Companie and him that m^r Wm Burrell for the Companie and James Marshe for him shall have the pvsing of the said accoumpte and loke what shalbe found to be dewe to him shalbe p^d him by warraunt to be geaven to one of the threīs.

1601 15 May. John Adye for Tymber.

Order is geaven to y^e said m^r Ald^r hollyday thrēr to pay vnto Wm Allom Lighterman for lighteradg of goodes sent to the shippes in full paym^t the somme of tenn pound(^s sterlinge.

10^li to Wm Allom for lightteradge.

The 22th of May 1601.

Mr Ald^n Wattes Go^r   Mr John Highelord
Mr Ald^n Hollyday   M
Mr Rich : Staper   Mr Roger Howe
Mr Olyuer Style   M^r Jo Combe.

1601 22 May.

AT this meeting m^r Rogér howe and Mr Combe did exhibite to the Comitties present divers accoumptes and papers concerninge ther busines in the West Cuntrey w^ch [the] are conteyned in 48 severall pticler Writinges [made] by way of Inventory noted vnder the handes of the said Comitties All wch writinges are deliuered over to the bookekeap to drawe in to ferme of accoumpte armed.

Mr Roger Howe. M^r Jo: Combe.

Geven a warrant vppon ald^rman Bayning ffor paym^t of l 39. 16. 6 to Mr Richard wryte in ffull payment of his accōpt ofcharge disburced ffor the vse of this voyadg as p the pticulers therein.

l 39. 16. 6^d. to Mr Richard Wryte.

Two severall Warraunt(^s directed to the Pursevant that attendeth vppon the Companie for the warning of divers of the adventuro^rs wch are behinde wth ther supplies to appeare before the LL : to aunswere ther Contempte.

Warrauntes for the Comitting of suche as deny ther suplies.

A warraunt geven vppon Ald^n hollyday to pay to lewis Tate Black Smithe in full paiment of iron worke for the red dragon and Susan the somie of two [three] hundred [and] twentie and seven poundes sterling.

227^li to Lewis Tate Blacke smithe.

Order is geaven to Ald^n holliday to pay vnto Agnes Haselton to relieve her husband Richard haselton hurt in

xl^s to Rich: Haselfoote.

<small>1601
22 May.</small>

the hecto^r in the Companies service the some of fowrtie shillinges.

<small>29 10 0
to Charles
Anthony
for geaving
of stampes.</small>

Order is geaven to Ald^r holliday thr̃er to pay vnto Charles Anthonie her Ma^{rs} Geaver for stampes made for the East Indie moneis the some of twentie nyne poundes x^s sterling.

<small>1601
29 May.</small>

A Gen^ral Court holden the 29th of May 1601.

Mr Aldⁿ Wattes gou^r   Mr Wm Chambers.
Mr Rich. Wyseman.   Mr Wm Harryson
Mr Rich : Staper.

<small>John Bate
disfraun-
chesied.</small>

WHEREAS ther hath bene some question betwene the Company and m^r John Bate touching the bringing in his contribution of 200^{li} by him sett downe wherin he hath wthstoode the Company for some dislyke he hath conceyved of the voyage and hath resolved not to be of the Company.

<small>John Jackson made
free.</small>

And whereas m^r John Jackson clotheworker is content to supply all suche payment^s as m^r Jo Bate shuld pay for his Contribution and supplies and to take the [place and] freedome of this felowship in the place of the said m^r Bate. Therfor this Court have agreed that the said m^r Bate shalbe disfraunchesied and from henceforth be holden an adventuro^r or brother of this Company and that m^r John Jackson shalbe admitted to the freedome of this felowship. whervppon the matter being put to question by erection of handes, the said Mr Bate is disfraunchesied and the said [John] m^r John Jackson admitted a free man to enioy all benyfites of freedome incident to this felowship as freely as yf he had bene nõiated in the Pattent.

<small>W^m. Smythe</small>

Whereas ther hath bene some question betwene the Comitties and m^r Wm Smyth touching his adventure by him sett downe wherin he pretendeth an agreem^t made wth him that for the paym^t of Cv^{li} [to be made to] *he shuld* stand an adventuro^r of C^{li} [he shuld] *and* be made free. wch agreem^t being denyed by the Comitties and the matter being referred by both ther Consent^s to the generalyty at a general Court to be descyded This Court being acquainted wth the question did fall into the delibation of the matter and in thende did resolve that they could not w{th}out [any] *a geñall preiudice* to the Company by suche an example yeld to the desire of the said Smythe and therfore did resolve that the said m{r} Smythe shuld be required to bring in the rest of his adventure and supplyes.

1601
29 May.

At this Court m{r} hughe hamersley haberdasher is admytted into the freedome and Liberties of this felowship and hath satysfied 200{li} for his adventure and xl{li} for his Supplies according to former orders.

Hugh Ham{r}sleys admission

At this Court humfrey Milward haber͠sher who hath formerly denied to bring in his supplies doeth at this Court assent to bring in the same by the last of Julie next.

humfrey Milward.

The 10{th} of June 1601.

1601
10 June.

M{r} Ald{n} Wattes. Go{r}   M{r} Rich : Wyche
M{r} Ald{n} Bannyng   M{r} Nichãs lynge.
M{r} staper   M{r} W{m} Harryson
M{r} olyuer style   M{r} Roger Howe.
M{r} Rich : Wyseman   M{r} John Highelord
M{r} Jo : Eldred   M{r} [John] Robt Bell.
       M{r} Robt Sandy.

T this Court m{r} frauncis Dent being desirous to set over his adventure and freedome vnto one George Bennet Salter doeth move the assent of the Comitties heervnto. But forasmuche as the name of M{r} frauncis Dent is pticlerly expressed in the pattent thes Comitties cannot w{th}out the consent of the geñ͠alie disfraunchies the one and admitt the other in his place. therfore the said Comitties have referred both the said pties to the next generall Courte.

fra: Dent
Geo: Bennett.

It is ordered that the Secretorie shall make out Billes of adventure and supplies to everie adventuro{r} and that the same be Delivered over to the two the͠rs to deliver to the parties that haue Cleared ther adventures and supplies w{th} the said the͠rs: and the thre͠r shall receave for the vse of the Secretorie for everic bill of adventure [the] vj{d}.

Billes of Adventure.

176   THE COURT RECORDS OF

The 23 of June 1601.

1601
23 June.

Mr Aldⁿ Wattes gou^r   M^r olyuer style.
Mr Wm Rumney *deputy*   Mr Rich: Wyseman
Mr Thomas Cordell   Mr John Highelord
          Mr Rich: staper.

Richard Taylby 73^{li}. 6. 8 assigned over to Mr Aty. 100^{li} assigned to the Moskvy Company of Rich: Taylbyes adventure.

m^d that this bonde is the 21 Julie 1601. dd to Mr Stap to deliv over to the said agent.

RICHARD Tailby one of the adventuro^{rs} hathe promysed to pay vnto m^r Atye vppon Satherday next the somme of 73^{li}. 6. 8. for part of his adventure and supply *by him vnp^d* the wch some is assigned over to the said m^r Atye for money owing him by the Company.

The said Richard Tailby is assigned over for C^{li} more of his adventure behinde to the Moskova Company to be p^d at michas next by a bonde made to the Agent in the penaltie of CC^{li}.

The 4th of July 1601.

1601
4 July.

Mr Gouernor   Mr Chambers   Mr Combe
Mr Deputye   Mr Highlorde   Mr Howe
Mr Aldⁿ Moore   Mr Sandy   Mr Lynge.
M^r wiseman   Mr Harrisson

v^{li} to M^r ffletcher.

T this Courte there was allowed to m^r fflecther v^{li} in consideracōn of Rackinge of syder.

Alsoe the rest of accompt of m^r Howe & m^r Combe beinge eyghtene poundes seven shillinge two pence is allowed them for there farther stay in the Countrey more then was expected.

A Gen^rall Court holden the 6. of Julie 1601.
Present.

1601
6 Julie.

Mr Aldⁿ Wattes Gou^r   Mr Aldⁿ Bannyng ⎫
Mr Wm Rumney Deputy   Mr Aldⁿ Holliday ⎬ thr̄ers
Sr John spencer knight   Mr Tho Cordell

M{r} fra: Chery   M{r} Nich: lynge.   1601
M{r} Roger Howe   M{r} Rich: Wyseman.   6 Julie.
M{r} W{m} Chamber.   M{r} Jo Eldred.
           M{r} Rich; Staper.
   w{th} the greatest p{t} of the geñ'alitie.

IT is ordered that all thes p{r}sons heer vnder named freemen
whose names are [heer] Left out of the pattent and
yet have p{d} their adventures sett downe and ther supplies of 4{s} the pound shall be admitted into the priviledges of
this felowship to enioy the same and all freedome thereof in as
Large and ample manner as yf they were Pattentees and [ther]
as yf ther names had bene conteyned in the pattent.

    Richard Bowdeler   Peter Helyn
    Henry Butler   Thomas Bramley
    Tho Hayes   Thomas Ball   Certen per-
    Rich Humble   Edmond Scott   sons made
                                                        free whose
    Antho Moseley   John Clenche   names are
    John Westwray   Jerom Davers   not in y{e}
                                                        Pattent.
    Hughe Hamersley   x{p}ofer Nicholles
    W{m} Kellett   John Leaman
    W{m} Albany   W{m} Allyn mercer.

   At this Court ffrauncis Dent on of the adventuro{rs} of this   Georg
felowship whose name is conteyned in the Pattent did present   Bennett
                                                               made free
to this Assemblie one George Bennett and praied that he might in the place
be admitted in his place beinge willing to assigne vnto him both of fraunces
                                                                 Dent.
his freedome and his adventure w{ch} is Two hundred and ffowrtie
poundes *in his* adventure sett downe and supplies w{ch} this Court
Assented vnto and in place of the said ffrauncis Dent have re{d}
the said George Bennett and admitted him in to this ffreedome
as freelie as yf he had bene noiated in the Pattent.
   It is moved by the auditors of the geñ'all [Court] Accoumptes The Erle of
                                                                  Cumber-
of the Company that whereas the Erle of Cumberland hath as-   land his sup-
signed v{Cli} lxx{li} of his adventure to m{r} Ald{n} Bannyng w{ch} doeth *owe* plies.
supplies at the rate of 4{s} the tt. that some order may be taken
therin that ether the same may be aunswered by the one or the
other Wheruppon m{r} Ald{n} Bannyng doeth consent voluntaryly

1601
6 Julie.

that yf the said Erle be moved for the said Supplies and do not assent to pay it and charge it vppon mʳ Aldⁿ willing him to pay it that then he will aunswer the same otherwyse he thinketh he can not be iustlie charged wᵗʰ thes supplies nether did the Court at this tyme resolve to charge him vntill the said Erle hath bene moved herein.

that the supplies & adventures may be called for & psecuted

It is ordered that all suche of the brethren of the Companie as are behinde wᵗʰ ther adventures or supplies shalbe prosecuted wᵗʰ all expedition by Complaint vnto the LL : to thende that the voyage may be cleared of all debte and imputation.

Certen of the Pattentees disfrainchesed
Sʳ Edw: Michelborn Robt: Towerson Georg Vtley

At this court accordinge to the condicion or proviso in the Pattent of the Companies priviledges for suche as are noiated in the Pattent and do not bringe in ther adventures sett downe thes severall psons videlt . Sʳ Edward Michelborne Robt Towerson and George Vtley whose names are conteyned in the said Pattent and have not brought in ther somes of money by them sett downe for ther severall adventures. are by the geñall Consent of this Assemblie disfraunchesied out of the ffreedome and priviledges of this felowship and vtterlie disabled from takinge anie benifite or proffit therby.

      Sʳ Edward Michelborne ⎫
      Robert Towerson   ⎬ disfraunchesed.
      George Vtley.   ⎭

The Election of the Governoʳ Deputy & Comitties of the Company.

The priviledges of this felowship appointing the Elecc̃on of the governoʳ Deputie & comitties of this [ffelowship] Companie vppon the first day of Julie or wᵗʰin six daies followinge This Court proceaded to the Elecc̃on of the said severall officers and by scruteny and geñall consent did make choice of thes severall psons to the severall offices following and havinge chosen them did before they were severally placed and admitted to ther severall places minister vnto them respectively the severall othes ordeyned and agreed vppon by [the] this geñall assembly and [herein] at this Court inregestred to stand for [a] standing̃ thes to be ministred [hereafter] to the governoʳ his deputie and Comitties hereafter from tyme to tyme to be chosen for the governing̃ of the affaires of this felowship.

M·r· John Wattes Aldeman Elected governo·r· for to governe y·e· affaires of the Companie for one whole yere. 1601 6 Julie.

M·r· William Rumney Elected Deputie Governo·r· to governe the affaires of the Companie for one whole yere. Governo·r· Deputy gove·r·.

    Comitties   Comitties   Comitties

S·r· John spencer knight   M·r· Roger Howe Ju·r·
M·r· Ald·n· Bannyng Ju·r·   M·r· W·m· Chamber Ju·r·
M·r· Ald·n· Hollyday   M·r· John Eldred J
M·r· Ald·n· Cambell   M·r· Rich: Wyche
M·r· Richard Staper. Ju·r·   M·r· John Highelord
M·r· Thomas Cordell Ju·r·   M·r· W·m· Harryson Ju·r·
M·r· W·m· Garway   M·r· Nich: lynge Ju·r·
M·r· Rich: Wyseman Ju·r·   M·r· W·m· freeman Ju·r·
M·r· John Harby Ju·r·   M·r· Nich: leat Ju·r·
M·r· John Newman   M·r· Nich: Salter
M·r· Thomas Symondes   M·r· Thomas farrington Ju·r·
M·r· Thomas Allabaster.   M·r· W·m· Greenwell.

The oathe of the Governo·r· of the Companie
and of his Deputie.

Yo·u· shall swere that yo·u· shalbe trewe Liegeman to o·r· Soveraigne Ladie the Queenes Ma·ie· and to her heires & successors Kinges & Queenes of England and yo·u· shalbe faithefull and trewe to the fellowship or Companie of the merchaunt(·s·) of London tradinge into the East Indies and to their successors, the good state of the said Companie yo·u· shall favou·r· & affecte and y·e· priviledge of y·e· same to yo·u· power endevo·r· to maintayne & preserve. yo·u· shalbe carefull to see & provide y·t· an equall and indyfferent hand be caryed in the Goverm·t· of this fellowshipp and in the affayres thereof to all the adventurers that shall adventure or putt in stocke in anie of the voiages sett owte or to be sett owte. by this fellowshipp that w·th·owte favo·r· affection or partialitye all chardges may indyfferently *be* rated and all paym·tes· groweinge to the adventure·s· maie indifferently be answered soe farre as yo·r· knowledge in the state of the affaires of this fellowshipp may directe yo·u· or the aucthoritie of yo·r· place may conveniently beare yo·u· soe helpe yo·u· god.

1601
6 Julie.

The oathe of Comitties for direction of the trade.

Yo^u shall swere that yo^u shallbe trewe Liedgmen to o^r Soveraigne Ladie the Queenes Ma^{ie} and to her heires and Successors Kingε and Queenes of Englande And yo^u shalbe faithfull and trewe to the Governo^r & Companie of m̃chauntε of London tradinge into the Easte Indies and to their successors yo^u shall wth yor best advise and Councell assiste m^r Governo^r of this fellowship and his deputie from tyme to tyme in the affayres of this Companye that an equall and indyfferent hand be carried in the Goverm^t of this fellowshipp and in the busines thereof yo^u shall deale faithfully and equally in the orderinge & disposinge of the adventures stocke trade & merchandize of this fellowshipp Comitted to yor direction or truste in all voiadges wherein yo^u shalbe ymployed as a Comittie. and that wthowte favo^r or affection to anie man haveinge no singler respecte to yor self to the preiudice of the said fellowshipp or anie the said adventurers thereof, yo^u *shall* indifferently *to* knowledge rate & apportion all chardges & burthens of this fellowshipp accordinge to the proporc̃on of eũye mans stocke or adventure & yo^u shall alsoe order & appointe wth like indifferency and pportion to yor best Skyll & knowledge all paymentε groweinge dewe to the said adventurers vppon their stockes or adventures So helpe yo^u God.

1601
20 Julye.

The xxth of Julye 1601.

Mr Aldⁿ Wattes Go^r :   Mr Niclas Lynge
Mr Wm Rumney Dep :   M^r w^m freman
Mr Rich : Staper   M^r w^m Grenewell
Mr Ric : Wyseman   M^r w^m Harison
M^r Jo : Highlorde   Mr Thomas farrington.
Mr Niclas Leate   Mr Thomas Symondes.

Wm Brett
16.16.11^d
for timber.

ORDER is geiven to Aldⁿ Bannynge Thr̃er to paye vnto William Brett in full for timber & other pvisiones delivered to the Assention the som̃e of sixtene poundε sixtene shillingε and eleven pence as p bill of pticlers may appeare.

It is ordered at this assemblie that ther shalbe allowed to m⁺ Wᵐ Burrell. for his paines takeñ in the provisioñ of timber for the shipping of the voyage and for the Surveying of the worke of the same shippes the sōme of xvˡⁱ.

Whereas Mʳ John Ellicot of Excetoʳ beinge an adventeroʳ of CCˡⁱ doeth owe 20ˡⁱ for his supplies and being imployed by the Company to provide Spanishe Ryalles in the West Cuntrey hath geaven in a geñ'all accoumpte to yᵉ Company of all his provision wherby he resteth debtoʳ to the voyage 32 11 8. It is ordered that a lře shall be written vnto him [for the] from the geñ'alty to sende vp his supply and a more pticler accoumpt of his imployments that this Reckoning may be cleared.

1601
20 Julye.

15ˡⁱ . oˢ . oᵈ
to Mʳ Wᵐ
Burrell for
his travell
about yᵉ
shippes.
Johñ
Ellycott of
Excetoʳ.

Gen'all Court.   The 24 of Julie 1601.

Mʳ Aldⁿ Wattes Goʳ   Mʳ Tho Farrington
Mʳ Aldⁿ Cambell   Mʳ Wᵐ Harryson
Mʳ Rumney dep.   Mʳ Nich: Leete
Mʳ Rich: Staper   Sʳ *John Spenser*
Mʳ Tho Cordell   Mʳ Wᵐ freeman
Mʳ Roger Howe   Mʳ Nich: Lynge
Mʳ Wᵐ Grenewell   Mʳ Rich Wyche

wᵗʰ the most part of the geñ'alty.

1601
24 Julie.

AT this Coʳte one Mʳ Robt Bayly one that hath sett downe his adventure of CCˡⁱ and pᵈᵉ the same to [the] this felowship. and being vnwilling to [supply] bring in any supplie is wylling to assigne over his said CCˡⁱ and to relinquishe his fredome [vnto Sʳ John Spencer knight] surrendring vp the sum [to] in to the handes of this Sosciety Wheruppon Sʳ John Spenser [was] being present in Court doeth vndertake to accepte of his said adventure and offreth him Ciiijˣˣˡⁱ for the same wᵗʰ mʳ Bayly [doe] is content to accepte. and doeth in open Court Renownce his fredome and theruppon this Court doth accepte his surrender. and doe assent and agree that Sʳ John Spencer shall have the nōiation of a freeman to be

Robt Bayly.

Sʳ Jo Spenser.

1601
24 Julie.

made free of this felowship and to enioy the priviledge thereof in as ample manner as anie *other* brother of this felowship Soe as the said Sr John Spencer do bring in to one of the theirs: of this Company the some of xl^{li} for the supplies wch the said Mr Baylie was to pay/ The wch the said Sr John doeth presentlie promyse and vndertake to pay.

discovery of the north west passage to ye East Indies.

At this Court motion is made to the genalyty by occasion of a lre written by one George Waymoth a navigato^r touching his attempte to be made for the discovery of the north west passage to the Est Indies whether the genalyty be willing to vndertake the said discovery and to supply the provision of 2 or 3 pinaces fytt for suche an enterprise yea or [noe]. And yf not vppon the genall charge then whether the genalyty wilbe content that private men shall deale therein. geaving them the benefite of the said discovery [yf they finde yt] *by the sole trade thereof* for certein yeres [and sole trade therof] wthout impechem^t *yf they discover the passage*. But this matter requiring further deliberation then [present] this present assembly can stand vppon It is agreed that the [matter] *resolution hereof* shalbe respited vntill the next genall Court and then to be further considered vppon and in the meane tyme to be disgested by every pticler man howe he can enclyne him self to the enterprise And it is also moved that this genall assembly would be thinke them selfes of anewe supply of shipping to seconde the former shippes sent out to the Est Indies *by the cape of Bona Speransa* wth a Convenient adventure to be [sent] provided for this yeres voyage whether it be the half [of] or a thirde part of the valewe of the last adventure . and lyke order was taken therin as in the former motion that eche man do advyse him self herein betwene this and the next genall Court.

1601
7 Aug.

A generall Court holden the 7th of August 1601.

Mr Aldⁿ Watts governo^r Mr Wiseman
Mr William Rumny Dep Mr Highlorde
Mr Thomas Cordell Mr Howe.
Mr Richard Stapers Mr Greenewell

THE EAST INDIA COMPANY

Mr Leate Mr Linge
Mr Harrison M^r farringeton
wth the most pte of y^e gen'ality.

1601
7 Aug.

QUESTION beinge made for the findinge out of the Northwest passage whether itt shalbe a vyage to seeke itt, or not. beinge put to handes it was consented vnto for a vyage.

Norwest passage.

And beinge put to the question whether the mony shouldbe levyed by the powle or by the pound it was by erectinge of hands ordered that the mony should bee levyed by the pound accordinge to y^r first adventures sett downe in the booke for ye first East India vyage wthout supplie *none* to bee enforced, but every man to adventure y^t will, and to allowe xii^d the lⁱ. And all those that doe not subscribe his name to his Adventure [betwene this and   ] shalbe exempted from this trade of the north-west. And every man to bringe in thone haulfe by Michellmas & the rest by Christmas next.

These psones vndernamed are appointed Comittees to sett downe the chardge of this vyage for 3 pinyces & to make report vnto the next Court.

Comitties for ye Northwest passage
Mr Governor Mr Stapers
Mr Deputy Mr Greenewell
Mr Cordall Mr Howe
Mr Wiseman.

All this aforesaid notwthstandinge it was in the end concluded that Mr Governor should [prvse our] *pvse y^e* Charters betwene this and the next Court to see whether [wee] have authority to compell any of the Company to paye his mony towards this vyage or the next vyage by the straights of [Magelano] *Bona Speransa*.

The first of [August] *September* 1601.
Mr Aldⁿ Wattes go^r Mr Thomas Cordell
Mr Wm Rumey dep. Mr Wm Greenewell
Mr Rich: Staper. Mr Tho: farrington
Mr Rich: Wyseman. Mr Georg Waymouthe
M^r Adⁿ Bannyng. Mr Highelord.

1601
1 Sept.

1601
1 Sept.
North west passage.

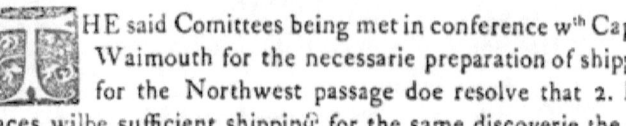HE said Comittees being met in conference wth Capten Waimouth for the necessarie preparation of shipping for the Northwest passage doe resolue that 2. Pinnaces wilbe sufficient shipping for the same discouerie the one of 50 and the other of 40 tuns. To be manned wth 30 men videlt the one wth 16 the other wth 14 men. The charge of all wch by estimation will amount to the valewe of 3000^li or therabout℔.

Georg Waymouth.

These Comitties haveing conferred wth the said m^r waymouth touching his enterteynment in the said voyage [It is] *he is* agreed wth all to goe for the some of one hundred pound℔ to be deliuered him to prepare his instruments and other necessaries: and yf he discover the passage then vppon his retorne to share by way of Contracte for this discovery the some of v^cli [more] referring him self to the favo^r of the Companie for suche further gratification as they shall thinke he deserveth wth this that yf he retorne and do not pforme the discovery he will aske nothing for his paines and travell.

George Waymouth.

1601
2 Sept.

A Gen^rall Courte the 2 of September 1601.
Present.

Mr Ald^n Wattes gouer^r   Mr Nich: lynge
Mr Wm Rumney dep: Mr Wm Garway
Mr Tho: Cordell   Mr John Highelorde
Mr Rich: Staper   Mr Tho farrington
Mr Rich: Wyseman   Mr Wm Grenewell.

wth the greatest part of the gen^ralyty.

16^li. 10^s. 0 to Symon furno^r for Gunpowder.

ARRAUNT is geaven to m^r Ald^r Bannynge to pay vnto Symon Furno^r vppon a rest of accoumpte for powder by him deliūed to the shippes in full Clearing of all Reckoninges the some of sixtene poundes tenn shilling℔.

The Northe west passage.

At this Court the Comitties appointed at the last generall Courte made report of ther conference wth Captein Waymouth touching the Discoverie of the Northwest Passage and of ther opinions of the Charge of the preparation of 2 pinaces wth they thinke will come to the Charge of three thowsand poundes as appeared by the pticlers of the same estimated by the said Comitties and read to the generalitie W^{ch} being conceaved by the generalyty they did well allowe thereof and did agree that the said pinaces and all preparation and furniture therto belonging shalbe taken in hand and a booke sent abroade to the adventure^{rs} to sett downe ther somes vnder ther handes at the rate of xij^d the pound according to the agreem^t of the last generall Court.

1601
2 Sept.

At this Courte Nathaniell Martin on that had sett downe for his adventure the some of two hundred poundes and never brought in the same but desired that a nother should take his place was by erecting of handes dyscharged and dismyssed of the freedome of this fellowship. And in his place Mr John Morice Clotheworker was receaved and by erection of handes admitted vnto the said freedome in as large and beneficyall manñ as any other freeman of the Company.

Nath: Martin. John Morice made free.

A Geñ'all Courte holden the 13 of September 1601.
Present.
Mr Ald^n Wattes gouerno^r M^r Jo: Highelord
Mr Wm Rumney deputy   Mr Wm Greenewell
Mr Rich: Staper   Mr Wm Harryson
Mr Rich Wyseman   Mr Nich: Iynge
    wth the greatest part of ye geñ'alyty.

1601
13 Sept.

WHEREAS ther is some question made or doubte conceaved that the Muskovia Companie may by vertue of ther previledges claime the interest of the North west passage, the wch this Companie are in hand to discover, the wch yf it shuld be discovered at the charge of this soscyetie may be [claymed] *stode vppon* by the said [Courte] Companie of Moskovia merchaunt^{es} by ther priorytie of graunt for the clearing of wch doubte it is thought

Moskovia Company

1601
13 Sept.

convenient that certen psons of this felowship shall conferre wth the governo^r and others principall merchaunt^s of the said Companie to knowe whether they will pmitt this felowship to enter into the discoverie of the said passage and wholie relinquishe all Claime of previledg therunto duringe the Contynuance of the pattent graunted vnto vs And to that ende [it is resolved by this Courte that] the psons herevnder named are apointed to require the [Consent] answer and Consent of the said Muskovia Companie in this behaulf and thereof to make report to the Generalytie at the next generall Court.

  Mr Gouerno^r   M^r ferro^r
  Mr Deputy   M^r [w] Grenewell
  Mr Wyseman   Mr Harryson
    Or anie 4 of them.

A seconde voyage by the Cape of bona esperanza.

And it is agreed by the geñall consent of this Court that ther shalbe presently sett out a seconde voyag^e to the East Indies by the Cape of bona speranca and [to that end] all expedition to be vsed to see what will be contributed to [that end] furnishe the same. to wch end a booke is to be prepared for the adventur^{rs} to sett downe their sommes of adventure vnder their handes to see howe the Contribucōn will arise But it is resolved by the generall Consent of this Co^rte that none shalbe received to adventure vnder the valew of one hundred poundes sterlinge but as muche above that valewe as anie man shalbe pleased to adventure and it is further agreed that none shalbe vrged to beare or bringe in anie further supply above his adventure sett downe.

1601
14 Sept.

    xiiij September 1601.

  Mr Aldⁿ Watts go^r   M^r Jo: Highlord
  Mr Wm Rumney dep: Mr Wm Grenewell
  Mr Ald: Holliday   Mr Wm Harrison
  Mr Wm Garway   Mr Niclas Linge
    M^r W^m freeman.

T this Co'te assemblyd the Comitties abovenamed did agree vppon a title or preface to the booke of Contribuc͂on to be sent abroad wch beinge sett downe some of them bargaine to sett downe vnder their handes their owne voluntary Contribuc͂ons and havinge so donne deliverd the Booke to the officer to be Carried to All the severall freemen of this fellowship to sett downe their severall adventures in this second voyage.

1601 14 Sept. A Booke of the adventures in ye seconde voyage.

A Generall Court holden the xiij^th of October 1601.
Present.

Mr Ald: Wattes Go^r:
Mr Wm Rumney dep:
S^r Jo: Spencer knight
Mr Richard Staper
M^r W^m grenewell
Mr Wm Harrison
Mr Thomas Cordell
Mr Tho: farrington
Mr Nicħas Leet
wth the greatest part of the Gene'alitie.

1601 13 Oct.

RDER is geaven to Mr Ald'man Baiiinge Thr̃er to pay vnto Beniamyn Decro Agent of the Muskovia Companie for the full rest of Cordage bought of the same Companie and in full payment of all debt{ owinge to the same Companie the soi͂e of fifty seven poundes sixteene shilling{ and eight pence.

li s d. 57. 16. 8. to ye Moskovia Company for ye rest Cordage

At this Co'te Sr John Spencer Knight accordinge to the lib'tie geaven vnto him at a generall Co'te the 24th of July last. for the makinge of a ffreeman whensoever he shall present him *to* [of] this societye dothe in pformaunce of the said Lib'tie geaven him present vnto this Court one Joseph Jackson Clothewo'ker to receave the said freedome vppon whose presentm^t this Courte do accept him into the freedome of this fellowshipp to enioy the same in as ample [manner] and beneficiall manner as any other brother of this Companie doeth or ought to enioy the said ffreedome.

Joseph Jackson's admission.

At this Co te Mr Deputie doeth make reporte to this assemblie that accordinge to the order geaven at the Last generall

1601
13 Oct.

Touching the Northwest passage.

Courte touchinge the Northwest passage to move the Muscovia Companie to relinquishe their Claime into the said passage for the tearme of xv yeares to the end this Company may proceade therein. he the saide m^r Deputie accompanied wth m^r Grenwell did since the said Last Courte reporte to the Governo^r and divers of the said Muskouia Companie assembled togeather and propounded vnto *them* the mocõn of this fellowshipp touchinge the said passage who gave them this aunswer that they havinge an inheritaunce in the same [said passage] would not by any meanes relinquishe their owne interest therein. for any tearme but yf this Companie would be willinge to joyne wth them in the discoverye of the said passage they would receive as manie of this Companie as will venture wth them and geave them the freedome of the said passage and all placẽ discovered therby in ppetuity wch aunswer beinge Considered of at this Court It is supposed that vnder this offer the Muskovia Companie may be at libertie to venture what they list, and so will supply them selves litle or nothinge and the whole or the greatest pte of the adventure will lye vppon this Companie and the discoverye beinge made at their Charge a trade shalbe putt into the other Companies handes for litle or nothinge disboursed or adventured by them for avoidinge of wch doubt It was propounded to the generalitie whether they would be willinge to adventure wth the Muskovia Companie suche sommes as they had already sett downe yf the Muskovia Companie wilbe Content to seclude *for the terme of xv yeres* all suche of ther owne felowship as will not joine in adventure wth the brethren of this Companie in the discoverie or findinge out of the said passage. Whervnto this Companie do agree and vppon that condition do yelde that all suche somẽs of money as they have already sett downe towardes the furnishinge of the voyage for the said Northwest shall be ioyned wth the adventurors of the Muskovia Companie that will proceade together wth them in the said voyage and do require that the booke may be carried abroade amongest the residewe of the Companie that have not yet sett downe ther contributions . And it is ordered that the meane While m^r Deputie and the residewe of the Comitties appointed at the last generall Court shall repaire to ẙ Governoʳ and Companie of the Muskovia merchauntꝭ at ther generall Court to conferre wᵗʰ them and to agree that ther shall noe more of that Companie claime the benyfyte of the freedome of the said passage yf it be discovered duringe the terme of xv yeres. then suche as shall ioine wᵗʰ this Companie in the contribution And that all suche of this felowship as shall adventure in the said voyage the sõme of xˡⁱ shall have the freedome of the said discovery to them and ther posteritie vnder the Comõ seale of the said Muskovia Companie for ever.

1601
13 Oct.

This Companie havinge alsoe heretofore resolved to sett out a seconde supply to the East Indies [of one] by the cape of bona Esperansa, and the booke having bene carried abroade amongest the breethren of this Companie to sett downe the Contributions it appeareth that the Whole adventure already sett downe doeth not exceade the valewe of Eleven thowsand poundes. wᶜʰ carrieth noe convenient proportion to sett out any voyage at all. And it *is* Notyfied to this Coʳt by Mʳ Governoʳ that he beinge of late wᵗʰ my L Admirall and Mʳ Secretary at the Court they enquired of him what was the cause that the Companie were so slacke in secondinge ther former voyage consideringe that the Duche nation had soe honorably gone throughe wᵗʰ ther voyage and retorned againe wᵗʰ soe good successe notinge vnto them that this Companie were not soe respective of her maᵗˢ honoʳ and the honoʳ of ther owne Cuntrey as were fytt they shuld be. Whervppon it was aunswered by some of the Companie that one especiall hinderaunce of the [slacke] proceading of this voyage is that it is doubted that for some private respectes the Comitties may be drawen in the preparation of the shipping for the voyage [to fall in to] to preferre suche shippes as shall not be so serviceable as were convenient. Ffor the avoidinge of wᶜʰ inconvenience. and to geave furtheraunce to the speady preparation of the voyage It is ordered that Noe ship shalbe prepared or enterteyned for the said voyage vntill the name of suche ship be notyfied to the generalitie at a generall Court and the geñall consent of the Companie geaven to certen Comitties to contract for [the] everie or

A seconde suply to yᵉ East Indies.

1601
13 Oct.

anie suche ship soe p̄sented and offered to ther consideratioṇs. And it is also ordered that the booke shalbe carried abroade to the breetheren of this felowship by some men apointed that shalbe able to p̄swade and encorage them to proceade in the said adventure.

xp̄ofer Cletherowe made free.

At this Court xp̄ofer Cletherow was admitted into the freedome of this ffelowship in the place of Rob̄t Bowyer supplyinḡ in his default. the som̄e of Two hundred and ffourtie poundes. wch he had sett downe in the booke of adventures. And for that the said Rob̄t Bowyer did not bring in his money according to the pattent and the ordenaunces of the Companie. he the said Rob̄t Bowyer is [disfranchesed] *excluded* and the said xp̄ofer Clethero admitted in to the said freedome in as large and ample manner as any brother of this felowship and holden a Contributo^r of the som̄e of CC and Fourtie poundes in Principall and supply.

Rob̄t Bowyer disfraunchised or excluded.

1601
5 Nov.

A Gen^rall Courte *the 5 of November* 1601.
Present

Mr Aldⁿ Wattes Govr   Mr Rich: Stapers
Mr Wm Rumney dep.   Mr Tho: farrington
Mr Aldⁿ Cambell   Mr Wm Grenewell
Mr Wm Carway   Mr Nich: lynge
            Mr Nich: leete
And the greatest part of the geñalyty.

The Northwest Passage.

T this Court m^r Deputie maketh report [to this Court] that since ther last geñall assemblie the muskovia Companie have mett together aboute the motion. [to enter into] *of* the discovery of the Northwest passage and do finde that the said Companie seme to have no liking to Joine wth this Companie in the said discoverie. but rather will deale in the same them selves. yet they assigne noe tyme for the doing thereof nor for anie thinge that appeareth doe goe aboute to deale therin wth anie expedition. Wherevppon this Companie thinking *it* not fitt that [suche] an

enterprise of suche importaunce shuld be staked doe resolve to vrge the expedition of the same voyage (beinge of soe great a consequence to the Comoñ wealthe) [and therefore do resolve] ether to be pformed by that Companie or *by* this Companie And to that ende this Companie do entreat the psons herevnder named as Comitties for this felowship to offer Conference wth sixe of the Muskovia Company to enter into [the] a Course howe this passage may be proceaded in. and yf it shall appeare vppon the conference that the Muskovia Companie will vndertake this discoverie them selfes and enter into it to leave them to ther proceadinge therin yf otherwyse to prove them whether they will ioyne wth this felowship according to the former conditions ppounded and yf they will do nether then that a relation may be made to the LL. of her ma^{ts} most honorable privy [the] Councell of ther refusall and ther hinderingof this company in the said discovery entended by them. And to thende the cause may not receave any delay that the muskovia Company may be required to geave ther directe aunswer *in writing* to this motion propounded.

1601
5 Nov.

Comitties.

Mr Governo^r Mr Cordell
Mr Deputy   Mr Grenewell
Mr Ald^n Cambell   Mr Bell
M^r olyver style   Mr Nich: leat.

At this Co^{r}te was rec͠ed a l͠re from the LL^p of the Councell notyfying͠ her Ma^{ts} mislike of the slacknes of the Companie in the secondinge of ther former viage to the East Indies by the Cape of Bona Speransa propoundinge vnto them thexample of the duche who doe prosecute ther viages wth a more honorable resolution But forasmuche as the Assemblie at this Court was not soe ample as the importaunce of the matter requireth it was thought fitt another Court shuld be called vppon Munday in the after noone to consider more deliberatly vppon ther honors l͠res and the same co^{r}t to be warned vppon a paine of xx^s vppon everie one that maketh default.

The Councelles lre for ye seconding of the first voyag to the East Indies.

1601
9 Nov.

A Gen'all Court [1601] holden the 9 of November 1601.
Present.

Mr Aldⁿ Wattes go^r
Mr Aldⁿ Hollyday
Mr Aldⁿ Cambell
Mr Tho. Cordell
Mr Rich: Stapers
Mr Rich: Wyseman

M^r Jo: Highelord
Mr Roger Howe
Mr Rich: Wiche
Mr Nich: leate
Mr John Eldred
Mr Wm Harryson

M^r W^m freeman.
Wth the greater nomber of the gen'alyty.

The Northe west passage.

T this Court the Northwest passage being againe brought in question vppon occasion of some speeche had wth some of the muskovia Company since the last Court And vppon some occasion of better opinion conceaved of the strength of o^r owne previledg^e then form̃ly wee had touching o^r interest in the same previledg^e It is resolved by this Geñ'all Court that the same vyage shalbe attempted and those [that] of the Companie that have not already written be solicited to wryte to thende the contribution may be made full. and yf anie of the Companie will deny to [for] adventure in this discovery according to the former ordinaunces that they shalbe secluded from anie benyfite of trade by the said passage, during the terme of the pattent of the previledg^e. and the trade to be wholie in them that do adventure in the same And it *is* further ordered that yf the said passage be discovered that then *the* trade made that way shalbe carried and handled from tyme to tyme during the [previledges] *contynuaunce of o^r pattent* in a proportionall sorte. videlt according to ye proportion of every mans adventure . to thende that every adventuro^r may have that advancem^t or previledg of *his* adventure in every viage according to the rate or quantety of his [adventure] *stocke ventured* in this viage of dyscovery and not otherwise.

Clement Moseley his stocke assigned to

Whereas Clement Moseley Citizen and mercer of loⁿ one of the adventurors of this felowship is nowe deceased. havinge adventured in this first voyage sett out by the Companie by the cape of bona speransa the some of 220^{li} in stocke and suply. did in his lief tyme assigne over the one moytie of his said adventure vnto Edmund Helmes of Burford in the Countie of oxon gent. in consideration of the some of one hundred poundes [by] him owing [by] *to* the said Edmund as by the said assignement shewed forthe and testified vnto the governo^{rs} deputie and others, of the Companie bearing date the 20th of may last appereth And whereas also the said Clement Moseley did alsoe assigne and sett over the other moitie of his said adventure vnto John Moseley gent in consideration of a certen debt owing by the said Clement vnto the said John, as by the said assignment done the day and yere abovesaid appeareth lykewyse testyfied to the said governo^r deputie and others. The interest of both wch assignments is by the said severall Assignees passed over vnto Elizabeth Moseley late the Wief of the said Clement Moseley in consideration of the some of Cij^{li} x^s by her paid to the said Edmund Helmes . and in consideration of Cij^{li} by her p^d to the said John Moseley as by the severall conveyhaunces thereof appeareth. Therfore the said Elizabeth is to be made Credito^r of the some of 240^{li} of Stocke and supplie When soever she shall have p^d the some of xx^{li} wch is behinde of the supply wch was to have bene brought in by the said Clement Moseley.

1601
9 Nov.
Eliz Moseley.

The 20th of Novemb^r 1601.

1601
20 Nov.

THIS day by order of Mr Governo^r a warraunt was made to Mr Ald^n Bannynge Thr$\bar{e}$r to pay to Mr Abraham Campion for the rest of Accoumpte and debt Dewe by the Companie to him for beare for y^e voyage the somme of Thirtie nyne poundes ij^s iiij^d.

Mr Campion for beare.
39. 2. 4.

The 4 of December 1601.

1601
4 Dec.

Mr Ald^n Wattes go^r Mr Tho: farrington
Mr Rich: Stapers   Mr Wm Grenewell
Mr John Highelord   Mr Rich: Wyche
            Mr Wm Harrison

1601
4 Dec.

An Englisheman brought home out of the East Indies in the Duche shippes.

PPON advyse written to Mr Aldⁿ Wattes from Midleboroughe touching the arryvall of 2 Dutche shippes retorned from the East Indies *full laden* wth Pepper wch have brought home from the Est Indies 13 men [w^{ch}] who have bene deteyned prysoners ther for the space of 4 yeres amongest wch ther is one Englisheman [w^{ch}] who hath the Language of Sumatra. and thexperience of the trade of divers Ilandes therabout? It is thought meet by thes Comitties that Mr Alderman take some private and secret course by writing to procure the said Englyshman to come over that some conference may be had wth him touching the state of the trade of those partes.

1601
22 Dec.

A Generall Court the 22th of December 1601.

Mr Aldⁿ Wattes gov^r   Mr Rich Staper
Mr Aldⁿ Cambell   Mr Wm Chamber
Mr Wm Rumney   Mr Wm Harryson
        Mr Tho : farrington
wth a great Companye of the generalyty.

Touching y^e question of the North west passige betwene this Comp. & the Muskovia Company.

HIS generall Court were at this assemblie made acquainted that since the last gen^{all} Court Mr Governo^r [and the] Mr Aldⁿ Cambell and Mr Rumney and others having acquainted the LL : of the Councell that by reason of the difference betwene the Muskovia Companie and this Companie for the interest of the Northwest passage the preparation of the discoverie of the same passage wch this Companie were in hand wthall was staied   It pleased ther LL : therfore for the Clearing of the said difference and the furthering of the said voyage to wryte ther l^res to the muskovia Companie. ether to joine wth this Companie in the said discovery or els to bring ther pattente to the Counsell board and to shewe ther Clayme *vnto the said priviledges.* vppon wch l^res the Muskovia Companie Som̃oned them selfes together and conferred vppon the same L^res and of the Worthines of the said enterpryse and theruppon resolved to joine wth this Companie

in the same discoverie, and to conferre vppon as manie of this
Companie as would adventure therein jointlie wth them all benyfyte of priviledge that lyeth in them to impart vnto [them]
the said adventurers. By wch consent of the Muskovia Companie all the former question and difference being cleared It
is nowe Resolved that all expedition possible shalbe vsed by
this Companie to goe on wth the said discovery, and the booke
to be carried abroade, that men may sett downe ther adventures
according to former orders and agreem^ts, viz at the rate of xij^d
the pound of ther [last] *first* contribution *sett downe* in the
viage by the Cape of bona Esperansa. or els to be pemptoryly
exempted out of all benyfyte that may growe by the discovery
of the said north west passage, not only during the Contynuance
of [the] o^r priviledges to the East Indies but for ever hereafter
And to thende that noe man shall excuse him self hereafter that
he hath not bene offered the Libertie of adventures in the said
discovery It is ordered that every adventure shall ether sett
downe vnder his owne hand his adventure. or els vnder his owne
hand sett downe his voluntary refusall to adventure therein.
And it is further ordered that all the Contributions *of the breethren of this Company* for this Discovery [*disbursed by the bretheren
of this Company and wch are not fre of the Musko : Company*] shalbe
brought in to m^r Rumey Deputy governo^r of this Company by
the xx^th of January next, and that from tyme to tyme both in
the meane tyme and afterwardes the Comitties appointed for [the]
both the Companies to meete together. and to capitulate and
agree in the proceading of the said [preparation] voyage and of
the Conditions therto belong as shalbe convenient for all the
adventuro^rs. But forasmuche as ther is a doubte conceaved
whether ther can be be vnytinge out of two companies *of* divers
selected persons free of them bothe to [holde a priviledg] *become
a Company to enioy a trade* wch shalbe but a part of a priviledge
drawen out of the graunt of one of the said Companies therfore
it is ordered that the opinion of some lerned Counsell shall be
taken whether this voyage may be in this sort proceeded in as
hathe bene purposed and enioyed by vertue of suche an agreem^t
as shalbe made by Consent of the adventuro^rs amongest them

1621
22 Dec.

1601
22 Dec.

selves or by any Warraunt that can be deryved from other of the said former Companies.

1601
5 Jan.

A Gen^ral Courte holden the 5th of January 1601.

M^r W^m Ruṁney dep gov^r   Mr Tho: Farrington
Mr Aldⁿ Cambell   Mr Wm Garway
Mr Rich: Staper   Mr Wm Greenewell
Mr Tho: Cordell   Mr Wm Harryson

wth the greatest part of the gen^ralyty.

The opinion of lawe geaven y^t this Company have the right of the Northwest passage.

INCE the last Courte, according to the Direction and resolution then holden for the satisfaction of the Companie touching the interest and previledge of the Northwest passage wch hath bene in Dispute and question betwene this Companie and the Moskovia Companie, ther hath bene a [course taken] the opinion of lerned Councell had touchinge the same. and it resolved for lawe that the interest of the same passage is expresselie in this Companie. And it is alsoe resolved [that One Company cannot graunt] touching the doubte that hathe bene formerlie propounded whether that a gen^rall Company out of ther gen^rall previledges thereof might graunt a part of ther previledges ether to a nother Companie or to anie private persons [and yet the psons to whom suche graunt is made] that a Companie cannot divide [the] and dismember ther previledg^e reteyning part

Comitties apointed to expedite the Northwest passage & to devyse ordinaunces to further ye same & other busines of the Company.

of them, and letting one other part So as nowe the doubte and questions formerlie a foote being Cleared and the interest thereof appearing to be in this Companie It is finallie resolved that the said viage shall wth all expedition be prepared aswell for that the shortenes of the tyme requireth expedition as that the Companie are ingaged in ther Credite to the lords to enter into it [soe as] as sone as it shall appeare that they have sufficient interest in the said previledge by ther pattent And to thende that [the] bothe the said voiages may be the better expedited and that the gen^rall governm^t of this felowship may be the better directed thes persons herevnder named are apointed by the gen^ralyty to [travell both in the said preparation and also in the] conceav[ing] of suche reasonable lawes and ordinaunces [for the] as may both further the said acc͠on and better guide all other occasions that may concerne the priviledges of the Companie W^{ch} lawes and ordinaunces being soe conceaved and prepared the same to be brought to the next geñall Court to receave ther allowance and confirmation [therof at] by the consent of the geñalyty wch shalbe at a geñall Court vppon tuesday in the after noone.

1601
5 Jan.

Comitties.

Mr Rumney deputy	Mr Chery
Mr Aldⁿ Cambell	Mr Grenwell
Mr Rich: Stapers	M^r farrington
Mr Garway	Mr Harrison
Mr Cordall	Mr Clerke

Or anie 4 of them.

At this Court was read a l're or [warraunt] *Certificat* vnder the hand and seale of the right ho: the Earle of Cumbland wherby it appeareth that he hath assigned over the some of two hundred and thirtie poundes to m^r Alderman Holliday out of his hono^{rs} adventure wth the Companie and therby requireth that the same may be putt of from his L^{ps} Accompte and Mr Aldⁿ Hollyday made Credito^r for so muche vppon wch Certificat this Court hath agreed that the Bookeap shall geave credite vnto Mr Aldⁿ Holliday for the same money.

230^{li} of the Earle of Cumblands [debte] adventure assigned to Ald^r Hollyday.

A Gen^rall Court holden the xjth of Januarie 1601.

1601
11 Jan.

Mr Wm Rumney Deputy	Mr Rich: Wyche
Mr Aldⁿ Cambell	Mr Tho: farrington
Mr Richard Staper	Mr Wm Harryson
Mr Wm Greenewell	M^r Jo: Eldred
Mr Niclias leet	M^r Jo: Highelord

wth ye greater part of the gen^ralyty.

[A]T this Court] According to the geñall order taken at the [geñall] last geñall Courte touching the devysing and conceaving of lawes and ordinaunces for the better governm^t of the state of the trade, [and] the

Lawes and ordinaunces presented to be Confirmed.

1601
11 Jan.

Comitties then appointed did at this Court present [certen] ther opinions by certen ordinaunces [already] by them devysed and offered the same to the Consideration of the Gen'alytie wch severall ordinaunces being *divers tymes* distinctly read and waighed *and in some pointes reformed* by this Court in ample number assembled and throwghly digested and severally putt to Scruteny and erection of handes the same severall lawes are agreed vppon establyshed and confirmed for standing lawes and ordinaunces to be holden and observed by this Soscyety vppon the *severall* paines and penalties therin severally Limited the teno^r of wch Lawes Do followe in thes wordes videlt :

Whereas the Queenes most excellent Ma^{ie} by her graces lres Patent⸱ vnder ye great seale of England bearinge date ye xxxith day of December in ye xliijth yeare of her ma^{tes} raigne hath incorporated this society by ye name of y^e [Company] goǔno^r and company of the m̃chaunt⸱ of Loⁿ tradinge into ye East Indies and hath geven them yⁿ sole trade of ye said Indies by all such waies and passages as they shall thinke meete to visit those part⸱ eyther by yⁿ way and passage already found out wch is by ye cape of bona Esperansa or by such waies and passages as shalbe hearafter found out by yⁿ part⸱ of America to enioy ye said trade for ye terme of xv^{en} yeares from ye feast of ye nativity of o^r Lord god 1600 And wheras this society in ye settinge forth of their late viage by ye Cape of Bona esperansa toward⸱ ye Iland⸱ of Sumat' Java and other ye part⸱ therabout⸱ entendinge to trade those Iland⸱ and places for Pepper Spices gould and other m̃chandizes wch are likest yeald ye most profitable returne for ye Adventuro^{rs} in ye same viage have sett forth ye greatest pte of theire adventure in English money Coyned of purpose for ye said voyage and other forreine coine Currant in those Ilands wch moneyes and coyne they could not p'pare but wth great difficultie and trouble and not wthout some mislike of ye transportacõn of treasure out of land They therfore beinge desirous to vse ye priviledges to them graunted rather for ye good of ye Cõenweale of theire Countrie then for theire private benefite and to maintayne the trade of ye East Indies if it be possible by ye transportacõn and vent of Cloth and other y^e

native Commodities of this Realme wthout any money at all or eles soe litle as may be conveniently tollerated Do resolve to attempt ye discoũy of a Passage by seas into ye said East Indies by ye Northwest thorough some pte of America wch if they shall fynd navigable Then shall they by that passage arrive in ye Countries of Cataia & China beinge the Eeast ptẽ of Asia and Africa Climatẽ of that Temperature wthin all likelihood will aforth a most liberall vent of English clothes and kersies to ye generall advancement of y^r trafficke of m̃chandize of this realme of England And to thend to putt in execuc̃on as well this theire resoluc̃on of ye discoũy of ye said passage as otherwise to bringe them selues and theire trade generally to a conformitie and order They do accordinge to ye libertie to them geven by ye said l̃res Pattentẽ for ye makinge of lawes constituc̃ons orders & ordinances for ye better advancement and continuance of theire trade and traffique make ordeine and constitute these seũall lawes constituc̃ons orders and ordinances followinge vizt.

First it is ordered and decreed by and wth ye generall consent of this Co^rte for standinge and vnchangeable decree that wth all convenient expedic̃on there shalbe preparac̃on made for ye attemptinge of ye discoũy of ye Northwest passage to ye East Indies wherin shalbe vsed two shippes or pinnaces of such burthen and makinge as shalbe hearafter considered of and resolved to be fitt for ye said voyage and manned victualled [and] furnished and provided wth such numbers of men munic̃on furniture victuall m̃chandize and other thingẽ as ye Com̃ittees hearafter nominated and appointed for ye prouision therof shall thinke meete And for ye levyinge of such [moyties] moneis as shall defray ye charges of the preparac̃on of ye said shippes or pinaces and all other thingẽ incident to ye said voyage And for ye bringinge of ye said moneys It is ordered that eũy brother of this felowshippe that hath contributed and adventured in ye former voyage to ye East Indies by ye Cape of Bona esperansa shall contribute to the settinge furth of this p^rsent voyage after the rate of xij^d at ye least for eũy pound of his former adventure by him adventured or wherin he is intereressed wthout supplie.

1601
11 Jan.

And if any brother of this felowshipp shalbe willinge voluntarily to bringe in a greater contribuc̃on then after ẙ said rate of xij^d in ye pound of his said adventure in ye former voyage it shalbe at his pleasure And to thend to stirre vp men y^u rather to enlarge theire said Contribuc̃ons to this enterprise It is alsoe ordered and agreed that after what rate or proporc̃on soeũ any man shall contribute in this discoũy Yf the passage be found out that he shall in all voyages hearafter to be made by ye said passage be aportioned or stinted in his adventures accordinge to ye same proporc̃on or rate and noe otherwise. And It is alsoe

the bringing in of ye money.

ordered that the said Contribuc̃on shalbe brought in by eũy ye Contributors in this manner vizt The one halfe before ye xxth day of January next comminge And ye residue or soe much therof as shalbe found necessary at ye goinge away of ye shippes to be paid to ye handẽ of Mr Ald Cambell appointed Thr̃er for ye same voyage Prouided allwaies that if any brother of this felowshippe shall deny to bringe in his said contribuc̃on at ye rate of xij^d ye pound of his former adventure *or do not bring in the same* at or before the daies and tymes before limited that then he or they that shall make default on that behalfe shall

forfeit v tymes the valew.

satisfy and pay for a fyne by way of deducc̃on out of his stocke adventured in ye last voyage fyve tymes ye valewe of ye Contribuc̃on by him payable by vertue of this act The same to be imployed to ye full furnishinge of ye said discoũy And if there remaine an oũplus to ye vse of ye adventurors in this intended voyage proportionably according to theire seũall adventures.

It is alsoe ordered and decreed by ye generall consent of this Co^{r}te concerninge ye generall trade of this Society and ye preparac̃on of all Viages Contribuc̃ons and generall adventures of this felowshippe hearafter to be sett forth That if any daies or tymes be limited and appointed by order of any generall

To pay contribucons &c. at the tymes limited. Or to be fined in the dis-

Co^{r}te for ye bringinge in of any Contribuc̃ons adventures or supplies and that default be made in ye pforminge of those payments Contribuc̃ons and supplies at ye daies limited by any of ye adventurors or Contributo^{rs} of such voyages that ye stockẽ or adventures of such Contributors shalbe taxed and charged

to answeare to yᵉ cōen treasure or vse of this society such
damages charges and allowances for not performinge of such
paymentᵗˢ at yᶜ daies limited as yᵉ Auditoʳˢ of yᵉ Company for yᵉ
tyme beinge appointed to audit yᵉ generall accomptˢ shall fynd
to be equall and yᵗ the goūnoʳ Deputy and Comittes or yᵉ most
of them shall censure to be fitt to be paid wᵗʰout any abatement.

1601
11 Jan.
cretion of the Companie or of the Auditoʳˢ appointed.

It is alsoe ordered and agreed by like generall consent of this
Society that if any brother of this Company shalbe sumoned
or warned by yᵉ officer of this felowshippe therto appointed To
appeare at any generall Coʳte of this Society or at any other
meetinge of mʳ Goūnoʳ his Deputy and yᵉ Comittees and yᵉ
said sumons or warninge geven to yᵉ ptie himselfe or left at his
house Yf then such person shall make default and not appeare
at all or not appeare at yᵉ howre assigned he shall forfeite for
eūy default of non apparance xijᵈ and for eūy default of comminge late vjᵈ vnlesse he can give a sufficient reason of his
absence or late comminge and yᵉ same to be allowed by yᵉ
generall consent of yᵉ assembly or yᵉ more part of them pˢent
eyther at a generall Coʳte or meetinge of Comitties.

For absence 12ᵈ & late coming to courtes vjᵈ.

12. 9 in the third waste booke.

For yᵉ better and more orderly proceedinge in yᵉ deliberaċōn
of matters propounded in geñall Coʳtes eyther for yᵉ establish-
inge of any actˢ or ordinances or in any other matters concerninge yᵉ Company Is ordered yᵗ it shall not be lawfull for any
brother of this Company to speake to any one matter propounded aboue three sundry tymes vppon peine of forfeiture of
iijˢ iiijᵈ for eūy such excesse in speach.

Not to speake in any matter propounded aboue 3 tymes pena iijˢ iiijᵈ.

It is alsoe ordered by late consent of a generall Coʳte that if
any brother of this Company shall in any Contenċōn or argument houlden wᵗʰ any other pson eyther in generall Coʳte or
meetinge of Comittees vse any vnciville or intemperate speaches
or behavioʳ and soe censured by yᵉ geñall Coʳte or yᵉ persons
assembled in Comitte he shall forfeite for eūy such offence xˢ.

No vncivill speaches or behauioʳ in Courtes pena 1ˢ.

And for yᵉ avoydinge of confusion of speach or discoʳse in
yᵉ deliberaċōn of matters to be handled in any geñall Coʳte or
meetinge of Comiities concerninge yᵉ affaires of yᵉ Company
It is ordered that noe brother of this felowshippe shall interrupt
any other in his declaraċōn or discoʳse of any matter declared

That none do interrupt an other in his speaches in Courtes pena ijˢ vjᵈ.

1601
11 Jan.

or disco'sed to ye Company nor duringe such declaracōn or disco'se hold p'uate whisperinge speach or talke wth any other to ye disturbance of him that speaketh But if he be disposed to answear or reply to ye speaches propounded then to direct his answear or reply to mr Goūno' or his Deputy vpon peine of forfeyture for eūy such offence ijs vjd.

That eu'y one keepe silence being comanded by Mr Gou'no' or deputie by the stroke of the Hammer pena vjd.

It is alsoe ordered for ye pacificacōn of contencōn in argument in geñ'all Co'tes and other meetingẽ and of lowde or confused speaches that when mr Goūno' or his Deputy commandeth scilence by ye stroake of ye hammer that then eūy eūy person keepe scilence vpon peine of forfeiture of vjd for eūy offence.

For refusall of paym't of fines ymprisonm't.

And It is alsoe ordered that if any brother of this felowshippe shall vppon commandment or demaund of mr Goūno' o' his Deputy refuse to pay such fynes or forfeytures as he shall have fallen into by ye breach of any of ye ordinances or actẽ of this felowshippe or do not pay them beinge required that then such person shalbe coīmitted to prison there to remaine duringe ye pleasure of Ye generaltie.

Not to depte Courte but by licence pena xijd.

And It is further agreed that if any brother of this society shall at any geñ'all Co'te or meetinge of Coīmitties depart out of ye Co'te or meetinge before ye Co'te shall breake vp or ye busines be ended except it be by licence asked of mr Goūno' or Deputy and by theire licence graunted that he shall forfeite for eūy default departinge wthout licence xijd.

All fines to be ymploied to the genall vse of the Companie.

And It is lastly ordered yt all fynes and forfeytures forfeyted and lost by any brother of this felowshippe by ye breach of any ordinance now heretofore or hearafter to be made shalbe paid and geven to ye generall and cōen vse of this Society and to be imployed to ye bearinge of ye cōen charges of ye same and to ye releefe of ye poore To dispose accordinge to order from tyme to tyme to be geven in that behalfe.

At this Courte the psons heervnder named are apointed and elected to be Comitties to further the expedicōn of the voyagẽ of the Northwest passage and to prepare the shippinge and all other provisions belonging to the voyage at the best and easiest rates and prises that they can and whatsoever they shall doe

therin the Companie to allowe thereof and the thēr to defray 1601
suche Charges as [They sh] the said Comitties or anie 4 of 11 Jan.
them vnder ther [warr] handes shall geave him warrant to pay.

   Comitties for ye Nortweast passage.

Mr Wm Rumney deputy   M^r olyver Style
Mr Rich: Staper   Mr Wm Harryson
Mr Tho^m Cordell   Mr Wm Grenewell
Mr Rich: Wyseman   Mr Nich: Leat.

    The 25 of January 1601.   1601
      Present.   25 Jan.

Mr Aldⁿ Wattes go^r   Mr Roger Howe
Mr Rumey deputie   Mr Rich: Wyseman
Mr Aldⁿ Cambell   Mr Wm Chamber
Mr Tho Cordell   Mr Nich: lynge
Mr Rich: Staper   Mr Tho Farrington
Mr John Harby   Mr Wm Harrison
    Mr Nich: Leat.

ARRAUNT is geaven to Aldⁿ Hollyday on of the Thērers of the voyage sett out by the cape of Bona Speransa to pay to Mr Robt Bell the somme of xiij^{li} iij^s ij^d to him owing by the Companie for charges [of] *by him disbursed for* wharfage at Wiggens key and for Cutting of leade as appeareth by the pticlers thereof.

Like warraunt is geaven to the said Alderman to pay vnto m^r Aldⁿ Bannyng the other thēr of the said voyage the some of iiij^{li} vij^s v^d for so muche money by him disbursed above his receiptes for the affaires of the Companie.

The Comitties assembled have at this tyme geaven vnto 200 mkes to
Richard Wright Secretarie of this felowship for and in respecte the Secre-
of his great travell taken in the begininge of the [the settling of tarie.
the] procuringe of the previledges of this fellowship and in all
thinges concerning the viage and the trade the some of two
hundred markes.

1601
25 Jan.
x^li p annu
to the Bedle
agmented to
xiij^li p annu
thr.

At this meeting the said Comitties have agreed to geave vnto Thom̅s Evettsett the Bedell of this felowship for his service to the Companie the yerelie salarye of Tenn poundes [the] his tyme to begynn at xpi̅u̅s last.

Ther is graunted vnto m^r Waymouthe towardes the provision of instrument̑s for the northwest passage the som̅e of thertie poundes to be p^d him by m^r Ald^n Cambell.

[Ther is] Warraunt is geaven to m^r Ald^n Holliday *Thr̅er* to pay vnto Beniamyn Deycro Agent of the Muskovia Companie. the somme of One hundred and Nyne pound̑s sixteene shillinges Eight pence in full paiment of Cordage delifed by him for the furnishinge of the shippes sett out by the Cape of Bona Esperansa to ye East Indies.

17 of Febr : 1601.

1601
17 Feb.
30 paid
Mr Wey-
mouthe.

WARRAUNT was geaven by the psons heervnder named to m^r Ald^r Cambell Thr̅er for the voyage by the Northwest passage to pay to George Waymouth for provisions for the same voyage the som̅e of thertie pound̑s.

The Comitties who signed the warraunt were

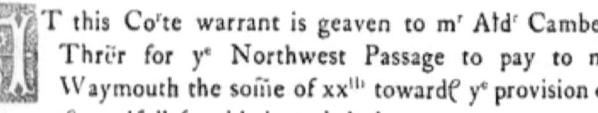

1601
17 Mar.

The xvij^th of March 1601.

m^r Cordell
m^r Jo^n El-
dred

m^r Ald Watt̑s governo^r	m^r Wych
m^r Rumney deputy	m^r Chambers
m^r Ric^d Staper	m^r Ffreeman
m^r Oliver Style	m^r Waymouth
m^r Leat	m^r Barrell

20^li paid
George
Wey-
mouthe
to buy In-
strumentes.

AT this Co^rte warrant is geaven to m^r Ald^r Cambell Thr̅er for ye Northwest Passage to pay to m^r Waymouth the som̅e of xx^li toward̑s ye provision of Instrument̑s needfull for this intended viage.

A generall Co^rte houlden the xviij^th of March 1601.   1601
                                                               18 Mar.

m^r Ald Watt^es governo^r   m^r Ric Leat
m^r Rumney dep :   m^r Ffarrington
m^r Ric^d Staper   m^r Wyche
m^r Tho : Cordell   m^r Ffreeman
                  m^r Lynge
        wth y^e most pt of y^r generality.

T is agreed] At this Co^rte [that] one Wm Nelson *grocer is* [shalbe] admitted into this freedome havinge already paid his adventure *of* 200^li *and supplies of* 40^li to m^r Ald Holiday Thrër [and] *who* is received into ye said freedome wth ye full consent of both Assistant^es and generalty. . . And it is to be noted and Remembred for the Charging of the Accomptes of the Company that the said Wm Nelson gave to this Companie the somē of xxx^li sterling for ther consent to admitt him to *be an* adventuro^r wth them [and in] and to have the freedom of this felowship.

This Co^rte do [likewise] *apoint and* entreat m^r Leat and m^r Lynge to take paines to [warne ye persons that] *move all suche brethren of the Companie as* have not already [dis]contributed their full alottm^t *of xij^d in the lb* toward^es ye discovery of the Northwest Passage vppon peine of forfeture of ye penalty *mencōed* in an act of Co^rte [afore mencōed] *of the xj^th of January last.* That they beinge in their *said rate* [allottm^t] of xij^d vpon ye pound To m^r Ald Cambell Thrër, before ye last of this p̄sent moneth.

Thomas Yerworth is enterteyned to be Purser of one of the shippes apointed for this viage to be made for ye discoūy of ye Northwest Passage and is content to accept of [ix^lb] *v^th* in hand part of his wages to beginn from this [Co^rte and] *day at the rate of* forty shilling^es [to be paid him for every] *a* moneth [imploym^t] yf ye discovery be [found] *made and* if not *then at the rate of* xx^s a moneth *duringe his imploym^t in the voyage* And ye said Yerworth is to give security for his [imploym^t] *good behavio^r in the execution of his Charge of Purser in this imploym^t* in a bond of [C markes] one hundred pound^es.

25th of March 1602.

1602 25 Mar.

WARRANT was geaven by the Persons herevnder named to m^r Aldⁿ Cambell Thrǖr for ye viage by ye Northwest Passage *to pay to John Drewe enterteyned to goe as m^r of a ship for discoũy of y^e said Passage* the somē of fyve poundℓ wch is to be delivered him by way of Impſt in part of paym^t of his wages agreed vppon for y^e viage.

The Comīttes who signed the warrant were

27th of March 1602.

1602 27 Mar.

WARRANT was geaven by y^e Persons herevnder named to m^r Ald Cambell Thrǖr for y^e viage by y^e Northwest Passage To pay to Thomas Yerworth Purser of [y^e] y^e *a* shipp appointed to goe for discovery of the said Passage the somē of fowreskore poundℓ wch is to be paid for clearinge of y^e carpenters wages who were lately imployed about y^e [p̄paracōn] *worke* of the said shipps.

The Comittees who signed the warrant were

John Wattℓ governo^r	Ric Staper.	Nic Leat
Wm Rumney Deputy	Tho: Cordell	Wm Harison.

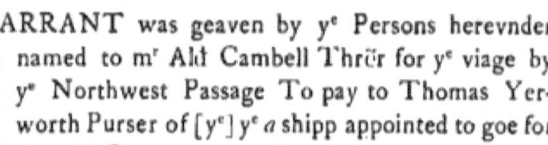

A Gen^rall Court holden the 29th of Marche 1602.

1602 29 Mar.

Mr Aldⁿ Wattes governo^r	Mr John Eldred
Mr Wm Rumney deputy	Mr Tho: farrington
Mr Aldⁿ Cambell thēr	Mr Niclias Leete
Mr Rich: Staper	Mr Tho: Cordell.

wth ye greatest part of the genēalyty.

Touching the suply for the north-west passage.

THIS Co^rte was warned vpon occasion of ye want of bringinge in of the rate of xij^d ye pound by former Co^rtes agreed vpon to furnish ye viage by ye Northwest Passage wch want beinge signified to this Assembly and an accompt made vnto them how far ye Company are engaged in their provision

already wch appeareth to be above ye some of 700^{li} all wch or 1602
ye most part therof would be lost yf they should not proceade 29 Mar.
and ye Company discredited in their not proceadinge in their
discovery the same beinge made soe publique aswell to o^r owne
Country as to Strangers in forrein part₴ Therfore this Co^rte
do agree for ye better furtheringe of this viage wch for ye hono^r
of o^r Country may not be left of And for ye better encoraginge
of those that have already supplyed their xij^d in ye pound accordinge to former orders that whatsoever hath bene sett downe
and brought in by any brother of ye Company [or shalbe brought] *or*
shalbe sett downe and brought in by any brother of this Company
toward₴ ye furnishinge of ye said viage to ye Northwest Passage
shalbe demed part of ye adventure and stock by him or them
adventured and contributed in ye viage already made by ye Cape
of BONA ESPERANSA and that every adventuro^r or supplyer shall
receave vpon such adventure as he shall bringe in for to be
imployed in this discovery such benefite and profitt proporcōn-
ably wth ye rest of his adventure already brought in to ye viage
to ye East Indies as though he had put in soe much stock and
supply in ye former viage And to thend the Act of ye xjth of
January *last* for ye forfeture of fyve for one to be forfeted by
such as shall not pay their rate of xij^d the li. to this discovery
shalbe ye better confirmed and *fortified* [forfeted] It is ordered
that suite shalbe made to ye LL : of the Councell acquayntinge
them wth ye necessity of this Co^rse entreatinge their hono^{rs} to
give vs an order vnder their hand₴ mencōninge their likinge
of this Co^rse taken by the Company and promisinge vs their
readines to aid vs in ye execucōn of o^r said act sith ye same is
intended for ye comōn benefite and hono^r of ye realme And to
the~~ ~~^e consent of all such as were p^rsent at this Co^rte may
appeare to ye Generalety of ye Company wch are absent every
of ye said persons now p^rsent have vnder their hand₴ sett downe
such somēs as they will Contribute in this discovery willinge y^t
ye same beinge brought in and received by ye Thr̃er of this
viage may be indorsed vppon their bills of adventure wch are
already geaven them vnder ye comōn seale of ye Company w^{ch}
is alsoe agreed vpon And yet notwthstandinge It is agreed y^t

208   THE COURT RECORDS OF

1602
29 Mar.

day shalbe continued accordinge to yᵉ order of yᵉ last Coᵣte to such as yet have not brought in their Contribuc̃on of xij ᵈ yᵉ pound that they shall have that tyme viz' the last of this moneth to bringe in their mony to the Thr̃er and after y' day the said Thr̃er shall not receive yᵉ said xij ᵈ yᵉ li. of any man that hath not already paid it wᵗʰout Consent of a generall Coᵣte.

1 of Aprill 1602.

1602
1 Aprill.

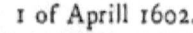 WARRANT was granted to *ye Thr̃er to pay to* Austyn Bandicott Butcherᵣ for 45ᶜ 3 qters of Porke beinge 49 hogẽ bought of him at xxiiij' the hundred the som̃e of fyftie fowre poundẽ eighteene shillings.

An other warrant was granted the day abouesaid to [Thomas Yerworth] mʳ Aldᵣ Cambell Thr̃er to pay to Thomas Yerworth the som̃e of thirtie poundẽ wᶜʰ is to be paid to certen workemen at Ratcliffe and Lymehouse and for salt and mariners board wages where they lye.

An other warrant was granted the same day to the said Thr̃er to pay to mʳ Richard Staper the som̃e of xxviij ˡⁱ xviij ˢ wᶜʰ the said mʳ Staper hath disbursed for lxiiij hydes to make yᵉ marinoʳˢ Cassockẽ Breaches and gownes

The seconde of Aprill 1602.

1602
2 Aprill.

Mʳ Aldⁿ Wattes governoʳ	Mʳ Wᵐ Chambers
Mʳ Wᵐ Rum̃ey deputy	Mʳ Wᵐ Harryson
Mʳ Rich: Staper	Capten Waymouthe
Mʳ Nicl̃as Leet	Mʳ Aldⁿ Cambell
Mʳ Wᵐ farrington	

xiij ˡⁱ xixˢ 6ᵈ
pᵈ to Mʳ Wᵐ
Rumey.

 ARRAUNT is geaven to Mʳ Aldⁿ Cambell thr̃ to pay vnto mʳ Wᵐ Rumney deputy the somme of xiij ˡⁱ xixˢ vjᵈ for so muche delivered [him] *by his servauntẽ to mʳ Burrell* in gilderns lying wynd bound at Holland after the preparin̄g of the 2 shippes for the northwest passage.

Another Warraunt is geaven to the said Ther to pay vnto [Captein Waymouth] Mr Rob̃t Sandy merchaunte the som̃e of threescore pound^e sterling for so muche taken vp by exchaung by Captein Waymouthe at Exceto^r of one Mr Newcombe to be p^d here in London to Mr Rob̃t Sandye wch money was taken vp for the hiring of marinors.

1602 2 Apr.

lx^{li} to Mr Sandy by exchaunge.

At this Assemblie the victualling and preparation of thing^e necessarie for the 2 shippes was agreed vppon to be devyded amongest the severall Comitties herevnder named assigning them to ther severall charge in preparing of the pticulers and severall kindes of Vittualls and other thinges as followeth viz

Provision of Victualles & other necessaries.

| Sacke & Cassalia
Wyne
Vinegar
Candelles
Lanthornes | to | Mr Ald^n Wattes
Mr Wm Harryson
Mr Wm Chambers
Mr Greenwell |

| Pease
Butter
Holland Ling
Stockfishe
Cheese
Otemeale
Oyle
Iron̄ Stoves
Wood
Baysalte
Musterseede | to | Mr Ald^n Cambell
Mr Wm Rumney
Mr Nich: Leat
Mr Nich: Lynge |

| Bread
Beare
Aquavite
Porke
Beef
Rice
Water Caske
Baricos
Meale | to | Mr Cordall
Mr Staper
M^r farrington
Mr Wiseman |

1602
2 Apr.

At this Assemblie Thomas Stephens is agreed wthall to take the charge of the keepinge of the bookes of Accompte of the Companie and to have for his salarye yearely for the same the somme of thirtie poundes to be p^d him quarterly.

1602
5 Apr.

The vth of Aprill 1602.

THIS day a warraunt was made to Mr Aldⁿ Cambell thrẽr of the voyage throughe the Northwest passage to pay vnto Thomas Yarworth Purser of the Discovery. the somme of one hundred poundes. to pay for ancors and other necessaries for the same ship for wch he is to geave an accoumpte.

The Comittees who signed ye warraunt were

Aldⁿ Wattẽ governo^r   Mr Nic. Leat
Mr Ric. Staper   Mr Harison
            M^r ffarrington.

1602
10 Apr.

The 10th of Aprill 1602.

THIS day a warrant was [granted] geaven to m^r Ald Cambell Thrẽr for the viage by ye Northwest passage to pay to Joⁿ Drewe enterteyned to goe as m^r of the Godspeede in this intended viage ye somme of ten poundẽ in part of his wages.

1602
11 Apr.

Pleno robore per assensu curiæ tamen fere.

[The 11th of Aprill 1602.

[THIS day a warrant was made to m^r Ald Cambell Thrẽr for ye viage by ye Northwest Passage to pay to Thomas Yerworth appointed to goo as Purser in one of ye ships for this intended viage the somme of one hundred pounds [wch somme is] to be paid for Sea Coales, wood, lead, and dyvers other necessaries And the said Yerworth to be accomptable.]

[An other Warrant was granted to the said Threr the same day for one hundred pound℈ to be paid to Capten Waymouth by pcells as he shall have occasion to call for it beinge for dyvers mens wages who are to be answeared therw^th.]

1602
11 Apr.

The   day of   1602.
Anno Rn^o Elizabethe xliiij^th.

1602.
April.

Articles of Agreement Indented made betweene the governo^r and company of the merchant℈ of London tradinge into y^e East Indies on y^e one ptie and George Waymouth of   in the County of   marino^r on the other party ..
the   day of Aprill 1602.

HERAS the said governo^r and company of the merchant℈ of London tradinge into y^e East Indies vpon great deliberacōn had and taken of the longe and tedious course wch hath benne hetherto houlden by all such as do trade or sayle from these part℈ of the world in to ye East Indies alonge the coast of Europe and Africa by ye Cape of BONA ESPERANSA and of the great adventures wch are borne in soe longe a viage by many kinds of daungers offered therin and beinge moved wth great hope that ther is a possibility of discovery of a neerer Passage into ye said East Indies by seas by ye way of the Northwest yf the same were vndertaken by a man of knowledge in Navigacōn and of a resolucōn to put in execucōn all possibility of Industrie and valo^r of the attayninge of soe inestimable benefite to his native cuntry and his *owne* perpetuall [fame] *hon^r* Have to that end [made] enterteinned the said George Waymouth a man in their opinion qualified and fitt to vndertake and attempt the performance of this discovery vnto whom they have dd before hand the some of one hundred pounds to furnish himselfe wth convenient instrument℈ of navigacōn accordinge to his owne choice and vnto whose direcōn they have committed two ships [*sufficientlie manned*] the one called the Discovery the other the Godspeede beinge manned victualled

1602
April.

p̄pared and furnished wth all thingẽ necessary and convenient for such a viage and therin bestowed and supplyed all kindẽ of provisions accordinge to his owne desire wherby both the said George Waymouth and his company are provided of victualle apparell and furniture for the space of [two yeares] 16 *monethes* and [hath] *have* alsoe laden aboard the said ships a convenient proporc̃on of severall kindes of merchandize In consideracõn wherof it is agreed between the said parties to these p^rsents in manner and forme followinge vizt.

The said George Waymouth doth promise covenant and agree to and wth the said governo^r and company of the merchantẽ of London tradinge into the East Indies that he and his Company shall and wilbe ready by the   day of next ensuinge the date hereof to depart from ye Port of London and as wynd and weather will permitt shall and will directly sayle towardẽ the coast of Groynland into that part of the open Seas wch is described in sundry generall mappẽ by ye name of FRETUM DAUIES and shall passe on forward in those Seas by ye northwest or as he shall fynd the Passage best to lye towardẽ the partẽ or kingedomes of Cataya or China *or ye backside of America* w^thout geavinge over the proceadinge on his Co^rse soe longe as he shall fynd those seas or any pte therof navigable and any possibility to make way or passage through them And shall not himselfe returne or voluntarily suffer any of his company to returne back againe vnto or towardẽ the Coast of England for any lett or impediment whatsoever vntill he and they have bestowed one yeare at ye least from the tyme of their departinge hence in goinge forward seekinge [and] soundinge and attemptinge the performinge of this intended viage.

And further the said George Waymouth doth promise grant and agree to and wth the said governo^r and company that he the said George Waymouth shall and will *not onlie well enterteyne and entreat but also* quietly permitt [and] suffer [*well entertaine and entreat*] such merchantẽ or pursers as the said governo^r and Company shall place or appoint to goe in the said ships or eyther of them to keepe a Register and accompt of all such goodẽ wares merchandizes provision & furniture as are shipped and laden in any yᵉ said shipᵱ how the same is bestowed bartered changed spent or otherwise disposed and alsoe to keepe an accompt of all other thingᵱ that shalbe bought bartered exchanged or receaved in liewe of any thinge that shalbe sould or made away and alsoe to make notes jornallᵱ and observacõns in wrytinge of their continuall proceadingᵱ in the said viage vntill their returne for England for yᵉ direccõn and helpe of posterity that shalbe occasioned or willinge hearafter to make a newe attempt vpon the same discovery [*and that he shall conceale what he hath discoũed therin from all other persons*] And further that he the said George Waymouth shall wᵗʰin [twenty] 10 daies after his returne in to England [*wᵗʰout concelemᵗ*] whether he do performe the said discovery or not *wᵗʰout concelement of anie thinge wᶜʰ he hath discovered in the voyage* deliver a declaracõn in wrytinge vnder his hand vnto yᵉ governoʳ of the said Company or his deputy conteyninge a report of all and every his proceadingᵱ in yᵉ viage worthie of note or memory for yᵉ good of yᵉ Company and for yᵉ helpe of such as shalbe disposed hearafter to proceade in the same passage and shalbe ready from tyme to tyme duringe yᵉ space of 40 daies after his arrivall & returne to London *vppon warninge or Somõns geaven him in that behaulf* to come before yᵉ governoʳ & deputy of yᵉ said Company for yᵉ tyme beinge and [x persons of the greatest adventure of yᵉ said Company] *the Comitties and such others of yᵉ Company as it shall please yᵉ governõ* [*and the Comittees or ten at yᵉ least*] *to call vnto them* in [this intended viage] & *will* truly relate vnto them such thingᵱ as passed in yᵉ said viage wherof they or any of them shall desire to be enformed wᵗʰout denyall or refusall in that behalfe *and shall not discover the secretᵱ or course of his proceading in the voyage to anie other pson or psons whatsoever then to the said Governor deputie and Comitties*.

1602 April.

And the said governoʳ and company of the merchantᵱ of London tradinge into yᵉ East Indies for them and their successoʳˢ do in consideracõn of the ᵱmises promise covenant and agree to and wᵗʰ the said George Waymouth to satisfy and pay vnto the said George Waymouth or his assignes wᵗʰin fortye daies after his returne in to England and after sufficient proofe

1602 April.

and testimonial by him made that he hath passed thorough the Northwest passage into ye East Indies and arrived at any Port wthin the dominions of the kingedomes [and] *or* Empires of Cataya [or] China *or Japan* the some of fyve hundred pound₷ of lawfull English mony wthout fraude or Covyn.

And lastly the said George Waymouth doth promise and agree that vnlesse in this intended viage he shall discover and passe through the same Northwest Passage and shal make sufficient proofe and give good testimoniall that he hath passed through the same passage and arrived in some part of the said East Indies in ye dominions or kingedomes of Cathayia and China or one of them that then nether he the said George Waymouth nor his assignes shall or will demand or require of the said governo^r or company or any of them any Salary wages or reward for his viage or travell in ye discovery of ye said Passage in regard the said viage was vndertaken by ye said governo^r and company ptly by his perswasion and vpon his resolucōn to adventure his travell and life therin for ye good of his Cuntrey to wch his resolucōn the said Company were content to add the adventure of ye settinge furth of ye viage to their great charge.

In witnes &c.

1602 14 Apr.

A generall Co^rte houlden the xiiijth of Aprill 1602.

m^r Ald Watt₷ Governo^r	m^r Wiseman
m^r Rumney deputy	m^r Harison
m^r Ric Staper	m^r Leat
m^r Farrington	m^r Lynge
m^r [Harison] Chambers	m^r Burrell.

T this Co^rte warrant was made to m^r Ald Cambell Thr̄r for y^e viage by y^e Northwest Passage to pay to William Russell Butcher the some of one hundred eleven pound₷ 5^s for beefe and Porke bought of him to furnish the occasion in this intended viage.

Mr Wiseman and m^r Lynge be entreated to audit the accompt₷ of Tho: Yerworth for 210^{li} wch he hath disbursed [for].

Another warrant was made to the said Thrẽr for one hundred and fyfty pound℥ to be paid to m^r w^m Chambers beinge for provisions of clothe and dyvers other necessaries. 1602 14 Apr.

Another warrant to the said Thrẽr for to pay to m^r Nicholas Leat the some of 150^{li} for provision of [lyke] further necessaries. And he to be accomptable.

Another warrant was made to ye said Thrẽr for payment of 150^{li} to m^r Staper to be disbursed to dyvers persons *for their wages* as they shall call for it. *And he to be accompt.*

[By this Court [*assembly*] it is *alsoe* ordered that the Pursers of the ships shall deliver the bills of *all* their provisions to m^r Burrell to receive allowance: and noe man to make provision for the store of the ship℥ but to have [direction from him] *allowance therof* vnder his hand.

The 20th of Aprill 1602.

1602 20 Apr.

Mr Aldⁿ Wattes governo^r
Mr Wm Ruñey deputy
Mr Tho Cordell
Mr Rich: Staper
Mr Wm Chamber

Mr Nich: Leat
Mr Tho: farrington
Mr Wm Harrison
Mr Wm Freeman
Mr Roger Howe.

ARRANT is geaven to Mr Aldⁿ Cambell thẽr of the North West passage, to pay vnto Josephe Page Baker [for] vppon an accompte of Biskett [deliuered and] to be delivered for the provision of the voyage the somme of three score poundes.

Joseph Page Baker 60^{li}

22th: of Aprill 1602.

1602 22 Apr.

ARRANT geaven to the said Thrẽr to pay vnto Thomas Yerworth 100^{li} to be vsed and disbursed vpon necessary provisions for this intended viage And the said Yerworth to give accompt therof.

The 24th of Aprill 1602.

[Mr Aldⁿ watt^s governo^r] M^r ffarrington
Mr Rumney deputy Mr Leat
Mr Ald Cambell Mr Harison
Mr Howe Mr Stapers
Mr Chambers Mr Wiseman

IT is agreed at this Co^rte by [that] John Cartwright of London Preacher wth y^e governo^r deputy and company of merchant^s of London tradinge into y^e East Indies to sayle and goe wth Cap: George Waymouth vpon a viage for ye discovery of ye Northwest Passage for ye wch ye said Cartwright is to have of the said company 3^{lb} p moneth. beginninge his sallary from ye depture of ye ship^s appointed for ye said discovery from Gravesend And if it happen that discovery be not made wherby ye said ship^s or one of them may returne from ye kingedome of China or ye kingedomes of Cataya then ye said Joⁿ Cartwright is only to have for his sallary the one halfe wch is xxx^s p moneth to be paid him at his returne But over and above ye said governo^r and company hath paid him the some of fyfteene pound^s of lawfull mony of England the wch ye said company doth give him for his pparacōn and furnishinge of *him selfe for* the said viage and in testimony of his agreement faithfully to be performed on both pts wherin the said Joⁿ Cartwright doth promise the said Comp: to do his best endevo^r in all thing^s [And further the] *The* said Cartw: is contented to enter into such covenant^s for his imployment in ye said viage as by ye said company shalbe thought good to be devised.

Edward Pullison is enterteyned to goe in this p̱sent viage as Purser of *one of* the Pynnaces [for this intended viage] for ye discovery of ye north west Passage and is content to accept of v^{li} in hand part of his wages to beginne from this day at ye rate of forty shilling^s a moneth if ye discovery be made and if not then at ye rate of xx^s p moneth duringe his imployment in ye viage And the said Pullison is to give security for his good be-

havio' in ye execucōn of ye charge of Purser and otherwise if he be further imployed in a bond of C^h.
1602
24 Apr.

Warrant is geaven to m^r Ald Cambell Thrēr for ye viage by ye northwest Passage to pay to m^r Wm Chambers ye soīne of one hundred pound€ wch is to be disbursed vppon necessary provisions [in] *to furnish* this [intended] viage and the said m^r Chambers [wil] *to* be accomptable therfore.

Warrant is geaven to ye said Thrēr to pay to m^r Ric^d Stapers the soīne of two hundred pound€ most part *of soe much* disbursed by y^e said m^r Stapers vpon necessaries and the residue to be disbursed as occasion shall serve for wch ifthe Stapers wil be accomptable.

A Geñ'all Court the last of Aprill 1602.

1602
Last of Apr.

Mr Ald^n Wattes governo^r
M^r W^m Ruīney deputy
Mr Tho: Cordell
Mr Rich: Staper
Mr Rich: Wysem.m
Mr Wm Chambers
Mr Nich: Leat
Mr Nich: Lynge
Mr Wm Harryson

The greatest part of the gen^r'alyty.

T this Co^rt the preparation of the viage for the North west passage being made and the shippes ready to dept certen articles of agreem^t [were] made betwene the Companie and Capten Waymouth were read, and ther were also read the Queenes l^re written to the Empero^r of China and Kathia wch being above the Court were made acquainted that divers of the Company that had not brought in ther moneys for the [said provision] provision of the said discovery allotted vppon ther adventures viz. ther xij^li in the pounde whervppon it was ordered that [the] auditors should be chosen and the accompte of the charge of the voyage [shuld] brought vnto them to be audited, [and] wch done reporte of the said accompte *to be made* at the next geñ'all Court and therw^th all the names of suche as have not brought in ther moneys to be [do] published [as] *to* that geñ'allyty, to thend the Company may [not onlie geave]

Articles of agreement
wth Georg Weymouth read.

1602
Last of Apr.

take order what further supply shalbe brought in to pforme the whole charge of the voyage and what further course shalbe taken wth those that have not brought in ther supplies according to order and thes psons heervnder named [may] *or any 4 of them* were apointed to be auditors for the said accompte. [viz.]

Auditors

M^r fra Chery	Mr Rob̃t Bell
M^r olyver Style	Mr Nich. pierd
Mr Humfrey Basse	Mr Aug: skynner
M^r fra: Tayler	Mr Morice Abbott
Mr Hughe Hamersley	Mr Rob̃t Carrell
M^r Jo: fletcher	M^r Jo: Combes

or any 4 of them.

Warrant geaven to ye Thrẽr to pay to Capten George Waymouth the som̃e of fyfty pound℘ sterlinge wch is allowed by y^e company for y^e bearinge of the charges and dyett of him and his servant℘ attendinge y^e p̃paracõn of y^e viage before the goinge forth of the ship℘ [Takinge his acquittance.]

1602
3 May.

The 3 of May 1602.

Mr Rum̃ey deputy	Mr Nic̃las Leet
Mr Rich: Staper	M^r Jo: Newman
Mr Wm Harryson	Mr Tho: farrington
Mr Rich: Wyseman.	

Watches compasses and other Instrum̃ẽtes cost 30^li.

WARRANT is geaven to m^r Ald^n Cambell thẽr of the voyage to the northwest to pay vnto Robert [and other] Grynkin for watches Compasses Rum̃yng Glasses and instrument℘ for the shippes vses the som̃e of xxx^li sterling.

Warrant is geaven to The Thrẽr to pay to m^r Leat the som̃e of xx^li to disgage the mariners cloathes.

Warrant is geaven to the said Thrẽr to-pay to Jo^n Davies a couper *for caskes &c.* 50^li 11^s 8^d and to take his acquittance.

Warrant to the said Thrẽr to pay to Adam Wood vij^li 8^s for deales ores and other provisions &c Takinge his acquittance.

THE EAST INDIA COMPANY

Warrant to y[e] Thrẽr for payment of vi[li] x[s] to w[m] wood-   1602
field Smith for [Iron] settinge on of Iron hoopes and such like   3 May.
worke takinge his acquittance.

Warrant to the Thrẽr to pay to Tho: Robinson for three cables and Skeytes 29[li] 18 Takinge his acquittance.

Warrant to the Thrẽr for payment of 92[li] 10[s] *the 3. of June next* to m[r] Skelton Chaundlo[r] for butter candles Powder and such like provisions [the] Takinge his acquittance.

Post meridiem eiusd diei.

m[r] Rumney deputy   m[r] ffarrington
m[r] Stap   m[r] Harison
m[r] Cordell   m[r] newman
m[r] Leat   m[r] Greenwell
m[r] Chambers   m[r] Burrell

DEPUTY reported vnto *this assembly* [these cõmittees] beinge [spoken of] enformed by m[r] Chambers [of] *how* some dislike *was* taken against y[e] Purser Tho: Yerworth notw[th]standinge after some further dispute it was [concluded] *agreed* he should be continued.

It [is by these comittees likewise] *was alsoe* thought convenient [that] and [fully] *therfore* agreed [was] *vpon in respect of* some difference dependinge [betwe] about y[e] other Purser Pullison that if by the Captaine [ther] *it* shalbe thought needfull to imploy him then the agreem[t] wth him y[e] 24th of Aprill 1602 to stand in force otherwise to be discontinued.

Warrant granted to M[r] Ald. Cambell Thrẽr for y[e] viage by y[e] Northwest Passage to pay to m[r] Johnson the somē of xi[li] vj[s] and viij[d] for bay Salt vsed in this p̄sent viage and to take his acquittance therfore.

A Geñal Court holden the 18th of May 1602.   1602
Mr Ald[n] Wattes governo[r]   Mr Rich: Stapers   18 May.
Mr Ald[n] Cambell thrẽr   M[r] Wm Chamber
Mr Tho: Cordell   Mr Nich: Lynge
     Mr Nich: leat

1602
18 May.

WHEREAS M{r} Ald{n} Cambell ther for the voyage by the Northwest passage is bounde by coveñnt vnder his hand and seale to John Drewe marino{r} for the payment of his wages xx nobles a moneth so longe as he shalbe in the voyage yf the passage be discovered and yf he discover not the said passage v marke a moneth and xv{li} moreover to be p{d}.

Vppon the xv{th} of marche This court doeth agree that a bonde vnder the Comon seale of the Companie shalbe made to m{r} James Cambell sonne to m{r} Tho: Cambell *in the penaltie of CC{li}* to save the said m{r} Thoñis Cambell harmeles from the said Coveñnte.

Supplies to be brought in.
Newe billes of adventure conteyning every mans stock and all supplies in one grosse some.

At this Court day is geaven to all the voluntarie suppliers for the setting forthe of the voyage *by the north west passage* w{ch} have supplied above the rate of xij{d} the lt. to bring in ther voluntary contribution by the [last] xx{th} of this moneth. And it is also ordered by this Co{rt} that all the ratable supplies of xij{d} the lt. for the northwest voyage and the voluntary supplies of encrease shalbe endorsed vppon everie adventurors bill of adventure by the ther *or otherwyse noted vnder his hand* And that bill to be [being] brought to the Secretorie and newe billes to be made vnder the coñion seale *for every suche adventuro{r}* w{ch} shall conteyne in one grosse soñie the severall adventures and the severall Supplies of everie brother of the Companie [ether] brought in and p{d} ether *fo{r}* the voyage by the Cape of bona Speransa. or [by] for the voyage by the Northwest passage w{ch} bill being sealed w{th} the comon seale shall be a testimony to every adventuro{r} what he is interest in the voyage sett forthe by the Cape of Bona Speransa according to the ordenaunces of the Company.

Fryday come sennight is apointed for the Auditors to meete together and that day to finishe the Accomptes of the northwest voyage to thende the Company may be informed at the next geñ{r}all court what is the whole charge of the same voyage.

Warraunt is geaven to [the] M{r} Cambell ther to pay vnto Thoñis Barbo{r} for canvesse [and] provided for to make sayles for the 2 flyboat{s} of the northwest voyage the soñie of 143{li}.

The lyke warraunt is geaven him to pay to Robert Hewghes saylemaker for making of sayles the some of thirtie and two poundes tenn shillinges.

Another warraunt is geaven to the said ther to pay to Arnold mabancke for pullies for the two fflye boates the some of [tenn] Nyne poundes and tenn shillings.

Another warraunt is geaven to the ther to pay vnto Thomis Tyler painter the some of thirteene poundes six shillings and eight pence for worke done by him about the two pinaces.

Another warraunt is geaven to the said threr to pay vnto Roger ffrythe Smythe for yron worke for store for the said shippes the some of xix^{li}.

Another Warraunt geaven to the said ther to pay to Richard Hall Blacksmith for yron worke for the two flyboates the some of xxvj^{li}.

Another Warraunt geaven to the said ther to pay to George Gryce carriage maker iij^{li} viij^s.

Warrant to the Threr for payment of two and twenty pound(' six shilling(' to xpofer Tompson Smith for *Iron* worke &c. [done by him] about the Pynnaces.

Warrant to the Threr for payment of 12^{li} to w^m Denham for Pullies &c.

Warraunt for payment of 120^{li} 3^s to Abraham Campion for provisions of Beare.

Warrant for payment to Nic. Symonson carpinter for worke vpon the discovery the some of 58^{li} 13^s and for tymber and a boat 13^{li} in all 71^{li} 13^s.

Warrant for payment of 7^{li} 11^s. to Mr Skelton for powder sent in to the downes for the further provision of the Pynnaces.

20th of May 1602.

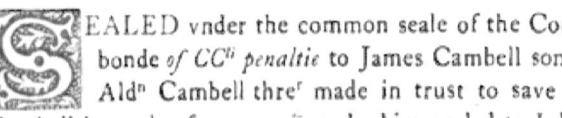

EALED vnder the common seale of the Companie a bonde *of CC^{li} penaltie* to James Cambell sonne of m^r Ald^n Cambell thre^r made in trust to save Mr Ald^n Cambell harmeles for a coveñnte by him sealed to John Drew mariner for his wages in the voyage by the Northwest passage.

1602
20 May.

Warrant geaven to mʳ Ald Cambell Thrēr for yᵉ viage by yᵉ Northw. to pay to mʳ Ric: Wright Secretary to this felowship for charges by him disbursed about yᵉ procuringe of yᵉ queenes lres the some of 4ˡⁱ 15ˢ.

1602
21 May.
To the Threr for viage by yᵉ northw:

21ᵗʰ of may 1602.

ARRANT to *pay to* Xp̄ofer and Thomas nicolls the some of thirtie fowre poundℓ seaven shillingℓ and ten pence for provisions of [ropes] cordage.

An other for mʳ Savage to receive the some of three poundℓ for spare maystℓ.

1602
23 May.

23ᵗʰ of may 1602.

ARRANT to pay to mʳ Richard Stapers the some of 40ˡⁱ 15ˢ 8ᵈ for soe much restinge due vnto him as appeareth by accompt audited.

Warrant to pay to Wᵐ Deyns Iremonger for provisions of spittℓ and such like necessaries received of him for the Pynnaces vse the some of 30ˢ 8ᵈ.

1602
26 May.

26ᵗʰ of may 1602.

ARRANT to pay to Joⁿ Makesfield Brasier for corkℓ and pottℓ of brasse copper kettles and other *like* necessaries the some of 17ˡⁱ 17ˢ.

Warrant to pay to Joseph Page Baker for biskett for both shipℓ and for biskett bagℓ yᵉ some of 41ˡⁱ 8ˢ.

Warrant to *pay to* Mʳ Ald Wattℓ governoʳ the some of forty two poundℓ for 30ᶜ of Iron hoopes at 28ˢ p centū.

Warrant to pay to Tristram Eldrich the some of 4ˡⁱ 7ˢ wᶜʰ is by him to be repaid to severall psons poore men for lodginge & *other* charges the mariners heretofore *have put them vnto.*

2 of June 1602.

WARRANT to pay to Peter Wright the some of forty three shilling℈ for lanthornes and other thing℈ for the Pynnaces.

Warrant to pay to Wm Thomas the some of twenty six shilling℈ for lanthornes for the vse aforesaid.

Warrant to pay to Smalwood a locksmith for lock℈ staples & other thing℈ the some of thirtie seaven shilling℈.

Warrant to pay to Joseph Pett Shipwright for [sheathinge] worke vpon the Godspeede the some of fyfty two pound℈.

3 of June 1602.

WARRANT to pay to m^r Ric Staps the some of 7^{li} 8^s 8^d beinge already disbursed by him to Joⁿ ffranklyn for [his] charges in caryinge of a l̅r̅e to Capten George Waymouth in to the Downes 28^s and 8^d and for the hyre of one Stace a Pylott to goe wth the Capten to Newcastle the some of 6^{li} wch both amount to y^e s^d some of 7^{li} 8^s 8^d.

8th of June 1602.

WARRANT to pay to w^m Hedger of wappinge for a boate made for y^e discovery wth rudder Irons and ringe bolt℈ the some of five pound℈ ten shilling℈ *in full payment* agreed wthall by m^r Burrell [in full satisfac̃on therof].

18th of June 1602.

WARRANT to pay to m^r nic Leat the some of fyfty one pound℈ 3^s 3^d and is for *monyes* [merchandize & soe much he hath] laid out more then he hath rec^d for *provisions of* merchandize [and other provisions] sent in ye two ship℈ for discovery wch he is to give accompt of to the Audito^{rs}.

1602
18 June.
129ˡⁱ 9ᵈ

Warrant to pay to John Fletcher for cordage the some of 129ˡⁱ 9ᵈ in full paymᵗ.

Warrant to pay to wᵐ Kymber for wharfage the some of 3ˡⁱˢ.

1602
28 June.

A Coʳte the 28ᵗʰ of June 1602.

 mʳ Rumney deputy   mʳ Wiseman
 mʳ Eldred   mʳ Harison
     mʳ Lynge.

IT is geaven in charge to the officer to warne a generall Coʳte to be at ffounders hall the sixt of July *next* to give their consents to the Elecc̃on of governor dep: and comittees accordinge to certen clauses conteyned in yᵉ Pattent limitinge a tyme of this said elecc̃on.

Order geaven to the bookekp to finish the accomptſ for the northwest *passage* and to charge every pticuler mans adventure last supplyed for discovery of yᵉ said northwest Passage together wᵗʰ his former adventures by yᵉ Cape of Bona Spe: [Speransa and to be entered in yᵉ bookes creditors for one entire some] *creditoʳ to yᵉ stock in one entire some in yᵉ bookes therfore appointed.*

1602
2 July.

A. Coʳte the 2. July 1602.
 Mʳ Governor   Mʳ deputy
    Mʳ farrington.

To the Thrᵉʳ of the viage by the Northwest.

WARRAUNT to pay to ffaithe may wief to John May one of the vj mʳ mattſ the some of xxxˢ in pte of his wagſ he beinge in the Suzan.

A Warraunt to pay to X͠per Thompson for plates for the 2. pinckſ thirteene shillingſ tenn pence.

A Warraunt to pay to Wᵐ Edward Plum̃er for Lead and sodar for the Pinckſ the somme of eight pound eight shillingſ.

A Warraunt to pay mʳ John Wattſ Governoʳ for thirty hundred of Iron hoopes at xxviijˢ p C. forty two poundſ.

A Warraunt to pay Mʳ Rumney deputy for boate hier and other charges forty six shillingſ eight pence.

A Generall Court holden the vj July 1602.

1602
6 July.

Mr Alderman
Watt(Gouernor.
Mr Rumney deputy
m^r Richard Staper
Mr Richard Wisemam
Mr Robte Chamberlaine
Mr Frauncis Cherrie

Mr Thomas farrington
Mr Niclias Leate
Mr Wm Harrison
Mr John Higelord
Mr Wm Chambers
Mr Rich: Wiche
Mr Nihas Leate.

Mr Nihas Linge

wth the most pte of the Generalitie.

THE preveledges of this fellowshipp appointinge the Elecc͠on of the Governo^r Deputie and Comitties of this Companie vppon the first day of July or wthin sixe daies followinge *was reade*. This Co^rte proceaded to the Elecc͠on of the said severall officers and by scruteny and generall consent did make choice of these severall psons to the severall offic(followinge and havinge chosen them did before they were severallie placed and admitted to their severall plac(minister vnto [them] *so many of them as were then present* respectively the severall othes ordeyned at the last Generall Co^rt of Elecc͠on.

S^r [Ald] *John* Harte Alderman Elected Governo^r for to governe the affaires of the Companie for one whole yeare.

Mr William Rumney reelected Deputie Governo^r to governe the affaires of the Companie for one whole yeare.

Committies
Mr Aldⁿ Watt(Ju͠r
Mr Aldⁿ Cambell Ju͠r
Mr Thomas Cordell [Ju͠r.]
Mr Wm Garrway Ju͠r
M^r Rc Wiseman Ju͠r
Mr Stapers Ju͠r
M^r Jo: Coombe Ju͠r
M^r Jo: Harby
Mr Wm Chambers Ju͠r
M^r Jo: Eldred Ju͠r

Committies
Mr Rich: Wiche Ju͠r
M^r Jo: Higelord Ju͠r
Mr Wm Harrison Ju͠r
M^r W^m dale Ju͠r
Mr George Booles Ju͠r
Mr Tho: Horton Ju͠r
Mr Nilias Linge Ju͠r
Mr Tho: farrington Ju͠r
Mr Wm Greenwell Ju͠r
Mr Geo: Smithes Ju͠r

1602
6 July.

Mʳ Humfrey Basse Juʳ   Mʳ Giles Parsloe Juʳ
Mʳ Humfrey Walcott Juʳ   Mʳ Wᵐ ferrers Juʳ
Mʳ Robte Chamberlaine elected Thrēr for the Companie.

Mʳ Richard Wrighte readmitted and contynued in the place of Secretary for the Companie for this yeare ensuinge.

Thomas Stephens admitted bookekeap for keepinge their generall accomptẽ for this yeare ensuinge demeaninge him selfe honestlye and faithfullie in his place.

Thomas Euesett readmitted to the place of Beadle for this yeare ensuinge.

Oathes.

A Warrant to pay to Tristrum Eldred Purser of the 2 Pinckẽ for paines taken in the Companies affaires the some of vj^{li} xiij^s iiij^d.

※

1602
28 July.

A Generall Courte holden the xxviijth of July 1602.

Mʳ Rumey deputy   Conmitties
Mʳ Alder : Cambell   Mʳ Wᵐ Grenewell
Mʳ Aldⁿ Holliday   Mʳ Robᵗᵉ Chamberlaine Thrēr
Conmittees.   Mʳ Humfrey Basse
Mʳ Wᵐ Harrison   Mʳ Wᵐ dale.
Mʳ George Booles
              wth ye most pte of the Generalitie.

Mʳ Alderman Cambell new elected Gouernor.

AT the Last General Coʳte Sʳ John Harte beinge by a generall consent elected Governoʳ of this Companie desired since to be excused alleadginge his age weakenes of body and many other important businessẽ of his owne. This Court therefore now proceaded to a new eleccon of a Governoʳ and by scruteny and generall consent did make choice of Mʳ Alder : Cambell to guide the affaires of the Companie this ensuinge yeare who [respectively] tooke his oathe before his admission.

At this Court one Peter Wellington humbly desired to be admitted a freeman of this Companie in place of one Peter Helms lately deceased the rather for that the widowe of the said Peter had assigned over to him the stock and profittẽ thereof, the *stocke and* proffitt^e arysinge by the said stocke is graunted to him. but his freedome altogether denied him.

Thomas Stephens likewyse humblie desired his freedome of this Companie but his sewte is defferred till further triall be made of his sufficiency and faithfull dischardge of that trust reposed in him about the Companies affaires.

Att this Court the Cassiers of the late Thrẽrs of this Company complained they had susteyned Losse by receavinge and painge out the Companies moneis some more some lesse And it was ordered they should be aunswered whatsoever they could iustly say they had Lost.

Warrant is geaven to [John Bowen] Mr Chamblen thre^r to pay vnto John Bowen six [five] q^{re} rent [of] for the Companies meeting^e at the founders Hall *to be* ended at [Midsommer last] *Michãs next* the somme of vj^{li}.

The 16th of September 1602.
Present.

m^r Ald^n Cambell Gover^r m^r Chambers
m^r Rumney dep: m^r Harison.
m^r Cordell m^r Bolles
m^r Stap m^r Leate
m^r Chamblen Thrẽr m^r Toomes
m^r Wiseman m^r Dale
M^r ffarrington.

[T]HE Company after readinge of the Jornall sent from Capten Waymouth and] *At this Court a Journall sent [directed] from Capten Waymouth was was read wch gave* Intelligence *beinge* [geaven] *to this assembly* [of the said] *how ye 2* Pinnaces [were] sent *forth for Discovery of a passage to the Est Indies by the Norw : are returned* & arrived at Dartmouth. *It is therfore* agreed by scruteny the [y] *said Pinnaces* shalbe brought about to London wthout sale of any of their provisions And thervpon ordered coīīission should be sent to Capten Waymouth for ye bringinge of the said Pynnaces about signifyinge

1602
16 Sept.

to him such thing℘ as remaine therin may serve for a seacond discovery   And further if the said Capten himselfe be sick he cannott fulfill the content℘ of the said Comission then to [be further] *give order* as in the discrecōn of y*e* said Capten shalbe thought most fitt for the speedy bringinge of them about.

Order l̃res should be writt to the 2. Pursers *to this effect* That sith it hath pleased god to [crosse them] *send them noe better successe* in this their [viage] intended discovery they would *the rather therfore* be carefull for y*e* preservinge of such thing℘ as remaine in the Pynnaces to serve for a seacond [di] adventure And to vse what industry they may in the speedy bringinge of them about.

Order geaven to Thomas Evesett to warne a generall Court at founders hall to morowe by two of the in y*e* afternoone.

1602
17 Sept.

A Gen'all Court The 17*th* September 1602.
Present.

m*r* Rumney Dep :   m*r* ffarrington
[m*r* Ofield] m*r* Wiche   [m*r* Mosley]
[m*r* Wright] m*r* Lynge   m*r* Greenewell
       And the most pt of the Generalty.

T this generall court m*r* Cartwright *Preacher* beinge called to satisfy the Company of their returne soe suddenly did [in breefe referr that their] refer them to the readinge of Captein Waymouth's Journall w*ch* he had delivered vnto the Governo*r* and beinge demaunded further whether he could give intelligence of any thinge more then the said Capten in his Journall had signified alleadged in answear his ignorance in navigacōn by reason wherof he could not further satisfy them.

M*r* Deputy gave intelligence to the Company how the Comittees at the last Court thought meete to send downe comission to Capten Waymouth for the speedy bringinge of the Pynnaces about to London w*th*out breakinge of bulke as alsoe to direct l̃res to the 2. purse*rs* for the safe p̃servacōn [as] of such thing℘ as did belonge to the place they were appointed in wch course beinge liked of by the said Company lres to to that end were sealed vnder the comon seale and sent to Dartmouth where the said Pynnaces are now at anker.

A Comittie the 29 of September 1602.
Mr Aldⁿ Cambell gouerno^r   Mr John Eldred
Mr Wm Rumney deputie   Mr Wm Harryson
Mr George Bowles   Mr Nichas Lyng

HES Comitties have assembled them selfes together vppon occasion of the longe stay of the cōming aboute of Captein Waymouth and doe thinke it convenient that yf they do not heare from him wthin thes 3 or 4 daies that then ther shall care be taken of a fitt man to goe downe to take for ther cōming away.

The xiijth of [September] *october* 1602.
m^r Rumney deputy   m^r Dale
m^r Chamblen Thrēr   m^r Lynge
m^r Combes   m^r Walcott
m^r Harison   m^r Smith
      m^r Horton.

R COMBES m^r Harison m^r Farrarr m^r Wiche m^r Lynge are entreated to take the paines to see the discharge of the two [shipp(?)] Pynnaces [lately] sett forth for a discovery to the East Indies by the northwest Passage *lately arrived at Dartmouth and* now [retorned againe into] the Port of London.]

The two Pynnaces lately arrived at Dartmouth beinge now come into the river of Thames according to direcc̄on [of] from the Company It is [now] thought meete for the discharge and safe preservac̄on of all provisions remayninge therin that some of the Comittees should survey the discharge of both the said Pynnaces And to that end m^r Coombes m^r Harison m^r Lynge

1602
13 Oct.

m^r Wiche and m^r ffarrar beinge thervnto entreated have assented accordingly.

1602
18 Oct.

A Generall Court houlden the 18th of October 1602.

Present

m^r Governor	m^r ffarrington
m^r Boules	m^r Eldred
m^r Dale	m^r Lynge
m^r Harison	m^r Smithers

wth the most pt of the Generalty.

HIS Court beinge assembled vppon occasion that the two Pynnaces or barkes were neere discharged according to order geaven by the last assembly of comittees Mr Governor thought meete to propound severall questions to the generalty [about] *touchinge* the sale of the barkes and all other provisions therin and about ; wch wth assent of the said Generaltie are agreed vppon as hearafter followeth on the other side.

1. Imprimis The stronge beere to be sould after the rate of fowre pound℘ p tonne to such of the Company as will buy it yf not to them to others at the same rate.
2. It ñt they who have the caske in wch the beere is shall pay for the same caske at the rate of 20^s p tonne.
3. All those wch will have the said beere shall fetch it from thence by to morowe night oreles by Wednesday night at the furthest.
4. Their Sack℘ to be laid vp in a seller for some [foure] 6. daies the caske beinge filled *wth ye same wine* [vp] and after that tyme sale to be made therof.
5. That there be a dry warehouse provided for their beefe and Porke and therof sale to be made.
6. It is in conclusion agreed that these provisions aforenamed the two barkes and all other thing℘ whatsoever in or about the said barkes shalbe sould. and for the pformance therof the Generaltie doe refer the sale of all to m^r Governo^r

dep: and Comittees to do therin as in their opinions shall seeme best for the vse and behoofe of the Company.

Mʳ Ald Holiday havinge in his handę of the Companies money to the valewe of 38ˡⁱ 6ˢ 9ᵈ [as appeareth by account] would stay in his handę some [sixe] 8 or [seaven] 9 poundę *therof* wᶜʰ was alledged to be [laid out by] *geaven away by* his wife but this Court not assentinge thereto have generally agreed that he shall bringe in the said somē of 38ˡⁱ 6ˢ 9ᵈ to the Thrēr.

The said Alderman Holiday beinge in arrerages for monies wᶜʰ he should have supplyed towardes the discovery by the northwest It is agreed that he and all others who have not supplyed towardę the said discovery according to the ordenances of the Company in that behaulfe provided shall have *such somēs* defaulted out of their adventures *into yᵉ East Indies* by the Cape of Bona Esperansa as by an order of the xjᵗʰ of January 1601 was sett downe for such as did [incurre] offend contrary to the tenor of that lawe and to be put to accompt.

A Court 23ᵗʰ of October 1602.

mʳ Ald Cambell goʳ mʳ Coombes
mʳ Rumney dep: mʳ ffarrington
mʳ Wiseman mʳ Parsloe
mʳ Bowles mʳ Stapers
   mʳ Lynge.

ARRANT granted to mʳ Robert Chamblen Thrēr to pay to such marinors as were hyred from Dartmouth to London to bringe the Pynnaces about such severall somēs as shouldbe subscribed by mʳ Governor or mʳ Deputy vnder the said warrant.

Mʳ Wiseman havinge assented vppon request made for the sparinge of some convenient place to bestowe the chestę wherein the merchandizes were put at the sendinge out of the two Pynnaces It is thought convenient that the said chestę shalbe caried to mʳ Wiseman's house & there to be vewed by the Comittees whether any of the quantety hath beene dimīnished.

The 25th of October 1602.

Mr Aldⁿ Cambell go^r
Mr Wm Rumey deputy
Mr Robt Chambleyn
Mr John Harby
Mr Gorg Bowles
M^r Jo: Eldred.
Mr Rich: Wyseman

Mr Tho: farrington.
M^r [Giles] *Humfrey* Walcott
Mr Wm Harryson
Mr Rich: Wyche
Mr Gyles Parslowe.
Mr Tho: Horton
Mr Wm Greenewell

M^r Jo: Combe.

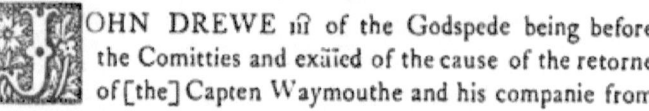OHN DREWE m^r of the Godspede being before the Comitties and exâied of the cause of the retorne of [the] Capten Waymouthe and his companie from ther voyage of the north west passage wthout anie discovery performed doeth confesse that Cartwright the minister was the principall pswader [defrauder] of the Companie n the ship called the discovery for ther retorne for England and geaving over of the voyage, and that [the] Capten Waymouth being the governo^r and generall of the voyage retorning homewardes he the said drewe and his companie were to followe ther geñ'all, and for the more certen proof that the said Cartwright was the pswader of the Companies retorne he saieth that the Boteson the Guñer and the Carpenter and others of the Companie of the discovery did signifie soe muche to the said Drewe, and as he thinketh will averr soe muche before the Company.

It is agreed that a demaund shalbe made [to] *at the handes* of the said Cartwright for the gowne and apparell delivered him to have bene vsed yf the voyage had bene made to the partes of Cathaia or China and yf he shall deny to deliver them then the opinion and direction some lerned counsell what acçon will best lye against him for the recovering thereof.

John Lane m^r mate of the Godspede beinge demaunded of the cause of the retorne of Captein Waymouth and his Companie from the northwest voyage doeth alledge that Mr Cartwright the minister as he him self did confesse and Justifie *to this John Lane* that he was the pswader and mover *of* the Company to retorne for England and to geave over the voyage.

A Gen'all Courte the 24 of November 1602.

M' Aldⁿ Cambell [Thẽr] Go^r
Mr Wm Rumney deputy

Comitties
Mr Wm Chamber

Mr Humfrey Walcott
Mr Thomas farrington
Mr George Bowles
Mr Nichas Lynge
Mr Wm Harryson

wth a greate part of the Gen'alyty.

A GENERALL order was geaven to the Bookeaper of this Companie to charge all suche brethren of this ffelowship as are anie way indebted to the Company in the accomptes of the Company as debtors for suche somes as they are in arrerages to thende yf the said money be not aunswered before the shippes returne ther said debtes may be defaulted vppon ther severall stockes.

At this Co'te the generalyty were informed by the relation of m^r Governo^r and m^r deputie of ther proceading against Capten Waymouth before the LL : of the Counsayll touching his retorne from the voyage of the northwest soe sone wthout *anie* discoverie. and what order was taken by ther handes in that cause. and doe further relate what was done by the commission's apointed by the LL : before whom the said Captein Waymouth was called. and demaunded vppon interr̃. whose aunswere was taken to those interr̃. and sett downe in wryting wch aunswere was read at this gen'all courte wherin he gave the reason of his retorne and did expresse in writinge the [hope of] possibylyty [of] and hope of [the] divers Inlettes that treat [to the] throughe the coast of America [to] in to the Southseas or the East Indies vppon wch disco'se and consideration of the great benyfyte that might growe to this comon wealth yf possybly a discovery may be made this Court were resolved that a newe attempte shalbe made wth [and] both ships [at the least] to see what can be done by the said Inlett[e] and to imploy the said Captein againe [therin] *in one of ye said ships* the rather for that he is very confident that ther will a passage be founde throughe some of [them] said Inlettes And because the Company having entred thus farre to finde and discover a passage

1602
24 Nov.

they meane to make this present attempte a finall proof whether ther be any passage or not. And therfore they doe agree by geñ'all consent to place another sufficyent man or captein to take charge of the second ship and to sett them forthe bothe to proceade in this discovery leavinḡ them to proceade therin ether Jointly together or severally apart eche of them taking ther severall co^rses according as [they shall thinke meet] *shall hearafter be agreed vppon* And for the preparation of the said shippes and all necessaries for the said voyage and for the calculation of the charge the better to informe the geñalyty at ther next meetinḡ the persons heervnder named are appointed and entreated to take paines herein viz.

    Mr Gou^r   Mr Chambers
    Mr Deputy   Mr Harryson
    M^r [Ald.] Will. Bannyng   Mr Greenewell
    Mr Cordell   Mr Combe
    Mr Garway   Mr Lynge.
    Mr Staper   or any 4 of them.

Warrant granted to m^r Robert Chamb̄len Thrēr to pay to Thomas Smith for keepinge of the two Pynnaces at the rate of twelve shillingꝑ p moneth the soñe of xxiiij^s the one halfe therof beinge dewe to him vppon S^attrday last and thother halfe is for a moneth next ensuinge.

1602
29 Nov.

29 prd mensis.

Warrant granted to m^r Robert Chamb̄len *Thrēr* to pay to John Drewe m^r of the Godspeede 5^{li} John Lane xxx^s Thomas Boarne iij^{li} and John Branskom xlvj^s viij^d [They] ffor their imployment in the late intended discovery all amountinge to the soñe of xj^{li} xvj^s viij^d They acknowledginge the same in full of all demaundꝭ.

THE EAST INDIA COMPANY

4th of [August] december a^o prd

ARRANT to the Threr aforesaid for payment of 6^{li} 13^s 4^d to Thomas Yerworth beinge in full for his imployment as purser of thone of the two Pynnaces sett out for discovery of the northwest Passage and [alsoe] for his dyet and attendance about the discharge of them.

A Court at founder(s Hall xiijth December 1602.

Mr Gouerno^r   Mr Deputy   Mr Chamberlaine Threr

Comitties   Comitties
Mr Staper   Mr Wiche   Mr Farrington
   Mr Higlorde   Mr Geo: Booles   Mr Linge.

MR CHAMBERLAINE informethe this Assemblie that m^r Stephen Hodsonn one of the Brethren of this Company had paide vnto him x^{li} for his supply toward(s the discovery of the Northwest passadge and desired the Company to have him excused for non payment thereof till now for that he haith bene in the cuntry all this Sũmer and never hard thereof.

Order is geaven to Thomas Euesett to warne a Court vppon Weddnesday morninge next. this Court not concluding of any thinge for want of a greater Assembly.

21th of December 1602.

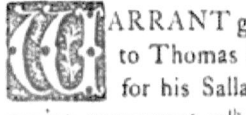ARRANT granted to m^r Robt Chamblen Threr to pay to Thomas Stevens Accompt keep for the Company for his Sallary dewe to him accordinge to the Companies agreement wth him beinge vnpaid for 3. quarters [rent beginninge] wch is since the 17th of March last amounteth to the soũe of 23^{li} 6^s 8^d.

[A generall Co^rte holden the 4th of Januarie 1602.
Mr Aldⁿ Cambell governo^r   Mr Aldⁿ Rumney deputy]

1602
30 Dec.

30. of December 1602.

M^r [Governo^r] Aldⁿ Cambell governo^r
Mr Aldⁿ Romney deputy

Comitties

Mr Rich : Staper	Mr Nichas Lynge
M^r Jo : Combe	Mr Edw : Harryson
Mr Wm Garway	

T is thought fitt by m^r Governo^r m^r deputy and the [said] comitties above menc̃oed that one of the companies barkes shalbe sett forth againe for the Northwest. So as they shall lyke well of [the] a newe conference wth Captein George Waymouth or some others.

1602
4 Jan.

A Gen^ral Court holden the 4th of January 1602.

Mr Aldⁿ Cambell governo^r	Mr George Bowles
Mr Aldⁿ Rumney deputy	M^r W^m ferro^r
Mr Robt Chamberlayn thẽr	Mr John Combe
Mr Rich: Wyche.	Mr Parslowe
Mr Wm Garway	Mr Wm Harryson
Mr John Eldred	Mr Wm Greenwell.

wth an ample nomber of the gen^ralyty.

T this Co^rte vppon relation made by m^r Governo^r and [his deputie] *Mr Aldⁿ Rumney* and vppon conference had in this Assemblie vppon the greatnes of the charge that the entended voyage by the Northwest will bring vppon the Company yf both the^r barkes [of the Companie] shuld be set forth [in] and furnished for that discovery. It is resolved for the avoydinge of the excessive charge [that] of the double p̄paration of both the shippes that a computation shalbe made vppon the preparation and furnishinḡ of on of them and to see how the victualles and furniture of them both [will] beinge laid together will sett forthe and defray a voyage by one of them wthout further charging of the Companie wth anie other suply And to

that ende this Co'te [*being aboute to make*] *have made againe* [have
made] choice of the persons heervnder named as well to consider
of the state and valewe of the p̃paration [of] and furnishinge of
oñ ship to this enterprise and of the meanes already provided to
defray the charge thereof as to confer wth Capten Waymouth
and to see what resolution he holdeth to proceade in the said
discovery, or wth some other fytt for the Enterprise who having
[entered] advysed thervpon are intreated at the next geñ'all
Co't to reporte ther opinions [and the] what they [fynde] conceave and fynde fytt and possyble to be done in this voyage according to the meaning of this Co't.

1602
+ Jan.

Comitties.

Mr Governo^r   Mr Grenwell
Mr Deputy   Mr Harryson
Mr Garway   Mr Hamersley
Mr Cordell   Mr Jennynges
Mr Staper   Mr Clerke
         or any 4 of them.

An Assembly the 7th of January 1602.

1602
7 Jan.

m^r Governo^r   m^r Stap
m^r Ald. Rumney dep: m^r Greenewell
m^r Garwey   m^r Hamersley
m^r Cordall   m^r Jennynge͡s
         Mr Clarke.

ACCORDINGE to the order of the last generall Court
the Coñiittees abovenamed beinge mett together
have thought meete in the proceadinge for the settinge out of one vessell for a discovery by the northwest *first*
to sett downe the provisions for the two Pynnaces formerly
sent forth and to make an estimate of the p̃ticulers therof aswell in respect they may take of the said provisions soe much
as shalbe found fitt for the furnishinge of one as alsoe by sale
of the residewe not found fitt to supply all other necessaries for
the setting out of the said vessell And to that end an estimac̃on

1602
7 Jan.

beinge made both of the *said 2* Pynnaces and all provisions therfore they do resolve for the supplyinge of all necessary provisions as men and victuall⁁ &c for setting out and furnishinge of one vessell to the northwest as shalbe reported to the next generall Court.

21 Jan.
1602

xxj^th of January 1602.

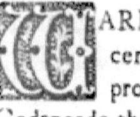ARRANT to Mr Chamblen Thr̃er for payment of certen porters for landinge and housinge of all the provisions out of the 2 Pynnaces the discovery and Godspeede the somme of fowre pound⁁.

Porters.

Thomas Evesed
xxv^s vij^d

Another Warrant to the said Thr̃er for payment of 25^s vij^d *to Thomas Evesed* beinge disbursed by him heretofore to m^r Popes man as appeareth by ye pticulers sent wth the warrant to the Thr̃er.

26 Jan.
1602

A General Court [of] the 26th of January 1602.
Present.

Mr Ald^n Cambell gov^er	Mr Rich. Wyche
Mr Ald^n Rumney dep^ie	Mr John Combe
Comitties	Mr Nich. Lynge
Mr Rich: Staper	Mr Humfrey Baese
Mr John highelord	Mr Wm Harryson
Mr Wm Dale	M^r W^m ferro^r
Mr Wm Chambers	Mr Humfrey Walcott

The greater part of y^e Gen^ralyty.

HIS Court beinge called together to receave the opinion of the Comitties appointed for [the] consultation of the setting forthe of one of the barkes latelie retorned from the Northwest passage the said Comitties do report that they finde some impediment that moveth them to stay the proceading in the said enterprise and [rather] thinke it rather for the good of the Companie that a carefull course be taken for the sale of bothe the barkes wth ther furnyture and other p̃paration

and mchaundize, and that the same be converted into money wch may ryse to a convenient some fytt to defray other necessarie charges vppon the retorne of the fleet sent out by the Cape of Bona Speranza, according to whose opinions the matter being putt to the consideration of this geñall Co^rte and a question made whether one of the barkes shalbe sett forthe againe [or not] or the viage vtterlie geaven over It appered by scruteny and the consent of the most part of the geñality that the voyage shall vtterlie be left of and [all] the preparation [both of] as well shipping victualling and other furniture as merchaundize *or so moche thereof as the Comitties shall thinke meet* putt to sale and made away in as prevalent a sorte as may be and to [thende] that ende the Comitties apointed at the last geñall Courte [are] for the setting forthe of one of the said barkes having acquainted them selves wth the kindes and particlaryties of the said goodes are intreated to make sale of them for the good of the Companye or of so muche thereof as they shall thinke meet. the names of wch Comittees do followe hearafter vizt.

26 Jan. 1602

Comitties.

m^r Governor
m^r Thomas Bramley dep:
m^r Ald Rumney
m^r Garwey
m^r Cordall
m^r Stap

m^r Greenewell
m^r Harison
m^r Hamersley
m^r Jennynge
m^r Clarke
or any 4 of them.

Forasmuche as m^r Aldⁿ Rumney having executed the place of deputie [of] to ye governo^r of this Company and is nowe chosen *an* Alderman and cannot attende the busines of this Company therfore this Court did proceade to the Election of a newe deputy to contynue vntill the next day of Election and divers persons being noiated and putt in election the choice of the place of the said deputie is fallen vppon Mr Thomas Bramley.

Mr Tho: Bramley chosen deputy.

At this Co^rte Thomas Stephens the bookekeap of this Company is admitted to the freedome of this felowship in as ample manner as anie brother of the Companie [and hathe taken his othe accordinglie] hath and injoyeth the same by vertue of thes previledges.

1602
28 Jan.

28th January 1602.

WARRANT to the Thr̃er for payment of xxiiij.ˢ to Thomas Smith for keepinge of the Two pynnaces at the rate of xij.ˢ p̃ moneth for Two monethes The one halfe therof beinge dewe the 20ᵗʰ of this present moneth and thother halfe is to the 20ᵗʰ of the next moneth.

17 Feb.
1602

The 17. of february 1602.

Mʳ Aldⁿ Cambell Goʳ	Mʳ wᵐ ferrers.
Mʳ Tho: Bramley deputy	Mʳ Rich: Wyche
Mʳ Wᵐ Chambers	Mʳ Humfrey Walcott
Mʳ Nich: Lynge	Mʳ Georg Smythes
Mʳ Dale	MʳTho: [Houghton] Horton.

Capten Waymouthe.

THES Comitties being̃ mett together to confer of some coʳse to be taken wᵗʰ Captein Waymouth who maketh demaundes of the Companie for charges and other moneys [by the] by him expended or otherwyse dewe as he pretendeth [wᶜʰ Capten Waymouth] and is contented to reserve him self and his demaundes to be arbitrably ended by 4. indifferent persons. forasmuche as he offreth his [action to be] demaundes to be arbitrably ended this assembly thinke it not fytt to refuse that coʳse and therfore do agree that whensoever he shall make choice of his arbitrators the Company will choose other arbitrators of like qualety: and for the better information of the [Comitties] Arbitrators thes persons are intreated to geave ther furtheraunce to solicite the state of the cause on the Companies behaulf.

Mʳ Governoʳ	Mʳ Chambers
Mʳ Ald: Rumey	Mʳ Harrison
Mʳ Deputy	Mʳ Wyche.

Edwd:
Pullyson
6ˡⁱ. 0. 0.

Warrant is geaven to Mʳ Thr̃er to pay vnto Edward Pullyson Purser of the Discouery in full discharge of his accompte and in full paymᵗ of all wages and demaundes the som̃e of sixe poundes.

Warrant is geaven to mʳ Thr̃er to pay vnto the Wyef of Thom̃ˢ Bowrne steward of the Godspede in full satisfaction of all demaundes the some of } xxˢ

THE EAST INDIA COMPANY

A Comittee 29th of March 1603.

Mr Ald. Cambell go^r	m^r Clarke
Mr Bramley dep:	m^r Boules
m^r Walcot	m^r Harison
m^r ffcrris	m^r Harby
m^r Lynge	m^r Wiche
m^r Wyseman	m^r Greenewell.

HESE Comittees above menčoned havinge debated whether the two barkes shalbe presently sould or [to] stay *made of* the sale therof till the fyue of Aprill next do resolve *by their execčon of hand℈* that the said Barkes shalbe kept till that [said] tyme And that a carpinter shall viewe them and do *therto* what is necessary for the keepinge tite of their orelop℈.

The said Comittees do alsoe resolve to make sale aswell of [all] y^r merchandize as all other thing℈ that are decayed or may decay at such prizes as shalbe thought convenient And wheras it is reported that cordage is *now* at a highe rate And *thought* we may be provided hearafter [at yf] *when* we shall have occasion for y^r vse of any at *a* more easy rate then we can now make sale of the companies cordage It is therfore agreed if such prizes may be had as is reported sale shalbe made of the said cordage accordingly.

Warrant was granted at this assembly by order from m^r Governo^r That m^r Chamblen Thrēr shall pay to Tho: Smith for keepinge of the two pynnaces for two monethes at the rate of xij^s p moneth the some of xxiiij^s The one halfe therof beinge dewe the xxth of this present moneth and the other halfe is to the xxth of the next moneth.

A Comittee the xxiiijth of May 1603.
Present.

m^r Governo^r	m^r Wiseman
m^r Harison	m^r lynge
m^r Jennyng℈	m^r ffcrris
	Mr Burrell.

1603
24 May.

WHERAS an order was taken by certen Comittees the xxixth of March last that the Two barkes should be sould after the fyue of May It is concluded that if the some of 600^{li} may be had for them viz' 300^{li} for one vessell wth his Inventorie and the like for the other It shalbe accepted of and not vnder but by the consent of the Governo^r and 4 Comittees.

1603
4 June.

4th of June 1603.

WARRANT to the Thr͡er for payment of xxiiij^s to Tho: Smith for keepinge of the Two pynnaces at the rate of xij^s p moneth for Two Monethes The one halfe therof dewe the xxth of the last moneth And thother halfe is to the xxth of this present moneth.

1603
6 June.

A Gen^rall Courte holden the vjth of June 1603.

Present	Comittes
Mr Aldⁿ Cambell governo^r	M^r olyuer Style
Comittees	Mr John Harby
Sr John Harte knight	Mr Robt Chamblayn
Mr Tho: Cordell	Mr Humfrey Basse
Mr George Bowles	Mr Wm Greenwell
Mr Rich: Staper	Mr Nich: lynge
Mr Rich: Wyseman	Mr Georg Smythes

Mr Tho: Horton
wth the greatest nūber of the gen^ralyty.

**T**HIS generall Co^rte being called together vppon occasion of the receipt of lr͡es re^d by a frencheman wch latelie departed at sea from one of o^r fleet the ship Assention wch lr͡es were written the one [from Ed. Highlord purser of the Assention and the other] from Roger Style Cape Merchant of the Assention. and the other from Ed: Highelord Purser of the same ship. bothe discoursing the state of the voyage bothe concerning the partes wch have bene visited for trade and

howe [they] many of [the] o' meñ are dead in the voyage. By wch discourses [in] this geñall Assemblie doe conceave good hope that the voyage will fall out suche as may minister incoragem^t to sett out another voyage for the further discovery of the partes of the East Indies.

1603
6 June

A Coñittee the ix^th of June 1603.

m^r Ald Cambell Go^r	m^r fferris
m^r Bramley dep:	m^r Stile
m^r Garwey	m^r Lynge
m^r Wiseman	Mr Bowles
m^r Smithies	Mr Giles Paslowe
m^r Clarke.	Mr Rich: Wyche

Mr Harrison.

1603
9 June

IT is resolved that lres shalbe written to the ffacto^rs & Company of the Assention and sent downe to the west cuntrey geving them to vnderstand the whole Companie here in care of the relief and comfort of all suche as are sicke in the ship and [for the] supply of anie wantes that they [or anie of ther Comp] stande fitt to be supplied [by] wth all the Companie here have written ther lres of credite to some of the principall merchant{es} of the Towne of Plymouth Dertmouthe and other the port{es} therabout{es} to take suche sicke and weake men on shore wch are desirous to leave the shippes. And to require the said ffactors and other officers of the shippes that forasmuche as this care is taken to furnishe ther wantes by the credite of the Companie here that they forbeare by anie pretence or want to breake bulke or make sale of anie thinge that doeth belonge to the *generall* adventure.

And it is alsoe ordered that according to the said lres soe to be written to the said factors and other officers in the ship Mr Robt Mydleton Mr Bateman and Mr Howe shalbe moved to make choice of suche mchaunt{es} in the said Townes of Plymouth Dartmouth &c. wth whom they are best acquainted to th ende that m^r Governou^rs lre may be directed to them subscribed

1603
9 June.

also w{th} ther handes entreating them to geave to the facto{r} Captein or principall in charge in the said ship credite for any suche moneys as he shall want for the vse of the ship. and to take in to ther townes suche sicke men as shall come on shore and to see them supplied w{th} suche relief as ther wantes require and the Companie vppon ther billes or advyse of the charges disbursed directed to m{r} Rob{t} Chambleyn will see them satysfied.

1603
16 June.

A General Court the 16{th} of June 1603.

Present.

M{r} Ald Cambell gov{r}   M{r} John Combe
M{r} Tho: Bramley deputy   [M{r} Humfrey Basse]
S{r} John Spencer   M{r} Geo: Smithes
M{r} Ald{n} Wattes   M{r} Humfrey Basse.
M{r} Ald{n} Hollyday   M{r} W{m} Chamber
M{r} Ald{n} Swynerton   M{r} Rich: Wyche
M{r} Ald{n} Hampson   M{r} W{m} Harryson
                                            M{r} Jo: Highelord
Comitties   M{r} Gyles Paslowe
M{r} W{m} Garway   M{r} Humfrey Walcott
M{r} Tho: Cordell   M{r} W{m} Dale
M{r} Rob{t} Chambleyn   M{r} W{m} ferrys
M{r} Rich: Wyseman   M{r} Nich: lynge
M{r} [olyuer] *George* Bowles   M{r} W{m} Greenewell

w{th} an ample nūber of the genñalyty.

The assention returned from the East Indies.

HER is propounded to this genñalyty the choice of a convenient place of receipte of the goodes retorned in the Assention w{ch} is nowe come in to the Ryuer. and for ther better direction what places are likelie to be hired for that p̄pose ther is nominated thes severall places or houses hereafter following [viz] out of which the comitties may make ther choice vppon the viewe of the fittest.

Warehouses {
The vault vnder thexchaunge
Sr John Spencers warehouse
The great house in Sething lane
Sr Edward osbornes house
The La : Barnes her house.
Mr Cartwrightes house.
}

1603
16 June.

At this Cou^rte the geñ'alyty have agreed that the coṁyttics according to the geñ'all trust wch is reposed in them for the managinge of the [trade of] merchaundize brought home in this voyage, shall appoint suche men as they shall thinke meet to goe aboarde the assention. and to attende ther from tyme to tyme vntyll the ship be vnladen.

Men to attende aboarde.

The generall Co^rte beinge broke vp the comitties did stay together in conference to geave order for the disposing of the ṁchandize aboard the ship : and ther vppon did resolve for the present that of these comitties the persons herevnder nōiated shall p̄sently goe downe to the ship and ther take order that noe marino^r or anie other shall presume to deliuer and carry from the ship anie thinge whatsoever vnlesse it be visited vppon paine of dẹteyning in the Companies handes the wages of everye suche marino^r or other officer :

Mr Bramley deputy
Mr Highelord

Mr Chambers
Mr Harryson.

And besides the comitties who are to take ther tornes as occasion shall serue to goe aboard the ship. these psons of the geñ'alyty herevnder named are appointed to goe downe and to take ther tornes of warding aboarde when they shall be appointed.

Mr Wm Jennyns
Mr Rich : Clerke
Mr Rich : Browne
Mr Taylby
Mr Barth : Haggett
Mr Roger Hemyng
Mr Wm Nelson
Mr Edm Nicholson

Mr Anth : Gibson
Mr Whyte
Mr Tho : Southewyke
Mr Geo : Bennett
Mr Ald^n Hollydaies man
Mr Ald^n Bannynges man
[cowcheman] Robt Barker.

1603
16 June.

M' Lytleford   M' W'" Wastall
            Ambrose Wheeler
         dẽi xvj° Junij 1603
    An Assembly of y' Comitties above named.

These 4 persons vndernamed are apointed to goe aboard the Assention to morrowe morning *the xvij*th *June* at 6 of the clocke and to contynewe ther vntill the next day the same howre viz:

    Edmund Nicholson   [Rich. Taylby]
    Ambrose Wheler.   [Robt Barker for]
    [Roger Hemmynge]   [M' Paull Bannynge]

for *Satherday* the 18th of June are apointed these psons vdlt.

    Roger Hemmyng   [M' Rich : Taylby]
    Robt Barker for   [M' W'" Wastall]
    M' P. Bannyng   [M' James Turno']
    [M' Antho Gibson]   [M' Ald" Hollydaies mañ]

For Sunday y' 19 of June are appointed to awaite aboarde these persons viz.

    Antho: Gibson   Rich : Taylby

For Monday the 20th of June are appointed to goe aboarde the ship. and to attende the from sixe in the morning vntill vj of the clocke the next day.

    M' Ja : Turno'   M' Rich : Clerk
    M' W'" Jennyns   [M' W'" Wastall]
    M' Ald" Hollydaies man   [M'   ]

For Tuesday y' 21th of June 1603 are apointed these persons viz.

    M' W'" Wastall   M' Barth : Haggett
    M' Rich : Broun   M' W'" Nelson

It is ordered that M' Style and the Purser doe attende aboard vntill the [that] shipp be discharged.

touching my L. Admiralles tythes.

It is thought meet by the Comitties above menc̃oed touchinge the tenthes belonging to my L. Admirall for the prise w'" the Companies shippes have taken in the East Indies. that his Lp̃ shalbe made acquainted w'" the advyse w'" Captein Lancaster

hath written in that behaulf wherin it may appere that the 1603
coṁodities taken are not vendable here but more fitter to be 16 June.
solde in the Indies.

M⁽ʳ⁾ Ferrers and M⁽ʳ⁾ Lynge are entreated by this assembly Canvas
to provide 50 or 60 peeces of Polldavies for the makinge of bagges.
baggꝭ for the bagginge of the pepper brought home in the
shippes And to putt them out to makinge. And alsoe to provide 6 sewtes of canves dublett and hose w⁽ᵗʰ⁾out pockettꝭ for
6. porters to be imploied in the fillinge of the pepp.

It is ordered that an entrie shalbe made in the custome house
of the goodes in the Assention consistinḡ of the pticlers viz.

      Pepper loose in the ship xxj m⁽ˡⁱ⁾   CCxm⁽ˡⁱ⁾
      Cloves 16 small baggꝭ cñ⁽ˡˢ⁾   xj C⁽ˡⁱ⁾
      Synamoñ 87 Cannasters cñ⁽ˡˢ⁾   vj mxxx⁽ˡⁱ⁾
      Gum lacre 67 baggꝭ cñ⁽ˡˢ⁾   iiij miiijxx⁽ˡⁱ⁾.

Warrant is geaven to m⁽ʳ⁾ Thrēr to pay vnto M⁽ʳ⁾ Midleton of M⁽ʳ⁾ Midleton v⁽ˡⁱ⁾ for
Plymouth for his paines rydinḡ hether w⁽ᵗʰ⁾ the first report of the ryding post
cõminḡ of the Assention out of the East Indies the soṁe of v⁽ˡⁱ⁾. from Plymouth.

            1603
            21 June.

      A Comittee the 21⁽ᵗʰ⁾ of June 1603
   M⁽ʳ⁾ Ald⁽ⁿ⁾ Cambell governo⁽ʳ⁾   M⁽ʳ⁾ John Eldred
   M⁽ʳ⁾ Tho : Bramley deputy   M⁽ʳ⁾ W⁽ᵐ⁾ ferrers
   M⁽ʳ⁾ W⁽ᵐ⁾ Garway   M⁽ʳ⁾ Tho : Horton
   M⁽ʳ⁾ George Bowles   M⁽ʳ⁾ W⁽ᵐ⁾ Harryson
   M⁽ʳ⁾ Humfrey Basse   M⁽ʳ⁾ W⁽ᵐ⁾ Greenewell
       M⁽ʳ⁾ Richard Wyche.

MR Governo⁽ʳ⁾ is moved by this Assemblie to take some other of the Companie to be bounde w⁽ᵗʰ⁾ him to the Customers for the Subsedye due to the kinge for the goodes brought home in the Assention . and for ther Indempnity they shall have an order of geñall co⁽ʳ⁾te and the companies coṁon seale to save them harmeles whervnto the said M⁽ʳ⁾ Governo⁽ʳ⁾ [is] doeth geave his assent and m⁽ʳ⁾ Eldred doeth agree to be bound w⁽ᵗʰ⁾ him.

M⁽ʳ⁾ Bowles and M⁽ʳ⁾ [Harryson] *Grenewell* are appointed and

248   THE COURT RECORDS OF

1603
21 June.

intreated to [goe] see the seullerage or vautes [in] *vnder* the exchaunge prepared and fytted to receave the said goodes . and to see the floores plancked and boarded for that purpose.

Mr Wm Grenewell and M^r wyche *and m^r Harryson m^r Horton* are appointed to be at the waterfall vppon Wensday and Thursday to see the goodes taken vp and sent to the [Exchaunge] Warehouses at the Exchaunge and the bookeap to be present wth them to make tickett^e for the carrmen.

Mr Bowles [and] Mr Eldred *Mr Lynge Mr Ferrers* are apointed to attende at the warehowses at thexchaung the same daies [and] to receave in the goodes and to waighe them and to vse the helpe of Tho: White to keepe a note of the waight.

for pilotage
vj^{li} to the
wief of
John May
purser in
the Susan
56^s.

Warrant is geaven to [M^r Thūr] *Tho: Stephens* to pay to the wyef of John May one of the m^{rs} Mates of the Susan for her relief in her husbandes absence a monthes wages coming to lvj^s *And to pay for pilotage for bringing vp the Assention into y^e ryver vj^{li}*.

1603
23 June

A Gen^rall Courte the 23th of June 1603.

Present

Mr Aldⁿ Cambell Governo^r   Mr Wm Chambers
Mr Tho Bramley deputy   [Mr Robt. Chambleyn Th.]
Mr Robt Chamberleyn   Mr Aldⁿ Hollyday
Comitties   Mr John highelorde
Mr Paull Bannyng   Mr Giles Parslowe
Mr Aldⁿ Wattes   Mr Wm Ferrers
Mr John Harby   Mr George Bowles

wth the greatest part of the gen̄ality.

WHEREAS ther is dewe to the kinge for custome ix^c and xvij^{li} poundes *or theraboutes* for the wch Mr Aldⁿ Cambell and Mr Eldred stande bounde by obligation in double the valewe by way of penaltie Therfore it is ordered for the indempnitie of the said Mr Aldⁿ Cambell and Mr Eldred that they shall have the com̄on seale of the company to save them harmeles ether made to them

selfes or to suche as they shall noīīte to have bondes made
vnto. w{ch} bondes this geñ'alyty will alway mainteyne for a good
securitie vnto them.

1603
23 June

It is ordered at this geñ'all Courte for the payment of the
marino{rs} w{ch} are come home in the Assention that moneis shalbe
taken vp at interest [and vppō] and that the geñ'alytie shall save
them harmeles that shalbe bounde for it. and geave *them* the
companies bonde vnder the cōen seale, vppoñ w{ch} order soe
taken by the geñ'alyty thes persons herevnder named being
present are entreated to geave ther bondes for the taking vp of
two thowsand poundes viz.

S{r} John Harte and M{r} Chamberleyñ for 1000{li} M{r} Paull
Baning Esquier and m{r} Ald{n} Wattes for 1000{li} to be contynued at interest for 3 monethes, [this Co{rt}te] the geñ'alytie
entendinge hereafter to take a co{r}se to levie by the pole and
vppon the rates of the pticler adventures, all suche soīnes of
money as the Companie shall have occasion to vse hereafter.

This Courte doe geave order and geñ'all coīnission to the
Comitties from tyme to tyme to proceade in sales of the goodes
nowe brought home and to take the best opportuncty in ther
discretions for that purpose and geñ'aly to pforme all thinges
incydent to the ordering and venting of the same coīnodities
And for the further helpe of the geñ'all busines It shalbe lawfull for m{r} Governo{r} and m{r} Deputy or ether of them from
tyme to tyme to apointe any one or two of the adventurors to
pforme anie pticler office or service w{th} the geñ'all busines
requireth.

    The 28{th} of June. Present
M{r} Bramley deputy   M{r} W{m} Dale
M{r} George Bowles   M{r} W{m} Harryson
   Ry Wright secretary

1603
28 June

Fowre obligations vnder coīnon seale of the Company sealed
in the presence of the psons above named videlt.

Two obligations of the penalties of 3000{li} a peece the one
to m{r} [John] James Cambell the other to m{r} John Eldred being

1603
28 June.

made to save them harmeles for 900ˡⁱ and seventeene poundes w^{ch} *they* are bounde for to the kinge for the custome of the goodes brought in the Assention the one half the xx^{th} of decemb next the other the xx^{th} June followinge.

Two other obligations of the penaltie of 1000 markes a pece the one to [mʳ] Sʳ John Hart and the other to Mʳ Roḃt Chamberlayn for the payment of 500 12ˡⁱ 10ˢ a peece to ether of them vppon the xxvij^{th} of September next at ther severall dwelling houses.

Billes of aduenture sealed.

	li.	s.	d.
21ᵗʰ of March 1600. To Stephen Hodgeson a bill of aduenture & supply at ijˢ the li.	240	0	0
10 June 1601. To Wᵐ Angell a Bill of adventure & supplies	240	0	0
13 June 1601. To Roger Hemyng a bill of adventure & supplies	240	0	0
17 June 1601. To John Eldred a Bill of adventure & supplies	600	0	0
To Humfrey Myllward a bill of adventure & supplies	240	0	0
To Richard Hearne a bill of adventure & supplies	240	0	0
14 August 1601. To [Richard] *Robert* Pennington a bill of adventure & supplies	240	0	0
17 June 1601. To Thomas Talbutt a bill of adventure & supplies	240	0	0
18 June 1601. To Roger Ofeilde a bill of adventure & supplies	360	0	0
To John Stoackly a bill of adventure & supplies	240	0	0
To William Megges a bill of adventure & supplies	240	0	0

		li.	s.	d.
18 June 1601.	To John Coucheman a bill of adventure & supplies	240	0	0
	To William Adderly a bill of adventure & supplies	240	0	0
	To Bartholmew Holland a bill of adventure & supplies	240	0	0
	[To Richard Gosson a bill of adventure & supplies	240	0	0]
	To Richard Humble a bill of adventure & supplies	240	0	0
	To Thomas Bootheby a bill of adventure & supplies	240	0	0
	[To William Jennyns a bill of adventure and supplies	240	0	0]
	To Andrewe Chamberlin a bill of adventure and supplies	240	0	0
	To Robte Offeley a bill of adventure & supplies	240	0	0
	To Clement Mosely a bill of adventure & supplies. *This bill is made to Eliz Moseley widowe*	240	0	0
	To Thomas Southacke a bill of adventure & supplies	240	0	0
	To William Quarles a bill of adventure and supplies	240	0	0
19 June 1601.	To Reynolde Greene a bill of adventure & supplies	240	0	0
	To Lawrence Waldoe a bill of adventure & supplies	240	0	0
	To Raphe Buzby a bill of adventure & supplies	240	0	0
	To William fferrers a bill of adventure & supplies	240	0	0
	To William Bonham a bill of adventure and supplies	240	0	0
	To Thomas Juxon a bill of adventure & supplies	240	0	0

		li.	s.	d.
19 June 1601.	To Thomas Shipton a bill of adventure & supplies	240	0	0
	To Edward Barker a bill of adventure & supplies	300	0	0
23 June 1601.	To George Whitmore a bill of adventure & supplies	240	0	0
	To Thomas Bramby a bill of adventure & supplies	240	0	0
	To Henrie Poulsteede a bill of adventure & supplies	240	0	0
	To ffrauncys Barker a bill of adventure & supplies	240	0	0
	To Richard Washer a bill of adventure & supplies	240	0	0
	To John Hodgson a bill of adventure & supplies	240	0	0
	To Humfrey Basse a bill of adventure & supplies	240	0	0
	To Wm Wollastone a bill of adventure & supplies	240	0	0
	To Humfrey Wallcott a bill of adventure & supplies	240	0	0
	To John Newman a bill of adventure & supplies	240	0	0
	To Samuell Armitage a bill of adventure & supplies	240	0	0
	To Henrie Bridgeman a bill of adventure & supplies	240	0	0
	To Wm Bond a bill of adventure & supplies	240	0	0
	To Thomas Horton a bill of adventure & supplies	240	0	0
	To John Swinerton a bill of adventure & supplies	360	0	0
	To Robte Waldoe a bill of adventure & supplies	240	0	0
	To Humfrie Style a bill of adventure & supplies	240	0	0

23 June 1601. To Thomas Farrington a bill of adventur & supplies	li. 240	s. 0	d. 0
To Wm Cotton a bill of adventure & supplies	240	0	0
To Edmond Nicholson a bill of adventure & supplies	240	0	0
To Raphe Gore a bill of adventure & supplies	360	0	0
To Oliver Stile a bill of adventure & supplies	560	0	0
To Richard Bell a bill of adventure & supplies	240	0	0
To Richard Piott a bill of adventure & supplies	240	0	0
To Robte Myldmay a bill of adventure & supplies	240	0	0
To John Buzbridge a bill of adventure & supplies	240	0	0
To Robte Coxe a bill of adventure & supplies	240	0	0
To Richard Peierce a bill of adventure & supplies	240	0	0
To Richard Ball a bill of adventure & supplies	240	0	0
To Robte Cobbe a bill of adventure & supplies	240	0	0
To George Coles a bill of adventure & supplies	240	0	0
To Robte Bucke a bill of adventure and supplies	240	0	0
To Richard Hale a bill of adventure & supplies	240	0	0
To Wm Hale a bill of adventure & supplies	240	0	0
To Wm Greewell a bill of adventure & supplies	240	0	0
To Robte Johnson a bill of adventure & supplies	240	0	0

		li.	s.	d.
23 June 1601.	To Andrewe Banninge a bill of adventure & supplies	240	0	0
	To Thomas Hewitt a bill of adventure & supplies	240	0	0
	To Robte Mydleton a bill of adventure & supplies	240	0	0
	To Wm Stoane a bill of adventure & supplies	600	0	0
	To Wm Cavendishe a bill of adventure & supplies	240	0	0
	To Samuell Hare a bill of adventure & supplies	240	0	0
	To Edmund Spencer a bill of adventure & supplies	240	0	0
	To Morrice Luellen a bill of adventure & supplies	240	0	0
	To Niclias Barmesly a bill of adventure & supplies	240	0	0
	To John Hewitt a bill of adventure & supplies	240	0	0
	To Jnº Cornelius a bill of adventure & supplies	240	0	0
	To James Turner a bill of adventure & supplies	240	0	0
	To Thomas Barbar a bill of adventure & supplies	240	0	0
	To Richard Poyntell a bill of adventure & supplies	240	0	0
	To James Deane a bill of adventure & supplies	360	0	0
	To Thomas Westrow a bill of adventure & supplies	240	0	0
	To Rowland Backhowse a bill of adventure & supp̃.	240	0	0
	To Bartholmew Barnes a bill of adventure & supplies	240	0	0
	To Ellis Crispe a bill of adventure & supplies	240	0	0

		li.	s.	d.
23 June 1601.	To Richard Clarke a bill of adventure & supplies	240	0	0
	To Raphe Hamer a bill of adventure & supplies	240	0	0
	To Jn° Hawkyns a bill of adventure & supplies	240	0	0
	To Thomas Henshawe a bill of adventure & supplies	240	0	0
	To Thomas Garway a bill of adventure & supplies	240	0	0
	To Thomas White a bill of adventure & supplies	240	0	0
	To George Candler a bill of adventure & supplies	240	0	0
	To Robte Bateman a bill of adventure & supplies	240	0	0
30 June 1601.	To Thomas Bostocke a bill of adventure & supplies	240	0	0
1 July 1601.	To John Clinche a bill of adventure & supplies	240	0	0
2 July 1601.	To Nicholas Leate a bill of adventure & supplies	240	0	0
	To Robte Sandy a bill of adventure & supplies	260	0	0
	To Richard Wyseman a bill of adventure & supplies	600	0	0
4 July 1601.	To Hughe Crompton a bill of adventure & supplies	240	0	0
6 July 1601.	To John Wollstenham a bill of adventure & supplies	240	0	0
	To Robte Gore a bill of adventure & supplies	240	0	0
	To John Leman a bill of adventure & supplies	240	0	0
7 July 1601.	To Allphonsus ffowle a bill of adventure & supplies	240	0	0
9 July 1601.	To Wm Romney a bill of adventure & supplies	240	0	0

	li.	s. d.
10 July 1601. To John ffletcher a bill of adventure & supplies	240	0 0
To Morrice Abbott a bill of adventure & supplies	240	0 0
14 July 1601. To Richard Tailbye a bill of adventure & supplies	240	0 0
21 July 1601. To John Cason a bill of adventure & supplies	240	0 0
To Thomas Allabaster a bill of adventure & supplies	240	0 0
To Nichas Pierde a Bill of adventure & supplies	240	0 0
22 July 1601. To Thomas Smithe a bill of adventure & supplies	360	0 0
To Roger Howe a bill of adventure & supplies	360	0 0
To John Westwraye a bill of adventure & supplies	360	0 0
To Edward Leeninge a bill of adventure & supplies	360	0 0
To Thomas Cambell Aldⁿ a bill of adventure & supplies	360	0 0
To John Wattes Aldⁿ a bill of adventure & supplies	600	0 0
To George Bowles a bill of adventure & supplies	300	0 0
To John Hart Knight a bill of adventure & supplies	600	0 0
To Edward Holmeden Aldⁿ a bill of adventure & supplies	1200	0 0
To John Spencer Knight a bill of adventure & supplies	360	0 0
To Robte Sampson Aldⁿ a bill of adventure & supplies	360	0 0
To Wm Offeley a bill of adventure *without* supplies	300	0 0
To John Middleton a bill of adventure & supplies	240	0 0

22 July 1601. To Nicħas Peird a bill of adventure and supplies	li. 240	s. 0	d. 0
To Giles Parsloe a bill of adventure and supplies	240	0	0
To Edmnd Scott a bill of adventure & supplies	240	0	0
To Edward Barkham a bill of adventure & supplies	240	0	0
To Anthonie Stratford a bill of adventure & supples	240	0	0
To Augustine Sknñ a bill of adventure & supplies	240	0	0
To Ambrose Wheler a bill of adventure & supplies	240	0	0
To Anthonie Moseley a bill of adventure & supplies	240	0	0
To Thomas Richardson a bill of adventure & supplies	240	0	0
To Wᵐ Burrell a bill of adventure & supplies	240	0	0
To Thomas Lydall a bill of adventure & supplies	240	0	0
To Samuell Backhowse a bill of adventure and suppˡˢ	240	0	0
To Richard Barrett a bill of adventure & supplies	240	0	0
To Peter Helinge a bill of adventure & supplies	240	0	0
To Nicħas Lynge a bill of adventure & supplies	240	0	0
To James Lancaster a bill of adventure & supplies	240	0	0
To Wᵐ Hynde a bill of adventure and supplies	240	0	0
To James Donkon a bill of adventure & supplies	240	0	0
To George Bennett a bill of adventure & supplies	240	0	0

	li.	s.	d.
22 July 1601. To Edward Walker a bill of adventure & supplies	240	0	0
To Robert Stratford a bill of adventure & supplies	240	0	0
To Gregorie Allen a bill of adventure & supplies	240	0	0
To Edward Harrison a bill of adventure & suppl:	240	0	0
To Wm Turner a bill of adventure & supplies	240	0	0
To Thoñis Ball a bill of adventure & supplies	240	0	0
To Edward Latterfeild a bill of adventure & supplies	240	0	0
To Anthony Gibson a bill of adventure & supplies	240	0	0
To Robte Bell a bill of adventure & supplies	240	0	0
To Ric^d Ironsyde a bill of adventure & supplies	240	0	0
To Nicħas Manley a bill of adventure & supplies	240	0	0
To Wm Chambers a bill of adventure & supplies	240	0	0
To Wm Millett a bill of adventure & supplies	240	0	0
To Wm Freeman a bill of adventure & supplies	240	0	0
To Wm Albany a bill of adventure & supplies	240	0	0
To Jefferie Kerby a bill of adventure & supplies	240	0	0
To Robte Key a bill of adventure and supplies	240	0	0
To Tho: Symondſ a bill of adventure & supplies	240	0	0
To Simon Lawrence a bill of adventure & supplies	240	0	0
To Nicħas Crispe a bill of adventure & supplies	240	0	0
To Barthol: Haggett a bill of adventure & supplies	240	0	0

	li.	s.	d.
22 July 1601. To Wm Smithe a bill of adventure and supplies	240	0	0
To Lewis Pope a bill of adventure & supplies	240	0	0
To Ric^d Bowdler a bill of adventure & supplies	240	0	0
To Robte Ducy a bill of adventure and supplies	240	0	0
To Robte Brocke a bill of adventure & suppl.	240	0	0
To Robte Carrell a bill of adventure & supl	240	0	0
To Richard Deane a bill of adventure & suppl.	240	0	0
To Richard Cokes a bill of adventure and supplies	240	0	0
To Niclias ffarrar a bill of aduenture and supplies	240	0	0
To James Cullymore a bill of adventure & suppl.	240	0	0
To John Harby a bill of adventure and supplies	240	0	0
To Roger Cotton a bill of adventure & supplies	240	0	0
To Robte Baylie a bill of adventure & supplies	240	0	0
To George Cater a bill of adventure & supplies	240	0	0
To Ric^d. Wiche a bill of adventure & supplies	240	0	0
To Wm Dale a bill of adventure & supplies	240	0	0
To Richard Burrell a bill of adventure & supplies	240	0	0
To Leonard White a bill of adventure & supplies	240	0	0
To George Hollman a bill of adventure & suppl.	240	0	0
To Henrie Archer a bill of adventure & suppl :	240	0	0

		li.	s.	d.
22 July 1601.	To Stephen Harvy a bill of adventure & suppl:	240	0	0
	To Josephe Salbancke a bill of adventure & suppl:	240	0	0
	To John ffryer a bill of adventure & supplies	240	0	0
	To Wm Wastell a bill of adventure and supplies	240	0	0
	To Humfrie Handford a bill of adventure & supplies	240	0	0
	To W^m ffysher a bill of adventure & supplies	240	0	0
	To Henrie Robinson a bill of adventure & supplies	240	0	0
22 Febr: 1600.	To Humfrie Robinson a bill of adventure & suppl.	240	0	0
22 July 1601.	To Wm Harrison a bill of adventure & supplies	240	0	0
	To John Greenewood a bill of adventure & supplies	240	0	0
	To John Humfrey a bill of adventure & supplies	240	0	0
	To Humfrey Smithe a bill of adventure & supplies	240	0	0
	To Roger Die a bill of adventure & supplies	240	0	0
	To Wm Cater a bill of adventure and supplies	240	0	0
	To ffrauncys Taylor a bill of adventure & sup:	240	0	0
	To John Combe a bill of adventure & supplies	240	0	0
	To Wm Palmer a bill of adventure & suppl:	240	0	0
	To John Highlorde a bill of adventure & supl:	240	0	0
23 July 1601.	To Rob^{te} Ducy a bill of adventure & supplies	240	0	0
	To Henrie Butler a bill of adventure [and supp^l.]	200	0	0
	To Jeremie Davers a bill of adventure &c	200	0	0
	To Wm Allen a bill of adventure &c	200	0	0

		li.	s.	d.
23 July 1601. To Thomas Heyes a bill of adventure &c		200	0	0
To Wm Palmer a bill of adventure &c		200	0	0
To Wm Starkye a bill of adventure &c		200	0	0
To Thomas Marshe a bill of adventure &c		200	0	0
To Raphe Allen a bill of adventure &c		200	0	0
14 August 1601. To Richard Chamberleyn a bill of àdventure &c.		240	0	0
To Richard Champion a bill of adventure &c		240	0	0
To Robt Chamberleiñ a bill of adventure &c		240	0	0
To George Chamberleiñ a bill of adventure &c.		240	0	0
To Frauncis Evington a bill of adventure &c.		240	0	0
To John Morrice a bill of adventure &c		240	0	0
28 August 1601. To Richard Stap a bill of adventure &c		800	0	0
To John Jackson a bill of adventure &c		240	0	0
To William Kellett a bill of adventure &c		240	0	0
9 October 1601. To Robte Robinson a bill of adventure &c		240	0	0
To John Watt℮ a bill of adventure &c		240	0	0
To Xpofer Cletherowe a bill of adventure &c		240	0	0
7 November 1601. To Hugh Hamersley a bill of adventure &c		240	0	0
19 November. To Eliz Moseley Widowe a bill of adventure		240	0	0
xxvijth of January 1601. To George Dorrington a bill of adventure & supplies &c		240	0	0
To Nic. Salter a bill of adventure and supplyes &c		240	0	0
To Richard Wragge a bill of adventure & supplies &c		240	0	0
John Wragge a bill of adventure & supplyes &c		240	0	0
To Willm Jennyng℮ a bill of adventure and supplyes &c		240	0	0
To Richard Gosson a bill of adventure & supplyes &c		240	0	0

	li.	s.	d.
17th of February 1601. Leonard Holiday Ald a bill of adventure and supp : &c	1440	0	0
xxvjth of February 1600. Roger Style factor a bill of adventure	40	0	0
2 of March 1601. Erle of Cumberland a bill of adventure	500	0	0
Countesse of Cumberland a bill of adventure	50	0	0
Ric Persons a bill of adventure	200	0	0
xth of March 1601. To Mr Leonard Holiday Ald a bill *of* adventure of ccxxxli assigned to him by Therle of Cumberland	230	0	0
xxvjth of Apirill 1602. To Mr Ald Moore a bill of adventure & supp :	480	0	0
To Xp̄ofer Nicholl℮ a bill of adventure and supp	240	0	0

[Memoranda on the fly leaves at the end of the volume.]
The 10ᵗʰ daie of August 1603.
A Comittie or Meeting of

Mʳ [P] Thomas Bramlye deputie Mʳ Wittm Chambers
Mʳ Pawle Banninge   Mʳ Hughe Hamerslye

HEIS Comitties have thought good to entertaine into their sʳrvice Elias Bradshawe for *the* consideracõn of tenne poundes for the yeare to be imployed in the busines of the East India company as they shall thincke good.

HEREAS ther is a viage preparing to the Est Indies sett forthe by certen merchantes the preparation whereof requireth much expedition to be vsed in Shipwrightℇ and ship carpenters wᵗʰ viage her maⁱᵉ doeth favor

A warraunt to take vp carpenters.

The names of such as have p̃sented themselues to bee employed as ffactoʳˢ in this voyadg :—

W ᵐ Garway   Wᵐ Skidmore
Robt Chambleyn   Robt Rickman

The Carnation of Colchester Mʳ Jo. Thurston bound from Loⁿ. to Colchester. bouyed vpon an Anker belonging to the Scourge. owner Stephen Johnes.

names of shipℇ.	men	tonnag	state of the adventure	
Red Dragon	180	600	68373ˡⁱ besidℇ the charge of the northwest.	tonnage
Hector	100	300		State of the Adventure
Assencõn	80	260		number of men in every ship
Suzan	80	240		
	440			

[Guift sent *cast* out] *Guift* sent out wth victualɫ and soe thought she was cast off at sea afterwardɫ.

Humfrey Robinson bound in for Tho. Yermouth

Tho. Yermouth to Humfrey Robinson

                            160 — —   500 — —
                                      350 — —

Tho Yerworth.

LETTERS.

To yr Ambassdr Mr Lyllo resident at Constantynople.   1599 Marche.

 HONORABLE. wee re[d] yr *Lo: Lrē*: of the 17 of November 99, wherbie it appeareth that the Graundsignior hath Roially graunted all caputulations, saving the consulage of foresteers wherin his redines *of assent* also appeared but that yo[u] were crossed by the Frenche Ambassadr, of whose proceading besides the advyse wth yo[u] wrote vs and [*of*] [wch] *whereof* mr Coltherst did in lyke sorte advertyse vs [in the said conten] *touching yo[r] crossinge and* contention for the [said] *said* foresteers. wee were made acquainted by [Mr Secretary] *Sr Robt*. Cycill. by occasion of a complaint wth the frenche ambassad[rs] lieges heer had made to her ma[ie] and wee were required to write vnto yo[u] as by order from her ma[ie] to desist all contention [for ye] w[th] the frenche [for] in that behaulf leaving the dutche and others to ther owne election to patronize them selfes [as] wher they seemed best [affection] affected w[th]out vrging or compelling them by comaundem[ts] procured. of w[ch] order geaven vs yo[r] [weare] *L. hath bene* ptelie advertysed [since] by a private Lrē written yo[u] by Mr Stap. But forasmuch as wee do collecte by the cowrse yo[u] [purpose] take in sending hether [Gr] *signis* Paull Pinder to her ma[ie] to acquainte her highnes wth the proceading of the frenche that ther [is] hathe bene some further and more indirecte working in this matter then yo[u] do [comitt to] *mencon in* yo[r] Lr̄es sent to vs and for that wee do observe by the ernest soliciting of the cause heer to her ma[ie] that the

M M

1599
Marche.

ffrench [leaveth] *omitteth* [noe] no meanes or oportunety [omitted] to prevaile in the obteyning his purpose. The matter being both an hono' and a benifite to [w^{ch}] *that* side *or part wch* [soever] prevaileth *in the contention* [wee thinke it.] *And albeit we are willed to signefie to your Lordshⁱ it is her ma^{ts} pleasure that yo^u should take no course to enforce the dutche or other fforesteers to come vnder yor consulage, yet wee thinke it* wysdome not to loose anie advauntage, but to reserve the cause in equall termes vntill yo^u receave a more absolute order in Comission ymediatlie from her ma^{ie} and therfore referre o^r selfes to yor L. approved care of the cause wch being entred in to so farre as it is would not be remisselie lost or lett [passe] pas.

And touching the accomptes and other pticlers *by yor L.* mencōned to be sent by *Signior* Paull Pinder wee hope wee shall receave them at his cōming whereof wee will wryte yo^u o^r [conceiptes] opinions as oportunety shall pmitt. the meane *tyme* wee propounde vnto yor L. [for] *in the name of the gertalyty* the accepting of o^r former motion wch is the allowaunce of 3000 cheskeens to begynne from m^r Bartons decease *for ye defraying of yor charges and expences* because the companie would gladlie stande vppon a certenty of ther charge as well for yor L as for *Mr. Coltherste* the Consull at Aleppo wherto wee *have* [found] *heretofore found* him inclynable. And wee move yo^u againe the rather for that yt appereth the graund signio^{rs} allowaunce is nowe aunswered and is lyke to be contynued wthout stay or question and also for that divers of yor frendes here did [not only] vndertake in yor *behaulfe that ye choice of you* [beinge chosen] that [behaulfe yor enterteynment] for her ma^{ies} ambassador should not only be a saving co'se to the comp. but that yo^u would willingly accept [therof] of the allowaunce of 3000 c^{ns} wch was supposed to be more then yo^u [could well expend] neade to expende but only in respecte of the first yeres charge vppon wch it was considered that yo^u should have it allowed yo^u from m^r Bartons death. Our care to avoide the *sending* [question vse] of Billes of exchaung made vppon vs [as] *ether for* venice [and here in] *or for*

England; and also all question of accepting the same, *when they come vppon vs vnexpected and wee vnprovided* hath moved vs to charge all o^r goodes. coṁing to Constantynople and Aleppo besides ther consulage wth ½ doller by way of lone vppon every kersey every Cth of tynn and every Cth of dry skynes *to be aunswered here at v' vj^d the doller* and *to* contynue the charge *thereof* for the supporting of bothe yor allowaunces because [wee] wee would be loth yo^u shuld seeke further of, for yor *necessary and convenient* supplies then the places of yor residences or neare thervnto. And wee doubt not but the said consulage and Lone together wth suche forestere consulage as shall occurre will liberally wth *an* ouerplus support [the needfull] yor nedefull and convenient expense. *wch said allowaunce of 3000 c^{ns} p anñ yf it please yo^u to accepte shalbe from tyme to tyme aunswerd yo^u by the Consull of Aleppo or see much thereof as shall make vp the consulage and Lone money collected at Constantynople to ryse to the said* [some] *soṁe of 3000 c^{ns}*.

1599 Marche.

Another motive that hath drawen vs in to ye takinǵ of this course of a sett and standynǵ charge is some trowbles that hathe happened vs of late by reason of a demaunde made by Mr John Bate to her ma^{ies} *privy* Counsull for the paym^t of v^{cli} by a bill of exchaunge sent by Mr Barton vppon the late L Ther^r for soe muche pretended by [him] *the said Bate* to be taken [vp vppon m^r Bates fact^r] *at Constantynople* [*vppon his*] *from his factor violently by cold of her ma^{ies} comission* [to serve his turne to] *to serve the ambassadors turne to* goe wth the graund signio^r in to *the* Hungaria *warres*, [wch demaunde] vppon wch wee were convented before ther hono^{rs} divers tymes and required to take some course to see him contented because *as they affirmed* m^r Barton was placed ambassador by o^r mediation. [and of w] and for the protection of o^r trade of whose service *ther honours alledged* her ma^{ie} had no vse, but wee [examyning the the wee] lokinge into the *manner of the* growinǵ of the debt founde that the greatest part of the said v^{cli} grewe vppon an accouṁpte betwene the said m^r Barton and m^r Bate and that only 400 Cheskeens was taken vp by cōmaundem^t [whereof] *wherein* [three] *divers* others besides Mr Bate were interessted [but] [*yet*] in conclusion

1599
Marche.

wee [have absolutely] *absolutelie* denyed to pay anie part of the said vth because the Bill came not vppon the companie, and also because ther are other billes of like kinde wch the said m^r Barton gave to other pticler men for divers great somes of money that would be required to be p^d by vs yf we shuld pay m^r Bates. [But of this matter] *Of wch proceading before the Counsell* wee doe the rather geave you a tast, because vppon o^r deniall [m^r Bate] to geave satisfacc̃on. [he seemeth] *Mr Bate seemeth* to [have a] *depend vppon some course or* meane to recover his debt in Turky ether vppon Peter Gallaunt *or* John Saunderson who deliuered the money or els by some other [meanes] *extraordinarie course* wch is doubted *by some* may concerne the companie or [preiudice] touche her ma^{ie} in hono^r whereof we pray yor L. have a care and to observe that ther be noe indirecte dealinge geaven way vnto no^r [wee] her ma^{ie} or the companie touched ether in damage or reputation by [defaulte] anie default or neglecte of the cause.

Wee do verie well allowe of yor L course taken fo^r the satisfaction of the dragoman, and do thanke yo^u for yor care in the prevention of his coming hether and for all other yor carefull and painefull offices done for the good of the Companie wch wee pray yor Lo. contynue.

[*It was vndertaken be shuld accepte of.*]

[For anie other speciall Other] For anie other speciall or pticler matter we have *not* at this tyme further to inlarge vnto yor L. other then [th] onlie this main and principall point wth wch wee of purpose *reserve for a conclusion* [conclude w^{ch} *is for the better y^r L. better remembring thereof*] which is this, that *it* hath bene moved both by yor frendes and others that wee shuld geave y^r L. this frendlie note (wch to yor modest disposition *and tractable nature* is thought to be sufficient) to have a care that the hono^r of y^r place doe not carry you *into the erro^r of y^r predecess^r. to deale in thinges imptinent to y^r impleym^t* [place] *nor that yo^u* [or   *move yo^u to carrie soe highe a course to*] *beare yor selfe aloft in so highe a course as that o^r people seeme to be despised by yor L.* [and] *Nether that the authorytie of yor commission be extended or stretched to the cõmaundinge of any mans goodes further then for yor necessarie supplie*

*according to our actes and ordenaunces [and contracte] and according 1599
to ye meanes wch shalbe apointed by vs for the aunswering of y^r* Marche.
*allowaunce agreeable wth [the] o^r contracte made to her ma^{ie} or by agreem^t
made betwene yo^u and vs* [too farre *too* farre into excessive expence
for that the charge therof is to be borne by vs that are m̃chaunt^e
who have bene reproved and for pmitting *some* of o^r Ambassad^{rs}
to runne into suche insolent co^rses of [ryott] excesse and ryot *as
they have done* and have not in tyme acquainted suche of her
ma^{ies} counseill as might have repressed the extremyty thereof
and for y^t wee have *not* taken good securyty for ther better
carriage and behavio^r of ther place.]

The exceading of wch Limites by m^r Barton was imputed
vnto vs by the Ll. of the Counseill as o^r fault for that wee [for that
wee] had not taken good securyty for him for his conteyninge
him self wthin some reasonable *boundes* [Limit^e] Thus not doubting of y^r L care both of yor *owne* hono^r and of that dewe regarde
wch is to be had of vs who are willing to beare all reasonable
charge that may conveniently be required to support the same
wee comitt yor [and] Lordship and the direction of yor affaires
to God.   London this   day of Marche 1599

Yo^r L. loving frendes.

More in the seconde Leafe following in the B. side of the leafe.

These being kepte vntill the   of marche. 99 we add for
further advyse to y^r L. touching the obteyning of foresteers,
that wee were [certefyed] required by m^r Secretary that excepte
ther were the like course taken wth the frenche ambassad^r at
Constantynople to restraine him from *vsing of any meanes by
procuring or inviting* [forcyble vrging] the Dutche and other nations
foresteers to come vnder his protection that yo^u shuld not *neade
to* geave way [to yor pre] or forbeare *any [lawfull] reasonable* [anie
meanes] *course* to procure them to come vnder yor protection.
and wee do not heare of any [course] *order* that hath bene taken
to restraine the frenche ambassado^r yor competito^r therfore o^r
advyse is that you geave him no advauntage but wee leaue yo^u
to yor owne wysdome and discretion to *proceade* [prevaile] therin
[as yo^u cañ best] by the best meanes yo^u can devyse to prevayle
in yor purpose Wee send yo^u here [in] inclosed the copies of o^r

1599
Marche.

severall actes of court vnder the hande or fyrme of o^r secretary concerning the Lone of ¼ doller vppon a kersy, C of tynn, C of cony skins &c to thende that yf anie fact^r for any of the Company shall ether deny or delay [to satisfie] to pforme o^r order *therin, or in the payment of consulage* that you may sease ther goodes and levy the sommes thervppon dewe by o^r orders. And otherwyse proceade wth them for their contempte of o^r actes [as shall stande wth good discretion] and the aucthoryty of yor place as [is] shall stande wth good discretion. And so as before we comytt yo^{ur} L. to the tuytion of the most highest.

London the   of marche/

To y^e Wo: m^r Richard Colthurst Consull for y^e Right
Wo. Companie of the Levant merchaunt℮.

R o^r hartie cōmendacōns premysed &c : yor last of the 29th of September wth [th] yor former therin recyted *we have rec^d* And wher yo^u seeme discoraged [by] to accepte of a certen allowaunce *from the companie* to bearg yor charge *in Aleppo* [*of consulage*] according to the offer made yo^u of the ½ Consulage *wch discoragem^t groweth as yo^u alledge* by reason of the Dutches ther discoverie of the East Indies. Wee see not [cause] anie reason whie that shuld be any iust discoragem^t *or cause* to *move yo^u to* chaunge yor *former* opinion for that wee o^r selfes whom the care of o^r trade concerneth more then this [pticler contracte] pticler contracte may concerne you are noe way doubtfull of anie preiudice that cañ [growe] spedelie growe vnto vs by ther discoverie for ther are manie impediment℮ that may hinder [a trade of soe] ther voiages of soe longe [and great] courses and great adventures. and may move the dutche m^rchaunt℮ rather to frequent a knowen and peaceable trade in Turkey then hassard the daunger of Seas and enemyes of soe longe a circuite and infestious clymates. [And besides] *Nether it is* o^r intention [is not] to tye yo^u to any inconvenience but for o^r better satisfaction in mainteyning a knowen charge. wee wishe yo^u to

accepte of it for a yere or too or so longe as yo⁰ shall finde yo⁰ may frugallie handle the matter for yo' owne good and o' [benefites] *ease bothe* wth wee wishe to concurre or els wee would be loth to move yo" therto. Wee rather incyte yo⁰ [heretofore] *to this course* for that wee doubt not but the Ambassado' will accepte of a sett allowaunce for y' defraying *of* his charges at Constantynople. to w^ch [ende] *effecte* wee have written him. And to thende that both a competent and convenient maintenanc' may be levied to defray both *his and* yo' charges wee have ordered by acte of Courte that all shippes that come for [ye Aleppo] Allexandretta Constantynople or other the portes of Turkey besides ther consulage shall by ther goodes contynue the Lone of ½ doller vppon a kersy and the like of every C of Tynn cony skines &c. returning *for* the somes lent [by] *billes of* exchaunge at *vs* [iiij] vj^d the doller. wch consulage and Lones together wth the helpe of the consulage of foresteers, we doubte not but the same wyll defray [all] bothe yo' *severall* charges wth an overplus. and wee have geaven order to y' said ambassado' to make over vnto yo" *his* billes [of exchaunge] for 3000 c^os yerelie. *or for so much as together wth his receipts of consulage and Lone at Consta:* shall make vp 3000 ch^rms whereof we pray yo" see him supplied. The vncertenty of his paiments and acceptation of his billes at venice besides, the repaiment of those billes by exchaunge here coming many tymes vnseasonably to ye Company when *wee* [they] were vnprouided hath moved vs to take order for the bearing of o' charge w'hin the compas of the places of o' trade or chiefest residence.

Touching *the* envyous and violent courses taken by the frenche ambassad', for the obteyning of the dutche foresteers besydes the advyse wch wee re^d both from [yo" and] [*M' Lello the Ambassad^r*] the Ambassador and from yo' self wee [founde] *hadd* some *notice* [*and*] [experience] heer, for the frenche ambassad' Liedges in London [being therein instructed] *by order and instruccons* from the ffrenche king. had made a great complainte to her Ma^ie against her *highenes* Ambassado' at Constantynople and by his [importunety] complaint soe farre prevayled wth her Ma^ie that her highnes gave order to vs *by m'*

1599 Marche.

1599
Marche.

Secretaries appointem to wryte to [the Ambass] Mr Lyllo that he shuld noe further contend for the said forresteers but to leave everie foresteer nation to ther owne voluntarie choice what [consull] protection they would *accept of* ether Englishe or ffrenche. but notwthstanding for asmuche *as* to prevaile in the obteyning of these foresteers is not onlie honorable considering the contention had therabout but alsoe profitable wee have written to ye Ambassado^r *to* preserve the cawse in equall termes. wthout preiudice vntill it shall appeare what further cowrse her ma^{ie} will directe vppon information brought over by *Signio^r* Paull Pynder [by] whom [the] Mr Lyllo sendeth over [over] of purpose to acquainte her Ma^{ie} with his proceadinges, and because yor [travell] favor wth the Bashawe may make muche to the obteyning the dutche consulage. wee pray yoⁿ vse all reasonable and fitt meanes to effecte the same or to pserve the state of the cawse wthout preiudice vntill her Ma^{ies} pleasure be knowen. and yoⁿ further thereof advysed.

We pray you contynue yor care to discouer and prevent the privie traffique of o^r facto^{rs} to Marcelles. *and to all other places* vppon frenche shippes or otherwyse *whereof yo^u have re^d any suspition by any report or other probable presumption* and yf yo^u shall finde any ground of suche practyses *we desire you to* take suche a cowrse therin as yo^u shall finde expedient, for the best prevention of suche mischiefes is to stay ther begynninges wherin wee doubt not yor [discretion and] good and discreete care.

For the matters written vnto you *out of percia* concerning Sr Anthony Shurley and his proceadinges. Wee concurre wth yo^u in opinion *therein* expecting little good of ther event wishing them better successe then wee [have looke for therin] by anie probabylyty cann hitherto coniecture. wee sende you here inclosed the copie of o^r severall actes of Court [wherin wee] wherby wee have contynued the Lone of ⅓ doller vppon o^r goodes firmed vnder the hand of o^r Secretery. Not doubting but the same being well executed. All necessarie [supplies for] charge and disbursement_ę will by this meanes and by the consulage largely be supplied. And thus having no other occasion to

inlarge further at this tyme wee cōmitt you to god. London 1599
this   of marche 1599.   Marche.

To oʳ verie Lovinge frend mʳ John Saunderson..
merchaunt [at] resident at Constantynople.

Per le exchaunge.

FTER oʳ verie hartie cōmendacions wee have reᵈ yoʳ Lres of the 17 November [p the   ] wᵗʰ yoʳ former therin related and touching yoʳ opinion of oʳ tolleration of the dutche for ther peaceable traffique in Turkey wee concurre wᵗʰ you and hold it fitt to enterteyne them kindelie. [wherby] *to thend* wee might receave benefite by ther consulage, but as yoᵘ have had some experience of the frenche Ambassadoʳ his opposition against ther cōminge vnder oʳ Consullage, soe hathe it appeared here by complaint made to her maⁱᵉ by the frenche Ambassadoʳˢ liedges [hee] howe they take to hart the obteyning of the dutche nation vnder [them] ther Ambassadoʳ in Turkey wherfore vntill [Sʳ] *Signiʳ* Paull Pinder hath bene heer and that her maⁱᵉ hath bene made acquainted wᵗʰ all proceadinges   Wee knowe not what corse to advyse therein.

Yoʳ care of the supplyinge the provision *and wantes* of Mʳ Lyllo her maⁱᵉˢ Ambassadʳ wee can not but take in verie thankefull part and think [oʳ sel] the Companie beholdinge to yoᵘ therein and for firme and sufficient *order* to be geaven yoᵘ for his furnishing according as is fitt wee [have] are also carefull yet do wee not see what *other* [*more*] *or* [firmer] or better cowrse wee can take therein then by geñ'all consent and order of Court to agree [vppon a course] to charge oʳ goodes [beinge vnder his aucthoritie and comaund] *comyng into Turkey ether to Constantinople Alexandretta or els wher* to beare suche a levie as wee by our consent have imposed vppon them, and howsoever some wilfull and vnbrideled yonge heddes have for some other respectes shewed their stomakes yet the order in it self is both firme and verie sufficient to [releve] afforthe suche [meanes of

1599
Marche.

supplie] [*the suche*] *payments* as therby wee intended, and noe doubt vppon better [considered] consideration of the matter wilbe so accepted and obeyed by those who haue most hotly opposed them selfes against it.

Wee resolving vppon all good and ready meanes to supply his L. accordinge to agreem^t do finde none soe apte as the contynuaunce of the Lone of ½ doller vppon everie kersye, every Cth of Tynn and Cth of Cony skins, that come into Turkey together wth the consulage of the same goodes. And therfore have ordered that the same Lone shalbe contynued and rep^d here againe by exchaunge at [iiij^s] v^t vj^d the doller. vntyll the companie shall vppon further consideration otherwyse advyse. and to that ende wee have written to his L. to make his billes [by exchaung] vppon the consull at Aleppo for the payment of *so much as wth the receipts at Consta: shall make vp* 3000 c^{ns} p ann^t as his occasions shall [move him] *nedefully import him* not doubting but the same together wth the graund signio^r his allowaunce (the contynuaunce whereof we nothing doubt) will very lyberally defray his expences. to ye contynuaunce of wch course of chardging o^r goodes wee were the rather induced to avoyde[th] bothe yor and the ambassado^{rs} trowble in seeking credite to supplie his occasions.

As touchinge the disposing of the Galata house wherin yo^u depende vppon o^r order wee [are of] wee thinke it fytt to be sold and made away to the best comoditie and advauntage. *And* wee wishe *the same* to be done yf it might be wthout bestowing anie further chardge thervppon, but yf yo^u thinke the Ruynes thereof being not in some sorte repaired would hinder vs more *in* the sale then. [some small charge the forbearing of] a matter of some small charg thervppon bestowed would amount vnto wee referre vs to yor good consideration [therin and leave it who doe] to take suche course therein as yo^u shall thinke may best advaunce *the* [o^r] sale still holding it for o^r full resolution that the same [is] shalbe sold away.

a secretery.

And wher yo^u write that the Ambassado^r is credito^r to the Company 1000 ch^{ns} when the accoumptes are come to o^r handes and wee see howe the same doeth ryse wee shall god willing geave his L. satisfac̃on.

Wee have considered of yor motion for allowaunce [of] for yor paines in the collecting of the consulage and Lone money. and have agreed *to* allow yo^u *fyve* vppon the 1000 of all moneys by yo^u collected according to o^r orders *praying you to accepte thereof in good part* and for yor better warraunt for the collection of the lone money wee sende yo^u herewth the copie of o^r severall actes contynued for the [collection] *levyinge* thereof firmed vnder the hande of o^r secretary.

1599 Marche.

5 p m^t for the allowaunce 50 ye embassado^{re} purchase.

This being kepte vntill the   of marche 99 [and] wee vppon further consideration of the disposing of the gallata howse do chang o^r former opinion touching the sale of the same. and do pray yo^u [to] carefully to consider of the necessarie wantes of repacons thereof, and to supplie the same as frugallie and carefully as yo^u can, and then to lett out the same for the most advauntage and benefite that it may reasonably make *by yerelie rent to suche of the company as shall neade it* bothe for the discharge of the Rent *wch we pay* and the benefyte of the company *by the overplus of the Rent that it may yeld*. Reteyninge the same still in the companies handes for that [may] many of vs are of opinion that ther may [may] be vse of the same howse bothe for the company in generall and for the^r factors in pticler in respecte whereof the sale of the same is altogether to be [respected] forborne. Thus having not at this tyme any further cause to inlarge, we comit yo^u to god London this [of]   of Marche 1599.   Y^r loving frends.

To my very lovinge frend Mr Byddell preacher [preacher] at Aleppo.

ince I was chosen to the place of the Governo^r of the Companie I re^d a lre from yo^u directed to the generaltie wch I publyshed at a generall Courte and the same being read [to the geñalyty] *the company have* [*they have*] according to yor desire [they have] agreed that what money soever shall fall out dewe vnto you besides that wch yo^u have re^d shall be aunswered to m^r Cockes after the rate of 50^{li} p

1599 Marche.

anit according to yᵉ Agreement betweene the Companie and yoᵘ and yoʳ wages to begynne at Micħas 1598 and that money wᶜʰ yᵒᵘ have *already* reᵈ *to* be rated vnto yoᵘ at vˢ the doller. And touching the money impresed vnto you wᶜʰ was xˡⁱ. albeit the same was entended by the Company to be only lent *to supply yᵒʳ neceessarie provision and to be* [and] discoumpted vppon yʳ wages yet for yoʳ better incoragemᵗ and comforte in yʳ charge they are content freely to bestowe it vppon yoᵘ as [a g] ther guift and gratuyty besides yʳ enterteynment agreed vppon. Not doubting but [that] according to the good opinion they have conceaved of yoᵘ and the good report they heare of yoᵘ hetherto yoᵘ will contyneue and proceade in yoʳ charge both [to] *in* the instruccõn of oʳ people [and in the repr] in knowledg of Religyon and in reprovinğ and rebukinğ whatsoever yoᵘ shall *ether* see or be dewly informed of to [be] deserve reproof or [admonis] admonition And soe cõmendinğ yoᵘ and yoʳ charge [to god] *to almightie god* wᵗʰ my harty cõmendacõns I conclude for this tyme.

    London this of Marche 1599.

          Yʳ Loving frende/

1599 10 Marche.

AFTER our hartie commendacons. [yoᵘ shall receave] wee sende yoᵘ *by* this ship the Exchaunge the pticlers of all the goodes laden in her for the companie as *the same are* [appereth by] *collected & [the notes] taken out of the* cockettℓ *and* thentries in the Custome Howse wᶜʰ wee pray yoᵘ to compare wᵗʰ the goodes discharged [in above] and yf yoᵘ shall finde any more then are pticlerly [entred] herein noted they goe wᵗʰout warraunt or assent of the Companie [Saving only wee have graunted to Mʳ Aldⁿ Hollyday part owner of the said exchaungē for his part of the shippes stocke licence to ship to ballettℓ of 24 kersers] Soe as what soever shalbe founde above the [said] same pticlers before menčõned [and above the Invoice herewith to *you* sent and inclosed] wee wishe yoᵘ to sease it to the Companies vse reteyning the one half of the valewe to [yoʳ self] the vse of the company and the other half betweene the

Consull and y{r} self [whereof and thereof also to geave vs advyse] geaving vs advyse what yo{u} finde soe shipped contrarie to order We are further to lett yo{u} vnderstande that divers of the Companie vppon the viewe of yo{r} invoices sent vs do averre that yo{u} do not carrie an equall course therin and therfore wishe that you shuld be admonished to beare an [equall] *even* hande in the generall service of the Companie that no man have cause to charge yo{u} w{th} partiall dealing hereafter it shall suffice that we note vnto yo{u} this erro{r} founde hoping yo{u} wilbe more carefull to avoide the like hereafter. You complaine that the mariners denie to bringe the goodes from the shippes to the magasine. and wishe vs to take some co{r}se to binde them therto. It appeareth by ther chartre ptie that they are to bring the goodes in to the magasine, and that is much as wee can tye them to doe [by chi'e partie] for anie further helpe for the stowing of [them] *the goodes being brought in* that yo{u} would require *of them* We doubt not but vppon well intreating of them or some small gratification geaven them they will not refuse to pforme you anie resonable [heipe wherin yo{u} are] labo{r} therin [w{ch} is] w{ch} is to be drawne from them by kinde vsage. You shall receave according to y{r} desire 2 lanternes w{ch} wee haue sent by this ship. further we have not at this tyme to enlarge but conclude with this note of remembraunce that yo{u} do certenlie and at large certefie vs from tyme to tyme by the shippes what yo{u} receave from hence or otherwyse brought in to Scanderona and what yo{u} ship from thence respecting noe man w{th} affection. but equally expressing althinges according to the Trueth and so bidd yo{u} hartely farewell.

London this 10th of marche 1599

1599
10 Marche.

To the right honorable the LL. and others her ma{ies} most honorable priuy Counsellers.

IGHT hl. yo{r} late suppliaunt{es} the m{r}chaunt{es} trading the Seignorie of venice whose shippes were arrested for *restitution of* the late prise taken by Englishe men of warre [do] having re{d} newe advyse from venice

[that sentence is geaven ther] that the arrest not only contynueth but is senten[sed]*ced* to stand *excepte pledg or securyty be geaven wthin viij daies for restitution of so muche of the goodes taken as shall be proved to belonge to venetians,* [and in default hereof] *and besides this sentence the englishe fact^{ers} ther resident do feare the arrest both of ther persons and all the goodes vnder ther handes* [vntill order be taken. Do most humblie renewe ther humble sewte to yor LL. to have consideration of the great damage and all o^r Englyshe merchauntes and ther goodes further threatened to be imprisoned and seased vntill securyty *or pledge* be geaven for the restitution of soe muche of the goodes as *shalbe proved to belong to Venetians*] In tender consideration whereof and for the avoyding [of further daunger] bothe of the present and further daunger threatened It may please y^r LL. to graunt a sequestration of the said *ship* spoiles and debtes thereof proceading to be deposited in some indifferent hand vntill [the] triall be made to whom the [goodes] prise *ship and* goodes belong vppon advyse [whereof] *of wch yor honors order sent to venice* y^r Suppliaunt^{es} doubt not but [some] a discharge of [thes] said shippes may be procured and yor said suppliauntes shalbe bounde to y^r ho. for y^r ho: favo^r extended to them herein.

1600 Sept.

A lrē in the behaulf of Ryland administrato^r to Ed Rose late facto^r Maryne.

To the wo^r. or verie Loving frend m^r Richard Colthurst Consull for the English nation resident at Alleppo.

AFTER our verie hartie comendacons. Vppon notice of the deathe of o^r late facto^r Edwarde Rose Lr̃es of administracon were graunted out of the prerogative court of Canterbury to [one] Humfrey Rylaunce who maried the said Rose his Sister in the behaulf of her and other two Sisters wch Rylance hath ernestlie solicited vs for o^r Lr̃es to yo^u for yor assistaunce in the Collection and recovery of the state of the said Edward Rose remayning in those ptes. to thende his freindes and kindred who are by nature and the Lawes of this Realme interested therin may receave that wch belongeth vnto them. Wee therfore beinge desirous to further

so equall and iust a motion Doe hereby verie hartelie pray yo᷎ᵘ 1600
and entreat yo᷎ᵃ by all the best meanes yo᷎ᵘ can [ether] *both* by Sept.
yo᷎ʳ [advyse] aucthority and [or] advyse to be ayding and
assysting to the said humfrey [Rylandes] Rylance or his assigne
deputy or attorney wᵗʰ shall solicite yo᷎ᵘ in his behaulf to deliver
in to [the] his or her handes all suche goodes moneys and merchandizes as yo᷎ᵘ shall [know] finde [and] *or* knowe [to knowe]
to belonge to the said estate. wᶜʰ yo᷎ᵘ may by some meanes
come by. together wᵗʰ all suche *private* bookes of the said Edw
Rose as do conteyne anie Remembraunces of his private debtes
or accoumptes *beinge severed from the Accomptes of the Companie.*
And yf in [oʳ] the bookes of oʳ shippinge belonging to oʳ trade
ther appeare anie thinge that may further the receaving or
recovery *of any debte* wᶜʰ is iustlie dew vnto him wee pray
yo᷎ᵘ [further] *assist* him therin by suche notes. sending vnto vs
the said Bookes by the next convenient meanes And thus [wᵗʰ]
wee cõmitt yo᷎ᵘ to god
    London this   of September 1600
        Yʳ verie Loving frend℮/

      ⱷ⸙ⱷ

  To my *very* Loving frend mʳ Jo Saunderson. 1600
                12 Sept.
FTER my verie harty cõmendacõns. I reᵈ [of] yo᷎ʳˢ of
the 25 of may, wᵗʰ a post script of the seventh of
June wherin yo᷎ᵘ make relation that yo᷎ᵘ had written
divers Lr̃es. whereof yo᷎ᵘ have reᵈ noe aunswere. and as touching
the [the] ambassadoʳˢ provision supplied by yoʳ [meanes] meanes
and credite, and his terme therein served wee toke knowledge
thereof by oʳ Lr̃es sent by thexchaunge and therin noted the
Companies *acceptation* [*of*] [acknowledgment] of yoʳ good service.
And ther resolution of the meanes howe [the said] his Lp̃ shuld
be supplied hereafter videlt by the Lone of ½ doller vppon
[a kersey] every kersy, every Cᵗʰ of tynne &c. together wᵗʰ the
Consulage money. to wᶜʰ Lr̃es I referre myself [because wee
have advyse of the aryvall] presumyng that longe since the

1600
12 Sept.

same are come to yo' handes and o' order [touching] in that behalf *beinge* written not only in the l̄res directed to yoᵘ but in his Lpˢ l̄re and alsoe in [the] oʳ L̄re directed to the Consull of Alleppo. And as touching the outrages rapyns and robberies of oʳ englishe men of warre in the straightꝭ wee have very ernestly enforced the complaint thereof *not onlie* to [yᵉ] the L. admirall but also to all the residewe of the LL. of the Councell: so as wee doubt not but that order wilbe taken hereafter for the prevention [thereof] of those mischiefes.

The Billes of exchaunge made vppon the Company for moneys [del] taken vp for his Lpˢ vse in the factors of mʳ Leet and mʳ Salter are accepted [to yoʳ Likinge] and shalbe [discharged] *satisfyed* as conveniently *as* they may. The late troubles offered to yᵉ company to supplant vs out of oʳ trade by others who were ready to vndertake to pay to her maⁱᵉ an imposition of vˢ vjᵈ vppon every Cᵗʰ of curraunce vj duckettꝭ vppon every but of [wyne] *muskadell* vˢ vppon every barrell of oyle whereof I make no doubt [yoᵘ have had advyse] *advyse hath come to Constantynople divers waies* hath bene the cause why yoʳ expectation hath not bene aunswered by L̄res from hence for that whiles these troubles held the Company were so disturbed [that they could] and so distracted that they could not resolve [whose] howe to directe ther owne *busines* nor assure them selfes of the having of the trade. But these [troubles] stormes being overblowen. wee hope wee shalbe able to hold a better corespondency [in the] not only in the entercoʳse of oʳ L̄res and advyses but in all other thingꝭ concerning the trade and government of the Company. The said troubles hath driven vs to vndertake the trade at the yerelie ferme of 4000ˡⁱ [p añ and] to be freed of all the said impositions and to have oʳ priveledges renewed, wᶜʰ priviledges are not yet vnder the great seale. by reason whereof we can not proceade to order oʳ government as wee hereafter entende. and therfore I am to pray yoᵘ to have patience touching yoʳ demaunde of increase of consideration vntill oʳ estate be setled [and] *and* a course resolved howe the Queenes ferme and all other oʳ needful charges shalbe supported And thus for this tyme [I cease cōmitting wth] I cease cōmytting yo^u to god. London the 12 of September. 1600.

     Yo^r loving frende
       T. Smythe Go^r.

    To Mr May at Constantynople.

[S^r I cōmende me verie hartely vnto yo^u yo^u]
. After my verie harty cōmendaćōns. Whereas yo^u were enterteyned by the company to goe for Aleppo and ther to preache the worde and minister the sacramentℓ to o^r nation ther resident [in] *the exercyse whereof* [in wch ministery ther] toke not soe good effecte as I for my part and the residewe of the company could have wished it had. Soe as by the discontentem^t and disagreement betwene o^r facto^{rs} and yo^u wee were occasioned to sende m^r Beddle [to minister at Aleppo] to supply yor place entendinge that yo^u shuld have come directly for England not wthstanding contrary to o^r expectation and order yo^u have gone vp to Constantynople, and ther remained ever since, the company still expecting yor returne for England wch at lengeth they pceaving yo^u entended not hath moved them at a Generall court to geave order for yor coming home. Therfore thes are to [pray and] require yo^u that [yo^u] vppon the receipte of thys my Lre by order of the Companie to yo^u directed in that behaulf [to] *you do* prepare yor self to come for England by the next and spediest meanes that shalbe offered yo^u by shipping or other [meanes] *wyse* by land soe that the Company be not occasioned by yor stay [ther] contrary to ther order to *growe into further* [encrease] myslyke towardes yo^u And soe [wishing y] as one vnaquainted wth yo^u yet wishing yo^u well I cōmytt yo^u to god
 London this 11 of September.

1600
11 Sept.

To ye L. Ambassado^r at Constantynople.

It may please y^r [hono^r] L to be aduertysed that I re^cd y^r generall l^re of the 21 June together wth the [inclosed] copies of the frenche Ambassadors proceading^s against y^r self and o^r nation [generally] wch proceadinges wee have exhibited to *m^r secretary and the residewe of* the Ll. of her ma^es Councell who do alledge that the frenche king [in the] doeth greatly wronge her ma^ie in the translation of her l^re written vnto him concerning the [plane speeche] motion of peace wth Spaine and the appointing of the place of the Comissioners meeting, alledging that the l^re is not to that purpose but muche falsefyed, as we doubt not but yor L shalbe better advertysed by m^r Secretary hereafter whom we meane to solicyte to wryte [to y^r L.] vnto *you* the trueth of that matter, Of the outrages of o^r men of warre in the Levant seas wee had informed both the L. Admirall and the residew of the Ll. before the frenche information came to o^r handes having re^cd severall advyses thereof [by both] from Aleppo and other places in the Levant, wherin wee hope ther wilbe some redresse vsed. and wee are sewters and are in hope to obteyne some warraunt of redresse of these peines to be graunted vnto vs in o^r priviledges, wch are nowe to be renewed Whereof and of the trowbles we have lately had touching the payment of impositions vppon curraunce wyne and oyles. and howe we are drawen to pay a ferme of 4000^li p ann^i to the Queene because I presume you are certefyed thereof by other meanes I forbeare to enlarge herein. [only] Only observing this to yor L. that the great trouble charge and heavy ferme nowe being laid vppon o^r trade will drive vs assone as we have o^r priviledges confermed a newe to devyse the best remidies wee may to governe the same in good order. Whereof wee will hereafter more at large acquainte *you* [yor L.] And so for this tyme I take my leave of yor L.

London this 11 of [M] September.

To Mr Colthurst Consull at Alleppo.

1600
11 Sept.

Y^{or} Last of the 22th of January written to Mr. Staper hath bene [publyshed to the Company] *considered of and deliuered over to me* wherby you seeme contented to be lymited to a certen allowaunce to begynne [for a yere] the seconde of ffebruary for a yere. wch we doubt not vppon the proof of one yere yo^u shall haue cause to accept for a longer tyme The charges of o^r trade by reason of the late disturbaunce offered vs and the great demaunde of impositions endevored to be raysed vppon vs, wch is nowe brought to a ferme of 4000^{li} p ann' whereof (because I knowe yo^u have bene advysed and certefyed [thereof] by other meanes I refrayne to make discourse) will necessaryly vrge vs to loke to o^r meanes [wh] howe this great charg and burthen wilbe supported and therfore we are to entreat [the] y^r best advyse and likewyse the advyse of others of best experience in the trade [howe] for o^r better direction therein. The outrages rcd by englishe men of warre in the Levant seas [hathe] *have* bene related by vs *both to my L. admirall and* to the LL. of the Councell wherin wee are promysed a course of redresse. Our priviledges being to be renewed vnder the Great Seale [and] wch is not yet done [maketh vs] will geave vs occasion and good warraunt when they are confirmed to advyse of some good courses of government howe o^r trade shalbe better guided *both heare and in Turkye* [and o^r great payment and charges defrayed] vntyll wch tyme we can *not* resolve of such advyse and directions as shalbe necessary for vs to consider of and to putt in execution. Therfore I will forbeare to enlarge any further at this tyme [but] *vntill some better opportunety* and so wth my very harty comendacōns comytt yo^u to god. London this 11th of September.

INDEX.

BBOTT, Maurice, assembly, 59; will bring in his money, 63; creditor, £100, p. 127; auditor, 218; bill of adventure sealed, £240, p. 256.
Accounts, *see also Bookkeeper, Auditors, Warrants.* Mr. Allabaster or Julinus Beamish appointed accountant, 25; Mr. Allabaster will supervise the accounts, 41; order for all pursers to bring in accounts, 97; several committees to clear accounts with creditors, 127; treasurer's accounts to be made up and audited, 156; all creditors to make up their accounts, 159; Mr. Howe and Mr. Combe to bring in their West Country accounts, 172; the general accounts to be audited, 172; arbitrators to settle Mr. Adye's timber account, 173; Thomas Stephens, book-keeper, 210; pursers in the North West voyage to keep accounts of all goods laden and how disposed of, 212-3.
Acts of Court of the Levant Co. for levies on goods entering Turkish ports to support the charges of the ambassador and consuls, 270, 272, 275.
Adderley, ⎫ William, adventurer with Thomas
Adderly,   ⎬ Henshawe, £300, p. 2; Mr. Hen-
Addersley, ⎭ shaw will pay, 63; bill of adventure sealed, £240, p. 251.
Admiral, *term as applied to the principal ship,* "*The Red Dragon,*" 136.
Admiral, *see Lord Admiral.*
Admiralty, Court of, damage done by the anchor of the Red Dragon, 128.
Admiralty, Sergeant of the, 141.
Adventures, ⎫
Adventurers, ⎬ *see also East India Co.*
List of, and amounts subscribed, 1-4; no ship or commodities to be received as portions of adventures, 6; factors and officers to be elected by a general assembly, 6; adventures to be paid in two instalments; not less than £200 admitted; levy of 12d. per £100 for petty expenses, 7; directors chosen with power to use the help of any adventurer when required, 12; order for adventure money to be brought in by the end of September, 1600, 15; the venture proves larger than expected, 27; probable withdrawal of many adventurers if gentlemen are employed, 28; no one to be refused who will adventure £200 until £55,000 is reached, 45; instructions for persons in the West Country desiring to adventure, 53-4; delay in bringing in adventure money, 60; adventurers attempting to withdraw to be certified to the Privy Council, 61; those in arrears to answer before the Privy Council, 62; names of persons wishing to withdraw, and their reasons, 62; names of those in arrears who promise to pay, 63; Robert Cobbe in arrears deposits security of bonds, 67; every mariner to receive two months' pay in adventures as his stock, 70; the amount of adventure given to the factors, 81; persons who refuse to pay to be called on for their reasons, that some course may be taken before engrossing the patent, 85; arrears to be paid in a week and defaulters to be held chargeable for damage, 93; committee to audit the treasurer's accounts in view of an increase of the general adventure if necessary, 107; adventurers not mentioned in the patent to be deemed equally as free as those named, 109; their names to be presented at the next court and then confirmed as freemen, 110; the adventure subscribed falls short £4,000 or £5,000 of what is necessary considering the great preparations of the Dutch: but as some have not paid and others will not pay as much as at first subscribed, the total falls short eight or nine thousand pounds of what is necessary to "make a good voyage;" deliberations to supply this want; levy of 2s. in the £ on all adventures agreed to; if the amount be raised by voluntary increase of stock the overplus of the levy to be proportionately restored; complaint to be made to the Privy Council of all who have disappointed the preparation of the voyage by their default, 110; the levy to be paid in six days on pain of forfeiture of double the value, but all those voluntarily increasing their stock to be exempt from the levy, 111; committee to wait on the Privy Council with complaint of the defaulters, 111; order in council for the defaulters to pay at once on pain of imprisonment, 112-3; the levy of 2s. in the £ confirmed, 113; every adventurer to have a bill of adventure under the common seal of the company, 113; committee to go to the Court with list of defaulters, &c., 115; an act touching the pay-

Adventurers, *continued*.
ment of the supplies of 21. in the £ and penalties for default, 137-8; two forms of bills of adventure read, 144-6; bills of adventure sealed, 152, &c., *see Bills of Adventure*; the state of the adventure on March 6, 1600, showing the amount not yet brought in, 156; order for a new supply of 21. in the £ with penalties by reduction of stock in default, 160-1; £9,000 set down not yet brought in, 160; Earl Cumberland assigns £200 stock to William Beerblock, 161; Mr. Megges's adventure in arrears, 162; order in council touching the adventures in arrears and ordering all defaulters to appear and be punished for contempt, 165; warrant for the summoning of those who have not paid, 169-70; list of defaulters, 170; defaulters committed, 170-1; John Bate assigns to John Jackson, 174; William Smyth refused his freedom for £105 and ordered to pay up the balance, 174; Mr. Hamersley and Mr. Milward bring in their adventures, 175; Mr. Dent named in the patent desiring to assign, is referred to a general court, 175; his assignment allowed, 177; bills of adventure to be delivered to all who have paid up in full, and 6*d*. to be paid for the same, 175; Richard Tailby agrees to pay £73 6s. 8*d*. to Mr. Atye, and £100 to the Muscovia Co. in part of his adventure, 176; the liability for the supplies due on Earl Cumberland's assigned stock, 177; all those in arrears to be prosecuted, 178; certain defaulters disfranchised, 178; John Ellicott ordered to pay up his supplies, 181; Robert Bayly assigns £200 stock to Sir John Spencer for £180, and Sir John to nominate a freeman, 181; voluntary levy of 12*d*. in the £ for the North West voyage, and when to be paid, 183; Mr. Governor to peruse the charter to see if power is given to enforce payments for the North West voyage or a second voyage by the Cape, 183; a book to be sent round for adventurers to subscribe for the North West voyage at 12*d*. in the £ on their original stock, 185; Nathaniel Martin disfranchised, and John Morice made free in his place, 185; a second voyage by the Cape resolved on, adventure not less than £100, 186; a book to be sent round for the freemen to subscribe, 187; Joseph Jackson made free on the nomination of Sir John Spencer, 187 (*see* 181); deliberations with the Muscovia Co. as to the respective rights to discover and use the North West Passage, 187-9, *see North West Passage*; adventure subscribed for the second Cape voyage insufficient (£11,000), 189; the book sent round again by men able to persuade and encourage the brethren to adventure, 190; Xpofer Cletherow disfranchised and Robert Bawyer admitted in his place, 190; stock of Clement Moseley deceased to be assigned to his wife on payment of £20 supplies in arrears, 193; £230 stock assigned to Mr. Holliday by Earl Cumberland, 197; dislike to the transportation of coin out of the country, 198; hopes of obviating this by the discovery of a North West passage, 198-9; laws and ordinances for general business and for the proposed voyage to the North West, showing amount of adventure to be raised, &c., &c., 198-202. *see East India Co.;* William Nelson admitted a freeman on paying £240 and £30 premium, 205; committee to persuade those who have not done so to pay their contributions for the North West voyage, 205; state of the North West voyage, and steps taken to encourage adventures by making every man's contributions become part of his original stock for the Cape voyage, and to bear profit accordingly, 206-8, *see East India Co.;* auditors appointed to ascertain the state of the North West adventure that further supplies may be called up and some course taken with defaulters, 217-8; day appointed for payment of voluntary supplies for the North West voyage; the rateable and voluntary supplies to be endorsed on the bills of adventure, and new bills made out shewing in one sum what is each man's interest in the voyage by the Cape, 220 (*see* 206-8); the book-keeper to enter up each adventurer's credits in a lump sum, 224; Mr. Holliday and others being in arrears with supplies for the North West voyage, it is ordered that the sums be defaulted from their stock for the voyage by the Cape, 231 (*see* 200 and 207); the book-keeper to charge up the accounts of all brethren debtors to the Co. that the amounts due may be defaulted on their stock if not paid before the return of the ships, 233; Stephen Hodson pays up £10 supplies, 235; the governor and deputy empowered to appoint any adventurer to perform any service which general business requireth, 249; list of bills of adventure sealed, with their dates and amounts, 250, *see also Bills of Adventure*; the state of the adventure, 263.

Ady } John, delay with timber at Woolwich,
Adye } 46; warrant £100 for timber, 114; committee to determine the reckoning for timber, 155; the account referred to arbitration, 173.

Africa, coast of, route to the East Indies by the Cape, 211.

Agreements, with Captain Davis, 37; with Captain Waymouth for the North West voyage, 211-4, 217; with John Cartwright, preacher, for the North West voyage, 216.

Albany, William, made free though not named in the patent, 177; bill of adventure sealed, £240, p. 258.

Aldermen adventurers, *see* Nicholas Mosley; Paul Bannyng; Leonard Holliday; Richard Goddard; John Moore; Edward Hownden; Roharte Hampson; Roharte Lee; Thomas Cambell; John Swinerton; John Wattes.

Aldeworth } Richard, adventurer, £200, p. 2;
Aldworth } assembly, 4.

Aleppo, Mr. Colthurst, consul, 265, *see Colthurst;* levy on certain goods entering, to support consuls' allowance, 267; letter of instructions to Mr. Colthurst, 270-2, *see Company of Levant merchants;* letter to Mr. Byddell, preacher, 275-6, *see Company of Levant merchants*.

Alexandretta, levy on certain goods entering, to maintain the charges of ambassador and consuls, 271, 273.

Allabaster, Thomas, assemblies, 22, 31, 39, 66, 77, 78, 80, 88; committees, 12, 26, 28, 32, 40, 58, 71, 72, 73, 77, 91, 124; general committee or directors, 63, 179; appointed accountan., 25; respecting the accounts, 41; order to provide moneys at Calais, 41; do. at Calais and Rouen, 58; warrant £500 for royals, 68; do. £500, p. 82; do. £500, p. 91; do. £500, p. 95; do. £700, p. 106; the conveyance of bullion from Calais, 84; commission

Allabaster, Thomas, *continued*.
for the provision of royals continued, 91 ;
order to provide no more royals, 102 ; several
warrants entered, 111 ; receives Norromborough ware, 138 ; bill of adventure sealed,
£240, p. 256.

Allen, Gregorie ; bill of adventure sealed, £240,
p. 258.

Allen, Raphe ; bill of adventure with William
Starkey, £400, sealed, 149 ; bill of adventure
£200, sealed, 261.

Allen, William, *mercer*, adventurer with
Richard Barrett, £200, p. 3 ; bill of adventure
sealed, £200, p. 149 ; made free, though not
named in the patent, 177 ; bill of adventure
sealed, £200, p. 260.

Allom, William, *lighterman*, order to be paid
£10 for lighterage, 173.

Allyn, George, admitted as an extra factor,
102.

Allyn, William, *see Allen*.

Altham, Mr., reads draft of the patent, 25.

Ambassadors, *see also Company of Levant
merchants*; letters from the Levant Co., to
Mr. Lyllo, English ambassador at Constantinople, 265, 282 ; rivalry with the French ambassador as to consulage, &c., 265-6, 269,
271-2 ; Mr Lyllo's allowance. 266-7, 271 ; the
late Mr. Barton was placed ambassador at the
request of the Levant Co., 267 ; credit supplied to Mr. Lyllo by Mr. Saunderson, 273,
279.

America, *see also North West Passage*; the
objects of the attempt to discover a North
West Passage through some part of America,
198, 199 ; the North West Passage supposed
to lead to "Cataya or China or ye backside
of America," 212 ; Captain George Waymouth's confidence in the discovery of a
passage to the South seas by divers inlets that
treat through the coast of America, 232.

Amounts of original adventures and names, 1-4 ;
total, 4.

Anchors, damage done to a ship by the anchor
of the "Scourge," 125, 128 ; warrant,
£30 10s., for two for the "Hector," 151 ; left
behind, 159 ; for the "Discovery," 210.

Ancients, streamers and flags ordered, 108,
149.

Aneys, Henry, *see Annis*.

Angell, William, assembly, 59 ; warrant, £50,
for fish, 92 ; to clear accounts with Mr. Holliday, 127 ; to bring in his account, 159 ; bill
of adventure sealed £240, p. 250.

Angells, *coin*, 106.

Annis, Henry, nominated factor, 77 ; recommended by the Lord Treasurer to be employed, 85.

Anthonie, Charles, order to be paid £29 10s.
for stamps for the East India money, 174.

Anys, *see Annis*.

Apsome, a place recommended for the purchase
of bisket, 48 ; do. cider, 49.

Aquavitae, 3½ tonne of caske required for, 30 ;
quantity for each ship, 35 ; committee to provide, 75 ; do. caske, 76 ; warrant £96 8s. for
482 gallons at 4s., p. 107 ; do. £30, p. 143 ;
committee to provide for the North West
voyage, 209.

Arbitration, price of the "Mare Scourge," 32 ;
Mr. Adye's account for timber, 173 ; Waymouth's demands for charges, &c. referred,
240.

Archbishop of Canterbury, *Privy Council*;
order in council, 164.

Archer, Henry, assembly, 60 ; bill of adventure
sealed, £240, p. 259.

Armitage, Samuel, assembly, 59 ; bill of adventure sealed, £240, p. 252.

Arms of the Company assigned by the king of
heralds, 171.

Assention, ship, tonnage, 260 ; 80 men ; Roger
Hankin, *master*; William Brand, *principal
factor*; Edward Highlord, *purser*; Christopher Newchurch, *surgeon*; Thomas Salterne,
second factor; Roger Style, *third factor*;
Philip Winchecomb, *fourth factor*. Viewed,
13 ; surveyors appointed, 14 ; inventory, 16,
22 ; William Leake, *purser*, guaranteed by
Mr. Garway, 33 ; rated 80 men, tonnage 260,
34 ; aquavitae, 35 ; warrant 100 markes on
account of repairs, 57 ; to be manned with 80
men, 72 ; warrant £200 on account of preparations, 85 ; the number of carpenters, caulkers,
gunners, stewards, cooks, surgeons and barbers to be employed, 89-90 ; warrant £100
for her provision, 91 ; William Brand to sail
as a principal factor, 94 ; ballast, 97 ; warrant
£20 to Christopher Newchurch, surgeon, for
furnishing his medicine chest, 98 ; warrant
£100 for repairs and preparations, 99 ;
officers appointed, 100 ; factors appointed,
101 ; warrant £100 for smithery, 104 ; do.
£100 to Mr. Garway, 105 ; do. £100 for timber, 114 ; do. £150 towards repairs, 114 ;
warrant to Robert Rickman, £133 6s. 8d., in
full payment of his 6th part of the ship, 115 ;
do. £333 6s. 8d. to William Skidmore, in full
of his sixth part, 117 ; committee to provide
stores, 117 ; warrant £150 to William Leake
for men's wages, 117 ; the amount of new
and Spanish money apportioned to be carried
and how packed, 122 ; warrant £100 to the
purser for necessaries, 126 ; do. £100 to Mr.
Garway for her provision, 140 ; do. £50 for
clearing away, 144 ; list of presents carried,
151 ; warrant £100 for wages and clearing
away, 154 ; do. £161 13s. 1d. for nails and
iron work, 157 ; do. £6 10s. for porterage
and lading, 158 ; ship's boat at Blackwall
ordered to be sold, 159 ; warrant £42 15s. for
canvas, 168 ; do. £22 4s for chandler's provisions, 169 ; do. £16 16s. 11d. for timber, &c.,
180 ; letters from Roger Style, *factor*, and
Edward Highlord, *purser*, brought home by
a Frenchman, 242 ; letters sent to the West
Country to the factors and officers, saying the
merchants of Plymouth and Dartmouth have
been instructed to attend to the sick and give
credit for the use of the ship : orders not to
break bulk or make sale of anything belonging to the general adventure, 243 ; arrival in
the river, 243 ; warehouses suitable for the
receipt of goods, 244-5 ; several committees
to attend on board in turns whilst unloading,
245-6 ; no mariner or other person to carry
anything from the ship "unless it be visited,"
on pain of detention of wages, 245 ; Mr.
Style and the purser to attend on board till
ship is discharged, 246 ; tithes due to the
Lord Admiral for a prize taken, 246-7 ; bags
to be made for the pepper, also suits without
pockets for the porters employed, 247 ; entry
to be made at the Custom House and list
of goods, 247 ; warrant £5 to Mr. Midleton
for riding with the first report of the return,
247 ; Mr. Governor and Mr. Eldred give
bond for the customs due to the king, 247 ; warrant £6 for pilotage into the river, 248 ; the
customs amount to £917 and Mr. Cambell

Assention, *continued*.
 and Mr. Eldred to be indemnified for their bonds given for payment of the same, 248; money to be taken up at interest for payment of mariners' wages, 249; memorandum, tonnage, 260; men, 80, p. 263.
Assignments of adventures and stock, Earl of Cumberland to Mr. Beerblock, 161; John Bate to John Jackson, 174; Francis Dent to George Bennet, 175, 177; Earl of Cumberland to Mr. Bannyng, 177; Robert Bayly to Sir John Spencer, 181; Nathaniel Martin to John Morice, 185; Xpofer Cletherow to Robert Bowyer, 190; Clement Moseley to Edward Helmes and John Moseley, and re-assignment to Elizabeth Moseley at a premium, 193; Earl of Cumberland to Alderman Holliday, 197.
Atterney, the Queen's; the patent of the Co., 88, 91; warrant £71 13s. 4d. for charges in drawing and engrossing the patent, 96.
Atye, John, *see Ady*.
Auditors, } Purser's accounts, 99; treasurer's
Audits, } accounts, 107, 136, 166; various trade accounts, 127, 146, 147, 148; accounts of the purser of the "Red Dragon," 147; Mr. Howe's and Mr. Combe's West Country accounts, 172; the general accounts, 172; power to inflict fines for delay in the payment of adventures, 201; Thomas Verworth's accounts, 214; the accounts of the North West voyage, 217, 220.
Axmouth, a fit place to buy cider, 49.

Babbington, Vrye, adventurer, £200, p. 3; assembly, 5.
Babington, Edwyn, warrant £100 for Canary wine, 95; do. £160, p. 103.
Babington, Richard, recommended as a purser, 39.
Backhouse, Rowland, adventurer with Bartholomew and Edward Barnes, £400, p. 3; bill of adventure sealed, £240, p. 254.
Backhouse, Samuel, bill of adventure sealed £240, p. 257.
Backhouse, Thomas, assembly, 5.
Bacon, William, warrant £16 0s. 10d. for masts, 157.
Baese, *see Basse*.
Bags, Polldavies to be bought and made up in the West Country, 86; biskett bags, 222; for pepper brought home, 247.
Baker, Captain Thomas; committee, 68; sent to join Captain Davis in the West Country to purchase provisions, &c., 29; commission for the provision of victuals, 38, 41; ordered to send up the ship's boat of the "Malice Scurge" from Plymouth, 40; commission for provisions altered, 46; commission for provisions, &c., 48-54; second commission, 54; money at Plymouth, 64; letter of advice as to money, &c., 64; letter sent to, 66; bills of exchange, 47, 68, 69, 80; letter from, 74; order to provide no more bread, &c., 88.
Bakers, *see Joseph Page*.
Ball, Richard, assembly, 59; bill of adventure sealed, £240, p. 253.
Ball, Thomas, made free though not named in the patent, 177; bill of adventure sealed, £240, p. 258.
Ballast, warrant £38 0s. 4d. for ballast and freight of two hoyes, 97; warrant £6 13s. 4d. for ballast, 121.
Bandicott, Austyn, *butcher*; warrant £44 18s. for pork, 208.

Baning, }
Baninge, } *see Bannyng.*
Banninge, }
Bannyng, Andrew, assembly, 60; warrant £213 6s. 8d. for oil, 111; bill of adventure sealed, £240, p. 254.
Bannyng, Paul, Alderman, adventurer £1,000, p. 1; assemblies, 4, 14, 20, 22, 26, 27, 28, 31, 33, 37, 39, 44, 45, 46, 47, 56, 57, 58, 64, 65, 67, 68, 69, 71, 73, 74, 76, 78, 79, 80, 82, 91, 107, 109, 113, 119, 121, 122, 123, 125, 128, 167, 168, 170, 171, 172, 175, 176, 183, 248; committees, 12, 26, 31, 37, 38, 40, 57, 58, 63, 67, 68, 71, 72, 73, 75, 76, 77, 80, 99, 114, 234; committees, per his coachman, Robert Barker, 245, 246; warrants paid as treasurer, *see warrants*; views ships, 13; sells the "Susan" on certain terms, 13; surveyor for the "Susan," 14; to treat for the "Cherubim," 15; guarantees Joseph Salmon as purser of the "Susan," 33; compounds for iron, 41; bills from the West Country, 50; signature to West Country commissions, 52, 54, 55; letter respecting Spanish money, 66; a mast for the "Hector," 71; to buy ling, 75; to buy oatmeal, 75; sale of the "Susan" made absolute, 120; required to pay £200 set down for Jeffrey Kerby, 126; entreated to raise £1,500 with Alderman Holliday on their credits, 146; to render accounts, 156; to be called on to bring in his account, 159; to be indemnified for the £1,500 raised at interest, 161; to deliver bills of adventure to all adventurers and to receive 6d. for each for the secretary, 175; the supplies due on £570 stock assigned to him by Earl Cumberland, 177; general committee and sworn, 179; order to be paid £4 7s. 5d. for disbursements, 203; requested to give his bond with Mr. Wattes for £1,000 as security for money to be raised at interest on the return of the "Assention," 249.
Barbar } Thomas, warrants for canvas £200,
Barber } p. 114; £100, p. 163; £200, p. 167; £309, p. 172; £143, p. 220; bill of adventure £240, p. 254.
Barbers, one to be carried in each ship, 90.
Barber, George, warrant £27 5s. 0d. for sails for the "Susan," 167.
Barber, Thomas, *see Barbar*.
Baricoes } eight dozen iron hooped required,
Baricos } 30; committee to provide, 76; do. for the North West Voyage, 209.
Barker, Edward, bill of adventure sealed, £300, p. 252.
Barker, Frauncis, assembly, 60; bill of adventure sealed, £240, p. 252.
Barker, Robert, *Alderman Bannyng's coachman*, committees, 245, 246.
Barkham, Edward, bill of adventure sealed, £240, 257.
Barks for the North West Voyage, *see ships, pinnaces, also "Godspeed" and "Discovery."*
Barley, Robert, adventurer with Thomas Haies and Mathew Hamoud, £300, p. 3.
Barme, Francis, elected one of the principal factors, 81.
Barmesly, *see Barnesley*.
Barnes, Bartholomew, adventurer with Rowland Backhouse and Edward Barnes, £400, p. 3; bill of adventure sealed, £240, p. 254.
Barnes, Edward, adventurer with Rowland Backhouse and Bartholomew Barnes, £400, p. 3.
Barnes, Francis, nominated factor, 77.

Barnes, The Lady, her house nominated as a suitable warehouse for goods brought home in the Assention, 245.

Barnesley, Nicholas, *grocer*, adventurer, £150, p. 2 ; assembly, 60 ; bill of adventure sealed, £240, p. 254.

Barrell, William, adventurer with Walter Porter, £400, p. 4 ; warrant to bring in his adventure at once, 170.

Barrels, *see Casks.*

Barrett, Richard, adventurer with William Allen, £200, p. 3 ; bill of adventure sealed, £240, p. 257.

Barrett, William, *see Barrell.*

Barrey, Gyles, bill of exchange, £40, p. 104.

Barrycods, *see Baricoes.*

Barton, Mr., late ambassador at Constantinople, 266 ; his bills of exchange on the Levant Co. in favour of Mr. Bate repudiated, and the accounts investigated, 267 ; appointed ambassador at the Levant Company's request, 267 ; remarks on his conduct, 269.

Bashaw of Turkey, 272.

Basse, Humfrey, assemblies, 226, 238, 242, 244, 247 ; auditor, 218 ; general committee and sworn, 226 ; bill of adventure sealed, £240, p. 252.

Bate, John, assemblies, 24, 31, 37, 39, 59 ; committee, 12 ; views ships, 13 ; signature to West Country commission, 52 ; declines to adventure and reason why, 62 ; warrant to bring in his adventure at once, 170 ; commitment warrant for non payment, 171 ; disfranchised and John Jackson admitted in his place, 174 ; bills of exchange drawn on the Levant Co. in his favour by Mr. Barton, repudiated, 267 ; the accounts investigated, 267 ; proposed course to recover his money, 268.

Bateman, Robert, adventurer with Thomas and Robert Midleton, £500, p. 2 ; assembly, 59 ; committee, 243 ; bill of adventure sealed, £240, p. 253.

Baylie, Robert, ? see Barley ; assigns his £200

Bayly (adventure to Sir John Spencer for £180, p. 181 ; bill of adventure sealed, £240, p. 259.

Baysah, 209, 219.

Beadle of the company, *see Thomas Evettsett*, salary £10, augmented to £12, p. 204 ; reappointed, 226.

Beale, Richard, assembly, 60.

Beamish, Julius, appointed accountant, 25.

Beans, 50 quarters required, 29 ; 30 tonne of dry caske required, 30 ; 20 quarters to be bought, 33 ; estimate of quantity and price, 34 ; price in the West Country to be ascertained, 49 ; 30 quarters ordered, 65 ; Lord Treasurer's warrant for the provision of peas and beans and transport from Cambridge and Norfolk, 66 ; committee to provide, 75 ; do. caske for, 70 ; warrant £100 for peas and beans, 82 ; do. £100, p. 96

Beare, Mr., to be conferred with as one of the chief masters, 90.

Beddle, Mr., *see Byddell.*

Beef, 26 ; 30 tonne of caske (hogsheads) required, 30 ; estimate of quantity and price, 34 ; committee for ordering, 68, 75 ; do. caske, 70 ; 120 oxen to be provided for making salt meat, 114 ; committee to provide for the North West voyage, 209 ; warrant £111 5s. for beef and pork for the North West voyage, 214 ; order for the sale of beef brought back from the North West voyage, 230.

Beer, 26 ; 170 tonne of caske (pipes) required, 30 ; estimate of quantity and price, 34 ; a barrel a day allowed to the workmen on the " Mare Scourge " to prevent their running from their work to the alehouse, 40 ; 240 tuns of beer ordered, 67 ; committee to provide, 75 ; do. caske : warrant £15 7s. for 59 barrels for the " Scourge," 154 ; [do. £200 on account], 155 ; do. £500, p. 171 ; do. £19 2s. 4d., 193 ; committee to provide for the North West voyage, 209 ; warrant £120 3s., 221 ; beer brought back from the North West voyage to be sold, 230.

Beerblock, William, *Goldsmith* ; £200 stork assigned to him by Earl Cumberland, 161 ; increases his adventure to £250, 162.

Beeston, Hughe, mortgagee of land belonging to Mr. Brodebent, Master of the " Red Dragon," 128.

Bell, Richard, bill of adventure sealed, £240, p. 253.

Bell, Robarte, adventurer with John Potter, £200, p. 3 ; assemblies, 5, 59, 64, 65, 67, 68, 78, 79, 80, 82, 83, 85, 89, 92, 93, 94, 95, 107, 108, 117, 118, 123, 125, 127, 139, 144, 168, 170, 175 ; committees, 67, 75, 76, 79, 86, 147, 191 ; surveyor of the " Mare Scourge," 33 ; General committee, 67 ; buys meal, 90 ; warrant £30 10s. for paper, 126 ; buys pewter, 127, ; warrant £13 3s. 2d. for wharfage, &c., 203 ; auditor, 218 ; bill of adventure sealed, £240, p. 258.

Bennett, George, *Salter* ; desires to become adventurer in lieu of Francis Dent, 175 ; the assignment assented to, 177 ; committee, 245 ; bill of adventure sealed, £240, p. 257.

Bennett, Widow Elizabeth, warrant £100 for iron, 119 ; do. £90 for nails, &c., 172.

Billett, Thomas, of Poole, bill of exchange, £200, p. 129.

Bills of Adventure, *see also Adventures.* Every adventurer to have a bill under the common seal, 113 ; Philip Grove to have a bill for the composition made with him, 139 ; two forms of bills read for factors and adventurers, 144-6 ; bills of adventure sealed, 148, 149, 150, 152, 153, 159, 250-262 ; bills to be delivered to all who have cleared accounts and 6d. each to be charged for the Secretary, 175 ; the contributions for the North West voyage to be endorsed on the bills, 207 ; new bills to be made out in a lump sum, 224.

Bills of exchange, *see Warrants*, instructions for drawing, &c., 50, 53 ; the Levant Co.'s desire to avoid bills from the ambassador at Constantinople, 266-7, 271 ; the trouble growing out of the bills drawn by the late Mr. Barton, 267-8 ; Mr. Saunderson's bills accepted, 280.

Bisket, *see Bread*, the provision of in the West Country, 21.

Bisket bags, 222.

Black Jacks, 105.

Blacksmiths, *see also Smiths*, Lewys Tyght, Lewis Tate, Richard Hall.

Blackwall, 159.

Boales, George, *see Bowles.*

Bourne, Thomas, *Steward of the " Godspeed,"* warrant £3 for wages for the North West voyage, 214 ; do. 20s. to his wife in full of all demands, 230.

Boats, *see also Ships, Pinnaces, Barks* ; the boat of the " Mare Scourge " ordered up from Plymouth, 40 ; new boat ordered, 46 ; the boat at

Boats, *continued*.
Plymouth to be inspected, 51; warrant, £100 for boats, &c., 115; the "Assention's" boat lying at Blackwall to be sold, 159; the two vessels for the North West voyage described as "flyboats," 220; warrant £13 for timber and a boat, 221; warrant £5 10s. for a boat for the "Discovery," 223; do. 46s. 8d. for boat hire, 224.
Bolles, George, *see Bowles*.
Bolton, appointed sailmaker to the "Mare Scourge," 40.
Bona Speransa, cape of, *see Cape*.
Bond William, *merchant taylor*, adventurer
Bonde with William Harrison, £200, p. 3; assembly, 59; bill of adventure sealed, £240, p. 252.
Bonds, *see also Guarantees, Security;* all factors to give bonds for their good behaviour, 105; amounts of the bonds for the factors, 105; Mr. Bannyng and Mr. Holliday indemnified for £1,500 borrowed on their credit, 161 (*see* 146); Richard Tailboy, adventurer in arrears, gives bond for £200 to the agent of the Muscovia Co., 176; Thomas Yerworth, purser, to give bond in 100 marks for his good behaviour, 205; Edward Pullison, do. do. 216-17; general bond to James Cambell in £200 to hold his father harmless against his covenant to pay the wages of John Drew, a master in the North West voyage, 220; the bond sealed, 221; Mr. Cambell and Mr. Eldred give their bonds for the payment of customs dues, 247; money to be taken up at interest on the bonds of Sir John Harte and others, 249; Mr. Cambell and Mr. Eldred to be indemnified by general bonds under the common seal, 248-9 (*see* 247); obligations of £3,000 each sealed to them, 249-50; obligations of 1,000 marks each, to Sir John Hart and Mr. Chamberlain, 250.
Bonham, William, bill of adventure sealed, £240, p. 251.
Bookkeeper, Thomas Stephens, *see also Accounts;* to charge all defaults in supplies against the stock, 161; to draw up the West Country accounts, 173; Thomas Stephens appointed, salary £30, p. 210; order to enter up each adventurer's credits in a lump sum, 224; Thomas Stephens re-appointed, 226; order to charge up the accounts of all brethren who are debtors to the Co., that such amounts may be defaulted from their stock if not paid before the return of the ship, 233; warrant for salary, 235; admitted a freeman, 239; to make tickets for the carmen removing the "Assention's" goods to the Exchange, 248.
Book of the adventurers in the North West voyage, 185.
Book of the adventurers in the second voyage by the Cape, 186-7, 190.
Book of the "Flemyng's" voyage, 125.
Booles, George, *see Bowles*.
Bootheby, Thomas, bill of adventure sealed, £240, p. 251.
Bostocke, Thomas, adventurer with John Ramridge, £200, p. 3; assembly, 5; surveyor for the "Assention," 14; bill of adventure sealed, £240, p. 255.
Boules, George, *see Bowles*.
Bover, James, warrant £24 19s. for spectacles, &c., 155.
Bowdeler, Richard, appointed auditor, 166; made free, though not named in the patent, 177; bill of adventure sealed, £240, p. 259.

Bowden, John, warrant £40 for sails, 168.
Bowen, John, warrant £6 for rent of Founder's Hall for the Company's meetings, 227.
Bowles, George, assemblies, 226, 227, 229, 230, 231, 232, 233, 235, 236, 241, 242, 244, 247, 248, 249; committees, 247, 248; warrant £46 17s. for Curraunce, 168; general committee and sworn, 225; bill of adventure sealed, £300, p. 256.
Bowles, Thomas, warrant to be paid £30 on a bill of exchange, 69.
Bowrne, Thomas, *see Bearne*.
Bowyer, Robert, warrant to bring in his adventure at once, 170; committment warrant for non payment, 171; disfranchised, and Christopher Cletherow admitted in his place, £240, p. 190.
Bradbanck, William, *see Brodebent*.
Bradbury, Robert, warrant £86 15s. 4d. for sails, 168.
Bradley, —, warrant £6 13s. 4d. for ballast, 121.
Bradshawe, Elias, employed at £10 a year, 263.
Bramley, Thomas, assemblies, 240, 241, 244, 247, 248, 249; elected Deputy Governor, 239; committee, 245; bill of adventure sealed, £240, p. 252.
Brand, William, *see Brunde*.
Branding iron for the shipping mark, 107.
Branskom, John, warrant 46s. 8d. for wages in the North West voyage, 234.
Brasiers: John Maxfield, 164.
Brass pots, 222.
Bread and biskett, estimate to be drawn up, 26; to be bought at Dartmouth and Plymouth, 29; estimate of quantity and price, 34; revised estimate, 46, 54-5; quantity to be bought in the West Country, 41, 52; quality, and how to be packed, 48; bakers to guarantee bread to keep sweet two years, 51; quantity ordered to carry the ships to the West Country, 67; committee to provide in London, 75; order for no more to be bought, 88; warrant £50, p. 157; do. £45 10s. 11d. p. 167; committee to provide for the North West voyage, 209; warrant £60, p. 215; do. £41 8s., p. 222.
Breeches. 118, 208.
Brende, William, *see Brunde*.
Brett, William, warrant £16 16s. 11d. for timber, 180.
Brewers, { Abraham Campion.
          { Anthonie Duffeilde.
Bridgehouse, 89.
Bridgeman, Henrye, *leatherseller,* adventurer, £200, p. 4; assembly, 59; bill of adventure, sealed, £240, p. 252.
Bridgewater, 73.
Brimstone, 142.
Broadbent, *see Brodebent*.
Brocke, *see Brooke*.
Brodebent, William, *Master of the "Red Dragon,"* a fit man to take charge in the voyage, 44; appointed to sail in the "Mare Scourge," 90, 100; order to be paid £100 on account, 104; is lent £100 on mortgage, 128; bill of adventure sealed in special terms, 153; repayment of his mortgage, 153.
Brooke, Roberte, adventurer with Augustine Skynner and Thomas Westray, £300, p. 3; bill of adventure sealed, £240, p. 259.
Broun, *see Browne*.
Browne and Co., order to supply cordage, pitch, tar, &c., 121.
Browne and Co., Richard, adventurers, £500, p. 3; assembly, 5; committees, 245, 246.

Brunde, William, nominated factor, 77; elected factor of the second sort, 82; will not accept as second factor, 93; chosen as a principal factor and nominated to the "Assention," 94, 100; warrant £100 for his provision to sea, 125; commission to take chief command in the event of deaths of Captains Lancaster and Middleton, 135; bill of adventure sealed, £200, p. 150.
Buck (Robert, assembly, 60; bill of adventure sealed, £240, p. 253.
Buckhurst, T., see *Lord Treasurer*.
Bullion, see *Coin*.
Burde, Mr., assembly, 30.
Burford in the County of Oxon, 193.
Burrage, William, confirmed as boatswain of the "Mare Scourge," 33.
Burrell, Richarde, adventurer, £200, p. 3; bill of adventure sealed, £240, p. 253.
Burrell, William, assemblies, 20, 22, 26, 27, 29, 30, 31, 39, 46, 59, 99, 156, 158, 167, 224, 234, 241; committees, 27, 155; surveyor for the "Hector," 14; general surveyor, 21; to provide timber, 21; warrant to take up carpenters and shipwrights, 40; nominates sail makers, 40; order for timber, 46; warrant £100 for timber, 47; order to take men from the "Susan" to finish the "Mare Scourge," 56; warrant £200 for timber, 65; order to see the ships "symented vppon ther sheathing" before leaving dock, 69; order to use a mast for the "Hector," 71; warrant £200 on account of the shipping, 74; do. £100, p. 85; order for timber, 89; warrant £80 for timber, 92; do. £100, p. 104; do. £100 for boats, &c., 115; to settle accounts with Mr. Wiseman, 127; warrant £100 on account, 157; to sell the "Assention's" boat, 159; to gather together in a warehouse all stores left behind, 159; to be called on for his account, 159; to enquire into Mr. Adye's account for timber, 173; order to be paid £15 for his pains in the provision of timber, &c., 181; all pursers to deliver him their bills to receive allowance, 215; agrees with William Hedger on the price of a boat for the "Discovery," 223; bill of adventure sealed, £240, p. 252.
Busbridge, see *Buzbridge*.
Busby, see *Buzbie*.
Bushea, a fit place to buy cider, 49.
Butchers } Austyn Bandicott, 238.
         } William Russell, 214.
Butler, Henry, made free though not named in the patent, 177; bill of adventure sealed, £200, p. 260.
Butter, estimate of quantity and price, 35; committee to provide, 75; do. for the North West voyage, 209; warrant, £14 5s., p. 125; do., £61 5s. 0d. for butter and cheese, 142; do., £92 10s. for butter, candles, powder, &c., for the North West voyage, 219.
Buzbie, Ralfe, *grocer*, adventurer, £200, p. 4; assembly, 59; bill of adventure sealed, £240, p. 251.
Buzbridge, John, *linendraper*, adventurer with James Turner, £200, p. 3; assemblies, 5, 39; compounds for iron, 41; warrant, £125 10s. for linen cloth, 97; do. £150 on account of iron, 104; do. £300, p. 111; bill of adventure, sealed £240, p. 253.
Buzby, see *Buzbie*.
Byddell, Mr., *preacher* at *Aleppo*, letter from the Levant Company, 275-6; see *Company of Levant merchants*, successor to Mr. May, 281.

Cables, 219.
Calais   ⎫ £3,000 worth of royals to be taken up
Callis   ⎬ there, 41; £5,000 do., 58, £500, p.
Callyce ⎪ 68; Mr. Allabaster commissioned to
Callys   ⎭ convey the bullion from thence, 84.
Cambell, James, bond of indemnity, £200, pp. 220, 221. See *Bonds*.
Cambell, Thomas, *alderman*, adventurer with Miles Huberd, £200, p. 2; assemblies, 5, 7, 9, 10, 181, 190, 192, 194, 196, 197, 203, 206, 208, 216, 219, 226, 227, 229, 230, 232, 233, 235, 236, 237, 238, 240, 241, 242, 244, 247, 248; appointed director, 6; committee, 5; general committee, 179; treasurer for the North West Passage voyage, 200; warrants as treasurer, see *warrants per Mr. Cambell*; all contributions for the North West voyage to be paid in to him by the end of March, 1601, p. 205; bound by covenant to pay the wages of John Drewe, 220; a bond of indemnity, £200, given to his son, 220; the bond sealed, 221; general committee and sworn, 225; elected governor, 226; Mr. Cartwright delivers to him Captain Waymouth's journal, 228; resolutions for the sale of stores from the two pinnaces, 230; warrant for payment of mariners hired from Dartmouth to London, 231; relates the result of proceedings against Captain Weymouth before the Lords of the Council, 233; thinks only one ship should go in the second North West voyage, 239; warrant to the Treasurer to pay 24s. for keeping the two pinnaces returned from the North West, 241; the pinnaces not to be sold under £300 each without his consent, 242; bound with Mr. Eldred as security for the payment of customs dues on the goods brought home in the "Assention," 247; is indemnified by a general bond of £3,000 under the common seal, 249; the bond sealed, 249; bill of adventure sealed, £360, p. 256, see also *Governors*.
Campion, Abraham, *brewer*, warrant, £200 for beer, 175; do. £300, p. 171; do. £39 2s. 4d., p. 193; do. £220 3s., p. 221.
Canary wine, see *Wine*.
Candell, Francis, *painter*, warrant, £30 for painting the "Red Dragon," 157; do £48, p. 172.
Candish, William, warrant, £150 for lead, 105; do. £9, p. 143.
Candishe, Captain, 72.
Candler, George, bill of adventure sealed, £240, p. 255.
Candler, Richard, recommends Thomas Wasse as a factor, 56.
Candles, *wax and ordinary*, estimate of quantity and price, 35; committee to provide, 76; do., for the North West voyage, 209; warrant, £200, p. 126, p. 142; do. £92 10s. for candles, butter, powder, &c., for the North West voyage, 219.
Candyshe, see *Candish*.
Cannons, 159.
Canterbury, 278.
Canvas, warrants, £200, p. 114; do. £100, p. 163; do £42 13s., p. 164; do. £200, p. 167; do. £300, p. 172; do. £143, p. 220.
Cahynge, George, adventurer with William Pauls, £100, p. 2.
Cape of Bona Speransa, 182, 183, 186, 191, 198, 199, 203, 214, 207, 211, 220, 224, 230.
Captains, *see also Masters*, Thomas Baker, John Davies, Captain Candishe, James Lancaster, John Middleton, George Waymouth.

"Carnation," ship of Colchester, 263.
Carpenters, *see also Shipwrights, see Edward Stephens, Nicholas Symonds*, 14, 27; warrant by the Lord Treasurer for taking up carpenters, 40, 263; number to be employed in each ship, 89; to be hired by Mr. Burrell and their wages agreed on, 89; committee to provide stores, 117; masts overcharged, 121, 157; committee to agree on disputed prices of timber, 124; Adam Wood, 168, &c.; Nicholas Symonson, 172, &c.; warrant £80 for wages for work on the ships for the North West Passage voyage, 206.
Carrell, Robert, *auditor*, 218; bill of adventure sealed, £240, p. 259.
Carriages, ? trucks, 163, 221.
Carriage Makers, John Hedland, 163; George Gryce, 221.
Carter, Richard, adventurer with Sir Stephen Soame, £400, p. 1.
Cartwright, John, *preacher, see also North West Passage and Waymouth*, engaged for the North West Passage voyage, 216; his salary contingent on the discovery of the passage, 216; his return and delivery of Captain Waymouth's Journal to the Governor, 228; can give no other particulars of the voyage, 228; accused of persuading Captain Waymouth to return and abandon the voyage, 232; ordered to give up the gown and apparel delivered to him to be used if the voyage had reached China, 232.
Cason, John, assembly, 60; bill of adventure sealed, £240, p. 256.
Cassalia Wine, 209.
Cashiers ordered to be repaid their losses in receiving and disbursing moneys, 227.
Cask, Caske, committee to provide and quantity required, 30; warrant £200, p. 41; do. £100, p. 92; the supply in the West Country to be ascertained, 49; warrant £100, p. 104; shipping mark, 107; warrant, £78 16s. 4d., p. 143; do. £61, p. 146; do. £57 15s., p. 147; do. £40 12s., £19 16s., and £36 19s., p. 148; do. £3 15s., p. 172; do. £30 11s. 8d., p. 218.
Cassocks, 138, 208.
Castle Soap ordered, 107. ? Castile.
Cataia ⎫ Proposed trade by the North West
Cataya ⎭ Passage if discovered, 193; supposed destination of the voyage if the passage is discovered, 212; Captain Waymouth to have £500 if he arrive at any port in Cataia, &c., 214; the salary of Mr. Cartwright, preacher, contingent on reaching Cataia, 216; Queen's letters to the Emperor, 217; Cartwright's gown for use in Cataia if reached, 232.
Cater, George, bill of adventure sealed, £240, p. 250.
Cater, William, assembly, 59; warrant, £28 14s. for Roan cloth, 97; bill of adventure sealed, £240, p. 260.
Caudell, *see Candell*.
Caulkers (Cawkers), number to be employed in each ship, 89; to be hired by Mr. Burrell and wages agreed on, 89.
Cavendishe, William, bill of adventure sealed, £240, 254.
Cecyle, *see Cycill*.
Cellarage under the Exchange used as a warehouse, 245, 248.
Chamberlain ⎫
Chamberlaine ⎬ *see Chamberleyn*.
Chamberlayn ⎪
Chamberlayne ⎭

Chamberlein ⎫ George, assembly, 59, bill of
Chamberleyn ⎭ adventure sealed, £240, p. 261.
Chamberleyn, Richard, bill of adventure sealed, £240, p. 261.
Chamberleyn, Robert, assemblies, 225, 226, 227, 229, 232, 235, 236, 242, 244, 248; warrants as treasurer, *see warrants per Mr. Chamberleyn*; nominated factor, 77; elected treasurer, 226; Stephen Hodson's supplies, 235; ordered to pay bills drawn by Plymouth merchants for expenses on the return of the "Assention," 244; requested to give his bond with Sir John Harte for £1,000 as security for money to be raised at interest for expenses on the return of the " Assention," 249; indemnified by a general bond under the common seal, 250; bill of adventure sealed, £240, p. 261.
Chamberlin, Andrewe, bill of adventure sealed, £240, p. 251.
Chambers, William, adventurer with William Stoane, £500, p. 2; assemblies, 4, 14, 20, 22, 24, 26, 27, 29, 31, 33, 37, 39, 46, 56, 58, 64, 66, 67, 68, 69, 71, 73, 76, 78, 80, 82, 83, 85, 86, 88, 89, 90, 91, 92, 93, 94, 95, 96, 98, 99, 100, 102, 103, 106, 107, 112, 113, 119, 121, 122, 124, 125, 128, 138, 139, 140, 142, 158, 170, 172, 174, 176, 177, 194, 203, 204, 208, 214, 215, 216, 217, 219, 225, 227, 233, 238, 240, 244, 248; committees, 12, 13, 22, 27, 30, 67, 69, 70, 76, 79, 120, 127, 128, 143, 209, 234, 240, 245; views ships, 13; feoffee in trust for ships bought, 32; warrant, £100 for casks, 33; to provide cider, 38; warrant £200 for casks and iron work, 41; the purchase of the "Mare Scourge," 45; signature to the West Country commission, 52; warrant, £100 for casks and hoops, 56; general committee, 63; warrant, £100 for casks, 92; recommends Walter Poyner as a factor, 97; warrant, £100 for casks, 104; warrant to pay 34s. 3d. to Captain Middleton, 142; auditor, 147; general committee and sworn, 179; do. 225; warrant, £150 for cloth, &c., 215; do. £100 for disbursement for the North West Passage voyage, 217; the dislike to Thomas Verworth, *purser*, 219; bill of adventure sealed, £240, p. 258.
Chamlettes, sixty pieces shipped without warrant, 123.
Champion, Richard, warrant to bring in his adventure at once, 170; bill of adventure sealed, £240, p. 261.
Chapman, George, warrant, £36 19s. for casks, 148.
Charters of the company, *see also Patent*, the charters to be perused to see if power is given to compel payments towards the North West Passage voyage or a second voyage by the Cape, 183.
Chaundler, Georg, assembly, 59.
Chaundlers, *see Francis Covell, Mr. Skelten, Simon Youans*.
Cheese, estimate of quantity and price, 35; committee to provide, 75; do. for the North West voyage, 209; warrant, £37 15s. 6d. p. 125; do. £61 5s. 9d. for cheese and butter, 147.
Cherie, Francis, *vintner*, adventurer, £200, 2; assemblies, 4, 10, 22, 68, 82, 86, 88, 94, 98, 100, 104, 109, 112, 119, 128, 144, 168, 177, 225; committees, 9, 10, 12, 69, 70, 115, 197; views ships, 13; general committees, 63; orders silver plate, 116; sells the ship "Guift" for £300, p. 147; auditor, 218.
"Cherubim," *ship*, 15.
Chery, *see Cherie*.

Cheskeens (Sequins), Turkish money, 266, 267, 271, 274.
Chests, for cloth, 118; Warrant, £11 1s., 138.
Chief command in the voyage; commission to Captain Lancaster, and others in succession, 132-7.
China, proposed trade by the North-West Passage, if discovered, 199; supposed destination of the voyage if the passage is discovered, 212; Captain Waymouth to receive £500 if he arrive at any port in China, &c., 214; the salary of Mr. Cartwright, *Preacher*, contingent on reaching China, 216; the Queen's letters to the Emperor, 217; Mr. Cartwright's gown to be used in China, if reached, 232.
Cicell, *see Cycill.*
Cider, the provision of in the West Country, 21; estimate of quantity and price, 34; Mr. Chambers to purchase what he can, 38; revised estimate, 46, 54 5; 100 tons to be bought in the West Country, 41, 52; instructions as to quality and preparation for shipment, 48; best places for buying, 49; 40 tons to be provided, 67; 60 tons to be provided in the West Country, 68; committee to provide casks, 76; £5 allowed to Mr. Fletcher for racking, 176.
Cinnamon, estimate of quantity and price, 35; quantity ordered and committee to purchase, 75; quantity brought home by the "Assention" and entered at the Custom House, 247.
Clarck, Walter, warrant, £105 12s. 4d. on Bill of Exchange, 102.
Clarke, *see Clerke.*
Claret wine, 169.
Clenche, John, brought in as an adventurer of £200 by Mr. Megges, 162; made free, though not named in the patent, 177; bill of adventure, £240, sealed, 255.
Clerke, Richard, assemblies, 237, 241; Committees, 197, 237, 239, 243 246; bill of adventure sealed, £240, p. 255.
Cletherow, Christopher, admitted adventurer and freeman in lieu of Robert Bowyer, 190; bill of adventure sealed, £240, p. 261.
Clinche, *see Clenche.*
Cloth, } *see also Cassocks, Gowns, Breeches.*
Clothes,
Committee to provide, 31; quantity to be sent out as merchandise with description and price, 36; warrant £19 6s. 3d. for chests for cloth, 118; do. £12 8s. 6d. for cloth work done, 159; proposed trade with China and Cataia by the North West Passage if discovered, 199; warrant £150, p. 215; do. £20 for mariner's clothes, 216; suits without pockets to be made for the porters employed to fill bags of pepper, 247.
Clothworkers, *see John Jackson, Joseph Jackson, John Morice, Nicholas Pearde, Edwarde Collins.*
Cloves, estimate of quantity and price, 35; quantity ordered and committee to purchase, 75; quantity brought home by the "Assention" and entered at the Custom House, 247.
Coals, sea coals for the North West Passage voyage, 210.
Cobbe, Robert, being behind with his adventure, offers security of bonds, 67; bill of adventure sealed £240, p. 253.
Cockain, Richard and Co., adventurers £3,000, p. 2.
Cockein, Richard, assembly, 4.
Cockes, Mr., touching the salary of Mr. Byddell, *preacher* at Aleppo, 275.

Cockes, Richard, *grocer*, adventurer £200, p. 2; assemblies, 4, 5, 59; bill of adventure sealed £240, p. 259.
Cockes, Robarte, *see Coxe.*
Cockeyn, (William, assemblies, 4, 7, 10; di-
Cockin,) rector, 6; committees, 8.
Coghill, John, a venturer with Henrye Parkehurste, £200, p. 3.
Coin, *see also Money*; petition to the Privy Council for leave to send out foreign money and to coin more in the mint when required, 8; petition to carry 5 mil. weight of bullion without charge, 10; warrant solicited to coin £5,000 in the Tower, 78; committee to provide £5,000 of bullion for coining, 80; Mr. Allabaster commissioned to convey bullion from Calais, 84; Lord Treasurer solicited for £5,000 bullion in the Tower, 87; order to coin £20 additional to be distributed to the lords and others, 114; respecting the £6,000 coming in the Tower, 120; inable to the transportation of treasure out of the country, 198.
Cokes, *see Cockes.*
Colchester, 265.
Cole, Elkana, nominated factor, 77.
Coles, Mr., warrant £200 on Bill of Exchange, 57.
Coles, George, assembly, 60; bill of adventure sealed £240, p. 253.
Colles, John, warrant £100 on Bill of Exchange, 88; do., £40, p. 104.
Colletton, fit place to buy cider, 49.
Collimore, Richard, nominated factor, 77; Roger Style appointed to take his place, 105.
Collins, Edwarde, *clothworker*, adventurer, £200, p. 2; assembly, 4.
Colthurst, Richard, *consul at Aleppo*; advices respecting the differences between the French and English ambassadors at Constantinople, 263; as to a fixed salary, 266; letters of instructions from the company of Levant Merchants, 270-2, 278-9, 283; *see Company, &c.*
Combe,   } John, *see Coombe.*
Combes,
Commissions, *see also Committees*; for the provision of victuals in the West Country, 28; Captain Baker's commission to buy victuals, &c., 38, 40; do. read and signed, 41; do. full copy, 47-52; to Mr. Allabaster's servant to take up royals at Calais, 41; West Country commission altered, 46; to Captain Davies to provide victual, &c., in the West Country, 52; to various committees for the provision of victuals, 77; to Mr. Allabaster to convey bullion from Calais, 84; to Captain Lancaster as chief in command of the voyage, and others in succession, viz.; power to correct offences; penalties for private trade; ships to be searched for private merchandise; penalties for deceit and fraud; instructions for leaving resident factors in the Indies; instructions for the devoving of the chief command in case of death, &c., 132-7; to Mr. Howe and Mr. Combe to go into the West Country to attend the discharge of the ships, 147, *see* 140; four commissions for the factors in succession, 133; to Captain Waymouth to bring his ships returned from the North West Voyage round to London from Dartmouth, 227-8; for the sale of the goods brought home in the "Assention," 249.
Committees, for the direction of the voyage generally, also to make suit to the Queen for sole privilege and for immunities from Customs and other favours, 6; to solicit the

Committees, *continued.*
Lords of the Council with a petition for privilege, &c., 8; to seek for ships, 8; to solicit the Lords of the Council for an answer to the petition, 9; to solicit the Lords of the Council for further favours, &c., 10; for the preparation and business of the voyage with power to use the help of any adventurer in any employment requiring the same, 12; to inspect the ships at Woolwich and Deptford, 13; to request the use of the docks at Woolwich and Deptford, 13; surveyors for the ships "Hector," "Assention," and "Susan," 14; for the provision of victuals and dollars in the West Country, 21; to find pinnaces in the river fit for the voyage, 22; to consider the estimate of victuals for the voyage, 26; to consider what merchandise is suitable to be shipped, 26; to survey the ship "Mare Scourge," 27, 33; to prepare a commission for the provision of victuals, &c., 28; to provide casks, 30; to provide clothes and kersies, 31; to arbitrate on the price of the "Mare Scourge," 32; to act as feoffees in trust for the ships bought, 32; to buy beans and mustard-seed, 33, 65; to compound with Captain Davies for the voyage, 37; to compound with Peter Francis, a native of Portugal, 38; to watch the preparation of the "Mare Scourge," 39; to act as remembrancer and in some sort prepare the business for the general committee, 40; to choose and appoint masters and mariners, 57; to treat with Captain Lancaster for taking chief command, 58, 66, 71, 73; general committee of 24 as mentioned in the patent, 63; to purchase biskett to carry the ships to the West Country, 67; to purchase beer, 67; to purchase cider, 68; to provide beef and pork, 68; to compound with Roger Hankin, *Master Mariner*, 69, 70; to review the estimate of victuals and the progress of the victualling, 72; several committees to purchase various kinds of provisions, &c., 75 6; to agree with Captain Middleton for the voyage, 77, 90; to solicit the Lord Treasurer's warrant for coining £5,000 in the Tower, and for providing bullion for the same; also to finish the patent; also to solicit the Lord Treasurer's warrant to transport provisions in the West Country, 78; to order small merchandise—knives, glasses, &c., 79; to provide lead and tin, 79; to provide £5,000 of bullion, 80; to buy Spanish meal taken prize by Lord Willoughby's ship, 86; to hire and compound with a master and officers, 87; to solicit the Lord Treasurer for £3,000 bullion in the Tower, 87; to confer with Mr. Beare to be one of the four chief masters, 90; to confer with Henry Napper as to his employment, 94; to confer touching letters to Potentates in the East to be solicited from the Queen, 91; to set down all names to be mentioned in the patent, 91; to audit the accounts of the pursers, 99; to audit the accounts of the treasurers, 107, 156, 166; to make complaint at Court against defaulting adventurers, 111; to purchase 120 oxen for making salt beef, 114; to go to Court with the names of defaulting adventurers, also to answer their petitions, 115; to provide silver plate, 117; to provide gunners', stewards', cooks', and carpenters' stores, 117; to enter all goods, pay customs, and make a cargazon of the whole, 118; to provide prunes, currants, and raisins, 118; to attend to the shipping of the money and victuals in the West Country, 120; to seal the bargain of sale of the "Susan" at £1,600, p. 120; to agree with the carpenters on disputed prices of timber, 124; to devise orders for the prevention of private trade, 124; to confer as to the damage done to a ship by the anchor of the "Scourge," 125; to take an inventory of all the furniture of the ships, 125; to agree with Captain Middleton, 127; several committees to settle accounts with various creditors, 127; to see to the discharge of the ships from the West Country, 128, 140; to wait on Lord Cumberland respecting the damage done to a ship by the anchor of the "Red Dragon," 128; to receive a mortgage from William Brodebent as security for £100 loan, 128; to entreat a warrant from the Lord Treasurer and Mr. Secretary for the removal of the plate and other presents from Mr. Governor's house, 141; to see the moneys entered in the Custom House, and waterborne to Gravesend and stowed in the ships, 142; to find a small ship to stow provisions and accompany the voyage part way, 143, 147; to audit the accounts of the purser of the "Red Dragon," 147; to go to Gravesend to see to the discharge of the ships, 147; to go to the West Country to see to the discharge of the ships, 147 (*see* 140); to settle disputed accounts for timber with Mr. Ady and other shipwrights, 155; to audit the accounts of the treasurer's, 156, 166; the general committee, 179; to set down the charge for three pinnaces, &c., for a voyage to find the North West Passage, 183; to confer with the Muscovia Company as to their rights in the discovery of the North West Passage, if made, 186; to expedite the preparation of the North West Passage voyage, and to devise laws and ordinances for the guidance of general business, 196-7; to prepare the shipping, &c., and forward the preparation of the North West Voyage, 202-3; to persuade adventurers to bring in contributions for the North West Voyage, 205; three committees to provide victuals and other necessaries for the North West Voyage, 214; to audit and report on the accounts of the North West Voyage, 217; the general committee elected and sworn, 225; to see to the discharge of the ships returned from the North West Voyage, 229; to prepare a second voyage to the North West, and to calculate the charges, 234; to consider the cost of equipping one vessel, and to confer with Captain Waymouth, 237; to attend to the sale of the ships and stores returned from the North West Voyage, 239; to investigate the demands of Captain Waymouth, 240; to make choice of merchants in Plymouth, Dartmouth, &c, to be instructed to give credit to the "Assention" on her return, 243; several committees to watch in turns the unloading of the "Assention," 245-6; to buy polldavies and make bags for the pepper, also suits without pockets for the porters, 247; to see the cellarage and vaults under the Exchange prepared to receive goods, 247, 248; to see the goods sent to the warehouse, 248; to attend at the warehouse and receive and weigh the goods, 248.

Common Seal of the Company. Ordered, 113; references to, 132, 141, 143, 247, 248, 249, 250; the seal of the Muscovia Company, 189.

INDEX   295

Company of Levant Merchants.
  Several drafts of letters in the East India
    Company's Record Book tending to show
    that the East India Company was partially
    an outgrowth of the Levant Company, as
    several persons mentioned appear to have
    been prominent members of both companies,
    notably, Sir Thomas Smith (*see* 62 and
    281), who was governor of both companies,
    265-83, *vid.*:—
  Letter to Mr. Lyllo, ambassador at Constan-
    tinople: instructions as to the differences
    with the French respecting consulage, &c.;
    orders to desist from all contention but to
    lose no advantage; Signior Paul Pinder
    sent home to acquaint Her Majesty of the
    doings of the French; complaints to the
    Queen by the French ambassador's lieges
    in London; private advices sent by Mr.
    Staper; accounts sent home by Signior
    Paul Pinder; amount of salary offered and
    how to be provided for; no bills of exchange
    to be drawn but a levy to be charged on all
    goods entering Constantinople and Aleppo
    to meet the charges of the ambassador and
    consul; troubles arising out of bills drawn
    by the late ambassador Mr. Barton in
    favour of John Bate and payment refused
    by the company; Mr. Bate's proposed
    course to recover his money; instructions
    to preserve the honour and credit of Her
    Majesty and the company and to avoid the
    errors of Mr. Barton; further instructions
    as to the rivalry with the French as to the
    Dutch consulage, &c.; Acts of Court and
    instructions for enforcing the levy on
    goods, 265-70.
  Letter to Mr. Colthurst, consul at Aleppo:
    he is dissatisfied with the offer of half the
    consulage, as he fears a falling off of trade
    on account of the discovery of the East
    Indies by the Dutch; it is thought the
    Dutch will prefer peaceable trade in Tur-
    key to the perils of the East India voyages;
    duties to be levied on goods entering Tur-
    kish ports to maintain his charges and those
    of the ambassador at Constantinople and
    thus avoid bills of exchange on Venice;
    instructions respecting the rivalry with the
    French as to Dutch consulage; orders for
    the prevention of private trade to Mar-
    seilles (Marcelles); Sir Anthony Shurley's
    doings in Persia; Acts of Court for the
    duties to be levied, 270-2.
  Letter to John Saunderson, merchant at
    Constantinople: the toleration of the Dutch
    trade in Turkey; the French rivalry as to
    the Dutch consulage, &c.; Signior Pinder
    sent home to acquaint the Queen as to the
    proceedings of the French; thanks for
    supplying the wants of the ambassador;
    proposed course for meeting the ambassa-
    dor's charges in future; instructions for
    selling, repairing, or letting the Galata
    House; the ambassador creditor for 1,000
    cheskeens; allowance for the collection of
    consulage, 273-5.
  Letter to Mr. Byddell, preacher at Aleppo:
    his salary £50 per annum; gratuity of £10
    allowed; his good character, 275-6.
  Letter to ———, factor at Scanderona (?):
    invoices sent of the goods shipped in the
    "Exchange;" orders to seize all goods not
    invoiced; complaints of impartial dealing;
    trouble with mariners refusing to carry
  goods into the magazines; all goods re-
    ceived or shipped to be certified to the
    Company, 276-7.
  Petition to the Privy Council respecting the
    Company's ships seized at Venice as resti-
    tution for the late prize taken by the
    English men-of-war, 277-8.
  Letter to Mr. Colthurst, Consul at Aleppo,
    to attend to the affairs of the late Mr. Ed-
    ward Rose, factor there, 278-9.
  Letter to John Saunderson: the ambassador's
    allowance and steps taken to support it;
    the trouble arising out of the action of the
    English men-of-war in the Straits; bills of
    exchange will be paid; troubles arising
    through the opposition of parties offering to
    pay imposts on certain goods to the Queen;
    the Company agree to pay £4,000 per
    annum to the Queen for a renewal of privi-
    leges and in lieu of imposts; Saunderson's
    demand for increase of salary, 279-81.
  Letter to Mr. May, ex-preacher at Aleppo,
    ordering him to come home at once, 281.
  Letter to the ambassador at Constantinople:
    the Queen's letter respecting peace with
    Spain falsified in translation by the French
    king; the outrages by the English men-of-
    war in the Levant; the payment of £4,000
    per annum to the Queen in lieu of imposts
    on wine, oil, &c.; privileges to be con-
    firmed, 282.
  Letter to Mr. Colthurst: as to his allowance;
    the payment of £4,000 per annum to the
    Queen; privileges about to be renewed
    under the great seal; the outrages by the
    men-of-war, 283.
Compasses, 218.
Comptroller, Mr. (Privy Council). Orders in
  council, 112, 164.
Constantinople. Letters to Mr. Lyllo, English
  ambassador, 265-70, 282, *see Company of
  Levant merchants*. Levies on goods entering Constantinople and Aleppo to support the
  ambassadors and consuls' charges, 267, 270,
  271, 273-4; letters to John Saunderson, Merchant, 273, 279.
Consulage. Differences between the French
  and English ambassadors at Constantinople,
  265-6, 269, 271-2, 273, *see Company of Levant
  merchants*; consulage at Aleppo thought to
  be affected by the discovery of the East
  Indies by the Dutch, 270; allowance to Mr.
  Saunderson for collection of consulage, 275;
  Mr. Colthurst's allowance, 283.
Consuls. Mr. Richard Colthurst at Aleppo,
  265, &c.; *see Colthurst and Aleppo*.
Cony skins, 271, *see Skins*.
Cooks, the number to be employed in each
  ship, 90; committee to provide stores, 117.
Coombe, }
Coombes, } John, adventurer, £200, p. 4.
  Assemblies, 59, 64, 65, 71, 73, 74, 77, 78, 80,
  82, 83, 85, 86, 88, 89, 93, 95, 99, 100, 103, 107,
  108, 115, 116, 117, 122, 124, 128, 140, 142, 143,
  144, 148, 170, 172, 173, 176, 227, 229, 231,
  232, 236, 238, 244; committees, 75, 76, 77,
  128, 228, 234; general committee, 63; buys
  vinegar, 115; warrant £14 12s. for vinegar,
  116; warrant £20 for attending to business in
  the West Country, 140; commission to go
  into the West Country and see to the discharge of the ships, 147 (*see* 140); orders to
  bring in his West Country accounts, 172;
  presents his account, 173; allowed £18 7s. 2d.
  with Mr. Howe for expenses in the country,

Coombes, John, *continued*,
176; appointed auditor, 218; general committee and sworn, 225; bill of adventure sealed, £240, p. 260.
Coopers, William Done, 139; John Davies, 218; John Spencer, 148.
Copper vessels, 164, 222.
Cordage ordered to be purchased of Browne and Co., 121; warrant £180 to John Lacy for cordage bought of the Muscovia Co., 126; bought of the Muscovia Co., 162, 170, 204; warrant £34 7s. 10d., p. 222; do. £120 9s., p. 224; the cordage returned from the North West voyage to be sold as current prices are high, 241.
Cordall, } Thomas, *mercer*, adventurer, £300,
Cordell, } p. 2.
Assemblies, 30, 37, 44, 46, 47, 56, 57, 58, 65, 67, 68, 69, 71, 76, 80, 82, 86, 88, 89, 90, 92, 93, 94, 98, 99, 100, 102, 103, 104, 106, 107, 108, 109, 112, 113, 116, 118, 122, 128, 139, 140, 142, 143, 144, 148, 150, 151, 152, 154, 156, 158, 162, 163, 172, 176, 181, 182, 183, 184, 187, 192, 205, 206, 215, 217, 219, 227, 237, 242, 244; committees, 6, 8, 10, 12, 4", 57, 58, 67^2, 71, 73, 75, 77^2, 87^2, 90, 91, 99, 107, 124, 128^2, 147^2, 155, 116, 183, 191, 197, 203, 209, 234, 237; surveyor of the " Mare Scourge," 33; appointed adventurer £500 by the Earl of Cumberland, 45; signatures to West Country commissions, 54, 55; general committee, 63; reports purchase of the " Guift," 147; assigned by Mr. Brodebent to pay the balance of his mortgage, 154; auditor, 166; general committee and sworn, 179; signature to treasurers' warrant, 206; general committee and sworn, 225.
Cornelis, } John, *goldsmith*, adventurer,
Cornelius, } £200, p. 3; assemblies, 5, 59;
Cornelys,   } bill of adventure sealed, £240, p. 254.
Cornwall, *see Devon and Cornwall*.
Cotton, Roger; bill of adventure sealed, £240, p. 259.
Cotton, William; bill of adventure sealed, £240, p. 253.
Coucheman, John; bill of adventure sealed, £240, p. 251.
Council, Lords of the, *see Privy Council*.
Counsels' opinion as to the respective rights of the Muscovia and East India Cos. in the discovery of the North West Passage, if made, 196.
Court of Admiralty, 128.
Courts, *see General Courts*.
Covell, Francis, supplies peas, 31; beans and mustard seed, 33; peas and beans, 65, 66; oatmeal, 75; warrant, £100 on account, 82; do. £100, 96; do. £17 4s. 11d., 105; do. £22 4s., 164; do. £22 4s., 169.
Covenants, *see Bonds*.
Cowper, John, *notary*, adventurer, £200, p. 3.
Coxe, Robarte, *grocer*, adventurer, £250, p. 1; assembly, 59; bill of adventure sealed, £240, p. 253.
Crane, John, warrant £4 9s. 8d. for pullies, 167.
Credit order for £1,500 to be raised at interest on the credit of Mr. Bannyng and Mr. Holliday, 146.
Cressell, Robert, nominated factor, 77.
Creswell, Robert, recommended as a purser, 39.
Crispe, Ellis, warrant £200 on bill of exchange, 68; bill of adventure sealed, £240. p. 254.
Crispe, Nicholas, adventurer, £200, p. 3; assemblies, 5, 59; bill of adventure sealed, £240, p. 258.
Crompton, Hughe, bill of adventure sealed, £240, p. 255.
Crosse, —, *vintner*, warrant £14 10s. for Malaga wine, 169.
Cryse,   } *see Crispe*.
Cryspe,   }
Cullymore, James, bill of adventure sealed, £240, p. 259.
Cumberland, Countess of, bill of adventure sealed, £50, p. 262.
Cumberland, Earl of, assemblies, 44, 47, 60, 87; offers the ship " Mare Scourge," 20; committee to survey and report on the ship, 27; declines £3,000 and offers her at £4,000, p. 29; will not take less than £4,000, but is offered £3,500, p. 30; accepts £3,700, p. 32; advises a chain pump for the ship, 44; seals bargain for the sale of the ship, 45; becomes an adventurer, 45; damage done by the anchor of the " Red Dragon," 128; assigns £100 of his adventure to Wm. Beerblock, 161; the supplies due on £570 of adventure assigned to Mr. Bannyng, 177; assigns £230 adventure to Mr. Holliday, 197, 262; bill of adventure sealed, £500, p. 262.
Currants,   } 118, 168; impost offered to the
Curraunce, } Queen in opposition to the Le-
Currents,   } vant Company, 280.
Custom House, committee to see the monies entered, 142; goods brought home by the " Assention " entered, and list of the same, 247; the entries of goods shipped by the " Exchange " to Scanderona, 276.
Customs. Suit made to the Queen for immunities from Customs, 6; petition to the Privy Council, 8-9; freedom of the Dutch from Customs, 9; committee to pay custom, 118; bonds given for the payment of dues on the goods brought home by the " Assention," 247; duties amount to £917, p. 248.
Cutteler, Thomas, *grocer*, adventurer £200, p. 3.
Cycill, Sir Robert, *secretary*, letters from the Privy Council to the Company, 60, 61; orders in council, 112, 164; the complaints of the French as to consulage, 265.

Dale, William, adventurer, £100, p. 2; assemblies, 59, 226, 227, 229, 230, 218, 240, 244, 249; warrant £112 on Bill of Exchange, 83; general committee, 225; bill of adventure sealed, £240, p. 259.
Dartmouth, provisions at, 29; Mr. Sandy, 70; recommended for the purchase of biskett, 48; dr. cider, 49; to be the place of assembly for all provisions bought, 49; return of the ships from the North West Passage Voyage, 227-9; mariners hired to bring ships to London, 231; letters to the principal merchants to give credit to the " Assention " on her return, 241.
Dassell, Thomas, nominated factor, 77; appointed third factor of the " Hector," 101; warrant £30 for wages, 104; bill of adventure £50 sealed, 153.
Davers, Jeremi or Jeremie, made free though not named in the patent, 177; bill of adventure sealed, £200, p. 260.
Davies, Captain John, assemblies, 14, 22, 24, 26, 27, 31, 33, 47, 143; committees, 22, 26, 68, 72; view ships, 13; sent to the West Country for provisions, 21; ordered to draw out an estimate of victuals for 500 men, 22;

INDEX 297

Davies, Captain John—*continued.*
letter to the Earl of Essex asking his approval of Captain Davies as Chief Director of the voyage, 25; presents his estimate of victuals, 26; compounds for his entertainment and profit in the voyage, 37 (*see also* 152); respecting the provision of seines, hooks, and lines, 49; do. victuals, &c., 51; commission for purchasing provisions, &c., in the West Country, 52, 54, 55; letter to, 66; letter from, 74; to sail in the "Red Dragon" as pilot-major of the fleet, 100; warrant £300 for salary, 127; bill of adventure sealed with profit contingent on the success of voyage, 152.
Davies, John, *Cooper*, warrant £50 11s. 8d. for casks, 218.
Davies Straits, Captain Waymouth's sailing orders, 212.
Davis, Captain John, *see Davies.*
Davyes, George, warrant £19 6s. 3d. for chests for cloth, 118; do. £11 1s., p. 138.
Deals, 164, 169, 171, 218.
Deane, James, *Draper*, adventurer, £300, p. 3; assembly, 59; bill of adventure sealed £360, p. 254.
Deane, Richard, assembly, 60; bill of adventure sealed £240, p. 259.
Decro, Benjamin, *Agent of the Muscovia Co.*, warrant £57 16s. 8d. for cordage, 187; do. £109 16s. 8d., p. 204.
Denham, William, *Shipwright*, warrant £6, p. 169; do. £12 for pulleys. &c., 221.
Denman, Mr., *Master of the Bridgehouse*; order to deliver timber to Mr. Burrell, 89.
Dent, Frauncis, assembly, 59; desires to assign his adventure to George Bennet, 175; the assignment allowed. 177.
Deodands for the "Hector," 169.
Deptford, committee to inspect ships there, 13; use of the docks requested, 13.
Deputy governors, Mr. William Rumney elected, 111, *see Rumney*; the oath of office, 179; powers at general courts, 200-2; Mr. Rumney re-elected, 225; Mr. Thomas Bramley elected in place of Mr. Rumney, 239; power to depute adventurers to perform any services required, 249.
Devon and Cornwall, letter from the Lord Treasurer to her Majesty's Receivers authorising credit to be given to the Company's agents, 38.
Deycro, *see Decro.*
Deyns, William, *Ironmonger*; warrant £30 8s. for necessaries for the pinnaces, 222.
Dickson, *see Dixon.*
Die, Roger, bill of adventure, sealed, £240, p. 260.
Directors of the voyage and their duties, 6, 12, 63; Captain Davies principal director, 25.
Discovery, one of the ships for the North West voyage; see also *North West Passage, Pinnaces, Ships, Waymouth, Verworth*; warrant £100 for anchors and other necessaries, 210; manned, victualled, and prepared according to Captain Waymouth's own desires, 211, 212; several warrants for the provision of stores and necessaries, 220-24, *see Warrants*; return to Dartmouth, 227-29; ordered to be sold with all stores, &c., 230; arrival in the Thames, 229; the boatswain, gunner and carpenter aver that Mr. Cartwright, the preacher, was the main mover for the return of the expedition, 232; warrant, £4, to the porters for landing and housing the stores, 238; warrant, £6, to Edward

Pullyson, *purser*, in full of his account and for wages, 240; the sale of the ship deferred, 241; ordered to be sold if £300 can be obtained, 242.
Disfranchisement of certain defaulting adventurers, 178; of Nathaniel Martin, 185; of Xpofer Cletherow, 190.
Dixon, ⎫ William, *purser of the "Red Dragon;"* warrant £50 for the use of the
Dixson, ⎬ ship, 105; do. £100, p. 108; do.
Dixsy, ⎭ £100, p. 111; do. £100 for the "Hector," 111; do. £150 for the "Red Dragon," 114; do. £250, p. 117; do. £250, p 120; do. £200, p 127; do. £200, p. 139; do. £100, p. 144; William Brodebent's account, 153; warrant £180 for mariners' wages, &c., 154.
Docks at Woolwich and Deptford; the use of requested, 13; the "Mare Scurge" at Woolwich, 27; dock charges to be paid, 80; ships ready to come out, 92.
Dollars, *see Spanish money, royals, &c.*; the provision of, in the West Country, 15; 1,000 dollars contracted for at 4s. 6d., p. 20; adventures received in dollars, 63; duties charged at Constantinople and Aleppo to be answered in London at 5s. 6d. the dollar, 267, 271; Mr. Byddell's salary to be rated at 5s. the dollar, 276.
Doncomb, Giles, adventurer with Richard Welbye £200, 4.
Done, William, *Cooper*, warrant £38 7s. 7d, p. 139.
Donkon, James, bill of adventure sealed £240, p. 257.
Dorrington, George, bill of adventure sealed £240, p. 261.
Downs, the, letter sent to Captain Waymouth, 223.
Dragon, ship, *see "Red Dragon."*
Drapers, *see Thomas Garwaye, William Garwaye, James Deane.*
Drewe, John, *master of the "Godspeed;"* appointed master of a ship for the North West voyage, 206; warrant £5 on account of wages, 206; do. £10, p. 210; Mr. Alderman Cambell, treasurer, bound by covenant for the payment of his wages, 220; bond of indemnity £200 sealed to James Cambell, 221; examined as to the causes of the return of the North West Expedition, 232; avers that Mr. Cartwright was the persuader for the return, 232; warrant £5 for wages, 234.
Drugs; Edmund Scott to go on the voyage in hope of his service in the choice of drugs, 109.
Duck, Thomas, warrant £29 for ancients and streamers, 149; do. £12, p. 163.
Duckett, John, adventurer with William Hallidaie, £200, p. 3.
Ducy, Robert, bill of adventure sealed £240, p. 259; do. 260.
Duffeilde, Anthonie, *Brewer*, warrant £15 7s. for beer, 154.
Dunkin, James, assembly, 60.
Dutch; their success in the East Indies; preparing for a new voyage; ships bought in England, 8; freedom from Customs, 9; their preparations, 110; return of their voyage with honour, 189; their example propounded to the East India Co. in a letter signifying Her Majesty's mislike to the delay in the second voyage, 191; an Englishman brought home out of the East Indies in the Dutch ships, 104; the rivalry between the English and French at Constantinople to obtain the

Q Q

Dutch, *continued.*
  Dutch consulage, 265, 266, 269, 271; the discovery of the East Indies by the Dutch as affecting the consulage at Aleppo, 270; trade in Turkey, 270, 273.
Dyckes, *see Dixon.*

East India Company: list of adventurers and the amounts subscribed, 1-4; formation of the company, royal assent, objects, rules to be made, 5; rules made, 6, *see Rules;* directors appointed, 6; suit to be made to the Queen for sole privilege and immunities and freedom from customs, 6; all officers or factors to be elected by a general assembly, 6; petition to the Privy Council for incorporation, privilege, &c., 8-10, *see Privy Council;* preparation of the voyage postponed by reason of the treaty of peace in hand with Spain, 10; the preparation resumed, 11, 12; general committee, 12; the adventure proves larger than expected, and hence more shipping required, 27; no gentlemen to be employed, 28; agreement with Captain Davies for his profit in the voyage, 37; remembrancers appointed to prepare the business for the general committee, 40; no adventure of £200 to be refused until £55,000 is reached, 45; general court summoned to take notice of a letter signifying Her Majesty's pleasure, 57; general court, 58-63, viz. the objects and proceeding of the company reviewed, 60; letter from the Privy Council confirming, privileges, with assurances of no hindrances to the voyage, 61; adventurers in arrears to be certified to the Privy Council, 61; the patent drawn up, 62 (*see* 108); election of Sir Thomas Smyth as first governor, 62; election of the general committee of 24, pp. 62-3; all business committed to the care of the governor and committee, 63; election of four classes of factors, 81-3; deficiency in the adventure, and steps taken to supply it, 110-11; order in council for defaulting adventurers to bring their money at once on pain of imprisonment, 112-13; common seal ordered, 113; every adventurer to have a bill of adventure under the common seal, 113; coining in the Tower (? special coinage), 114; resolution respecting prizes and prize money, 118; ordinances, laws, and decrees for the guidance of trade, 129, 131 (*see also* 197, 202); everything to be managed as a joint stock, and no private trade to be practised, 130; all private goods shipped to be forfeited to the common stock, 130; ordinances against fraud, 130; proposed leaving of factors to trade in the East Indies, 131; the commission to the general or principal merchant and to others in succession, 132-37, *see Commissions;* two forms of bills of adventure for merchants and factors, 144-46; £1,500 to be borrowed on the credit of Mr. Bannyng and Mr. Holliday, 146; the treasurer's accounts on March 6, 1600, showing amount of debts also of adventure not yet brought in, 156; being £9,000 in arrears, a supply of 2*s.* in the £ is ordered, with penalties by reduction of stock in default of payment, 160-61; order in council touching the discredit likely to arise by the remissness of the company in paying their debts, and ordering defaulting adventurers to appear and be punished for contempt, 164-65; resolution that great care be taken to remove all discredit, and for the better ordering of business, Alderman Wattes elected governor in place of Sir Thomas Smyth in prison, 166; auditors chosen for the treasurers' accounts, 166; an estimate to be made of the money in the treasurers' hands, 167; warrant for the summoning of all defaulting adventurers, 169-70; arms assigned by the King of Heralds, 171; disfranchisement of certain defaulters, 177, 181; election of governor, deputy, and committee, 178-79; the oaths of office, 179-80; letter received from Captain George Waymouth touching his attempt to be made for the discovery of a North West Passage to the East Indies, asking whether the company will undertake the enterprise, and if not whether they will allow private men to deal therein, giving them the benefit of the discovery, if made, by the sole trade for certain years, 182, *see North West Passage* and *Waymouth;* a second voyage by the Cape proposed, 182; the charters to be perused to see if power is given to compel payments towards the North West Passage voyage, or the second voyage by the Cape, 183; second voyage by the Cape resolved on, the adventure to be not less than £100, p. 186; adventure subscribed for the second voyage amounts to £11,000 only, which is insufficient, 189; enquiries by the Lord Admiral and Mr. Secretary as to the great delay in furthering the voyages as compared with the Dutch, and complaining that the company were not so respective of Her Majesty's honor as they should be, 189; the causes of the delay, 189; to avoid delay no ship to be prepared until approved by a general court, 189; the subscription book to be carried round by men able to persuade and encourage the brethren to adventure, 190; letter from the Privy Council notifying Her Majesty's mislike to the delay in the second voyage, and propounding the example of the Dutch, 191; general court summoned to deal with the matter, with penalty of 20*s.* for non-attendance, 191; return of two Dutch ships laden with pepper, 194; an Englishman brought home by the Dutch after being detained a prisoner four years, and knowing the language of Sumatra; Mr. Wattes is desired to induce him to come over to confer as to trade, &c., 194; committee appointed to expedite the second voyage by the Cape and the North West voyage, and also to devise laws and ordinances for the better guidance of general business, 196-97; laws and ordinances for the government of trade, &c., as devised by the committee and revised and agreed on by the generality, viz., preamble; by the Queen's letters patent the company have the sole right to the trade with the East Indies for 15 years, either by the Cape or by such passages as shall be hereafter found out by the parts of America; in the late voyage by the Cape the greater part of the adventure was taken out in English and foreign coin prepared with great difficulty and not without mislike to the transportation of treasure out of the country; therefore for the good of the country, and in order to carry on the trade with the Indies with little or no money, it is resolved to attempt to discover a passage through some part of America, so that by reaching Cataia or China, countries of temperate climate, a

East India Company, *continued*.
market would be found for a liberal sale of clothes and kersies to the general advancement of English trade; resolved therefore that the voyage to the North West be set forth with all convenient expedition; two ships or pinnaces to be employed; every adventurer to contribute at least 12*d*. in the £ on the amount of his adventure for the voyage by the Cape; if the discovery be made every man to participate in the benefit in proportion to his adventure, and in all future voyages in the same ratio only; dates for the payment of adventures; Mr. Cambell appointed treasurer; any one declining to adventure or being behind time in his payments to be fined 5 times the value of his levy at 12*d*. in the £ to be deducted from his original stock, such fines to be employed in the preparation of the voyage, and any surplus proportionately divided; all future contributions or levies for the general trade to be paid on the days appointed on pain of fines in the discretion of the company or of the auditors; penalty for absence from a general court, 12*d*.; for being late, 6*d*.; no one to speak on any one matter more than three times, penalty, 3*s*. 4*d*.; penalty for uncivil speeches or behaviour, 10*s*.; no one to interrupt another in a speech or disturb by private whisperings, but all replies to be directed to the governor or deputy on pain of penalty, 2*s*. 6*d*.; silence to be kept at the stroke of the hammer, penalty, 6*d*.; penalty for non-payment of fines, imprisonment; no person to leave a general court without leave, penalty, 12*d*.; all fines to be employed to the general use of the company or to the relief of the poor, 197-202; committee for the preparation of the North West Voyage, 202-3; the tardiness of payment of contributions for the North West Voyage reported at a general court; the expenses already incurred amount to £700, all which would be lost, and the company discredited at home and abroad if the voyage did not proceed: resolved therefore for further encouragement that all sums brought in shall be deemed part of the adventure for the voyage to the Cape, and shall bear profit and benefit in that voyage in proportion with the original stock; the act for the forfeiture of five times the value of the levy by defaulters confirmed and fortified, and ordered that suit be made to the Privy Council to approve the same; those present set down their contributions in writing that their consent may appear to those absent, and all contributions to be endorsed on the bills of adventure; all contributions to be brought in by the end of March, 1602, after which date no payments to be received without the consent of a general court, 206-8; committees appointed to provide victuals and other necessaries for the North West Voyage, 209; articles of agreement with Captain Waymouth with his orders and instructions, 211-14, viz., the company's desire to discover a nearer passage to the East Indies (*see* page 182, Waymouth's suggestions); Captain Waymouth considered a fit and proper person to attempt the discovery, and is allowed £100 to furnish his instruments to his own choice; two ships committed to his charge, the "Discovery" and the "Godspeed," manned, victualled, and furnished for 16 months to his own desires, and also laden with various merchandise; Waymouth agrees to be ready to sail by a certain date and to proceed towards the coast of Greenland into Davies Straits, thence to the north west "or as he shall fynd the Passage best to lye" towards the kingdoms of Cataya or China "*or ye backside of America,*" without giving up the attempt as long as he shall find those seas navigable, or any possibility of finding a passage, and will not return or suffer voluntarily any of his company to return till a year has been bestowed on the attempt; agreed for merchants and pursers to go in the ships to keep a register of goods laden and how disposed of, also to make notes, journals, and observations for the direction and help of posterity; within 10 days of his return to deliver a report of all his proceedings, and within 40 days on a summons to appear before the company and relate such things as they desire to be informed of, and will not discover the secrets of the voyage to any person whatsoever; within 40 days of his return the company will on proof of his having arrived at any port in China, Cataya, or Japan by the North West Passage pay unto him £500, but if the passage be not discovered it is agreed that he is to make no claim for salary, wages, or reward, seeing that the expense of the voyage was undertaken at his persuasion and on his resolution to adventure his life for the good of his country, 211-14; agreement with John Cartwright to go as preacher in the North West Voyage with salary contingent on the discovery of the passage, 216; the agreement with Waymouth read to the generality, also the Queen's letters to the Emperor of China and Kathia, 217; auditors chosen to report on the state of the adventure, that further supplies may be called up and some course taken with the defaulters, 217-18; day appointed for the payment of supplies for the North West Voyage; the rateable and voluntary supplies to be endorsed on all bills of adventure, and the secretary then to make out new bills showing in one lump sum what is every man's interest in the voyage by the Cape, 220 (*see* 206-8); order to the bookkeeper to enter up each adventurer's credits in a lump sum, 224; election of treasurer, secretary, book-keeper, and beadle, 226; election of governor, deputy, and committees, 225-26; the return of the North West expedition, 227, *see North West Passage;* Mr. Holliday and others being in arrears with supplies for the North West Voyage, it is ordered that the same be deducted from their stock, 231 (*see* pages 200 and 207); the book-keeper ordered to charge up the accounts of all brethren debtors to the company, that the amounts may be defaulted on their stock if not paid before the return of the ships, 233; proceedings against Waymouth before the lords of the council; deliberations and preparations for a second voyage; the idea of a second voyage abandoned, and the ships and stores ordered to be sold off; dispute with Waymouth as to his demands for charges, and the same referred to arbitration, &c., &c., 232-42, *see North West Passage;* Mr. Thomas Bramley elected deputy-governor in place of Mr. Rumney, 239; letters from the "Assention" brought home by a Frenchman

East India Company, *continued*.
who lately departed at sea from that ship, by which good hope is conceived of a successful voyage and encouragement given to set forth another, 242-43; letters to be written to the factors and officers of the "Assention" and sent into the West Country saying that orders have been sent to the principal merchants in Plymouth, Dartmouth, &c., to take any sick men on shore and supply their wants and to give credit for money required for the use of the ship; orders not to break bulk or make sale of anything belonging to the general adventure; committee to make choice of the merchants in Plymouth, &c., to be written to, to supply the wants of the ship, and the same to be reimbursed by the treasurer, 243-44; arrival of the "Assention" in the river, 244; warehouses for the goods, 245; committees to attend in turns to the unloading, 245-46; no mariner to remove anything from the ship "unlesse it be visited" on pain of detention of wages, 245; the tithes due to the Lord Admiral for a prize taken in the East Indies, 246-47; bags to be made for the pepper, also suits for the porters *without pockets*, 247; list of goods brought home and entry to be made at the Custom House, 247; Mr. Governor and Mr. Eldred give bond for the payment of customs, 247; customs amount to £917, and Mr. Cambell and Mr. Eldred indemnified for their bonds given for the payment of the same, 248; £2,000 to be taken up at interest for the payment of mariners' wages, and Sir John Harte and others asked to give their bonds to secure the same, 249; future monies required, to be raised by a levy by the pole and upon the rates of particular adventures, 249; order for the sale of the goods brought home, 249; the governor and deputy empowered to appoint any adventurer to perform any service which the general business requireth, 249; two obligations of £3,000 each sealed to Mr. James Cambell and Mr. John Eldred, who gave their bonds for the payment of customs, 250; two obligations of 1,000 marks each to Sir John Harte and Robert Chamberlayne for money taken up at interest, 250; several drafts of letters of the Levant Company written in the East India Company's record book tending to show that the East India Company was partially an outgrowth of the Levant Company, several persons mentioned appearing to have been prominent members of both companies; notably Sir Thomas Smith (*see* 62 and 281), who was governor of both companies, 265-83, *see Company of Levant Merchants*.

East Indies: the objects of the East India Company, 5, 60; the Dutch voyages, 8; letters from the Queen to potentates in the East, 91, 131, 134; resident factors, 97, 102; Mr. Hacklett, historiographer, reads his notes and is desired to furnish a list of places where trade is, 124; orders and instructions respecting the leaving of resident factors, 131; warrant £13 7s. 8d. to William Segar, *Herald*, for writing the Queen's letters to the kings of the East Indies, 139; the presents for the kings and how distributed in the ships, 151; warrant £20 10s. for making stamps for the East India monies, 171; Captain George Waymouth's proposed voyage for the discovery of a North West Passage to the East Indies, 182, *see North West Passage*; an Englishman, a prisoner for four years, brought home from the East Indies by the Dutch, 194; two Dutch ships returned laden with pepper, 194; abstract of the objects and aims of the company in reference to trade in the East Indies, 198, *see East India Company*; Waymouth's confidence in the discovery of a passage by divers inlets that treat through the coast of America, 233; the return of the "Assention," 242, &c., *see East India Company and "Assention;"* the discovery of the East Indies by the Dutch as affecting the Consulage at Aleppo, 270.

Eaton, Thomas, adventurer with William Essington, £200, p. 3.
Edmondes, Thomas, *Clerk to the Privy Council*, signatures to orders in council, 113, 165.
Edmonds, Richard, adventurer with Humfrey Wymers, £200, p. 3.
Edward, William, *plumber*, warrant £8 8s. for lead and soda, 224.
Edwardes, Thomas, adventurer, £200, p. 2; assembly, 4.
Eldred, John, adventurer, £400, p. 1; assemblies, 4, 24, 26, 27, 28, 31, 37, 44, 45, 46, 57, 58, 59, 64, 67, 71, 73, 76, 80, 82, 83, 92, 94, 95, 98, 102, 103, 104, 106, 108, 109, 113, 114, 119, 121, 122, 124, 125, 139, 144, 155, 156, 158, 160, 162, 164, 171, 175, 177, 192, 197, 206, 224, 229, 230, 232, 236, 247; committees, 12, 26, 31, 76, 120, 141, 155, 248; views ships, 13; feoffee in trust for ships bought, 32; purchase of the "Malice Scurge," 45; general committee, 63; recommends Thomas Eldred as a captain, 72; general committee and sworn, 179; ditto, 225; bound with Mr. Cambell as security for the payment of customs dues on the goods brought home in the "Assention," 247; indemnified by a general bond under the common seal, 248; the bond of indemnity in £3,000 sealed, 249; bill of adventure sealed, £600, p. 250.
Eldred, Thomas, *of Ipswich*, willing to be employed as a captain, 72.
Eldred, {Tristram, *purser of the two pinnaces*,
Eldrich, {warrant £4 7s. to be disbursed for mariners' lodgings, &c., 222; warrant £6 13s. for his pains taken in the company's affairs, 226.
Elections: of officers, 6, 8; of Sir Thomas Smyth as governor, 62; of three principal factors, 81; of four second class factors, 82; of third and fourth class factors, 83; of William Rumney as deputy governor, 111; of Mr. Alderman Wattes as governor, in place of Sir Thomas Smyth in prison, 166; of Mr. Wattes as governor, and Mr. Rumney as deputy, 179; of the general committee, 179, 225; of Sir John Harte as governor, and Mr. Rumney as deputy, 225; of Alderman Cambell as governor, in place of Sir John Harte, who declines, 226; of Thomas Bramley as deputy, in place of Mr. Rumney, 239.
Elington, Francis, warrant £600 for cloth, 45.
Elizabeth, Queen, *see Queen*.
Ellacott, {John, *of Exeter*, respecting money
Ellecot, {on the West Country, 50, 51, 53,
Ellecote, {54, 56, 64; bills of exchange, 38,
Ellecott, {65, 69, 83, 102, 108, 109, 115, 119;
Ellicott, {Spanish money, 66; warrant £500 for royals of plate, 105; to confer with Mr. Pope as to shipping the Spanish money, 119; as to Mr. Augustine Skinner's adven-

Ellacott, John—*continued.*
ture of £200 being received in royals, 124 ; bill of adventure sealed, £220, p. 149 ; ordered to render his account and pay up his supplies, 181.

Emerson, James, order to be paid £30 for aquavitae, 143.

Essex, Earl of, letter to, on behalf of Captain Davies, 25.

Essington, William, adventurer with Thomas Eaton, £200, p. 3.

Evesed, } Thomas, *beadle of the Company,*
Evesett, } warrants for general courts, 57;
Evettsett, } 228, 235 ; salary fixed at £10 per annum, 204 ; re-appointed, 226 ; warrant for 25s. 7d. disbursed to Mr. Pope's man, 238.

Evington, Francis, adventurer ; assembly, 59 ; warrant £120 on bill of exchange, 56 ; bill of adventure sealed, £240, p. 261.

Europe, Coast of, route to the East Indies, 211.

Exchange, *ship of the Levant Company,* letters sent, 273, 279 ; Mr. Holliday, part owner, 276 ; goods shipped and invoices sent, 276.

Exchange, the, warehouses under, 245 ; committee to prepare the vaults and receive goods, 248 ; committee to receive and weigh goods, 248.

Exeter, 56, 58, 66, 74, 81, 83, 84, 97, 102, 106, 119, 125, 181, 209.

Eydes, John, *of Exeter,* bill of exchange, £50, p. 83.

Factors, all to be elected by a general assembly, 6 ; Thomas Wasse recommended, 56 ; list of factors nominated, 77 ; the scale of remuneration fixed, 81 ; election of four sorts of factors, 81, 82, 83 ; to give security and to abstain from private trade, 86 ; Roger Style not being elected, offers to serve without salary, or to remain in the East Indies and learn the language, 86 ; the choice of factors to be discussed at a general court, 92 ; Mr. Brund recommended as a principal factor, 93 ; elected, 94 ; names of the principal factors appointed to each ship, 94 ; Walter Poyner recommended as an extra factor without salary to serve in case of death, or to be left resident in the Indies, 97 ; William Martin recommended and security offered as a resident factor in the Indies, 97 ; appointed to their respective ships, 100-1 ; bonus £50 to Robert Pope for his pains in the provision of victuals, &c., 101 ; list of extra factors to serve in case of death, or be left resident in the Indies, 102 ; Mr. Howe to answer letters from factors in West Country, 103 ; warrant £30 to William Wilford for salary, 103 ; Roger Style to take the place of Richard Collymore of the third class, 105 ; bonds to be given for truth and good behaviour, 105 ; amounts of bonds for the four classes, 105 ; warrant £50 to William Starky for his salary and preparation, 106 ; ditto £30 to Roger Style, 108 ; orders for the prevention of private traffic, 130 ; orders and instructions for factors left resident in the Indies, 131 ; form of bill of adventure read, 144-5 ; bills of adventure sealed, 148, 149, 150, 152, 153 ; four commissions sealed, 153 ; letters to the factors of the " Assention " on her return, 243 ; names of factors offering to be employed, 263 ; orders for the prevention of private trade from Aleppo to Marseilles,

272 ; difficulties at Venice by reason of prizes taken by English men-of-war, 278 ; orders to Mr. Colthurst to attend to the estate of Edward Rose, deceased, at Aleppo, 278-9 ; money taken up from Mr. Leet's and Mr. Salter's factors, for the use of the ambassador, 280.

Fans, 141.

Farrar, } Nicholas, *Skinner,* adventurer, £200,
Farrer, } p. 2 ; assemblies, 4, 59 ; committees, 186, 229, 230 ; bill of adventure sealed, £240, p. 259.

Farrington, Thomas, *Vintner,* adventurer, £200, 2 ; assemblies, 59, 180, 181, 183, 184, 187, 190, 193, 194, 196, 197, 203, 205, 206, 208, 214, 215, 216, 218, 224, 225, 227, 228, 230, 231, 232, 233, 235 ; committees, 197, 209 ; general committee and sworn, 179 ; do. 225 ; signatures to treasurer's warrants, 210 ; bill of adventure sealed £240, 253.

Feathers, 141, 151.

Fenton, Peter, *carpenter of the " Susan,"* deceit in the supply of masts, 121.

Ferries, } William, assemblies, 236, 238, 240,
Ferrers, } 241, 244, 247, 248 ; offers the ship
Ferris, } " Phenixe," 14 ; assembly, 59 ; general committee and sworn, 226 ; to provide bags for pepper and suits *without pockets* for the porters, 247 ; committee, 248 ; bill of adventure sealed £240, p. 251.

Ferror, Nicholas, *see Farrar.*

Ferror, } William, *see Ferries.*
Ferrys, }

Finchcoomber, William, nominated factor, 77.

Fines, various fines or penalties for breach of rules, 200-2 ; all fines to be employed to the use of the Co. or to the relief of the poor, 202.

Fish, estimate of quantity and price, 34 ; quantity to be bought in the West Country, 41, 52 ; revised estimate, 46, 54-5 ; as to quality and packing, 49 ; 1000 ling to be bought to carry the ships to the West Country, 67 ; committee to provide, 75 ; warrant £50, p. 92 ; stockfish for the North West Voyage, 209.

Fisher, William, assembly, 59 ; warrant £80 for oil, 114 ; bill of adventure sealed £240, p. 260.

Fishing tackle, 52.

Fitche, Mr., committee for merchandise, 26.

Flags, streamers and ancients ordered, 108 ; do. for the " Hector," 151.

Fleming, } Giles, bill for iron, 128 ; balance
Flemyng, } due to Richard Hart, assigned to Mr. Flemyng, 147 ; warrant £29 1s. 4d., p. 172.

Flemyng's Voyage, the Book of the, dedicated to the Co., 125.

Fletcher, Mr. } provision of cider, 38, 68 ;
Fletcher and Co. } order to settle accounts, 127 ; allowed £5 for racking cider, 176.

Fletcher, John, auditor, 166, 218 ; warrant £129 9s. for cordage, 224 ; bill of adventure sealed £240, p. 256.

Fletcher, Walter, adventurer, £200, p. 2 ; assembly, 5.

" Flyboats " for the North West Voyage, 220, 221.

Formation of the Co. and objects, 5.

Fortescue, Sir John, *Privy Councillor;* letter from the Privy Council to the Co. favouring the voyage, 61 ; orders in council, 112, 164.

Founders Hall ; used for the Company's meetings, 11 ; general court, 57 ; warrant £6 for six quarters rent, 227.

Fowle, Alphonsus, bill of adventure sealed £240, p. 255.
Franklyn, John, carries a letter to Captain Waymouth in the Downs, 223.
Frauncis, Peter, *of Bridgewater, a native of Portugal;* compounds for his entertainment in the voyage, 38; to sail in the "Susan" with Mr. John Havard, 117.
Free-brethren } of the Company, *see Freemen.*
Free-brothers }
Freeman, *see Freman.*
Freemen, *see also Disfranchisement;* adventurers not named in the patent to be deemed equally as free as those mentioned, 109; their names to be presented and then confirmed as free, 110; William Beerblock admitted by way of assignment of part of Earl Cumberland's stock, 161; John Jackson admitted in lieu of John Bate, 174; refusal to grant freedom for £105, p. 175; Francis Dent named in the patent desires to assign, and referred to a general court, 175; list of persons made free though not named in the patent, 177; disfranchisement of certain defaulting adventurers, 178; Robert Bayly assigns to Sir John Spencer, and renounces his freedom, 181; Sir John Spencer allowed to nominate a freeman, 181; John Morice made free in place of Nathaniel Martin disfranchised, 185; book sent round for all freemen to subscribe to the second voyage, 187; Joseph Jackson made free on the nomination of Sir John Spencer, 187 (*see* 181); Robert Bowyer made free in the place of Xpofer Clethrowe, 190; William Nelson admitted on paying £240 adventure and supplies and £30 premium, 205; freedom denied to Peter Wellington, 226-7; the freedom of Thomas Stephens deferred, 227; Thomas Stephens admitted, 239.
Freman, Ralfe, adventurer with William Freman, £300, p. 2; assembly, 4
Freman, William, adventurer with Ralfe Freman, £300, p. 2; assemblies, 180, 181, 186, 192, 204, 205, 215; general committee and sworn, 179; bill of adventure sealed £240, p. 258.
French; letters brought home from the "Assention" by a Frenchman, 242; rivalry between English and French ambassadors at Constantinople as to consulage, 265, 266, 269, 271, 272; complaints to the queen by the French ambassador, 265, 271, 273; Signior Paul Pinder sent from Constantinople to acquaint the queen of the doings of the French, 265, 272, 273; instructions to the English ambassador, 266, 269; do. to the consul at Aleppo, 271-2; orders for the prevention of private trade by French ships from Aleppo to Marseilles, &c., 272.
Fretum, Davies, route to the North West Passage, 212.
Frier, } John, assembly, 59; bill of adventure
Fryer, } sealed £240, p. 260.
Frythe, Roger, *smith,* warrant £19 for iron work, 221.
Furner, Symon, warrant £326 13*s.* 4*d.* for powder, 122; do. £371 15*s.*, p. 142; do. £16 10*s.*, p. 184.
Fysher, *see Fisher.*

Gallata House, instructions to Mr. Saunderson for its sale or letting, 274-5.
Gallaunt, Peter, *merchant in Turkey,* 268.
Gamond, John, *surgeon of the "Susan,"* warrant £20 to provide remedies, 98.

Gamrain, } Nathaniel, elected factor of the
Gamrym, } third sort, 83; to sail in the "Dragon," 101; warrant £30 for his entertainment, 139; bill of adventure sealed £50, p. 150.
Garrard, Samewell, adventurer with John Suzan, £200, p. 4.
Gartoeway, *see Garway.*
Garway, Thomas, *Draper,* adventurer, £200, p. 1; bill of adventure sealed £240, p. 255.
Garwaye, } William, *Draper,* adventurer, £500,
Garwey, } p. 2; assemblies, 7, 9, 10, 20, 24, 26, 27, 28, 31, 37, 46, 57, 58, 64, 68, 69, 73, 78, 80, 82, 85, 86, 88, 90, 93, 94, 98, 99, 102, 106, 107, 108, 114, 116, 118, 121, 138, 140, 142, 144, 148, 151, 152, 158, 164, 167, 184, 186, 190, 196, 236, 237, 244, 247; committees, 6, 8, 9, 12, 32, 58, 71, 76, 77, 87, 91, 106, 141, 147, 155, 197, 234, 237, 239; views ships, 13; surveyor for the "Assention," 14; to enquire price of peas, 26; desired to answer the Lord Treasurer's letter respecting the employment of Sir Edward Michelborne, 28; guarantees William Leake as purser of the "Assention," 33; warrant 100 markes towards repairs of the "Assention," 57; do. £200, p. 85; do. £100, p. 91; do. £100, p. 105; do. £130, p. 114; do. £100, p. 126; do. £100, p. 140; do. £50, p. 144; general committee, 63; warrant £194 5*s.* 6*d.* for oil, 114; buys steel, 138; assigned by Mr. Brodebent to pay balance of his mortgage to the company, 154; general committee, 179; do. and sworn, 225.
Gawldsmith, Mr., supplies meal, 90.
General Courts.
October 28, 1600. The objects and proceedings of the company reviewed, 60; letter from the privy council confirming priviledges, &c., 61; adventurers in arrears to be certified to the privy council, 61; the patent drawn up, 62, (*see* 108); election of Sir Thomas Smyth as first governor, 62; election of the general committee of, 24, 62-3; all business committed to the care of the governor and committee, 63.
December 8, 1600. Order for the bringing in of adventures in arrears, 93; Mr. Brund elected a principal factor, 93.
January 9, 1600-1. The patent read, 109; deficiency in the adventure and steps taken to supply it, 111; Mr. Rumney elected deputy governor, 111.
January 14, 1600-1. Order in council for adventurers in arrears to bring in their money at once on pain of imprisonment, 112-13; order confirming a levy of 2*s.* in the £, 113; the common seal ordered, 113.
February 10, 1600-1. Laws and ordinances enacted, viz., all things to be managed as a joint stock and no private trade to be practised, 130; all private goods shipped to be forfeited to the common stock, 130; ordinances against fraud, 130; proposed leaving of factors to trade in the East Indies, 131; the commission to the general or principal merchant and to others in succession, 132-37 (*see Commissions*); an act touching the bringing in of the supply of 2*s.* in the £, 137-38.
April 1, 1601. A new supply of 2*s.* in the £ to pay the company's debts, 160; the £1,500 taken up at interest by the treasurer to be discharged by the company, 161; William Beerblock admitted an adventurer for £200 by way of assignment of so much of the

General Courts, *continued*.
  Earl of Cumberland's stock and also made free, 161.
  April 11, 1601. Order in council touching the discredit likely to arise through the remissness of the company in paying their debts and ordering defaulting adventurers to appear and be punished for contempt, 164-65; resolution that great care be taken to remove all discredit, and for the better ordering of business Alderman Wattes elected governor in place of Sir Thomas Smyth in prison, 166; auditors chosen for the treasurers' accounts, 166.
  May 29, 1601. John Bate disfranchised, and John Jackson admitted a freeman, 174; respecting other adventurers, in arrears, 174-5.
  July 6, 1601. Certain persons made free whose names are not in the patent, 177; touching the supplies due on the Earl of Cumberland's assigned stock, 177; adventurers in arrears to be prosecuted, 178; certain freemen disfranchised, 178; election of governor, deputy, and committees and the oath of office, 179-80.
  July 24, 1601. Assignment of John Bayly's stock to Sir John Spencer, 182; letter received from Captain George Waymouth proposing that the company should undertake a voyage for the discovery of a North West Passage to the East Indies, 182.
  August 7, 1601. A voyage to discover the North West Passage resolved on, 183; a levy of 12*d*. in the £ to support the expence of the same, 183; committee appointed to estimate the expense, 183; the governor to peruse the charters to see if authority is given to compel contributions for the North West Voyage, 183.
  September 2, 1601. Two ships for the North West Voyage to be prepared forthwith and the subscription book to be sent round for adventurers to set down their sums at 12*d*. in the £, 185.
  September 13, 1601. Differences with the Muscovia Co. as to the respective rights of the two companies to the North West Passage if discovered, 186; a second voyage by the Cape resolved on, and the adventure to be not less than £100, p. 186.
  October 12, 1601. Respecting the differences with the Muscovia Co. as to the North West Passage, 187-89, *see North West Passage*; the second voyage by the Cape, complaints as to the delay, &c., &c., 189-90, *see East India Company*.
  November 5, 1601. *See North West Passage*, 190-91; letter from the privy council respecting the delay in the second voyage by the Cape, and propounding the example of the Dutch, 191.
  November 9, 1601. *See North West Passage*, 192; the assignment of the stock of Clement Moseley, deceased, 192-93.
  December 22, 1601. *See North West Passage*, 194-96.
  January 5, 1601-2. *See North West Passage*, 196-97.
  January 11, 1601-2. Laws and ordinances for the government of trade, &c., agreed on, 197-202, *see East India Company*; committee to expedite the North West Voyage, 202-3.
  March 17, 1601-2. William Nelson admitted an adventurer of £200 on paying £30 premium, 205; the supply for the North West Voyage to be brought in at once on pain of forfeiture, 205; Thomas Yerworth engaged as purser, 205.
  March 29, 1602. Touching the supplies for the North West Voyage, *see East India Company*, 206-8.
  April 14, 1602. Several warrants signed, 214-15.
  April 30, 1602. Articles of agreement with Captain Waymouth read, also the Queen's letters to the Emperor of China, 217; auditors appointed to ascertain the state of the adventure that further supplies may be called up and some course taken with the defaulters, 217-18.
  May 18, 1602. Bond of indemnity sealed to Alderman Cambell; supplies for the North West Passage to be brought in at once; new bills of adventure to be made out containing every man's stock and all supplies in one gross sum, 220; several warrants for necessaries for the North West Voyage, 221.
  July 6, 1602. Election of governor, deputy, and committees, &c., 225-6.
  July 28, 1602. Election of Mr. Cambell as governor, 226.
  September 17, 1602. The return of Waymouth, 228-9, *see North West Passage*.
  October 18, 1602. Certain stores, &c., returned from the North West Passage to be sohl, 230; Alderman Holliday's payments being in arrears, ordered that the same be deducted from his stock, 231.
  November 24, 1602. Proceedings respecting Waymouth's return, *see North West Passage*, 233-4.
  January 4, 1602-3. Deliberations as to a second voyage for the discovery of a North West Passage, 237-8.
  January 26, 1602-3. The North West Voyage abandoned and committee appointed to see to the sale of the ships and stores, 238-9; Mr. Thomas Bramley chosen deputy-governor, 239.
  June 6, 1603. Letter received from the purser of the "Ascention" homeward bound, 242-3.
  June 16, 1603. Proceedings respecting the return of the "Assention," *see East India Company and "Assention,"* 244-7.
  June 23, 1603. Customs Duties on the goods from the "Assention," 248; money raised to pay the mariners, 249; orders and commissions for the sale of the goods brought home, 249.

Georg, Giles, nominated factor, 77.
Gibbons, Roger, warrant £39 on bill of exchange, 79.
Gibson, Anthony, adventurer, committees, 245, 246; bill of adventure sealed £240, p. 258.
Gilderns, 208.
Ginger, quantity ordered and committee to provide, 75.
Girdeler, Francis Tailor, 169. (N.B. The Girdlers Company was incorporated in 1448.—*Bailey*.)
Glasses, to be ordered, 79; warrant £43 16*s*. 6*d*., p. 129.
Globe, *ship*, viewed, 13.
God, John, warrant £40 on bill of exchange, 82.
Goddard, } Richard, *Alderman*, adventurer,
Godderd, } £200, p. 1; assemblies, 4, 7, 9, 10; committees, 6, 8, 12.

Godspeede, **one of the ships for the North West Passage Voyage**, *see also Pinnaces, Ships, "Discovery," North West Passage, Waymouth.* John Drewe, *master;* Edward Pullison, *purser;* John Lane, *master's mate;* Thomas Boarne, *steward.* Warrant £10 to John Drewe in part of his wages, 210; manned, victualled, and furnished to Waymouth's own desires, 211-12; covenant for the payment of John Drew's wages, 220, **221**; several warrants for the provision of stores and necessaries, 220-1, *see Warrants;* return to Dartmouth, 227-9; arrival in the Thames, 229; ordered to be sold with all stores, &c., 230; Mr. Cartwright, *preacher,* accused of being the persuader of the return of the voyage, 232; various warrants for wages, 234-5; warrant £4 to the porters for landing and housing the stores, 238; warrant £20 to the wife of Thomas Bowrne, steward, in full of all demands, 240; sale of the ship deferred, 241; ordered to be sold if £300 can be had, 242.

Gelding, Robert, *of Radcliff, mariner;* order to be paid £300 for the "Guift," 154.

Goldsmiths, *see Richard Wiseman, John Cornelis, Richard Youxon, William Beerblock, George Smythes.*

Goods, *see Merchandise.*

Gore, John, adventurer **with William Gore,** £300, p. 3.

Gore, Raph, assembly, 59; **bill of adventure** sealed £360, **p 253.**

Gore, Robert, assembly, 59; **bill of adventure** sealed £240, p. **235.**

Gore, William, **adventurer with John Gore,** £300, p. 3.

Gossen, (Richard, ordered to clear accounts

Gosson, { with Mr. Holliday, 127; to bring in his account, 159; {bill of adventure sealed, £240, p. 251}; do. £240, p. 261.

Gover, John, warrant £96 8s. for aquavitae, 107.

Governor and Company, *see East India Company, also Company of Levant Merchants.*

Governors of the East India Company, *see also Deputy Governors;* Mr. Thomas Smyth elected first governor, 62; Mr. William Rumney elected deputy, 111; Sir Thomas Smyth being in prison and Mr. Rumney ill, Mr. Alderman Wattes elected governor, 166; Mr. Wattes re-elected with Mr. Rumney as deputy, 179; the oaths of office, 179; powers at a general court, 201-2; Sir John Harte elected governor, 225; Sir John Harte declines to serve and Mr. Cambell elected in his stead, 226.

Gowns, 208.

Grand Signior (*Turkey*); grants all capitulations except as to consulage, 265.

Grants of Privilege, &c., *see Patent, also Privilege.*

Gratuities, £100 in gold to be given, 106; £20 (or 20s. ?) to William Walter who dedicated to the company the Book of the Flemyng's Voyage, 125.

Gravesend, 44, **153**; ships to be surveyed there before sailing, 141; bullion to be shipped there, 142; Mr. Holliday to take down money for harbour wages and clearing expenses, 146; committee to see the discharge of the ships thence, 147; committee left there, 152; warrant to Mr. Rumney for travelling expenses, 158; Waymouth to sail from thence, 216.

Great Seal, warrant for expence of making, 107.

Greene, Lawrence, adventurer, £200, p. 2.

Greene, Reynold, adventurer with John Newman, £200, p. 2; assemblies, 4, 59; **bill of** adventure sealed £240, p. 251.

Greene, Robert, nominated factor, **77.**

Greenewell, *see Greenwell.*

Greenewood, John, bill of **adventure sealed,** £240, p. 260.

Greenland, *Groynland,* 212.

Greenwell, William, assemblies, 180, 181, 182, 183, 184, 185, 186, 187, **190,** 193, 196, 197, 226, 228, 232, 236, 237, 241, 242, 244, 247; committee, 183, 186, 191, 197, 203, 209, 234, 237, 239, 247, 248; surveyor of the "Malice Scurge," 33; auditor, 166; general committee, 179; do. and sworn, 225; bill of adventure sealed, £240, p. 253.

Greewell, *see Greenwell.*

Gregorie, Richard; warrant £40 on **bill of exchange,** 84.

Grenewell, *see Greenwell.*

Grocers, *see Nicholas Barnesley; George Bowles; Richard Burrell; Ralfe Buzbie; Richard Cockes; Robarte Coxe; Thomas Cuttelev; George Holman; Thomas Juxon; William Nelson; Edmund Nicholson; Robarte Sandye; Nicholas Style; Oliver Style;* warrant to pay the grocers' porters for loading the ships, 138.

Grove, Peter; warrant £70 **in full payment,** 71.

Grove, Philip, *second pilot;* assembly, 46; appointed pilot, 47; warrant £30 on account of wages, 56; committee on lead, 79; to sail in the "Hector" as second pilot of the fleet, 110; warrant £11 for boat hire, &c., 138; to have a bill of adventure for the composition made with him, 139; bill of adventure sealed £500, p. 148.

Groynland, Greenland, 212.

Gryce, George, *carriage maker,* warrant £3 8s. p. 221.

Grynkin, Robert, warrant £30 for watches, compasses, &c., 213.

Gryvell, Foulke, *treasurer of the navy,* asked for the use of the docks at Woolwich, 13.

Guarantees, Alderman Bannyng for Joseph Salaman, purser of the "Susan," 33; Mr. Stapers for George Parsons, purser of the "Hector," 33; Mr. Garwaye for William Leake, purser of the "Assention," 33.

Guift, *ship,* 120 *tons,* bought to accompany the fleet with victuals, 147-48 (*see* 143); warrant £300 in payment, 154; sent out with victuals and to be cast off afterwards, 264.

Gully Key, *wharf,* 138.

Gum Lacre, quantity brought home by the "Assention" entered at the Custom House, 247.

Gunners, number to be employed in each ship, 99; committee to provide stores, 117; warrant £30 12s. 4d. for stores, 157.

Gunpowder, 122, 142, 184, 219, 221.

Haberdashers, *see Hugh Hammersley; Humfrey Miltward; Thomas Smithe;* warrant to pay the haberdashers' porters for lading ships, 138.

Hackett, } [Richard], *historiographer;* assembly, 10; requested to give information as to places of trade in the East Indies, 123-24; warrant £10 for his advice and 30s. for maps, 143.

Haggett, Bartholomew, assembly, 60; respecting the payment of his adventure, 126; war-

Haggett, Bartholomew, *continued*.
  rant to bring in his adventure at once, 170;
  committees, 245, 246; bill of adventure sealed
  £240, p. 258.
Haies, *see Hayes*.
Haiward, John, nominated factor, 77.
Hakluyt, Richard, *see Hacklutt*.
Hale, Mr. *of the Bridgehouse*; order to deliver
  timber to Mr. Burrell, 89.
Hale, Richard, bill of adventure sealed, £240,
  p. 253.
Hale, Sergeaunt, *see Heale*.
Hale, William, bill of adventure sealed, £240,
  p. 253.
Hall, Richard, *blacksmith*, warrant, £30 10s.
  for anchors, 151; do. £26 for iron work, 221.
Halledaie, }
Halleday, } Leonard, *see Holliday*.
Hallidaie, }
Hallidaie, William, *Mercer*, adventurer with
  John Duckett, £200, p. 3.
Hallydaie, } Leonard, *see Holliday*.
Hallyday, }
Halmeden, Edward, *see Holmeden*.
Hamer, Ralfe, *see Hamor*.
Hamersley, Hugh; assemblies, 59, 237; com-
  mittees, 237, 239; surveyor for the "Assen-
  tion," 14; declines to adventure, 62; warrant
  to bring in his adventure, 170; offers to bring
  discharge of some account in lieu of adventure
  money, 170; pays his adventure £240, and
  admitted a freeman, 175; made free though
  not named in the patent, 177; appointed auditor, 218; bill of adventure sealed, £240, p. 261.
Hamond, Mathew, adventurer with others,
  £300, p. 3.
Hamor, Ralfe, *Merchant Tailor*, adventurer,
  £200, p. 2; assembly, 60; bill of adventure
  sealed, £240, p. 255.
Hampson, Robarte, Alderman, adventurer,
  £300, p. 1; assembly, 244.
Hanckey, *see Hankin*.
Handford, Humfrie, bill of adventure sealed,
  £240, p. 260.
Hangar, George, warrant £231 10s. for canary
  wine, 103.
Hankin, Roger, *Master of the " Assention ";*
  committee to treat with him, 69, 70; master
  of the "Assention," 97; warrant £36 0s. 4d.
  for ballast, &c., 97; to sail in the "Assention," 100; warrant £50 on account of wages,
  104.
Harbie, John, *Skinner*, adventurer, £200,
  p. 4; assemblies, 203, 232, 241, 242, 248;
  general committee and sworn, 179; do.
  225; bill of adventure sealed, £240, p. 259.
Harbour wages at Gravesend, 146.
Harby, *see Harbie*.
Hardway, John, warrant £57 13s. for casks, 147.
Hare, Samuel, bill of adventure sealed, £240,
  p. 254.
Harrison, Edward, assembly, 59; bill of adventure sealed, £240, p. 258.
Harrison, } William, adventurer with William
Harryson, } Bonde, £200, p. 3; assemblies, 20,
  22, 24, 26, 27, 28, 33, 37, 39, 46, 56, 57, 58, 59,
  64, 66, 67, 68, 73, 74, 77, 80, 82, 83, 85, 86, 88,
  89, 90, 91, 93, 94, 95, 96, 98, 99, 103, 104, 106,
  108, 113, 114, 117, 118, 119, 121, 122, 123,
  124, 125, 128, 138, 139, 140, 144, 150, 151,
  155, 156, 158, 160, 162, 163, 164, 167, 170,
  171, 172, 174, 175, 176, 180, 183, 185, 208,
  214, 215, 216, 217, 218, 224, 225, 226, 227,
  229, 230, 232, 233, 236, 238, 241, 244, 247,
  249; committees, 12, 22, 27, 30, 67, 75, 76,
  99, 107, 124, 127, 143, 147, 156, 158, 186, 197,
  203, 209, 229, 234, 237, 239, 240, 245, 248;
  views ships, 13, requested to provide peas
  and beans, 29; signature to West Country
  commission, 52; general committee, 63;
  warrant £378 for canary wine, 103; do. £70
  for vinegar, 114; to provide ship's stores for
  the "Assention," 117; audits accounts, 147,
  148², 158; to gather into a warehouse all
  stores left behind, 159; appointed auditor,
  166; general committee and sworn, 179; do.
  225; signatures to treasurer's warrants, 206,
  210; bill of adventure sealed, £240, p. 260.
Hart, Richard, warrant £100 for smithery, 104;
  balance of account to be paid to Mr. Flemyng, 147; warrant £161 13s. 1d. for iron
  work, 157.
Harte, Sir John, Knight, adventurer with
  George Boales, £1,000, p. 1; assemblies, 4,
  58, 111, 159, 164, 242; elected governor, 225;
  declines to serve on account of age, 226;
  gives his bond as security for money to be
  raised at interest, 240; indemnified for the
  same by a general bond under the common
  seal, 250; bill of adventure sealed, £600, 256.
Harvy, John, appointed auditor, 166 ("Harby).
Harvy, Stephen, bill of adventure sealed, £240,
  p. 260.
Harvy, William, of *Bridgewater*, warrant £50
  on bill of exchange, 73; do. £40, p. 74;
  do. £400, p. 141.
Haselton, Agnes, warrant 40s. to relieve her
  husband hurt in the "Hector," 173
Haselton, Richard, 173.
Havard, John, elected a principal factor, 81;
  appointed to the "Susan," 94, 100; to sail in
  the "Susan" with Peter Francis, 117; order to
  provide ship's stores for the "Susan," 117;
  warrant £250 for men's wages for the "Susan,"
  118; do. £100 for his entertainment in the
  voyage, 123; commission to take chief command in case of death of Captains Lancaster
  and Middleton, and Mr. Brund, 135; bill of
  adventure sealed, £200, p. 150.
Hawkyns, John, bill of adventure sealed, £240,
  p. 255.
Hayes, Thomas, adventurer with others, £300,
  p. 3; made free though not named in the
  patent, 177; bill of adventure sealed, £200,
  p. 261.
Heale, Sergeaunt, will provide money in the
  West Country, 45; draws bill on Warwick
  Heale (of Plymouth), £200, p. 47, 54; war-
  rant £200 for do., 55; warrant £50 for so much
  paid to the company's agent at Exeter, 119.
Heale, Warwicke, *see Heale, Sergeaunt*.
Hearne, Richard, warrant to bring in his adventure at once, 170; bill of adventure sealed,
  £240, p. 250.
Heckes, *see Hick*.
Hector, *ship*, 300 tons; Captain Middleton,
  first factor; Henry Napper, *master*; Philip
  Grove, *second pilot of the fleet*; George
  Parsons, *purser*; James Lovering, *surgeon*;
  William Starkey, *second factor*; Thomas
  Dassell, *third factor*; Thomas Tudd, *fourth
  factor*. Surveyors appointed, 14; inventory,
  15; warrant £100 for necessaries, 25; the
  purser guaranteed by Mr. Stapers, 33; rated
  100 men, 300 tons, 34; the aquavite shipped,
  35; warrant £100 for repairs and provisions,
  65; a mast ordered, 71; to be manned with
  100 men, 72; warrant £100 for her provision,
  79; do. £100, p. 88; number of carpenters,
  caulkers, gunners, stewards, cooks, surgeons

R R

Hector, *continued*.
and barbers to be employed, 89-90; Captain Middleton to sail in the "Hector," 94; warrant £100 for preparations, 96; warrant £25 to James Lovering, *surgeon*, for his medicine chest, 98; warrant £100 for repairs and preparations, 99; Vice Admiral's ship, 100; list of officers appointed, 100; do. factors, 101; warrant £200 for wax candles, &c., 104; do. £50 for iron work, 105; do. £60 to Xpofer Thompson, a smith, 111; do. £100 to Mr. Wyseman, 111; do. £100 to William Dixon, 111; do., £100 for timber, 114; committee to provide stores, 117; warrant £250, 117; do. £100 for provisions, 121; the amount of new and Spanish money carried in each ship and how packed, 122; warrant £100 for wages, 139; do. £2 13*s*. to Mr. Pope, Sergeant of the Admiralty, on a bill of charges for the burial of 'those slain in the "Hector," 141; warrant £100 to the purser for charges, 142; do. £20 to Henry Napper, *master*, for his pains in the preparation of the ships, 143; warrant £30 10*s*. for anchors, 151; list of presents to be carried, 151; warrant £100 for wages and clearing expenses, 154; do. £8 4*s*. for porterage and lading, 158; do. £6 for a pinnace, 167; do. £86 15*s*. 4*d*. for sails, 168; do. £3 15*s*. for caske, 172; do. 40*s*. to relieve Richard Haselton, hurt, 173; memorandum tonnage 300, men 100, p. 263.
Hedger, William, warrant £6 for a pinnace for the "Hector," 167; do. £5 10*s*. for a boat for the "Discovery," 223.
Hedland, John, warrant £16 1*s*. 8*d*. for carriages, 163.
Heighoo, Robert, warrant £42 15*s*. for canvas, 164, 168.
Helinge, Peter, warrant to bring in his adventure at once, 170; made free though not named in the patent, 177; bill of adventure sealed £240, p. 257.
Helle, *see Heale*.
Helmes, Edmund, *of Burford in Oxon*; Re the assignment of £100 adventure of Clement Moseley, deceased, 193.
Helms, Peter, deceased, 226; his stock assigned to Peter Wellington, 226.
Helyn, *see Helinge*.
Hemyng,   } Roger, assembly, 59; committees,
Hemmyng, } 245, 246; bill of adventure
Hemmynge,} sealed £240, p. 250.
Henshaw, } Thomas, adventurer with William
Henshawe, } Adderley, £300, p. 2; assemblies, 5, 59; will bring in Mr. Addersley's adventure, 63; bill of adventure sealed, £240, p. 255.
Heralds, warrant £13 7*s*. 8*d*. to William Segar, *herald*, for writing the Queen's letters to the Kings of the East Indies, 139; warrant 20 merkes to the King of Heralds for assigning the company's arms, 171.
Herbert, Mr. Secretary, 9, *see Privy Council*; letters from the Privy Council to the company, 60, 61; orders in council, 112, 164; committee to solicit a warrant to remove the plate from the governor's house, 141.
Hercules, *ship*, 99.
Hertrowe, 74.
Hewett, John, adventurer, £333 6*s*. 8*d*., p. 3; bill of adventure sealed, £240, p. 254.
Hewett, William, assembly, 59.
Hewghes, *see Hughes*.
Hewitt, John, *see Hewett*.
Hewitt, Thomas, bill of adventure sealed, £240, p. 254.

Hewys, Thomas, *Clothworker*, warrant £12 8*s*. 6*d*., p. 159.
Heyes, *see Hayes*.
Hiccocke, Thomas, adventurer, £100, p. 1; assembly, 4.
Hick, Baptiste, *Mercer*, adventurer, £400, p. 2; assembly 4.
Hickes, Thomas, nominated factor, 77; elected factor of the third sort, 83.
Hickock, *see Hiccocke*.
Hides, warrant £28 18*s*. for hides to make the mariners cassocks, breeches, and gowns for the N. W. voyage, 208.
Higelord, *see Highlord*.
Higboe, } *see Heighoo*.
Highoo, }
Highelord, } Edward, *purser of the* "*Mare*
Highlord, } *Scourge*," *afterwards of the* "*Assention*," warrant £100 for repairs of the "Scourge," 87; do. £200 for her preparation, 106; do. £180 for mariners' wages, &c., 154; letter from him from the "Assention" brought home by a Frenchman, 243; order to attend on board the "Assention" until ship is discharged, 246.
Highlord John, adventurer with John Marris, £200, p. 3; assemblies, 4, 59, 64, 66, 68, 69, 71, 73, 77, 80, 82, 83, 85, 86, 88, 89, 92, 94, 97, 99, 100, 103, 104, 106, 109, 112, 115, 123, 127, 138, 140, 144, 154, 155, 156, 158, 160, 162, 164, 167, 168, 170, 171, 172, 173, 175, 176, 180, 182, 183, 184, 185, 186, 192, 193, 197, 225, 235, 238, 244, 248; committees, 158, 245; appointed treasurer, 7; surveyor for the "Susan," 14; general committee, 63; to wait on Lord Cumberland as to damage done by the anchor of the "Red Dragon," 128; warrant, £14 7*s*. 4*d*. for money laid out, 162; general committee, 179; do. and sworn, 225; bill of adventure sealed, £240, p. 260.
Hilles, Peter, warrant £3 15*s*. for casks, 172.
Hilliard, Mr., contracts for dollars at 4*s*. 6*d*., p. 20; committee, 79.
Historiographer, *see Hacklett*.
Hodgeson, John, assembly, 60; bill of adventure sealed, £240, p. 252.
Hodgeson, Stephen, bill of adventure sealed, £220, p. 159; pays £10 supplies for North West voyage with apologies for delay, 235; bill of adventure and supplies sealed, 240, p. 250.
Hodgson, } *see Hodgeson*.
Hodsonn, }
Hogsheads, *see Casks*.
Holiday, *see Holliday*.
Holland, Bartholomew, assembly, 59; bill of adventure sealed, £240, p. 251.
Holland, Ling, 209.
Hollidaie,} Leonarde, Alderman, adventurer
Holliday, } £1,000, p. 1; assemblies, 4, 14,
Hollyday, } 20, 22, 24, 26, 27, 28, 31, 33, 46, 47, 56, 57, 58, 64, 65, 67, 68, 69, 71, 76, 78, 80, 82, 83, 85, 86, 88, 89, 91, 92, 93, 94, 95, 99, 100, 102, 104, 106, 107, 109, 112, 115, 119, 124, 127, 128, 144, 148, 150, 151, 158, 160, 167, 173, 176, 186, 192, 226, 244, 248; committees, 12, 32, 37, 38, 58, 68, 71, 73, 76, 77, 80, 91, 99, 141, 147; per his man, 245, 246; warrants for the payment of money as treasurer of the company, *see Warrants*; views ships, 13; bills from the West Country, 50; signature to West Country commissions, 52, 54, 55; general committee, 63; to buy fish, 75; as to the coining of £6,000 in the Tower, 120;

INDEX   307

Hollyday, Leonarde, *continued*.
  account of the new and Spanish money in his
  custody prepared for shipment, 127; to clear
  accounts with Mr. Angell and Mr. Gosson,
  127; to carry to Gravesend money for the
  clearing of the ships, 146; order to raise
  £1,500 on his credit and Alderman Bannyng's,
  146; to render accounts, 156; to be indemnified for the £1,500 raised at interest, 161;
  to deliver bills of adventure to every adventurer, 175; general committee, 179; £230
  adventure assigned to him by Earl Cumberland, 197; receives £240 adventure from
  William Nelson with £30 premium, 205;
  ordered to bring in £38 6s. 9d. balance of his
  treasurer's accounts, 231; being in arrears
  with his adventure for the North West
  voyage, ordered that the same be defaulted
  out of his East India stock, 231; (*see page*
  200); bill of adventure sealed, £1,440, p.
  262; do. £230 assigned to him by the Earl
  of Cumberland, 262; part owner of the ship
  "Exchange," 276
Hollywell,—nominated factor, 77.
Holman, George, *Grocer*, adventurer, £150,
  p. 1; assemblies, 4, 60; bill of adventure
  sealed, £240, p. 257.
Holmden, (Edward, *Alderman*; adventurer
Holmeden, { £500, p. 1; assemblies, 74, 76,
Holmenden, (79, 80, 119; general committee,
  63; bill of adventure sealed, £1,200, p. 256.
Holway, Nycholas, warrant £50 on bill of
  exchange, 58.
Honey, barrels required, 30; estimate of
  quantity and price, 35; committee to provide,
  35; warrant £21 1s. for 32 jars, 125.
Horton, Thomas, assemblies, 50, 229, 232, 240,
  242, 247; general committee and sworn, 225;
  committee, 248; bill of adventure sealed,
  £240, p. 252.
How, (Roger, adventurer, £200, p. 3; assem-
Howe, (blies, 5, 7, 9, 10, 28, 31, 37, 39, 46,
  47, 56, 57, 58, 64, 66, 67, 69, 73, 74, 79, 82, 85,
  86, 88, 93, 98, 100, 102, 104, 109, 118, 122, 124,
  140, 142, 170, 172, 173, 175, 176, 177, 181, 182,
  192, 203, 215, 216; committees, 6, 8, 12, 28,
  40, 41, 75, 76, 99, 120, 127, 183, 243; views
  ships, 13; sent to the West Country for
  dollars and victuals, 15, 21; warrant £500
  for use in the West Country, 29; feoffee in
  trust for the ships bought, 37; provision of
  victuals, 38; purchase of the "Malice
  Scurge," 45; signature to West Country
  commissions, 52, 54, 55; warrant £200 to pay
  to Sergeaunt Heale for a bill of exchange on
  Plymouth, 55; do. £50 to pay to Laurence
  Waldo for a bill on Exeter, 55; general committee, 63; to answer letters from Plymouth,
  64; letters to Captains Baker and Davies,
  &c., 66, 74; to see to the making of bags,
  86; to write into the West Country to provide no more bread, &c., 88; warrant £600
  on bill of exchange, 102; to answer letters
  from West Country factors, 103; buys vinegar, 115; to clear accounts with Mr. Sandy,
  127; warrant £20 for attending to business
  in the West Country, 140; commission to go
  into the West Country, 147; to bring in his
  account, 159, 172; presents his West Country
  account, 173; allowed with Mr. Combe £18
  7s. 2d. for expenses in the country, 176;
  general committee and sworn, 179; bill of
  adventure sealed, £360, p. 256.
Howse, Richarde, adventurer with Henry
  Robinson, £200, p. 3; assembly, 5.

Huberd, Miles, adventurer with Thomas
  Cambell, £200, p. 2.
Hughes, Robert, appointed sailmaker of the
  "Mallyce Scurge," 40; warrant £49, p.
  167; do. £32 10s. p. 221.
Hule, Hugh, admitted as an extra factor, 102.
Hull, peas and beans to be bought there, 29.
Humble, Richard, made free though not
  named in the patent, 177; bill of adventure
  sealed, £240, p. 251.
Humfrey, John, bill of adventure sealed, £240,
  p. 260.
Hurleston, Thomas, nominated factor, 77.
Huse, *see Hughes*.
Hylliard, Edward, appointed surveyor of the
  works on the "Malice Scurge," 40; to
  prevent the workmen from running to drink,
  40.
Hynde, William, bill of adventure sealed, £240,
  p. 257.

Impositions on certain goods offered to the
  Queen by persons attempting to supplant the
  Levant Co., 280; £4,000 per annum agreed to
  be paid to the Queen by the Levant Co. in
  lieu of impositions, 280, 282.
Incorporation of the East India Co.; petition to
  the Privy Council, &c., 8; *see East India Co.
  and Privy Council*.
Indemnities, *see Bonds*.
Instruments (naval), £30 granted to Captain
  Waymouth, 204; do. £20, p. 204; £100 al-
  lowed to Waymouth, 211; warrant £30,
  p. 218.
Interest, £1,500 to be borrowed, 146; £2,000
  do. 249.
Inventories of the ships "Hector," 15; "Assention," 16, 22; "Susan," 17; "Malice
  Scurge," 42.
Ipswich canvas, 164.
Iron, 30 tons to be sent out in the ships, and
  price, 36; 20 tons purchased, 41; quantity
  increased to 50 tons, 99; warrant £150,
  p. 104; do. £100, p. 104; do. £300, p. 111;
  do. £100, p. 119.
Iron hoops, quantity and price in the West
  Country to be ascertained, 49; warrant £36,
  p. 129; do. £6 10s., p. 219; do. £42, p.
  222; do. £42, p. 224.
Ironmongers, *see William Deyns, Nicholas
  Leatt, James Waters, John Woodwarde*.
Iron stoves for the North West voyage, 209.
Ironsyde, Richard, assembly, 60; bill of adventure sealed, £240, p. 258.
Ironsyde, Thomas, will bring in his money,
  63.
Ironwork, *see also smiths, iron iron hoops, &c.*;
  warrant £200, p. 41; do. £50 for the
  "Hector," 105; payment of a smith's bill
  stopped because he hath not paid for his iron,
  128, 147; warrant £100 for the "Red
  Dragon," 157; do., £161 13s. 1d. for the
  "Assention," 157; warrant £100, p. 163;
  do. £27, p. 168; do. £29 1s. 4d., p. 172;
  do. £227, p. 173; do. £19, p. 221; do.
  £26, 221; do. £22 6s., p. 221.

Jackson, John, *Clothworker*, admitted adventurer in lieu of John Hate, £200, p. 174; bill
  of adventure sealed, £240, p. 261.
Jackson, Joseph, admitted a freeman on the
  nomination of Sir John Spencer, 187 (*see*
  181).
Jamryn, *see Gamryn*.
Japon, Waymouth to receive £500 if he arrive

Japan, *continued.*
  at any port in Japan by a North West Passage, 214.
Java, 198.
Jaymes, Edwarde, adventurer, £200, p. 3.
Jennynges, William, assemblies, 59, 237, 241;
Jennyns, committees, 237, 239, 245, 246; [bill of adventure sealed, £240, p. 251]; do., 261.
Jewels, Mr. Hacklett, *historiographer*, reads out of his notes and books divers instructions, 124; instructions to the principal factor, 132, 133.
Johnes, Stephen, owner of the ship "Carnation" of Colchester, 263
Johnson, John, offers to serve as a master, 27. do. £12 6s. 8d., p. 219.'
Johnson, Patrick, warrant £38 for salt, 121;
Johnson, Robert, bill of adventure sealed, £240, p. 253.
Johnson, Thomas, *runaway servant of the Earl of Oxford*, order not to be allowed to go in the voyage, 125.
Joint stock, *see East India Co., and Adventurers*, all things to be managed as a joint and common stock, and no private trade to be allowed, 130, 133.
Jones, Thomas, bill of exchange for £200 paid to the company at Plymouth, 68.
Journals, the pursers of the North West voyage to make notes, journals, and observations for the direction and help of posterity, 213; journal from Captain Waymouth, 227.
Juxon, Thomas, *grocer*, adventurer £200, p. 3; bill of adventure sealed, £240, p. 251.

Kathia, *see Cataia.*
Kellett, William, warrant to bring in his adventure at once, 170; made free though not named in the patent, 177; bill of adventure sealed, £240, p. 261.
Kempe William, warrant £30 on bill of exchange from Plymouth, 80.
Kerby, *see Kirby.*
Kerseys, Committee to provide, 31; quantity
Kessies, to be sent out, description and price, 35; proposed trade with China and Cataia by the North West passage if discovered, 199; duties at Constantinople and Aleppo to support the ambassador's and cunsuls' charges, 267, 270, 271, 274, 279.
Key, Robert, bill of adventure sealed, £240, p. 258.
King James I., customs due on goods brought home in the "Ascension," 247, 248, 250.
King of Heralds, *see Heralds.*
Kings of the East Indies, letters to, 91, 131, 134, 139.
Kintalles, weight for bread, 41.
Kirby, Jeffrey, Mr. Bannyng required to pay the £200 set down for Jeffrey Kirby, 126; bill of adventure sealed, £240, p. 258.
Knives, 70.
Knowles, Sir William, Privy Councillor, 60.
Kymber, Mr., *wharfinger*, warrant £34 16s. 8d. for lighterage and porterage, 158; do. £3, p. 224.

Lacy, John, warrant, £188 for cordage, 126.
Lacy, William, *of Hertrowe*, warrant £110 on bill of exchange, 74.
Lading of the ships, warrant to pay the porters, 158.
Lambard, Henry, warrant £10 5s. 8d. for Black Jacks, 105.

Lamps, five dozen required, and price, 35.
Lancaster, Captain James, *chief commander in the voyage*, assemblies, 14, 22, 24, 26, 27, 28, 31, 33, 39, 44, 45, 46, 47, 56, 57, 64, 71, 73, 74, 76, 78, 80, 82, 83, 86, 88, 89, 90, 91, 92, 94, 95, 96, 98, 99, 100, 102, 103, 104, 106, 107, 109, 113, 114, 117, 118, 119, 142, 143, 144; committees, 12, 22, 26, 27, 28, 30, 37, 40, 57, 67, 69, 72, 75, 87, 91, 94; views ships, 13; warrant £200 to buy iron work and caske, 41; signature to West Country commission, 52; committee to treat with him for taking the chief command, 58, 66, 71, 73; general committee, 63; warrant £100 on account for his entertainment, 89; order to agree with the carpenters, caulkers, and gunners, 90; nominated as principal factor to sail in the "Scourge," 94, 100; instructions as to the mariners' shares of reprisals, 119; motion for £100 to be paid to the purser of the "Hector" for provisions, 121; his commission and instructions for the voyage, 132; the Queen's approval of his appointment, 132; authority by letters patent to correct and chastise offenders, 132; private traffic not to be permitted, but all trade to be reckoned as a joint and common stock, 133; measures to prevent private trade, 133; penalties for embezzlement and fraud, 134; instructions for factors to be left resident in foreign parts, 134; instructions for the devolving of the chief command in case of death, &c., 135; warrant £200 for his entertainment, 139; do. £11 7s. 8d. for money disbursed, 139; purchase of the ship "Guift," 147; bill of adventure sealed, £1,500, p. 150; bill of adventure sealed, £240, p. 257.
Lane, John, *master's mate of the "Godspeede,"* examined as to the cause of the return of Captain Waymouth, 232; warrant 30s. for wages, 234 (*see* 205).
Language of Sumatra. An Englishman knowing the language brought home by the Dutch, 194.
Lant, John, *of Exeter*, warrant £150 on bill of exchange, 81.
Lanternes, 157, 209, 223.
Lanthornes,
Latterfield, Edward, bill of adventure sealed, £240, p. 258.
Launches, *see pinnaces.*
Lawrence, Simon, bill of adventure sealed, £240, p. 258.
Laws, decrees, and ordinances of the company, *see also Rules and East India Company*, 129, 197-98, 198-202.
Lead, quantity to be sent out and price, 36; committee to provide, 79; warrant £224 2s., p. 95; do. £150, p. 105; do. £49, p. 143; warrant for payment of charges for cutting lead, 203; warrant for lead for the North West voyage, 210; do. £8 8s., p. 224.
Leake, William, purser of the "Assention," 33; warrant £150 for men's wages, 117; do. £100, p. 154.
Leaman, John, made free though not named in the patent, 177.
Leanyng, Edward, assembly, 59.
Leat, *see Leatt.*
Leate,
Leathersellers, *see Henrye Bridgeman.*
Leatt, Nicholas, *Ironmonger*, adventurer, £200, p. 1; assemblies, 4, 7, 9, 10, 59, 180, 183, 187, 190, 192, 197, 203, 204, 205, 206, 208, 214, 215, 216, 217, 218, 219, 225, 227;

Leatt, Nicholas, *continued*.
committees, 6, 8, 10, 191, 193, 205, 209; surveyor for the "Hector," 14; appointed auditor, 166; general committee and sworn, 179; signatures to treasurer's warrants, 206, 210; warrant £150 for necessaries provided, 215; do. £20 for mariners' clothes, 218; do. £51 3s. 3d. for disbursements, 223; bill of adventure sealed, £240, p. 253; money taken up at Constantinople from his factor for the use of the ambassador, 280.
Lecheland, Mr., *of Culleton*. Price of peas, 54.
Lee, Robarte, *Alderman*, adventurer, £300, p. 3.
Leeninge, Edward, bill of adventure sealed, £360, p. 256.
Leet, *see* Leatt.
Leman, John, bill of adventure sealed, £240, p. 255.
Letters to the Earl of Essex asking his consent to Captain Davies being appointed chief director of the voyage, 25; from the lord treasurer recommending Sir Edward Michelborne to be employed, 28; from the Lord Treasurer to the receivers of Devon and Cornwall, authorizing credit to be given to the company's agent for purchasing provisions, 38; letters commending several men to be employed as pursers, 39; from Mr. Pope with advice of proceedings in the purchase of provisions, 64; do. from Captain Baker, 64; from Mr. Ellycot as to the provision of royals in the West Country, 64; replies to Captain Davis, Captain Baker, Robert Pope, Mr. Ellicott, and Mr. Sandy, 66; from the West Country as to the proceedings of the business, 74; from the Queen to potentates in the East Indies, 91, 131, 134, 151; warrant £13 7s. 8d. to William Segar, *herald*, for writing the Queen's letters, 139; from the Privy Council respecting adventurers in default, &c., 164-65; the Queen's letters to the Emperor of China, &c., for the North West voyage, 217; warrant £4 15s. for charges for the Queen's letters, 222; warrant 28s. 8d. to John Franklyn for carrying a letter to Captain Waymouth in the Downs, 223; to the pursers of the North West voyage to preserve all things suitable for a second voyage, 228; letters from and to the purser of the "Assention," respecting the return of that ship, 242-43; to the merchants of Dartmouth and Plymouth to give credit to the officers of the "Assention," 243-44; *see East India Company*; several drafts of letters in the East India Company's Record Book, tending to show that the East India Company was partially an outgrowth from the Levant Company, 265-83; *see Company of Levant merchants, viz.*: to Mr. Lyllo, English ambassador at Constantinople, 265-70, 282; to Richard Colthurst, consul at Aleppo, 270-72, 278-79, 283; to Mr. John Saunderson, merchant at Constantinople, 273-75, 279-80; to Mr. Byddell, preacher at Aleppo, 275-76; to Mr. ———, merchant at Scanderona (?), 276-77; to Mr. May, preacher at Constantinople, 281.
Letters Patent, *see Patent*.
Levant merchants, *see Company of*.
Levant seas. Outrages by English men-of-war, 280, 282, 283.
Levies of 2s. in the £ to make up deficiency in the total required, 110; to be brought in within 6 days on pain of forfeiture of double the value, 111; levy confirmed, 113; act touching the bringing in the 2s. in the £, 137; voluntary levy of 12d. in the £ for the North West adventure, 183; 12d. in the £ for the North West voyage and penalties for default, 199-200; proposed levy by the poll and upon the rates of particular adventures to raise money hereafter required, 249; levy on certain goods entering Constantinople and Aleppo to support the ambassador's and consuls' charges, 267, 270, 271, 272, 274, 279.
Lieth, Thomas, warrant £68 18s. for pewter, 129.
Lighterage, 158, 173.
Lighterman, William Allom, 173.
Limehouse, 208.
Linen cloth, warrant £125 10s. for, 97.
Linendrapers, *see John Buckbridge, see also Drapers*.
Ling, *see Fish*.
Ling, Holland Ling, 209.
Linge, *see Lynge*.
Lioness, *ship*, viewed, 13.
List, of adventurers and amounts subscribed, 4; of caske required, 30; of provisions required, 34-5; of merchandise to be carried, 36-7; of timber borrowed from Her Majesty's storehouse at Woolwich, 71-2; of factors nominated, 77, 101; of silver plate and presents, 141, 151; of provisions for the North West voyage, 209; of bills of adventure sealed, 250-62.
Locks, } Mr. Smalwood, 223.
Locksmith, }
Lodgings for mariners, warrant £4 7s., p. 222.
Lokar, Edward, nominated factor, 77.
Looking-glasses, to be provided as presents, 116, 141, 151.
Lord Admiral, letters from the Privy Council to the company, 60, 61, 164; wine given to him in lieu of deodand claimed for the "Hector," 169; touching the tithes due for the prize taken in the East Indies, 246; respecting the outrages by the men-of-war in the Levant seas, 282.
Lord Chief Justice, 61, 112.
Lord Keeper, 112, 164.
Lord Mayor of London, Sir Stephin Soame, 1.
Lords of the Council, *see Privy Council*.
Lord Treasurer (? T. Buckhurst, *see* p. 38), 9, 60, 61, 112, 164, *see Privy Council*; letter recommending Sir Edward Michelborne to be employed, 28; letters to the receivers of Devon and Cornwall to extend credit to the company's agents, 38; warrant for providing peas and beans in Cambridgeshire and Norfolk, 66; letter recommending Henry Aneys to be employed, 85; respecting bullion in the Tower, 87; committee to solicit warrant to deliver the silver plate out of Mr. Governor's house, 141.
Lovering, James, *surgeon of the "Hector"*; warrant £25 to provide remedies, 98.
Luellen, Morrice, bill of adventure sealed, £240, p. 254.
Lydall, Thomas, bill of adventure sealed, £240, p. 257.
Lyllo, *Mr.*, resident English ambassador at Constantinople, letter of instructions, 265, *see Company of Levant merchants*; his salary, 271; contentions with the French as to the Dutch consulage, 271-2; credit for his wants supplied by Mr. Saunderson, *merchant*, 273, 279; creditor of the company for 1,000 chesskeens, 274.
Lymehouse, *see Limehouse*, 208.

Lyng, } Nicholas, adventurer, £100, p. 2; as-
Lynge, } semblies, 4, 7, 9, 59, 64, 68, 77, 78, 79, 80, 82, 83, 88, 91, 92, 93, 94, 95, 96, 99, 100, 107, 108, 112, 118, 122, 124, 128, 129, 140, 142, 143, 155, 158, 162, 164, 167, 168, 170, 171, 175, 176, 177, 180, 181, 183, 184, 185, 186, 190, 203, 205, 214, 217, 219, 225, 228, 229, 230, 231, 233, 235, 236, 238, 240, 241, 242, 244; committees, 6, 8, 97, 128, 156, 158, 205, 209, 214, 229, 234, 248; surveyor for the "Assention," 14; general committee, 63; buys cloth, &c., 97; warrant £20 for charges, 111; general committee and sworn, 179; do. 225; requested to provide bags for the pepper brought home in the "Assention," and suits without pockets for the porters, 247; bill of adventure sealed, £240, p. 257.
Lypson, Derick, warrant £40 for steel, 138.
Lytleford, Mr., committee, 246.

Mabanck, Arnold, *pulleymaker*; warrant £56 7s. 9d. for work done, 163; do. £9 10s. for pulleys, 221.
Macy, William, bill of exchange, £112, p. 88.
Magelano, Straits of, 183.
Makesfield, John, *brasier, see Maxfield*.
Malaga wine, 169.
Malice Scurge, } *see* " *Mare Scurge*."
Mall Escourge, }
Mallett, Justice, *see Mullett*.
Mallett, William, warrant £70 on bill of exchange, 85.
Malyce Scurge, *see* " *Mare Scurge*."
Manley, Nicholas, bill of adventure sealed, £240, p. 258.
Maps, three maps supplied by Mr. Hacklett, 143; Fretum Davies and Greenland, 212.
Marche, *see Marsh*.
Mare Scurge, *ship*, afterwards re-named the "Red Dragon;" 600 tons, Admiral ship of the fleet. Captain Lancaster, *General of the Fleet*; Captain Davis, *Pilot Major of the Fleet*; William Broadbent, *Master*; Robert Pope, *Second Factor*; Nathaniel Gamram, *Third Factor*; Xpofer Stradling, *Fourth Factor*; William Burrage, *Boatswain*; Ralph Salter (?) *Surgeon*. Motion for buying her from the Earl of Cumberland, 20; her tonnage found to be too great, but recommended for the second voyage, 20-1; surveyed and price inquired, 27; £3,000 offered for her, but declined; offered at £4,000; to be re-surveyed and price considered, 29; £3,500 offered and declined, 30; price settled at £3,700 by arbitration, 31-2; surveyors appointed, 33; William Burrage, boatswain, ordered to see to the preparation of the ship, 33; rated, 200 men, tonnage, 600, p. 34; quantity of aquavitæ, 35; committees to watch her preparation, 39; a barrel of beer a day allowed to the workmen to prevent their running from their work to the alehouse, 40; ship's boat lying at Plymouth to be sent up, 40; sailmakers appointed, 40; inventory of the ship, 42; a chain pump advised, 44; the bargain and sale sealed with the Earl of Cumberland, and manner of payment, 45; a new long boat ordered, 46; the boat lying at Plymouth to be inspected, 51; men required to complete the ship to be drawn from the "Susan," 56; warrant £1,000 for repairs, 65; do. £100, p. 70; quantity of timber borrowed from Her Majesty's storehouse at Woolwich, 71; to be manned with 180 men, 72; warrant £100 for timber, 74; do. £80 for preparations, 74; do. £100, p. 84; do. £50 for repairs, 87; do. £100, p. 87; do. £4 recompense to a poor man for the bulging of his crane, 88; number of carpenters, gunners, caulkers, stewards, cooks, surgeons, and barbers to be employed, 89-90; the Pilot-Major and Mr. Bradbanck, *Master*, to sail in the "Scurge," 90; Captain Lancaster appointed principal factor, 94; ordered to be launched and re-named the "Red Dragon," 96, *see henceforth* "*Red Dragon*;" the "Carnation" of Colchester buoyed on an anchor belonging to the "Scurge," 263.
Margann, *see Morgan*.
Mariners, *see also Masters*; William Tavernor engaged, 68; all mariners to be paid two months' wages in advance and two months' wages in adventure stock, 70; number of men in each ship, 72; to be engaged by the committee and masters, 78; as to prizes and prize money, 118; warrant for board wages, 208; hiring of mariners in the West Country, 209; warrant £28 18s. for hides to make mariners' cassocks, breeches, &c., for the North West Voyage, 208; warrant £20 for clothes, 218; warrant £4 7s. for mariners' lodgings, &c., 222; warrant to pay mariners hired at Dartmouth to bring to London the ships returned from the North West voyage, 231; penalty for removing goods without leave from the "Assention," 245; money to be raised at interest to pay mariners' wages, 249.
Marris, John, adventurer with John Highlord, £200, p. 3.
Marseilles (Marcelles), orders for the prevention of private trade from Aleppo, &c., 272.
Marshe, Daniel, assembly, 59; offers to bring in his money if he can be employed, 63; nominated factor, 77.
Marshe, James, warrant £9 15s. for deals, &c., 169; order to enquire into Mr. Adye's account for timber, 173.
Marshe, Thomas, bill of adventure sealed, £200, p. 261.
Masters, *see also Captains*; John Johnson offers as a master, 27; William Brodebent thought suitable, 44; Roger Hankin to be compounded with, 69, 70; Thomas Eldred recommended, 72; no master to be employed till seen and spoken with, 72; to engage other officers and mariners, 78; committee to hire and compound with, 87; Mr. Bradbanck to sail in the "Scurge," 90; committee to treat with Mr. Beare, 90; the choice of masters to be discussed at a general court, 92; appointed to their respective ships, 100; Samuel Spencer of the "Susan," 116; the terms of Mr. Brodebent's bill of adventure, 153.
Masters' mates, John May, 224.
Martin, Nathaniel, assembly, 59; declines to adventure, 62; John Morice adventures £200 in his place, 185.
Martin, Roger, admitted as an extra factor, 102.
Martin, William, *of Exeter*, respecting money in the West Country, 51, 53, 54; his son recommended to be employed, 97.
Martyn, *see Martin*.
Masts for the ships: "Hector," 71; overcharge by the carpenter of the "Susan," 121, 157; warrant £16 6s. 10d., p. 157; do. £150, p. 164; do. £3, p. 222.
Maxfield, John, *brasier*, warrant £11 10s. for

Maxfield, John, *continued*.
copper vessels, 164; do. £17 17s. for brass pots and copper kettles, 222.
May, Faith, *wife of John May*.
May, John, *master's mate of the "Susan,"* warrant 30s. to Faith May in part of his wages, 224; do. 56s., p. 248.
May, Mr., *preacher at Aleppo*, letter ordering him home, 281.
Mayflower, *ship*, viewed, 13.
Meal: an estimate submitted, 26; estimate of quantity and price, 34; revised estimate, 46, 54-5; quantity to be bought in the West Country, 41, 52; instructions as to quality and packing, 48; warrant to buy the Spanish meal taken prize in Lord Willoughby's ship, 86; no more to be bought, 88; committee to provide for the North West Voyage, 209.
Medicine, warrant £32 to Raphe Salter for furnishing his chest, 95; do. £25 to James Lovering, surgeon of the "Hector," 98; do. £20 to Christopher Newchurch, surgeon of the "Assention," 98; do. £20 to John Gamond, surgeon of the "Susan," 98.
Megges, William, order to bring in £100 balance of his adventure, 162; bill of adventure sealed, 250.
Men-of-war, outrages by English, in the Levant, 280, 282, 283.
Mercers, *see William Allen, Thomas Cordell, William Halliday, Baptiste Hick, Clement Moseley*.
Merchandise: committee to consider what is suitable for the voyage, 26; quantity and description to be shipped, 36; total value, 37; committee to consider and order small merchandise, glasses, knives, &c., 79; shipping mark, 107; committee to enter and pay customs, &c., 118; sixty pieces of chanelettes shipped without warrant, 123; all merchandise to be accounted for as a joint and common stock, 130, 132; rules for the prevention of private trade, 130, 133; the kinds to be sought in the East Indies, 198; the object of the attempted discovery of the North West Passage was to create a market for English goods in the temperate climates of Cataia and China, 199; a convenient quantity laden in the two ships for the North West Voyage, 212; the pursers to keep an account of the same, 212-13; warrant £51 3s. 3d., p. 223; the merchandise returned from the North West Voyage to be carried to Mr. Wiseman's house and inspected, 231; ordered to be sold, and a committee appointed to attend to the sale, 239, 241; committee to attend to the unlading of the "Assention," 243; list of goods brought home in the "Assention," 247; committee to prepare the vaults under the Exchange to receive goods, 247-48; committee to see the goods sent to the Exchange, 248; committee to receive and weigh goods at the Exchange, 248; order and commission for the sale of the goods, 249.
Merchants, *see Factors, Adventurers*; letters to merchants in Plymouth and Dartmouth to give credit to the "Assention" on her return, 263.
Merchant Tailors, *see William Boude, Ralfe Hamor, John Robinson, senior*.
Michelborne, Sir Edward, recommended by the Lord Treasurer to be employed as a chief commander, 28; resolution of the committee to employ no gentlemen, 28; disfranchised, 178.

Middleton, *see Midleton*.
Midleborough, advice from thence of two Dutch ships returned laden with pepper, 194.
Midleton, Mr., *of Plymouth*; warrant £5 for riding post from Plymouth with first report of the return of the "Assention," 247.
Midleton, Henry, recommended as a purser, 39; appointed surveyor of the works on the "Mallice Scurge," 39; order to prevent the workmen running to drink, 40; warrant £100 for charges for the "Mace Scurge," 36; nominated factor, 77; warrant £100 for the "Scurge," 78; elected factor of the third sort, 83; warrant £300 for the provision of the "Scourge," 95; appointed second factor in the "Susan," 101; warrant £100 as purser of the "Red Dragon," 104; warrant £50 for his entertainment, 141; bill of adventure sealed, £100, p. 152.
Midleton, Captain John: assemblies, 33, 37, 39, 44, 57, 59, 64, 67, 68, 71, 74, 77, 78, 80, 83, 86, 88, 89, 90, 92, 93, 94, 95, 96, 98, 100, 103, 104, 106, 107, 108, 109, 117, 118, 121, 122, 123, 139, 140, 142, 143, 144; committees, 30, 57, 72, 86, 94; surveyor for the "Susan," 14; do. "Mare Scourge," 27; commends Henry Midleton as a purser, 39; general committee, 63; committee to agree with him for going on the voyage, 77, 90; nominated factor, 77; elected a principal factor, 81; to sail in the "Hector," 94, 100; ordered to provide ship's stores for the "Hector," 117; his commission, 135; appointed to take chief command in the event of the death of Captain Lancaster, 135; warrant £100 for his entertainment, 140; do. £8 3s. 7d. for disbursements, 140; do. £34 3s., p. 142; directs £100 to be paid to the purser of the "Hector," 142; bills of adventure sealed, £400 and £220, p. 150; receives £38 10s. from Mr. Rumney for mariners' wages, 158; bill of adventure sealed, £240, p. 256.
Midleton, Robert, adventurer with others, £500, p. 2; assemblies, 4, 59; warrant £27 6s. 6d. for sugar, 149; committee, 243; bill of adventure sealed, £240, p. 254.
Midleton, Thomas, adventurer with others, £500, p. 2; assemblies, 4, 9, 28; committees, 6, 8, 9; recommends Robert Creswell as a purser, 39.
Mildmay, Robert, assembly, 59; warrant to bring in his adventure at once, 170; bill of adventure sealed, £240, p 251.
Millett, William, bill of adventure sealed, £240, p. 257.
Milward, Humfrey, *haberdasher*, assents to bring in his supplies, 175; bill of adventure sealed, £240, p. 230.
Money. *See also Dollars, Bullion, Coin, Royals, Warrants, Adventurers*; no sum above £10 to be disbursed by the treasurers without a warrant, 24; money in the West Country, 45; instructions for taking up money and giving bills of exchange, 50; money wanted to pay wages, 92; committee to attend to the shipping of money in the West Country, 120; £6,000 coined in the Tower, 120; amount of new and Spanish money apportioned to be carried in each ship and how packed, 122; to be entered at the Custom House and water-borne to Gravesend and stowed in the ships, 142; order for £1,500 to be taken up at interest, 146; warrant £29 10s. for stamps made for the East India monies, 174; the mislike to

Money, *continued*,
the transportation of so much coin out of the country, 198; money to be raised at interest for payment of mariners' wages returned in the "Assention," 249.
Moone, Richard, money supplied in Plymouth, 64.
Moore, John, *alderman*, adventurer, £300, p. 1; assemblies, 7, 9, 58, 65, 68, 71, 82, 87, 80, 90, 93, 94, 96, 98, 99, 100, 102, 103, 115, 118, 123, 140, 144, 148, 150, 151, 159, 176; committees, 8, 58, 71, 73, 77, 91, 115, 147; appointed director, 6; general committee, 63; bill of adventure sealed, £480, p. 262.
Morgan, } Thomas, nominated factor, 77;
Morgann, } elected factor of the fourth sort, 83; to sail in the "Susan," 101; order to be paid £20 for his provision to sea, 126; bill of adventure sealed, £40, p. 152.
Morice, } John, adventures £200 in place of
Morrice, } Nathaniel Martin, 185; bill of adventure sealed, £240, p. 261.
Mort, royals to be procured there, 51.
Mortgage, £100 lent to William Brodelent, master of the "Red Dragon," 128; the same repaid, 153.
Moseley, Anthony, warrant to be paid £25 10s. for vinegar, 115; made free, though not named in the patent, 177; bill of adventure sealed, £240, p. 257.
Moseley, Clement, adventurer with Jerome Suger, £250, p. 2; assembly, 4, 59; deceased and assignment of stock, 192; bill of adventure, sealed, £240 to his widow, 251.
Moseley, Elizabeth, widow of Clement Moseley, 193; bill of adventure sealed, £240, p. 251; do. £240, p. 261.
Moseley, John, assignment of £100 of Clement Moseley's stock, 193; assembly, 228.
Moseley, Nicholas, *alderman*, adventurer, £300, p. 1; assembly, 4.
Moskova, } Company. *See Muscovia.*
Moskvy, }
Mosley, *see Moseley.*
Mullett, Justice, employed as a smith at Woolwich, 40; warrant £29 11. 4d. for iron work, 172.
Muscatel wine (muskadell), impost offered in opposition to the Levant Company, 280.
Muscovia, } Company, warrant £180 for cord-
Muskovia, } age, 126; do. £57 16s. 8d., p.
Muskovy, } 187; a target and headpiece, 141; respecting cordage, 162, 170, 204; £100 adventure in arrears from Richard Tailby assigned over for payment to the Muscovia Company, 176; touching the respective rights of the Muscovia and East India Companies to the benefit of the North West Passage if discovered, 185, 186, 188-89, 190-91, 194-96, *see North West Passage.*
Mustard seed, one tonne of dry caske required, 30; thirty bushels to be bought, 33; estimate of quantity and price, 35; committee to provide 30 bushels and caske, 76; committee to provide for the North West Voyage, 209.
Myddleton, } *see Midleton.*
Mydleton, }
Myldmay, *see Mildmay.*
Mylward, *see Milward.*

Nails, 157, 172.
Napper, Henry, "*master of the Hector;*" committee to confer with him touching his employment, 94; to sail as master in the "Hector," 100; warrant £20 for his pains and expenses in the preparation of the ships, 143.
Nelson, William, admitted an adventurer £240, and pays premium of £30, p. 205; committees, 245, 246.
Nets, fishing, to be bought in the West Country, 41.
Newcastle, 223.
Newcastleship, *ship*, viewed, 13.
Newchurche, Christopher, *surgeon of the* "*Assention;*" warrant £20 for providing surgeon's remedies, &c., 98.
Newcombe, Mr., bill of exchange £60 for money advanced to Captain Waymouth, 209.
Newman, John, adventurer with Reinold Greene, £200, p. 2; assembly, 218; general committee, 179; bill of adventure sealed, £240, p. 252.
Newton, a fit place to buy cider, 49.
Nicholles, Christopher, made free though not named in the patent, 177; bill of adventure sealed, £240, p. 262.
Nicolls, Xpofer and Thomas, warrant £34 7s. 10d. for cordage, 222.
Nicholson, Edmond, *Grocer*, adventurer, £200, p. 4; committee, 245, 246; bill of adventure sealed, £240, p. 253.
Nicholson, Edward, assembly, 59.
Norromborough, Ware, 79; warrant, £207, p. 138.
Northeover, Thomas, warrant, £40 on bill of exchange, 80.
North West Passage, *see also Waymouth and East India Co.*; letter received from Captain George Waymouth suggesting an attempt be made for the discovery of a North West Passage to the East Indies, asking whether the company will undertake the expedition, &c., 182; the matter adjourned for further consideration, 182; the voyage resolved on, 183; the adventure to be voluntary at the rate of 12d. in the £ on the amounts of original adventures, 183; committee to set down and report the charge for three pinnaces for the voyage, 183; the charters to be perused to see if power is given to compel payments towards this voyage, 183; conference with Waymouth; two pinnaces resolved on of 50 and 40 tons with 16 and 14 men and the total charge estimated at about £3,000, p. 184; Waymouth agrees to undertake the voyage for £100 for his instruments and to receive £500 if he discover the passage but to claim nothing if unsuccessful, 184; Waymouth's agreement reported to a general court and approved and the preparation of the voyage to be taken in hand, 185; a book to be sent round for adventurers to subscribe at 12d. in the £, 185; doubts arising as to the rights of the Muscovia Co. and fearing they might claim the benefit of the discovery if made, a committee appointed to enquire whether that company will relinquish their privileges during the continuance of the patent, 187; deliberations with the Muscovia Co. who decline to give up their rights, but offer to admit as freeman all those of the East India Co. who will contribute to a joint adventure, 188; proposal that the Muscovia Co. shall exclude from all benefit in the discovery for 15 years all their own members who will not contribute, and such of the East India Co. as will contribute £10 to have the freedom of the discovery under the seal of the Muscovia Co., 188-89; the Muscovia Co. having no liking to

INDEX   313

North West Passage, *continued*.
join with the East India Co. prefer to deal in
the discovery by themselves, but will assign
no time for so doing ; the importance of the
enterprise urged, and a committee appointed
to confer again, to the end that if the Muscovia Co. will undertake the discovery, they
may be left to proceed in it, but if otherwise
then to request them to join with the East
India Co. on conditions formerly propounded
and if they will do neither, a relation to be
made to the Privy Council of their refusal and
hindering of the East India Co. in the intended
discovery, and the Muscovia Co. to be required to answer in writing, 191 ; in consequence of a better opinion conceived of the
strength of their privileges, the East India
Co. resolve to attempt the voyage alone ; ordered that adventurers shall write their contributions at once, and any person refusing, to
be excluded from all benefit during the term
of the patent, and all profit in the discovery to
rest proportionately in those who will adventure, 92 ; the Privy Council learning that by
reason of the difference between the two
companies the preparation of the voyage is
delayed, wrote to the Muscovia Co. to either
join with the East India Co. or else bring
their patent before the Council to show their
claim to their privileges, 194 ; the Muscovia
Co. thereupon agree to act jointly with the
East India Co., 195 ; the subscription book to
be sent round that everyone may set down
his adventure or else refuse, and those who
refuse to be exempted from all benefit in the
discovery for ever, 195 ; the amounts adventured to be brought in within a month, 195 ;
the committees of both companies to meet
from time to time to agree on the preparations of the voyage, &c., 195 ; doubts arising
as to the powers of either Co. to subdivide
themselves and unite partially with each
other, it is ordered that counsel's opinion be
taken thereon, 195 ; counsel's opinion that
the interest in the discovery rests expressly
with the East India Co. and that no company
can divide their privileges or grant a portion
of their rights to another company, 196 ;
finally resolved that the voyage shall be prepared and a committee appointed to expedite
the same and to devise laws and ordinances
for the general guidance of business, 196-97 ;
the laws and ordinances devised and the main
object of the proposed discovery set forth together with the details for the preparation of
the voyage, 198-202, *see East India Co.*;
£30 allowed to Waymouth for his instruments,
204 ; warrant £30 to Waymouth for provisions, 204 ; do. £20 for instruments, 204 ;
committee to persuade adventurers to pay
their contributions on pain of the penalty
enacted, 205 (see 209); Thomas Yerworth
appointed a purser with wages contingent on
the success of the voyage and to give bond
for his good behaviour, 205 ; John Drewe
appointed a master, 206 ; warrant £80 to
Thomas Yerworth, purser, for carpenters'
wages, 206 ; state of the preparation of the
voyage and steps taken to encourage the adventure, &c., 206-8, *see East India Co.*;
warrants for pork, mariners' wages, &c , 208 ;
warrant £28 18*s*. for hides to make the
mariners' cassocks, breeches, and gowns,
208 ; mariners hired at Exeter, 209 ; committee to provide victuals, &c., 209 ; warrant

£100 for anchors and other necessaries, 210 ;
warrant £10 to John Drewe, master of the
"Godspeed," in part of his wages, 210 ; warrant £100 to Thomas Yerworth for sea coals,
wood, lead, &c., 210 ; do. £100 to Waymouth for men's wages, 211 ; articles of agreement with Waymouth containing his orders
and instructions for the voyage, 211-14, *see
East India Co.*; agreement with John
Cartwright, *preacher*, with salary contingent
on the success of the voyage, 216 ; articles of
agreement with Waymouth read to the
generality, also the Queen's letters to the
Emperor of China, &c., 217 ; auditors appointed to ascertain the state of the adventure, that further supplies may be called up
and some course taken with the defaulters,
217-18 ; Waymouth allowed £50 for his expenses prior to sailing, 218 ; warrant £30 for
watches, compasses, &c., 218 ; do. £20 for
mariners' clothes, 218 ; do. £50 11*s*. 8*d*. for
casks, 218 ; do. £7 8*s*. for deals, oars, &c.,
218 ; do. £6 10*s*. for iron hoops, &c., 219 ;
do. £29 18*s*. for cables and skeyts, 219 ; do.
£92 10*s*. for butter, candles, powder, &c.,
219 ; do. £11 6*s*. 8*d*. for bay salt, 219 ; dislike to Thomas Yerworth, purser, 219 ; differences with the other purser Pullison, 219 ;
Mr. Cambell indemnified for his bond given for
the payment of John Drew's wages, 220 ; day
appointed for the payment of supplies and
new bills of adventure to be made out, showing in a lump sum what is every man's interest in the voyage by the Cape, 220, (see
resolutions on pages 206-8) ; day appointed
for the auditors to complete the accounts that
the whole charge may be made known, 220 ;
warrant £143 for canvas for sails, 220 ;
several warrants for sails, pullies, iron work,
beer, timber, powder, &c., 221-24, *see Warrants*; the book-keeper to complete the accounts for the North West voyage and to enter
up each adventurer's credit in a lump sum,
224 ; journal from Waymouth announcing
return to Dartmouth ; orders to bring the
ships to London without sale of provisions ;
letters written to the pursers to preserve all
things useful for a second voyage, and general
court summoned, 227-28 ; Mr. Cartwright on
being asked to state the reasons for the return, can give no further information than
Waymouth's journal, 228 ; the ships ordered
to London without breaking bulk, 228 ; Waymouth's delay in coming to London, 229 ;
ships' arrival in London and committee appointed to see to their discharge, 229 ; certain provisions to be sold, also the two ships
and their belongings, 230 ; Mr. Holliday and
others being in arrears with their supplies it
is ordered that the amount be defaulted from
their stock, 231 (*see* page 200) ; the merchandise brought back to be taken to Mr.
Wiseman's house and inspected, 231 ; John
Drewe, master of the "Godspeed," and John
Lane, master's mate, and others aver that
Cartwright was the chief cause of the return,
231 ; ordered that demand be made of Cartwright for the gown and apparel delivered to
him, 232 ; proceedings against Waymouth before the Privy Council ; his hopes of the discovery of divers inlets that treat through the coast
of America to the Southseas or East Indies ; a
new and final voyage resolved on and Waymouth reappointed chief in command ; his
confidence in the discovery of a passage ; a

S S

314　　　　　　　　　　　　　　INDEX

North West Passage, *continued*.
suitable captain to take charge of the second ship to proceed with Waymouth or separately as may be agreed; committee appointed to see to the preparation of the ships and calculate the charges, 233-34; various warrants for wages in the late voyage, 234-35; Stephen Hodsonn pays his supplies, 235; a new voyage with one ship only thought advisable, and conference to be had with Waymouth, 236; to save new expense it is suggested that the stores, &c., brought back by the two ships may be sufficient to equip one ship for a new voyage; committee to consider and confer with Waymouth or some other fit person, 236-37; the committee decide to use such old stores as are fit and by sale of the residue equip one ship for a new voyage, 237; at a general court the committee report against a second voyage and suggest it be abandoned and that the ships, &c., be sold, that money may be raised to defray the charges on the return of the fleet by the Cape, and by general consent the voyage is abandoned, and the ships, victuals, merchandise, &c., ordered to be sold and committee appointed to effect the sale, 239; demands by Waymouth for charges, moneys expended or otherwise due as he pretendeth, and the same agreed to be settled by arbitration, 240; the sale of the ships deferred, but all perishable merchandise to be sold at once, and prices being high at present all cordage to be sold at once, 241; the ships to be sold if £300 each can be obtained, 242.

Norwich stuff, quantity to be shipped and price, 36.

Notary, *see John Cowper*.

Number of men and tonnage of ships, for the East India voyage, 34; for the North West voyage, 184.

Nutmegs, estimates of quantity and price, 35; quantity ordered and committee to purchase, 75.

Oars (ores), 218.

Oaths of office for the Governor, Deputy and committees, 179-80.

Oatmeal, 12 tonne of dry caske required for, 30; estimate of quantity and price, 35; committee to provide, 75; do. caske for, 76; committee to provide for the North West voyage, 209.

Objects of the East India Company, 4, 198.

Objects of the proposed attempt to discover a North West passage, 199.

Obligations, *see Bonds*.

Ofeilde, Roger, *see Owfield*.

Offeley, Robert, assembly, 59; declines to adventure, 62; bill of adventure sealed, £240, p. 252.

Offeley, William, the elder, adventurer, £200, p. 4; bill of adventure sealed, £300, p. 256.

Officers, all officers to be elected by a general assembly, 6, 8; committee to hire ships' officers, 87; list of officers appointed to each ship, 100; the officers to be called on for an account of the provisions supplied to each ship, 126.

Oil, estimate of quantity and price, 35; committee to provide sweet oil, 76; do. rape oil, 76; do. casks for, 76; warrant, £213 6s. 8d., p. 111; do. £80, p. 114; do. £194 5s. 6d., p. 114; a barrel allowed to Samuel Spencer, master of the "Susan," 123; committee to provide for the North West voyage, 209; impost offered to the Queen in opposition to the Levant Company, 280.

Onnyslowe, Leonard, warrant £40 12s. for casks, 148.

Orders for the payment of money, *see Warrants*.

Orders in Council, *see Privy Council*.

Ordinances, for the guidance of the traffic of the voyage, 129-31; for the guidance of general business, 197-202; *see East India Company*.

Ordnance, quantity carried in the "Mare Scurge," 43-4.

Osborne, Sir Edward; his house nominated as a convenient place for storage of goods brought home in the "Assention," 245.

Osseley, *see Offeley*.

Owfield, Roger, adventurer, £300, p. 3; [assembly], 228; bill of adventure sealed, £360, p. 250.

Oxen, 120 to be bought for making salt beef, 114.

Page, Joseph, *baker*; warrant £80, p. 149; do. £50, p. 157; do. £45 10s. 11d., p. 167; do. £60, p. 215; do. £41 8s., p. 222.

Painter, John, *of Dartmouth*, bill of exchange £110, p. 70.

Painters, *see Francis Candell, Thomas Tyler*.

Palmer, William, assembly, 59; warrant to bring in his adventure at once, 170; bill of adventure sealed, £240, p. 260; do. £200, p. 261.

Paper, warrant, £90 10s., p. 126.

Paragon, *ship*, viewed, 13.

Parkehurste, Henrye, adventurer with John Coghill, £200, p. 3.

Parkins, Thomas, warrant £20 1s. for honey, 125; do. £78 16s. 4d. for casks, 143.

Parrett, warrant £207 for Norromborough ware, 138.

Parsloe, } assemblies, 231, 232, 236, 244, 248;
Parslowe,} general committee and sworn, 220; bill of adventure sealed, £240, p. 257.

Parsons, George, purser of the "Hector," 33; warrant £100 for provisions, 121; do. £100 for men's wages, 154.

Paslowe, *see Parsloe*.

Patent of the East India Company; petition to the Privy Council for leave to prepare a grant of privilege, &c., 10; Mr. Altham reads the draft of the patent, 25; the patent drawn, 62; committee to finish it, 78; adventurers in arrears to be dealt with before engrossing, 85; the patent read and the secretary ordered to solicit the Queen's attorney to make an end to the same, 88; committee to set down all names to be mentioned, 91; warrant £71 13s. 4d. to Mr. Attorney and clerks for drawing and engrossing the patent, &c., 96; warrant £50 for other charges in passing the patent, &c., 107; the patent read to the generality, 109; all adventurers not mentioned to be deemed equally as free as those named, 109; an adventurer named in the patent desiring to assign, is referred to a general court, 175; the assignment allowed, 177; list of persons made free though not named in the patent, 177; disfranchisement of certain defaulting adventurers, 178; reference to the patent as set forth in the preamble of the general laws and ordinances,

INDEX

Patent of the East India Company, *continued*— 198; power to make laws and ordinances, 199; the charters to be perused to see if the Company have power to compel payments towards the North West voyage and the second voyage by the Cape, 183; conferences with the Muscovia Company in reference to the respective rights to the North West Passage if discovered, 189; counsel's opinion that the East India Company have the right to the North West Passage under their patent, 192; limited time for the election of governor, deputy, and committees, 224.

Paule, William, adventurer with George Canynge, £100, p. 2.

Payment of money, *see Warrants*.

Peace with Spain, 10.

Pearde, Nicholas, *see Pierd*.

Peas, to be provided, 26; one hundred quarters required, 29; 30 tonnes dry caske required for peas and beans, 30; 60 or 70 quarters ordered, 31, 65; estimate of quantity and price, 34; price in the West Country to be ascertained, 49; instructions for buying in the West Country, 54; Lord Treasurer's warrant for the provision and transport of peas and beans from Norfolk and Cambridge, 66; committee to provide, 75; ditto, for the North West voyage, 209; committee to provide casks, 76; warrant £100 for peas and beans, 82; do. £100, p. 96.

Peierce, Richard, bill of adventure sealed, £240, p. 253.

Peird, *see Pierd*.

Penalties, for private trading and fraud, 130, 132, 133; for breach of the general laws and ordinances, 200-2; for default in the payment of adventure or supplies, 200, 207.

Pennington, Robert, warrant to bring in his

Pennyton, } adventure at once, 170; bill of adventure sealed £240, p. 250.

Pepper, estimate of quantity and price, 35; committee to provide 12 lbs., 75; two Dutch ships returned laden with pepper, 194; one of the articles to be traded in, 198; bags to be made and suits *without pockets* for the porters employed to fill in the pepper brought home in the "Assention," 247; quantity brought home in the "Assention" entered at the Custom House, 247.

Persia, Sir Anthony Shurley's doings in Persia, 272.

Persons, George, *see Parsons*.

Persons, Richard, bill of adventure sealed £200, p. 262.

Petitions of the East India Company to the Privy Council, *see Privy Council*.

Petition of the Levant Company to the Privy Council respecting their ships seized at Venice for restitution of the late prize taken by English men of war, 277-78 (*see also* 280, 282, 283).

Pett, Joseph, *shipwright*; warrant £42 for work on the "Godspeed," 223.

Pett, Peter, *shipwright*; warrant £17 12s. 6d., p. 169.

Pewter, warrant £68 18s., p. 129.

Phipps, Humfrey, warrant £20 for vinegar, 115.

Phoenix, *ship*, viewed, 13; offered for £1,400, and to be taken back for £700 after the voyage, or for £1,200 without return, 14; time taken to consider the matter, 21.

Piece, Nicholas (? Pierd), assembly, 59.

Pierd, } Nicholas, *clothworker*, adventurer,
Pierde, } £100, p. 1; assembly, 4; surveyor

for the "Hector," 14; to clear accounts with Mr. Sandy, 127; ordered to bring in his bill, 159; appointed auditor, 218; bill of adventure sealed, £240, p. 256; do. £240, p. 257.

Pilotage, warrant £6 for bringing the "Assention" into the river, 248.

Pilot Major of the Fleet, *see Captain Davies*.

Pilots; Philip Grove appointed and his pay fixed, 47; the pilot-major to sail in the "Scurge," 90; pilots appointed to their ships, 100; warrant £300 for salary to John Davies, pilot-major, 127; bill of adventure sealed to Philip Grove, 148; do. to Captain Davies, 152; warrant £6 for the hire of one Stace, a pilot, to go with Captain Waymouth to Newcastle, 223.

Pinder, Signior Paull, sent home by Mr. Lyllo, English ambassador at Constantinople, to acquaint the Queen with the doings of the French, 265, 272, 273; ambassador's accounts sent home by him, 266.

Pinnaces, *see Ships*; "Godspeed;" "Discovery;" committee to find suitable ones in the river, 22; no pinnaces to be used, but small lancher pinnaces to be carried in the ships, 28; "The Pynnace" rated at 40 men, tonnage 100, p. 34; proportion of aquavitæ, 35; a pinnace for the "Hector," 167; pinnaces for the North West voyage, 182; committee to set down the cost of three pinnaces, &c., 183; two pinnaces of 50 and 40 tons manned with 16 and 14 men resolved on, 184, 185; two ships or pinnaces finally resolved on, 199; Edward Pullison, *purser*, of one of the pinnaces for the North West voyage, 216, *see Pullison*; various warrants for the provision of sails, iron work, beer, pullies, timber, powder, &c., 221, *see warrants*; return to Dartmouth and ordered to London without breaking bulk, 227; all stores suitable for a second voyage to be carefully preserved, 228; arrival in the Thames, 229; ordered to be sold with all stores, &c., 230; warrant to pay the mariners hired at Dartmouth, 231; warrants 24s. to Thomas Smith for keeping the pinnaces, 234, 240, 241, 242; various warrants for wages in the late voyage, 234; the two "barks," order to be sold, 239; the sale deferred, 241; to be sold for £300 each, 242.

Piott, Richard, assembly, 60; bill of adventure sealed, £240, p. 253.

Pipes, *see Casks*.

Pitch, tar, cordage, &c., ordered to be bought of Browne and Co., 121.

Planks, 169.

Plate, *see silver plate*.

Platters, 157.

Plompton, warrant £67 9s. for rape oil, 119.

Plumber, *see William Haward*.

Plumes of feathers, 141, 151.

Plymouth, 29, 80; the "Mare Scurge's" boat lying there to be sent up, 40; recommended for the purchase of biscuit, 48; wine there and the price, 50; letters to the principal merchants to give credit to the "Assention" on her return, 243-4; warrant £5 to Mr. Midleton for riding with the first report of the return of the "Assention," 247.

Poalstedd, Henrye, adventurer with Georg Whitmor, £200, p. 4; assembly, 60; bill of adventure sealed, £240, 252.

Pockets; suits without pockets for the porters to fill bags with pepper brought home in the "Assention," 247.

Polklavies, to be bought for making bags, 86; 50 or 60 pieces to be bought to make bags for pepper, 247.
Polsted, see Poalstedd.
Pountell, Richard, assembly, 59; to bring in his bill, 159; bill of adventure sealed, £240, p. 254.
Poole, 129.
Pope, Lewis, bill of exchange, £40, p. 104; bill of adventure sealed, £240, p. 259.
Pope (Mr.), serjeant of the admiralty, warrant £2 13s. for the burial of those slain in the "Hector," 141.
Pope, Robarte, committee, 68; sent to join Captain Davies in the West Country, 29; commissions for buying provisions, &c., in the West Country, 41, 46, 48, 52, 53, 54; bills of exchange, 54, 57, 58, 68, 73, 74, 79, 81, 82, 84, 85, 88, 89, 104, 115, 129, 141; letters touching provisions and money, 64, 66, 74; nominated factor, 77; elected factor of the second sort, 82; letter from Mr. Howe to provide no more bread, &c., 88; paid £50 for his trouble in the West Country, 101; appointed second factor in the "Red Dragon," 101; Mr. Howe ordered to give him a remembrancer for the managing of business, 103; to confer with Mr. Ellicott as to shipping the Spanish money, 119; bill of adventure £100, sealed, 152.
Pork; estimate of quantity, 26; 40 tonnes of cask required, 30; estimate of quantity and price, 34; cheap in the West Country, 54; committee for ordering, 68, 75; do. for caske, 76; warrant £54 18s., p. 208; committee to provide for the North West Voyage, 209; warrant £111 5s. for pork and beef, for the North West Voyage, 214; pork brought back from the North West Voyage to be sold, 230.
Port of London, 229.
Portage; warrant £34 16s. 8d. for lighterage and portage of goods to the ships, 158.
Porter, Walter, adventurer with William Barrell, £400, 4.
Porterage, £1 for lauding goods from the "Godspeed" and "Discovery," 238; clothes to be made without pockets for the porters to fill bags with pepper, 247.
Portman, Sir Hugh, warrant £400 on bill of exchange from Hewghe, the West Country, 68; do. £1,000, p. 115.
Portman, John, warrant £200 to be delivered by him to the company's agent in the West Country, 87.
Post; letters to and from Exeter, 66, 74.
Pots of brass, 222.
Potter, John, adventurer with Robert Bell, £200, p. 3.
Poulsteede, see Poalstedd.
Powder, see Gunpowder.
Poyner, Walter, recommended by Mr. Chambers as a factor, 97; admitted as an extra factor, 102.
Poyntell, see Pountell.
Preachers, see Thomas Pullyn, John Cartwright, Mr. Ryddell.
Premiums on the sale or assignment of Clement Moseley's stock, 193; William Nelson pays £10 on his admission as an adventurer of £240, p. 205.
Presents for the Kings of the East Indies, 36; looking glasses, 116; silver cups, &c., 118;

list of plate and other presents, 141; how distributed among the several ships, 151-2.
Prices and quantity of provisions for the voyage estimated, 34.
Princes and Potentates in the East Indies; letters from the Queen, 91, 131, 134, 139; presents for, 141, 151.
Prisoners in the East Indies, 194; an Englishman brought home by the Dutch, 194.
Private trade, all factors to abstain from, 86; sixty pieces of Chamlettes shipped without warrant, 123; committee to devise orders to prevent, 124; ordinances for the prevention of, 130; do. from Aleppo to Marseilles, &c., 272.
Privilege, see also Patent; suit to be made to the Queen for sole privilege for as many years as can be obtained, 6; committee to solicit the Privy Council, 8; petition to the Privy Council, 8; petition for leave to prepare a grant of privilege, 10; privileges promised, 11-12, 25; 200 marks awarded to Richard Wright, Secretary, for his pains in procuring the privileges, &c., 203.
Privy Council, committee to solicit privilege, &c., 8; petition praying for privileges and incorporation as a company, that the shipping when ready be not stayed for any service; for leave to send out foreign money and to coin the same in the mint; for freedom from customs, &c., 7-8; the enterprise favoured by the Council and recommended to the Queen, 9; committee to solicit an answer to the petition, 9; committee required to attend and receive their lordships' orders, also to tender a petition praying that the voyage may proceed without impeachment; leave to carry out 5 m¹. weight of bullion without charge, and for leave to prepare a grant of privilege, &c., 10; by reason of a treaty of peace in hand with Spain their lordships decline to give a warrant for the proceeding of the voyage without impeachment, October, 1599, 10; in September, 1600, their lordships favour the enterprise and obtain the royal assent to favours sought in the petition, 11-12; general court summoned to take notice of a letter signifying Her Majesty's pleasure, 57; general court, 58-63; letter promising no hindrance shall be given to the voyage, 60; all adventurers in arrears to be certified to their lordships, 61; the patent, 62; a complaint to be lodged against all adventurers in arrears, 110; order in council for defaulting adventurers to bring in their money at once on pain of imprisonment, 112-13; order in council touching the remissness of the company in paying their debts and ordering all defaulting adventurers to appear and be punished for contempt, 164-65; warrant summoning all adventurers who refuse payment to be brought before their lordships and list of such defaulters, 169-70; defaulters committed, 170-1; complaints of the hindrances offered to the North West Voyage by the Muscovia Company, 191; letter signifying Her Majesty's mislike to the delay in the second voyage and propounding unto them the example of the Dutch, 191; suit to be made for an order approving the company's act for the forfeiture of five times the value of the levy for the North West voyage to be made on the stock of all defaulters, 207; proceedings touching the return of Captain Waymouth from the North West voyage, 233; petition of the

INDEX 317

Privy Council, *continued*.
  Levant Company respecting their ships seized at Venice as restitution for the late prize taken by the English men-of-war, 277-78, *see also* 281, 282, 283.
Privy Seal, 107.
Prizes and prize money, resolution respecting, 118; tithes due to the Lord Admiral, 246-47.
Prockter, James, warrant £100 on bill of exchange, 73.
Profit of the voyage to be allotted in proportion to the adventure, 146; respecting the North West voyage, 200.
Prosperous, *ship*, viewed, 13.
Provisions, *see Victuals*.
Prunes, 118.
Pulleymakers, *see Arnold Mabanck, John Crane, William Denham*.
Pulleyn, Thomas, *preacher*, warrant £26 13s. 4d. for his provision to sea, 116; bill of adventure £50 sealed, 150.
Pulleys, 167, 221.
Pullison, } Edward, engaged as one of the
Pullyson, } pursers for the North West voyage, 216; salary contingent on the discovery of the passage, 216; to give a bond of £100 for his good behaviour, 216; only to be employed if the captain thinks it needful, 219; warrant £6 in full of wages and demands, 240.
Purnell, John, warrant £50 for royals, 64.
Pursers, *see the various ships*. Francis Wilson recommended, 27; the fidelity of the pursers of the "Susan," "Hector," and "Assention," guaranteed, 33; letters commending several men to be employed, 39; order to bring in accounts, 97; committee to audit and certify accounts, 98; wages fixed 40s. a month at sea, 20s. a month and board wages in harbour, 116; the "Scourge" to have two pursers, 116; Thomas Yerworth appointed one of the pursers for the North West voyage with wages contingent on the discovery of the passage and to give a bond of 100 marks for his good behaviour, 205; Edward Pullison, do. do., 216; Yerworth, purser of the "Discovery," 210; in the North West voyage pursers to keep a register and account of goods laden and disposed of, also to make notes, journals, and observations for the direction and help of posterity, 213; to deliver their bills of provisions to Mr. Burrell to receive allowance, 215; dislike taken to Thomas Yerworth, 219; differences with Edward Pullison, 219; warrant £6 13s. 4d. to Thomas Yerworth for his wages and expenses, 235; do. £6 to Edward Pullison, 240.
Pywell, John, warrant £7 10s. for head peces and morrens, 149.

Quarles, William, bill of adventure sealed, £240, p. 251.
Quays, *see Wharves*.
Queen (Elizabeth), *see also Privy Council*; suit to be made for sole privilege, also immunities from customs, &c., 6; letters to potentates in the East Indies, 91, 131, 134, 157; letters to the Emperor of China and Kathia to be carried in the North West voyage, 217, 222; letter respecting peace with Spain, 282; £4,000 per annum to be paid by the Levant Company in lieu of imposts, 280, 282, 283.

Radcliff, *see Ratcliffe*.
Raisins, 118.
Ramridge, John, adventurer with Thomas Bostocke, £200, p. 3.
Ranton, Nicholas, warrant £50 on bill of exchange, 84.
Rape oil, 2½ tonne of caske required, 30; estimate of quantity and price, 35; warrant £67 9s., p. 119.
Ratcliffe, }
Ratclyff, } 147, 154, 208.
Reddereth, committee to inspect ships lying there, 13.
Red Dragon, *ship*, the "Mare Scourge" renamed, *see also "Mare Scourge*;" the "Scourge" ordered to be launched and renamed the "Red Dragon," 96; Admiral ship, 100; list of officers, 100; list of factors, 101; warrant £100 to Henry Middleton, purser, 104; do. £100 to William Bradbanck, master, 104; do. £50 to William Dixson, purser, for the use of the ship, 105; do. £200 to Edward Highlord, purser, for preparations, 106; do. £50 to Edward Stephens on account for timber, 106; do. £100 to William Dyckes on account of necessaries, 108; do. £100 to William Dixon, purser, 111; do. £150 to William Dixsy, purser, for repairs, 114; ordered to have two pursers, 116; committee to provide stores, 117; warrant £250 to William Dixson, purser, 117; do. £250, p. 120; the amount of new and Spanish money appointed to be carried and how packed, 122; Mr. Wattes to inquire into the damage done to a ship by the anchor of the "Scourge," 125; warrant £200 to William Dixon, purser, 127; committee to wait on Lord Cumberland respecting the damage done to a ship by the anchor of the "Red Dragon," 128; warrant £200 to William Dickson, purser, 140; do. £100 for clearing expenses, 141; the pursers' accounts to be audited, 147; warrant £7, for ancients and streamers, 147; list of presents to be carried, 151; Mr. Brodebent's bill of adventure, 153; warrant £180 for wages and for clearing away the ship, 154; do. £15 7s. for 59 barrels of beer, 154; do. £100 for iron work, 157; do. £18 for turnery, &c., 157; do. £13 2s. 10d. for porterage and lading, 158; do. £50 for shipwright's work, 163; do. £86 13s. 4d. for sails for the "Dragon" and "Hector," 165; do. £29 11s. 4d. for iron work, 172; do. £48 for painting work, 172; do. £227 for iron work for the "Dragon" and "Susan," 173; memorandum tonnage, 600, men, 180, p. 263.
Remembrancers, committee to act as, and prepare the business for the general committee, 40.
Rent, warrant £6 for 6 quarters' rent of Founder's Hall for the Company's meetings, 227.
Reprisals, resolution respecting mariners' shares of, 118; tithes due to the Lord Admiral, 246-47.
Rewler, Mr., called on to bring in his account, 159.
Rice, one tonne of drie caske required, 30; estimate of quantity and price, 35; committee to provide, 75.
Richardson, Thomas, surveyor for the "Susan," 14; bill of adventure sealed, £240, p. 257.
Rickman, Robert, warrant £133 6s. 8d. for his 6th part of the "Assention," 115; order to

Rickman, Robert, *continued.*
make Maurice Abbott creditor by Mr. Rickman for £100, p. 127.
Roan canvas, } warrant £28 14s., p. 97.
Roan cloth,
Robinson, Henrye, adventurer with Richarde Howse, £200, p. 3; assembly, 5; bill of adventure sealed, £240, p. 260.
Robinson, Humfrie, bill of adventure sealed, £240, p. 260.
Robinson, John, senior *Merchant Tailor,* adventurer, £200, p. 2.
Robinson, Robert, bill of adventure sealed, £240, p. 261.
Robinson, Thomas, warrant £29 18s. for cables, &c., 219.
Romney, *see Rumney.*
Rose, Edward, late factor at Aleppo, 278-79.
Rouen, £5,000 worth of royals to be provided there and at Calais, 58.
Rowe Buck, *ship,* viewed, 13.
Royal assent to the formation of the Company, 5; to the preparation of the voyage and the favours sought in the petitions, 11, 25, *see also Privy Council.*
Royals, } *see also Dollars and Spanish*
Royals of Plate, } *Money;* the provision of,
Royals of 8, } in the West Country, 21, 57; two adventures brought in in Spanish money Royals of 8 at xviij the £ profit, 31; Mr. Allabaster commissioned to take up £3,000 in Royals of Plate at Calais, 41; do. £3,000, p. 58; instructions for taking up in the West Country, 51, 53; may be taken in the West Country as payment of adventure money, 54; payment for, *see Warrants;* Mr. Ellycott buys Royals and sells to the Company at London rate, 64; his conduct deprecated, 65; letter to him expressing dislike to his course, 66; letter to Mr. Sandy advising him not to exceed the price of 12d., p. 66; warrant £500 to Mr. Allabaster, 68; do. £500, p. 82; Mr. Allabaster commissioned to convey bullion and Royals from Calais, 84; warrant £500 to Mr. Allabaster, 91; Mr. Allabaster's commission continued, 91; warrant £105 12s. 4d. to Walter Clark for Royals taken up at Exeter, 102; Mr. Allabaster to buy no more, 102; instruction concerning, 103; warrant £500 to Robert Stephen on account, 105; do. £700 to Mr. Allabaster on account, 106; instructions for shipping from the West Country, 110; committee to attend to the shipping in the West Country, 120; the amount apportioned to be carried in each ship and how packed, 122; Mr. Skinner's adventure, £200, received in Royals, 124.
Rudd, Richard, warrant £60 on bill of exchange, 84.
Rules for the working of the Company, *see also East India Company.* No ship to be received as a portion of an adventure; all shipping to be bought for ready money only; no commodities to be accepted as portions of adventure, but all to be bought by committees appointed; committee of 15 appointed for the direction of the voyage, 6; any adventurer to be employed by the directors in any service, 12; no sum above £10 to be disbursed by the treasurers without a warrant, 24; no gentlemen to be employed, 28; all business in the hands of the governor and committee, 63; committee to devise rules for the prevention of private trade, 124; laws and decrees for the guidance of the traffic of the voyage, 129; committee to devise laws and ordinances for the better guidance of general business, 197; the laws and ordinances devised, 197-202, *see East India Company.*
Rumney, William, adventurer, £200, p. 2; assemblies, 4, 64, 68, 71, 77, 78, 80, 82, 96, 99, 100, 103, 109, 114, 116, 118, 121, 122, 123, 124, 125, 126, 128, 129, 138, 139, 140, 142, 143, 144, 148, 150, 151, 154, 155, 156, 158, 159, 162, 163, 164, 171, 172, 176, 180, 181, 182, 183, 184, 185, 186, 187, 190, 194, 196, 197, 203, 204, 205, 206, 208, 214, 215, 216, 217, 218, 224, 225, 226, 227, 228, 229, 231, 232, 233, 235, 236, 237, 238; committees, 77, 147, 183, 186, 191, 194, 197, 203, 209, 234, 237, 239, 240; appointed treasurer, 7; general committee, 63; elected deputy governor, 111; warrant £42 8s. 11d. for disbursements, 158; on account of Mr. Rumney's bad health and Sir Thomas Smyth being in prison, Mr. Wattes elected governor, 166; elected deputy governor to Mr. Wattes, 179; the oath of office, 179; to receive all contributions for the North West Passage, 195; signatures to treasurers' warrants, 206; warrant £13 19s. 6d. for money delivered to Mr. Burrell, 208; the dislike to Thomas Yerworth, purser, 219; warrant £2 6s. 8d. for boat hire, 224; re-elected deputy governor, 225; orders to Captain Waymouth at Dartmouth to bring his ships round to London, 231; relates the proceedings against Waymouth before the Lords of the Council, 233; thinks that only one ship should be employed in the second North West voyage, 236; being chosen an alderman, resigns the deputy governorship of the company, 239; bill of adventure sealed, £240, p. 255.
Running glasses, 218.
Russell, William, nominated factor, 77.
Russell, William, *butcher,* warrant £111 5s. for beef and pork, 214.
Rutton, William, nominated factor, 77.
Ryalles, }
Ryalls, } *see Royals.*
Ryals, }
Rylance, Humfrey, administrator of Edward Rose, late factor at Aleppo, 278-79.
Ryvelles, Henry, warrant £61 for casks, 146.

Sack wine, 169, 209, 230.
Sailmakers, *see George Barbor, Mr. Bolton, John Bowden, Robert Bradbury, Robert Hughes, Hildebrand Sprusen.*
Sails, 163, 167, 168, 220, 221.
St. Mallowes, Royals to be provided there, 51.
Salamon, } Joseph, *purser of the "Susan;"*
Salbanck, } guaranteed by Mr. Bannyng, 33; warrant £100 for the "Susan," 41; order to let Mr. Burrell take men for the "Mare Scourge," 56; warrant 100 marks for the "Susan," 65; do. £80, p. 74; do. £66 13s. 4d., p. 79; do. £120, p. 92; do. £250, p. 108; do. £200, p. 117; do. £100, p. 129; do. £100, p. 148; do. £100, p. 154; bill of adventure sealed, £240, p. 260.
Salbanck, Robert, *see Salbanck, Joseph.*
Salt, estimate of quantity and price, 36; committee to provide 16 tons, 75; warrant £38 for 12 way of salt, 121; warrant for salt for the North West voyage, 208.
Salt beef, 120 oxen to be bought to make, 114.
Salter, Mr., money taken up from his factor for the use of the ambassador at Constantinople, 280.
Salter, Nicholas, assembly, 59; will bring in

INDEX   519

Salter, Nicholas, *continued.*
  his money, 73; general committee, 179; bill of adventure sealed, £240, p. 261.
Salter, Raphe, *surgeon,* warrant £32 for furnishing remedies, &c., 95.
Salter,   } Thomas, nominated factor, 77;
Salterne,   } elected factor of the second sort, 82; to sail in the "Assention," 101; warrant £50 for his entertainment, 120; bill of adventure sealed, £100, p. 149.
Salters, warrant to pay the Salters' porters for lading, &c., 158; George Bennett, 175.
Saltonstall, Sir Richard, adventurer with his children, £200, p. 3.
Saltpetre, 142.
Sampson, Peter, warrant £44 on bill of exchange, 58.
Sampson, Roberte, bill of adventure sealed, £360, p. 256.
Sandie, *see Sandy.*
Sandy (John), *of Exeter,* bills of exchange for money taken up in the West Country, 58, 70, 83, 84, 102, 106; letter to, respecting the price to be paid for Royals, 66; letter from, as to business in the West Country, 74; letter from, asking for Lord Treasurer's warrant to transport provisions, 78; letter to provide no more bread, 88.
Sandy, } Robert, *Grocer,* adventurer, £200, p.
Sandye, } 1; assemblies, 4, 59, 64, 65, 66, 67, 68, 69, 71, 74, 76, 78, 80, 82, 83, 85, 86, 88, 89, 94, 96, 98, 99, 100, 102, 104, 106, 107, 108, 109, 112, 113, 115, 116, 118, 119, 121, 123, 124, 127, 128, 138, 139, 142, 144, 148, 150, 151, 154, 155, 158, 160, 162, 164, 167, 168, 170, 171, 175, 176; committees, 75, 76, 79, 120, 127, 147; respecting the supply of Royals in the West Country, 57; general committee, 63; letter from Mr. Ellycott as to Royals, 64; reply to Mr. Ellycott, 66; warrant for £300 to be remitted to Exeter, 84; warrant £71 13s. 4d. for charges disbursed for the patent and warrant for coining, 96; recommends William Martin to be employed, 97; iron ordered, 104; orders lead, 105; to provide soap, 107; bill of exchange £100 from John Ellicott, 108; do. £100, p. 109; warrant £128 1s. 8d. for sundries, 115; buys vinegar, 115; to provide prunes, currants, and raisins, 118; to write to Mr. Ellicott and Mr. Pope as to shipping Spanish money now in the West Country, 119; respecting Mr. Skinner's adventure of £200 being received in Royals, 124; buys cheese, 125; to clear accounts with Mr. Peard and Mr. Howe, 127; buys pewter, 129; buys curraunce, 168; warrant £60 on bill of exchange, 209; bill of adventure sealed, £260, p. 255.
Saunderson, Edmond, *turner,* warrant £18 for turner's work, 157.
Saunderson, John, *merchant in Constantinople,* as to Mr. Bate's account, 268; letters from the Levant Company, 273, 279-80, *see Company of Levant merchants.*
Saundye, *see Sandy.*
Savadge, } Robert, warrant £210 for Canary
Savage, } wine, 104; do. £102 for wastes and deales, 171; do. £3 for a spare mast, 222.
Scanderona, 277.
Scott, Edmund, nominated factor, 77; adventures £200, and is employed in the voyage to choose drugs and spices, 109; made free, though not named in the patent, 177; bill of adventure sealed, £240, p. 257.
Scourge } *ship, see Mare Scourge.*
Scurge }

Seacoals, 210.
Seals, the Signet, Privy Seal, and Great Seal, 107; a Common Seal ordered, 113.
Seaton, a fit place to buy cider, 49.
Secretary of the Company, *see Wright, Richard.*
Security, *see Guarantees, Bonds;* all factors to put in security, 86, 105.
Segar, William, *Herald,* warrant £13 7s. 8d. for writing the Queen's letters to the Kings of the East Indies, 139.
Sething Lane, the great house in, nominated as a warehouse, 245.
Shaw, Leonard, warrant £52 for butter and cheese, 125.
Sheer, } John, *of Exeter,* bill of exchange £25,
Sheir, }   p. 106.
Shere, Thomas, *of Exeter,* warrant £60 for money advanced, 125.
Shipping, *see Ships.*
Shipping mark for all goods shipped by the Company, 107.
Ships and shipping, *see* "*Assention,*" "*Carnation,*" "*Discovery,*" "*Exchange,*" "*Globe,*" "*Godspeed,*" "*Guift,*" "*Hector,*" "*Hercules,*" "*Lioness,*" "*Mare Scourge*" (or "*Red Dragon*"), "*Mayflower,*" "*Newcastleship,*" "*Paragon,*" "*Phoenix,*" "*Prosperous,*" "*Red Dragon*" (or "*Mare Scourge*"), "*Rowe Buck,*" "*Susan;*" *see also Pinnaces, Masters, Mariners, Factors;* no ship to be received as portion of any adventure, 6; all to be bought for ready money only, 6; committee to purchase, &c., 6, 8; ships bought in England by the Dutch, 8; petition to the Privy Council that the shipping when ready be not stayed for any service, 8, 10; ships viewed at Deptford, &c., 13; surveyors appointed, 13; the provision of victuals in the West Country, 15; the surveyors to report the wants of each ship to the committee, and then by their orders supply the same, 21; Mr. Durrell ordered to supply timber, 21; more shipping required and the "Mare Scourge" surveyed, 27; bargains and sales of the ships to be made to feoffees in trust, 32; a computation of quantity and price agreed on for victualling, 34; number of men and tonnage of ships, 34; total bulk and value of provisions, 36; quantity and value of merchandise to be taken, 36-7; Alderman Watts's opinion to be taken on all proceedings, 67; biscuit and fish to be bought to carry the ships to the West Country, 67; order for ships to be "symented vppon their sheething" before they come out of the docks, 69; number of men to go in each ship, 72; officers and mariners to be engaged by the masters, 78; factors elected, 81-3; committee to hire masters and officers, 87; list of officers engaged, 89; the state of the ships to be discussed at a general court, 92; ships ready, 93; ballast, 97; shipping mark or brand, 107; committee to provide gunners, stewards, cooks, and carpenters' stores, 117; the bargain and sale of the "Susan" sealed at £1,600, p. 120; amount of new and Spanish money apportioned to be carried in each ship and how packed, 122; the Earl of Oxford's runaway servant to be sought for and not allowed to sail in any of the ships, 126; authority for the committee to call on all officers for an account of provisions brought into the ships, 126; committee to see the discharge of the ships from the West Country, 128, 140; all the ships to be examined that

Ships and Shipping, *continued*.
no private merchandise be shipped, 130; the commission to Captain Lancaster to the chief command and others in succession, 130-7, *see Commissions*; ships too heavily laden, suggestion for a small ship to accompany the fleet part way and stow the spending provisions; ships to be surveyed at Gravesend before deciding, 141; committee to see the moneys shipped, 142; ships reported overladen, 143; committee to find a small ship to stow the provisions and accompany the fleet part way, 143; £20 paid to Henry Napper, master of the "Hector," for his extraordinary pains in the preparation of the ships, 143; committee to see the discharge of the ships at Gravesend, 147; the "Guift" bought to accompany the fleet with victuals, 147-8; lighterage, wharfage, and porterage, 158; all stores, &c., left behind to be gathered together into a storehouse and sold, 159; £15 allowed to Mr. Burrell for his pains in the providing of timber and surveying the work, 181; pinnaces for the North West Voyages, 182, *see Pinnaces*, also *North West Passage*; committee to set down the cost of 3 pinnaces, &c., 183; two pinnaces of 30 and 40 tons manned with 16 and 14 men resolved on, 184, 185; no ships for the second voyage by the Cape to be prepared without the consent of a general court, 189; two ships or pinnaces to be employed for the North West Voyage, 199; two ships, the "Godspeed" and the "Discovery" selected and provisioned and furnished for 16 months under Captain Waymouth's own instructions, 211-12; all pursers to deliver the bills of their provisions to Mr. Burrell to receive allowance, 215; the ships for the North West Voyage described as "flyboats," 220, 221; do. pinnaces, 221; several warrants for stores and necessaries for the North West Voyage, 220-24, *see Warrants*; return of the pinnaces to Dartmouth, 227; arrival in the Thames, 229; ordered to be sold, 230, *see North West Passage*; committee to prepare ships for a second North West Voyage, 234, 237; conference as to the practicability of attempting a second North West Voyage with one ship, 236; the idea of a second voyage abandoned and ships ordered to be sold, 239; the sale deferred, 241; ordered to be sold if £300 each can be obtained, 242; the return of the "Assention," 242, *see "Assention"*: memoranda of tonnage and men employed, 263; orders for the prevention of private trade on French ships between Aleppo and Marseilles, 272; English ships seized at Venice, 277-78: outrages by English men-of-war in the Levant seas, 280, 282, 283.

Shipton, Thomas, bill of adventure sealed, £240, p. 252.

Shipwrights, *see William Denham, Joseph Pett, Peter Pett, Edward Stephens*; warrant by the Lord Treasurer for taking up shipwrights, 40, 263; committee to settle disputed accounts for timber, 155.

Shirts, 138.

Shirts of mail, warrant £36 10s. 10d. for 22, p. 123.

Shirley, Sir Anthony, his doings in Persia, 272.

Signet, 107.

Silver plate, warrant £69 8s. 2d. for a silver fountain and case, 116; a basin and ewer ordered, also two standing cups and two other pieces, 117; four standing cups ordered, size and price, 118; warrant £188 16s. 3d., p. 127; committee to solicit the Lord Treasurer for a warrant to remove the plate from Mr. Governor's house, 141; list of the plate and other presents, 141; how distributed among the four ships, 151.

Simes, Thomas, *of Charde*, respecting the providing of Royals in the West Country, 51, 53.

Skelton, James, *chandler*, warrant £9 for tallow, 171; do. £92 10s. for butter, candles, &c., 219; do. £7 11s. for powder, 221.

Skidmore, William, warrant £333 6s. 8d. for his sixth part of the "Assention," 117.

Skins, levy at Turkish ports to maintain the charges of the ambassador and consuls, 267, 270, 271, 274, 279.

Skinner, } Augustine, adventurer with Roberte
Skynner, } Brooke and Thomas Westray, £300, p. 3; assembly, 59; will bring in his money in dollars, 63; ordered to do so, 124; appointed auditor, 218; bill of adventure sealed, £240, p. 257.

Skynners, *see Nicholas Farrer, John Harbie, William Starky*; warrant to pay the porters employed in lading, 158.

Smalwood ( ), *locksmith*, warrant 37s. for lock staples, &c., 223.

Smith, (Sir) Thomas, alderman and governor of the company, *see Smythe*.

Smith, Thomas, warrant 24s. for keeping pinnaces returned from the North West Voyage, 234; do. 24s., p. 240; do. 24s., p. 241; do. 24s., p. 242.

Smithe, Humfrey, }
Smithe, Thomas, } *see Smythe*.
Smithe, William, }

Smithers, *see Smythes*.

Smithery, warrant £100, p. 104; do. £100, p. 104.

Smithes, George, *see Smythes*.

Smiths, *see Roger Frythe, Richard Hart, Justice Mullett, Lewis Tate, Christopher Thompson, William Woodfield*; payment of a smith's bill stopped because he had not paid for his iron, 128, 147.

Smithyes, George, *see Smythes*.

Smyth, Thomas, } *see Smythe*.
Smyth, William, }

Smythe, Humfrey, assembly, 59; bill of adventure sealed, £240, p. 260.

Smythe, John, admitted as an extra factor, 102.

Smythe, (Sir) Thomas, *Haberdasher*, adventurer, £200, p. 3; alderman, first governor of the East India Company, also governor of the Levant Company, *see 275 and 281*; assemblies, 26, 27, 33, 58, [65], 68, 69, 76, 80, 82, 83, 85, 87, 92, 93, 94, 99, 100, 104, 106, 107, 109, 111, 119, 122, 124, 126, 129; committees, 12, 37, 38, 73, 77, 111; elected governor of the company, 62; being still in prison Mr. Watts elected governor in his place, 166; bill of adventure sealed, £360, p. 256; letter to Mr. Byddell, preacher at Aleppo, 275; signed letter to Mr. Saunderson, merchant at Constantinople, 279-81.

Smythe, William, freedom refused for £105, and ordered to bring in the balance of his adventure, 174-75; bill of adventure sealed, £240, p. 259.

Smythes, George, *Goldsmith*, adventurer, £200, and will pay in Spanish money, 31; warrant £88 14s. 3d. for plate, 127; general committee and sworn, 225; assemblies, 229, 230, 240, 242, 244.

INDEX

Soame, Sir Stephin, Lord Mayor of London, adventurer, £200, p. 1; do. with Richard Carter and Co., £400, p. 1.
Soap ordered, 107.
Sole Privilege, *see Privilege*.
Southacke, Thomas, committee, 245; bill of
Southewyke, adventure sealed, £240, p. 251.
Southseas, Captain Waymouth's hope of the discovery of a passage "by divers inlets that treat through the coast of America," 233.
Spain: by reason of the treaty of peace in hand, the East India Company fearing delays, postponed the preparation of their first voyage from October, 1599, to September, 1600. p. 11; the alledged false translation by the French King of the Queen's letter to him respecting the motion of peace with Spain, 282.
Spanish money. *see also Royals, Dollars, West Country, &c.*; two adventures paid in, 31; the amount apportioned to be carried in each ship and how packed, 122.
Spanish Royals, or Ryalles, *see Royals*.
Speake, George, warrant £200 for money provided in the West Country, 66.
Spectacles, 155.
Speeke, *see Speake*.
Spencer, Edmund, bill of adventure sealed, £240, p. 251.
Spencer, Sir John, adventurer, £800. p. 1; assemblies, 109, 175, 181, 177, 244; general committee, 179; takes over the £200 adventure of Robert Bayly for £180, and to have the nomination of a freeman 181; nominates Joseph Jackson for a freeman, 187; his warehouse suggested for storing the goods brought home in the "Assention," 245; bill of adventure sealed, £360, p. 236.
Spencer, John, *cooper*, warrant £19 6s. for casks, 148.
Spencer, Samuel, to sail as master in the "Susan," 100; warrant £30 on account as agreed, 116; order to receive a barrel of oil, 123.
Spenser, *see Spencer*.
Spices, estimate of quantity for the voyage and price, 35; quantity ordered and committee to purchase, 75; Edmund Scott to go in the voyage in the hope of his service in the choice of drugs and spices, 109; mentioned as one of the articles to be traded in, 198; quantity brought home by the "Assention" and entered at the Custom House, 247.
Spits, 222.
Spruson, Hildebrand, *sailmaker*, warrant £13, p. 168.
Stace ( ), *pilot*, hired for £6 to go with Captain Waymouth to Newcastle, 223.
Stamps, warrant £29 10s. for stamps made for the East India monies, 174.
Stanfeld, John, warrant £110 on bill of exchange, 70.
Staper, Richard, adventurer, £500, p. 1;
Stapers, assemblies, 4, 7, 9, 10, 20, 22, 24, 26, 28, 30, 31, 23, 44, 45, 46, 56, 58, 63, 67, 68, 69, 71, 78, 80, 82, 83, 89, 90, 94, 96, 98, 100, 103, 106, 107, 108, 114, 116, 118, 119, 123, 124, 125, 126, 129, 138, 139, 142, 144, 148, 150, 155, 158, 159, 162, 164, 167, 171, 173, 174, 175, 176, 177, 180, 181, 182, 183, 184, 185, 187, 190, 192, 193, 194, 196, 197, 213, 204, 205, 206, 208, 214, 215, 216, 217, 218, 219, 225, 227, 231, 235, 236, 237, 238, 242; committees, 6, 8, 9, 10, 12, 31, 37, 38, 40, 67, 75, 77, 80, 87, 90, 91, 97, 118, 155, 156, 163, 197, 203, 209, 210, 234, 237, 239; views ships, 13; proposes the "Mare Scurge,"

20; guarantees George Parsons as purser of the "Hector," 33; commends Richard Babington as a purser, 39; compounds for iron, 41; signature to West Country commission, 52; general committee, 61; letter from Mr. Sandy respecting Spanish money, 66; compounds with William Tavernor, *Mariner*, 68; ordered to bring in his account, 159; receives bond for the payment of Mr. Tailby's adventure, 176; general committee and sworn, 179; do. 223; signature to treasurer's warrant, 206; warrant £28 18s. for hides, 208; warrant £150 to be disbursed for wages, 215; do. £200 for necessaries, &c., 217; do. £40 15s. 8d. for balance of account, 222; do. £7 8s. 8d. for disbursements, 223; bill of adventure sealed, £800 p. 261; a private letter written to Mr. Lyllo, ambassador at Constantinople, as to the complaints made by the French ambassador, 265; *see Company of Levant Merchants*.
Starkey, William, nominated factor, 77; elected factor of the second sort, 82; to
Starkie, sail in the "Hector," 101; warrant
Starky, £30 for his preparation, 106; bill of
Starkye, adventure £100 sealed, 143; bill of adventure sealed £200, 261.
Starky, William, *Skynner*, bill of adventure with Raphe Allen £400 sealed, 143.
Steel, warrant £40, p. 138.
Steephens, *see Stephens*.
Stephens, Edward, *Carpenter*, warrant £100 for timber for the "Mallice Scourge," 14; do. £50 for repairs, 87; do. £50, p 95; do. £50 for timber, 105; £50 for work on the "Red Dragon," 163.
Stephens, Richard, adventurer, £200, p. 2; assemblies, 4, 30.
Stephens, Robert, warrant £1,100 on bill of exchange from Mr. Ellicott, 56; do. £100, p. 58; do. £1,000, p. 65; do. £900, p. 69; do. £800, p. 102; do. £600, p. 102; do. £500, p. 105; do. £100, p. 105; do. £100, p. 109; do. £100, p. 115.
Stephens, Thomas, appointed book-keeper at a salary of £30, p. 210; re-appointed bookkeeper, 226; desires the freedom of the company, but his suit deferred, 227; ordered to charge up all debtors' accounts that the amounts due may be defaulted on their several stocks, 223; warrant £23 6s. 8d. for salary, 235; admitted to the freedom, 239; to make out carmen's tickets for the goods from the "Assention" sent to the Exchange, 248; warrant to pay 56s. to the wife of John May, master's mate of the "Susan," 248; do. £6 for pilotage of the "Assention" into the River, 248.
Stephins, *see Stephens*.
Stevens,
Stewards, *see Thomas Bourne or Bowrne?* the number to be employed in each ship, 90; committee to provide stores, 117.
Stile, *see Style*.
Stoackly, John, bill of adventure sealed, £240, p. 250.
Stoane, William, adventurer with William Chambre, £500, p. 2; assembly, 59; bill of adventure sealed £600, p. 234.
Stock, *see adventure*.
Stockfish, 209.
Stone, *see Stoane*.
Storehouses, *see Warehouses*, for the gathering together of things left behind by the ships, 159.
Stoves, for the North West Voyage, 20.

T T

Stradling,) Christopher or Percival, elected fac-
Stragling,) tor of the fourth sort, 83; to sail
in the "Red Dragon," 101; warrant £20 for
his preparation, 119; bill of adventure sealed,
£40, p. 152.
Straits of Magelano, 183.
Stratford, Anthonie, bill of adventure sealed,
£240, p. 257.
Stratford, Richard, warrant £50 on bill of exchange, 82.
Stratford, Robert, bill of adventure sealed,
£240, p. 258.
Streamers, ancients and flags, 108, 149, 163.
Style, Humfrey, assembly, 59; bill of adventure sealed, £240, p. 252.
Style, Nicholas, *Grocer*, adventurer, £200, p. 2; assemblies, 4, 7; appointed director, 6; committee, 8.
Style, Oliver, *Grocer*, adventurer, £300, p. 2; assemblies, 59, 64, 65, 67, 68, 71, 74, 76, 79, 80, 82, 83, 85, 88, 89, 90, 91, 92, 93, 94, 95, 96, 98, 99, 100, 102, 103, 104, 107, 108, 109, 112, 113, 115, 116, 118, 119, 124, 143, 144, 151, 154, 156, 159, 173, 175, 176, 204, 242; committees, 77, 107, 117, 124, 147, 191, 203; general committee, 63; respecting Roger Style, 86; adventures £200 on behalf of Roger Style, 105; appointed auditor, 166, 218; bill of adventure sealed, £560, p. 253.
Style, Persevall, seeks to be employed, 65.
Style, Roger, seeks to be employed; nominated a factor, 77; offers to serve as factor without salary, also to reside in the East Indies and learn the language, 86; appointed third factor in the "Assention," 101; to take the place of Richard Collymore, 105; Oliver Style adventures £200 on his behalf, 105; warrant £30 for his preparations, 108; do. £30 for his entertainment, 120; bill of adventure sealed, £50, p. 149; bill of adventure £40 sealed, 151; letter received from him from the East Indies, by which good hope is conceived of the success of the voyage and encouragement given for another voyage for further discoveries, &c., 243; order to attend on board the "Assention" till ship is discharged, 246; bill of adventure sealed, £40, p. 262.
Suckley, Mr., Lord Treasurer's secretary, 85.
Sugar, estimate of quantity of price, 35; quantity ordered and committee to purchase, 75; warrant £27 6s. 6d., p. 140.
Suger, Jerome, adventurer with Clement Moseley, £250, p. 2.
Sumatra, 194, 198.
Supplies, *see Adventures, also Levies*.
Sureties, *see Security, Guarantees*, all factors to put in, 86.
Surgeons, *see also Medicine*, the number to be carried in each ship, 90; warrant £32 to Raphe Salter for furnishing his medicine chest, 95; do. £25 to James Lovering of the "Hector," 98; do. £20 to Christopher Newchurch of the "Assention," 98; do. £20 to John Gamond of the "Susan," 98.
Surveyors for the ships "Hector," "Assention," and "Susan," 14; power with the advice of the carpenters to supply all defects and repairs, 14; Mr. Burrell appointed general surveyor, 21; all surveyors to report the wants of their ships to the committee, and then by their orders to supply the same, 22; for the "Mare Scourge," 27, 29, 32.
Susan, *ship*, 240 tons, 80 men; Samuel Spencer, *Master*; John May, *Master's Mate*; John Havard, *Principal Factor*; Henry Middleton, *Second Factor*; William Wilford, *Third Factor*; Thomas Morgan, *Fourth Factor*; John Gamond, *Surgeon*; Peter Fenton, *Carpenter*; viewed, 13; chosen and bought with her furniture of Alderman Banning, for £1,600, p. 13; surveyors appointed, 14; inventory, 17; Joseph Salaman, the purser, guaranteed by Mr. Bannyng, 33; rated 80 men, tonnage 240, p. 34; proportion of aquavitæ, 35; order to the purser to give up any men required to complete the "Mare Scourge," 56; warrant £50 on account of repairs, 57; do. 100 markes, 65; to be manned with 80 men, 72; warrant £50 for timber, 79; do. £66 13s. 4d. for necessaries and wages, 79; the number of carpenters, caulkers, gunners, stewards, cooks, surgeons, and barbers, to be employed, 89-90; John Havard to sail as principal factor, 94; warrant £20 to John Gamond, *Surgeon*, for furnishing his medicine chest, 98; officers appointed, 100; factors appointed, 101; warrant £250 for necessaries, 108; warrant £20 to Samuel Spencer, *Master*, on account, 116; Peter Francis, a Portugal, to sail in the "Susan," wages £5 a month, 117; committee to provide stores, 117; warrant £250 for men's wages, 117; the bargain and sale of the ship made absolute, and sealed at £1,600, p. 120; abuses and overcharges by the carpenter for masts, 121, 157; amount of new and Spanish money to be carried and how packed, 122; a barrel of oil allowed to the master, 123; warrant £100 to the purser for charges, 129; being found overladen, a committee appointed to find a small ship to accompany the fleet part way, 143, *see* 144; warrant £100 to the purser for clearing the ship, 148; list of presents to be carried, 152; warrant £100 for wages and for clearing away the ship, 154; do. £30 12s. 4d. for gunners' stores, 157; do. £100 for timber, &c., 157; do. £6 16s. 8d. for porterage and lading, 158; do. £27 5s. for sails, 167; do. £71 15s. for timber, 172; do. £227 for iron work, 173; do. 30s. to Faith May in part of wages of John May, *Master Mate*, 224; do. 56s. to the wife of John May for a month of his wages, 248; memorandum, 240 tons, 80 men, 263.
Suzan, John, adventurer with Samewell Garrard, £200, p. 4.
Swinerton,) Nicholas, junior, alderman, adventu-
Swynerton,) rer, £300, p. 4; assembly, 244; bill of adventure sealed, £360, p 252.
Symondes,) Thomas, adventurer, £200, p. 1;
Symonds,) assemblies, 4, 7, 9, 10, 180; appointed director, 6; committees, 8, 10; warrant £6 13s. 4d., p. 117; respecting the account with John Hedland, 163; appointed auditor, 166; general committee, 179; bill of adventure sealed, £240, p. 258.
Symonds,) Nicholas, *Carpenter*, assembly,
Symondson,) 30; warrant £50 for timber for
Symons,) the "Susan," 79; do. £80, p.
Symonson,) 92; do. £100, p. 157; do. £71 15s., p. 172; do. for work on the "Discovery," &c., £71 13s.
Syms, *see Simes*.
Synamon, *see Cinnamon*.

Tailby,) Richard, assembly, 50; promises to
Tailbye,) pay £73 6s. 8d. to Mr. Atye, and
Taileby,) £100 to the Muscovia Company as part payment of his adventure, 176; committees, 245, 246; bill of adventure sealed, £240, p. 256.

INDEX   323

Tailor, Francis, *Vintner*, warrant £18 for claret, 169;
Talbutt, Thomas, bill of adventure sealed, £240, p. 250.
Tallow, 171.
Tar, committee to provide casks, 76; ordered to be bought of Browne & Co., 121.
Tate, Lewis, *Smith*, warrant £100 for smith's work, 104; do. £100, p. 163; do. £227, p. 173.
Taverner, William, *Mariner*, compounds for his employment at £6 per month, 68.
Taylby, *see* Tailby.
Tayler, } Francis, appointed auditor, 218; bill of
Taylor, } adventure sealed, £240, p. 260.
Taylor, John, adventurer, £200, p. 77; nominated factor, 77.
Tayte, *see* Tait.
Terrell, Fraunces, adventurer, £200, p. 2.
Thames, River, the return of the ships from the North West, 229; the return of the "Assention," 244, *see also* Gravesend, Woolwich, Deptford, &c.
Thomas, William, warrant 26s. for lanthornes, 223.
Thompson, } Christopher, *Smith*, warrant £50
Thomson, } for iron work for the "Hector," 105; do. £80, p. 111; do. £100, p. 149; do. £14 4s. 2d., p. 163; do. £22 6s., p. 221; do. 13s. 10d. for plates, 224.
Thurston, John, master of the ship "Carnation," 293.
Timber, Mr. Burrell ordered to supply, 21, 46, 89; warrant £100, p. 47; do. £100, p. 74, do. £100, p. 86; quantity borrowed from Her Majesty's storehouse at Woolwich for the repairs of the "Scourge," 71; warrant £50 for the "Susan," 74; do. £80, p. 92; do. £80, p. 92; do. £50 for the "Red Dragon," 106; do. £100 for the "Hector" and "Assention," 114; committee to agree with the carpenters on the disputed prices of timber, 124; committee to agree with Mr. Ady and other shipwrights, 155; warrant £100 for the "Susan," 157; do. £50, p. 164; do. £100 for wastes and deales, 171; do. £71 15s. for the "Susan," 172; arbitrators appointed to agree on Mr. Adye's account, 173; warrant £16 16s. 11d. for timber, &c., for the "Assention," 180; £15 allowed to Mr. Burrell for his paines in the providing of timber and surveying the work, 181; warrant for timber for the "Discovery," 221.
Tin, quantity to be sent out in the ships and price, 36; committee to provide, 79; duty at Constantinople and Aleppo to support the ambassador's and consuls charges, 267, 270, 271, 274, 279.
Tithes due to the Lord Admiral on a prize taken in the East Indies, 246-7.
Tonnage of ships and number of men for the East India voyage, 34, 263; do. for the North West Voyage, 184, 185.
Toomes, Mr., assembly, 227 (? Coombes).
Toppesfelde, Mr., offers the ship "Phenixe."
Tower of London, as to coining, 78; bullion stored there, 87; coining, 114, 120.
Towerson, Robert, disfranchised, 178.
Trade, the chief articles of trade in the East Indies, 198; the object of the attempt to discover a North West Passage was to open up trade in English merchandise with China and other temperate climates, 199.
Treasurer, Lord, *see* Lord Treasurer.
Treasurers, *see also* Warrants, Bannyng,

Holliday, Cambell, and Chamberlaine, &c. John Highlord and William Romney elected, 7; immediate levy of 12d per £100 for petty charges, 7; to pay all sums by warrants signed by four of the committee, but not to disburse above £10 without a warrant, 24; Mr. Bannyng elected, 25; committee appointed to audit the accounts, 107, 156, 166; Mr. Bannyng and Mr. Holliday desired to borrow £1,500 at interest on their own credits, 146; the state of the accounts on March 6, 1600-1, showing amount of debts and amount of adventure not yet brought in, 156; indemnity for the money borrowed at interest, 161; conference as to money in hand to pay debts, 167; to deliver bills of adventure to all who have cleared their adventures and supplies and to charge 6d. each for the same, 175; Mr. Alderman Cambell appointed treasurer for the North West Voyage, 200; the treasurer for the North West voyage not to receive any contributions after the end of March, 1602, without the consent of a general court, 208; Mr. Robert Chamberlaine elected, 226; the cashiers ordered to be reimbursed for money lost in the receiving and paying of money, 227; Mr. Holliday ordered to bring in £38 6s. 9d. balance of his accounts and the sum of eight or nine pounds disbursed by his wife not allowed, 231.
Trowbridge, Thomas, money in the West Country, 73.
Tucker, Daniel, nominated factor, 77.
Tudd, Thomas, nominated factor, 77; elected factor of the fourth sort, 83; to sail in the "Hector," 101; warrant £20 for his preparations, 122; bill of adventure sealed, £40, p. 153.
Turkey, trade in, 268; the trade by the Dutch, 270, 273; duties on certain goods entering Turkish ports to maintain the charges of the ambassador and consuls, 271; Mr. Coltherst's favour with the Bashaw, 272.
Turner, Edward, adventurer with William Turner, £200, p. 3.
Turner, James, adventurer with John Buzbridge, £200, p. 3; assembly, 59; committee, 246; bill of adventure sealed, £240, p. 254.
Turner, William, adventurer with Edward Turner, £200, p. 3; assembly, 5; warrant £24 for money supplied in Plymouth, 64; bill of adventure sealed, £240, p. 258.
Turnery, 157.
Turnor, *see* Turner.
Tyght, Lewys, *Blacksmith*, warrant £100 for ironwork, 157.
Tyler, Thomas, *Painter*, warrant £13 6s. 8d. for work done, 221.

Uffington, William, warrant £86 for wax candles, 142.
Utley, George, disfranchised, 178.

Vale, Richard, warrant £24 19s. for spectacles, &c., 155.
Value, of the original adventures subscribed, 4; of the provisions for the voyage, 36; of the merchandise to be sent out, 37; of the goods brought home by the "Assention," 247.
Vaults under the Exchange used as a warehouse, 245, 248.
Venice, bills of exchange from the ambassador at Constantinople, 266, 271; petition to the Privy Council respecting the Levant Company's ships seized at Venice as restitution

Venice, *continued*.
for the late prize taken by English men-of-war, 277-8, *see also* 280, 282, 284.
Victuals, *see also* Bread, Butter, Beer, Beef, Pork, Cheese, Peas, Wine, Oil, &c., &c. The providing of, in the West Country, 15, 21; Captain Davies ordered to draw out a proportion for 500 men, 22; Captain Davies presents his estimate, which is referred to a committee, 26; peas, 26, 29; a commission to be prepared for Captain Davies, 28; committee appointed to go to the West Country and purchase, 29; the quantity of caske required for victuals, &c., 30; a computation agreed on for the victualling of the ships, quantity and price, 34-6; total bulk and value, 36; commission for Captain Baker to purchase, 38, 54; the quantities to be provided in the West Country, 41, 52, 54-5; prices to be certified, 49; commission for Captain Davies to purchase, 52-4; bills of exchange for the purchases in the West Country, *see Warrants*; letters of advice as to business in the West Country, 64; Admiral Wattes joined to the committee on victuals, 70; committee to review the estimate and the progress of the victualling, 72; quantities required and committees to purchase, 75-6; commissions given to the committees to purchase, 77; committee to solicit Lord Treasurer's warrant for transporting provisions in the West Country, 78; all ready for the voyage, 93; £30 paid to Robert Pope for his pains in the West Country, 101; committee to attend to the shipping of in the West Country, 120; the committee authorized to call on all officers for an account of all provisions supplied, 126; the ships appearing overladen it is suggested that a small ship be bought to stow part of the provisions and accompany the fleet part way, 141; the "Guift" bought, 147-8; all stores, &c, left behind to be gathered together and sold, 159; warrant £22 4s. for chaundler's provisions, 164; three committees appointed for the provision of victuals and other necessaries for the North West voyage, 209; the North West ships victualled, &c., after Captain Waymouth's own desires, 211-12; various warrants for stores for the North West voyage, 217-21; the stores returned from the North West voyage to be preserved for a second voyage, 228; certain provisions to be sold, 230; all ordered to be sold, 239.

Vinegar, 30 tonne of caske required, 30; estimate of quantity and price, 35; price and quantity in the West Country to be ascertained, 49; committee to provide, 76; do. casks for, 76; warrant £70 for 7 tons, 114; do. £25 10s., and £20, p. 115; do. £14 12s., p. 116; committee to provide for the North West voyage, 209.

Vintners, *see Mr. Crosse, Francis Cherie, Thomas Farrington, Francis Tailor*.

Voyage, first by the Cape to the East Indies, *see also Adventurers, East India Company, Ships, Pursers, &c.* Committee for the general direction of the voyage, 6, 63; Oct. 1599, the voyage postponed for a year, 11; September, 1600, on receiving the royal assent the preparation of the voyage determined on and committee appointed for its direction, 11, 12; Captain Davies principal director, 25; victuals, 22, 26, 28, *see Victuals;* merchandise, 28, &c., *see Merchandise;* more shipping required, 27; no gentlemen to be employed, 28; number of men and tonnage of ships, 34; quantity and value of provisions, 34-6; do. of merchandise, 36-7; number of men to go in each ship, 72; the hindrance and damage to the voyage by reason of certain persons not bringing in their adventure, 110; action of the Privy Council to compel adventurers to bring in their sums subscribed, 112-13; the amount of money apportioned to be carried in each ship and how packed, 122; all things to be managed as a joint stock and no private trade to be practised, 130; the commissions for the general or principal merchants, 132-7, *see Commissions*; ships appearing too heavily laden, suggestion for a small ship to accompany the fleet part way and stow the provisions, 141; Mr. Hacklett paid £10 for his advice and instructions and 30s. for 3 maps, 143; forms of the bills of adventure, 145; the return of the "Assention," *see "Assention."*

Voyage, second by the Cape to the East Indies. A second voyage proposed, 182; Mr. Governor to peruse the charters to see if power is given to compel any one to contribute to a second voyage, 183; a second voyage resolved on and a book to be sent round that adventurers may set down their contributions under their own hands, and not less than £100 to be received, 186; the title or preface to the book agreed on and ordered to be sent round to all the freemen, 187; the total subscribed amounts to only £11,000, which is insufficient, 189; enquiries by the Lord Admiral and Mr. Secretary as to the cause of the great delay in the second voyage as compared with the Dutch, 189-90; letter from the Privy Council notifying Her Majesty's mislike to the delays, and propounding the example of the Dutch, 191; a general court convened to deal with the matter and a penalty of 20s. imposed for non-attendance, 191.

Voyage to discover the North West Passage, *see North West Passage, Waymouth, East India Company, &c.*

Wages, *see also Warrants, Agreements.* Pursers 40s. the month at sea, and 20s. and board wages in harbor, 116; in the North West voyage contingent on the discovery of the passage, 205; agreement with Waymouth, 214; do. with Thomas Cartwright, preacher, for the North West voyage, 216; do. with Edward Pullison, purser, 216; covenant for the payment of the wages of John Drew, master of the "Godspeed," 220-1.

Walcott, Humfrey, assembly, 59, 229, 232, 233, 238, 240, 241, 244; general committee and sworn, 226; bill of adventure sealed, £240, p. 252.

Waldo, Laurence, assembly, 59; recommends Francis Wilson as a purser, 27; warrant £50 to be repaid at Exeter, 55; do. £25, p. 106; bill of adventure sealed, £240, p. 251.

Waldo, Robert, assembly, 59; bill of adventure sealed, £240, p. 252.

Walker, Edward, bill of adventure sealed, £240, p. 258.

Wallcott, *see Walcott*.

Walter, William, ordered to be gratified with £20 (? 20s.) for dedicating to the company the book of the Flemynges Voyage, 125.

Walthall, William, warrant £224 2s. for lead, 95.

INDEX

Walton, Richard, warrant £40 on bill of exchange, 84.
Wapping, 223.
Warde, Thomas, admitted as an extra factor, 100.
Warehouses, for the beef and pork returned from the North West voyage, 230; for the goods brought home in the "Assention," 245; committee to prepare the vaults under the Exchange, 248; committee to see the goods sent to the warehouses, 248; committee to receive and weigh the goods, 248.
Warner, Robert, warrant £100 for iron, 104; do. £43 16s. 6d. for glasses, 129.
Warrants. No sum above £10 to be disbursed by the Treasurers without a warrant, 24; warrant to take up shipwrights, 40; Lord Treasurer's warrant for the transport of peas and beans from Norfolk and Cambridge, 60; do. from the West Country, 78, 79; warrant for coining, 78; charges on the warrant for coining, &c., 96; warrant summoning the adventurers who have not brought in their payments, 169-70; two warrants warning defaulting adventurers to appear before the the Privy Council to answer for their contempt, 173; warrant to take up carpenters, 203.
Warrants entered in Mr. Allabaster's book £100 to John Bushridge for iron, 111; £100 to William Dixon, Purser of the "Dragon," 111; £20 to Xpofer Thompson, *smith*, for the "Hector," 112; £100 to Mr. Wyseman for the "Hector," 111; £20 to Nicholas Lynge for charges, 111; £23 6s. 8d. to Andrew Bannyng for oil, 111; £100 to William Dixon for the "Hector," 111.
Warrants to the Treasurer (no name): £100 to Mr. Wiseman for necessaries for the "Hector," 25; £100 to Mr. Chambers for casks and iron hoopes, 33; £100 to do. for casks and iron hoopes, 56; £30 to William Kempe on a bill of exchange from Captain Baker, 80; £20 to Mr. Governor to gratify William Walter, who dedicated to the Company the book of the "Flemyngs" voyage, 125; £2 to Mr. Worsenham, *Searcher*, for clearing the ships, 156.
Warrants per Mr. Banning, Treasurer: £4 to Mr. Altham for making the draft of the patent, 25; £500 to Mr. Howe, to be sent into the West Country for purchases, &c., 29; £200 to Captain Lancaster and Mr. Chambers for iron work and caske, 41; £100 to Joseph Salamon, necessaries for the "Susan," 41; £600 to Francis Elington for cloth, 45; £1,000 to the Earl of Cumberland on account of the purchase of the "Mare Scurge," 45; £100 to Mr. Burrell for timber, 47; £20 to Captain Davis for travelling expenses, 47; £50 to Laurence Waldo for a bill of exchange on Exeter, 55; £100 to Henry Middleton, Purser, for charges about the "Scourge," 56; £1,100 to Robert Stephens on bill of exchange from Exeter, 56; £200 to Mr. Coles on bill of exchange from the West Country, 57; 100 markes to Mr. Garway on account of the repairs of the "Assention," 57; £50 on account of the repairs of the "Susan," 57; £50 to John Purnell for Royals delivered at Plymouth, 64; £24 to William Turner on bill of exchange from Plymouth, 64; £1,000 to the Purser of the "Scourge" on account of repairs, 65; £1,000 to Robert Stevens on a bill of exchange from Exeter, 65; £100 to Richard Wiseman for repairs and provisions for the "Hector," 65;
£200 to William Burrell for timber, 65; 100 markes to Joseph Salbancke, *Purser*, for repairs, &c., on the "Susan," 65; £900 to Robert Stephens on two bills of exchange from Exeter, 69; £30 to Thomas Bowles on a bill of exchange from Captain Baker, 69; £110 to John Stanfeld on a bill of exchange from Dartmouth, 70; £100 to Purser of the "Malice Scurge" for preparations, 70; £40 to William Harvy on bill of exchange from Robert Pope, 74; £110 to William Lacy on bill of exchange from Robert Pope, 74; £80 to Joseph Sulman, Purser of the "Scurge," for preparations, 74; £150 to John Lant on bill of exchange from Robert Pope, 74; £100 to Henry Middleton, Purser of the "Scurge," for preparations, 78; £40 to John Wyndham on a bill of exchange from Robert Pope, 79; £30 to Nicholas Symons for timber for the "Susan," 79; £66 13s. 4d. to Joseph Salbanck for necessaries and wages for the "Susan," 79; £39 to Roger Gibbons on a bill of exchange from Robert Pope, 79; £100 to Richard Wyseman for the Hector's provision, 79; £40 to Thomas Northeover on bill of exchange from Robert Pope, 81; £150 to John Lant on bill of exchange from Robert Pope, 81; £40 to John God on bill of exchange from Robert Pope, 82; £100 to Francis Covell for peas and beans, 82; £500 to Mr. Allabaster for royals of plate, 82; £300 to Mr. Robert Sandy, to be repaid to Mr. John Sandy at Exeter, 84; £100 to Edward Highlord, Purser, on account of repairs of the "Scourge," 87; £112 to William Dale on a bill of exchange from Robert Pope, 88; £120 to Joseph Salbanck, 92; £80 to Nicholas Symundson for timber, 92; £50 to William Angell for fish, 92; £300 to Henry Middleton, Purser, for the provision of the "Scourge," 93; £224 2s. to William Walthall for lead, 95; £100 to Edwin Habington for canary wine, 95; £100 to Francis Covell for beans and peas, 96; £100 to Richard Wyseman on account of the preparation of the "Hector," 96; £73 13s. 4d. to Mr. Attorney and Clerks for drawing and engrossing the patent and warrant for coining, 96; £125 10s. to John Bushridge for linen cloths, 97; £100 to the Pursers of the "Hector" for repairs and preparations, 99; £800 to Robert Steveus on a bill of exchange from John Ellacott, 102; £105 12s. 4d. to Walter Clarck for royals of plate delivered in Exeter, 102; £30 to William Wilford, factor, for his salary, 103; £231 10s. to George Hanger for canary wine, 103; £378 10s. to William Harrison for canary wine, 103; £160 to Edwin Habington for canary wine, 103; £100 to Lewis Tate for smithery, 104; £100 to Henry Middleton, Purser of the "Red Dragon," 104; £50 to Roger Hanckey, Master of the "Assention," on account of his wages, 104; £100 to William Burrell, for the provision of the ships, 104; £40 to John Coles on bill of exchange from Lewis Pope, 104; £200 to Mr. Wyseman for wax candles and provision of the "Hector," 104; £30 to Thomas Dassell for his wages, 104; £100 to William Bradhanck, Master of the "Red Dragon," on account, 104; £150 to John Buzoridge on account of iron, 104; £100 to Robert Warner on account of iron, 104; £210 to Robert Savage for canary wine, 104; £100 to William Chambers towards the provision of caske, 104; £10 5s. 8d. to Henry Lambard for black jacks, 105; £50 to Xpofer Thomson, *Smith*, on account of iron work

Warrants per Mr. Bannyng, *continued.*
for the "Hector," 105; £17 4s. 11d. to Francis Covell in full of provisions made by him, 105; £50 to William Dixson, Purser of the "Red Dragon," for the use of the ship, 105; £500 to Robert Stephens on account of £700 taken up in royalles of plate, 105; £200 to Edward Highlord, Purser of the "Red Dragon," for preparations, 106; £50 to Edward Stephens on account of timber for the "Red Dragon," 106; £700 to Mr. Allabaster on account of £880 bills of exchange for royailes, 106; £96 8s. to John Gover for aquavitæ, 107; £250 to Joseph Salbanck, Purser of the "Susan," for necessaries, 108; £30 to Roger Style, factor, being the allowance for his provisions, 108; £100 to John Ady, Carpenter, on account of timber for the "Hector" and "Assention," 114; £80 to William Fisher for candy oil, 114; £70 to William Harrison for vinegar, 114; £200 to Thomas Bazar on account of canvas for the ships, 114; £133 6s. 8d. to Robert Rickman for his sixth part of the "Assention," 115; £128 1s. 8d. to Robert Sandy for sundry disbursements, 115; £200 to Robert Stevens on bills of exchange, &c., 115; £500 to Sir Hugh Portman on a bill of exchange from Robert Pope, 115; £233 6s. 8d. to William Skidmore for his sixth part of the "Assention," 117; £200 to Joseph Salbanck to be employed on the "Susan," 117; £67 0s. to Henry Plompton for rope oil, 119; £30 to Roger Style, factor, for his entertainment, 120; £250 to William Dixon, Purser, for the preparation of the "Red Dragon," 120; £6 13s. 4d. to —— Bradley for ballast, 121; £36 10s. 10d. to Mr. Wattes for 22 shirts of mail, 123; £20 1s. to Thomas Parkins for 32 jars of honey, 125; £52 to Leonard Shaw for butter and cheese, 125; £20 to Thomas Morgan, factor, for his provision to sea, 126; £180 to John Lacy for cordage bought of the Muscovia Company, 126; £300 to John Davies, Pilot Major, for his salary, 127; £200 to William Dixon, Purser of the "Red Dragon," on account of her provisions, 127; £100 to Joseph Salbanck, Purser of the "Susan," for the provision of the voyage, 129; £36 to Alderman Watts for iron hoops, 129; £207 to Frances Parrett for Norromborough ware, 138; £11 1s. to George Davyes for chests, 138; £200 to Captain Lancaster as per agreement, 139; £11 to Captain Lancaster for so much laid out by him, 139; £200 to William Dickson, Purser of the "Red Dragon," on account of her provision, 139; £78 16s. 4d. to Thomas Perkins, Cooper, for caske, 143; £20 to Henry Napper, Master of the "Hector," for his extraordinary pains in the preparation of that ship, 143; £100 to Joseph Salbanck, Purser of the "Susan," for the clearing away of the ship, 148; £19 16s. 4d. to John Spencer, *Cooper*, for caske, 148; £27 6s. 6d. to Robert Myddleton for sugar, 149; £100 to Nicholas Symondson for timber and planks for the "Susan," 157; £14 7s. 2d. to Mr. Highlord for disbursements, 162; £12 to Thomas Duck for streamers, 163; £50 to Edward Stephens, Shipwright, for work on the "Red Dragon," 163; £50 to Adam Wood for deals, masts, and timber, 163-4; £27 3s. to George Barber for sails for the "Susan," 167; £4 9s. 8d. to John Crane for pulleys, 167; £46 17s. to George Bowles, *Grocer*, for curraunce, 168; £6 to William Denham, Shipwright, in full of his bill, 169; £9 15s. to James Marshe for deales and planckes, 169; £22 4s. to Francis Covell, *Chaundeler*, for provisions for the "Assention," 169; £18 to Francis Tailor, *Girdeler*, for a tun of claret wine, 169; £9 to Jeames Skelton for tallow, 171; £500 to Abraham Campion on account of beer, 171; £71 15s. to Nicholas Symonson, Carpenter, in full for timber, 172; £39 16s. 6d. to Richard Wryte in full payment of his account for disbursements, 173; £16 16s. 11d. to William Brett for timber, &c., for the "Assention," 180; £16 10s. to Symon Turnor for powder, 184; £57 16s. 8d. to Benjamin Decro, agent of the Muskovia Company, for cordage, 187; £39 2s. 4d. to Abraham Campion for the rest of his account for beer, 193.

Warrants per Mr. Cambell, Treasurer of the North West Voyage: £30 to Captain Waymouth to provide his instruments, 204; £30 to do. for provisions for the voyage, 204; £20 to do. to provide needful instruments, 204; £5 to John Drewe, a master to go in the North West Voyage, as an advance on his wages agreed on, 206; £80 to Thomas Yerworth, purser, for clearing carpenters' wages, 206; £54 18s. to Austyn Bandicott, *Butcher*, for pork, 208; £30 to Thomas Yerworth, purser, to be paid to workmen at Ratcliffe and Lymehouse, and for salt and mariners' board wages, 208; £28 18s. to Richard Staper for hides to make the mariners' cassocks, breeches, and gowns, 208; £13 19s. 6d. to Mr. Rumney for so much delivered by his servant to Mr. Burrell in gildernes, 208; £60 to Mr. Sandy on bill of exchange, for so much taken up at Exeter by Captain Waymouth for the hiring of mariners, 209; £100 to Thomas Yarworth, purser of the "Discovery," for anchors and other necessaries, 210; £10 to John Drewe, Master of the "Godspede," in part of his wages, 210; £100 to Thomas Yerworth, purser, for sea coals, wood, lead, and divers other necessaries, 210; £100 to Captain Waymouth by parcels, as he shall call for it, for men's wages, &c., 211; £111 5s. to William Russell, *Butcher*, for beef and pork, 214; £150 to William Chambers for cloth and other necessaries, 215; £150 to Nicholas Leat for further necessaries, 215; £150 to Mr. Staper to disburse for wages as called for, 215; £60 to Joseph Page, Baker, for biskett, 215; 100 to Thomas Yerworth for necessary provisions, 215; £100 to William Chambers for necessary provisions, 217; £200 to Richard Stapers for necessaries and disbursements, 217; £50 to Captain Waymouth for his expenses attending the preparation of the voyage, 218; £30 to Robert Grynken for watches, compasses, running glasses, and instruments, 218; £20 to Mr. Leat for mariners' clothes, 218; £50 11s. 8d. to John Davies, *Cooper*, for casks, 218; £7 8s. to Adam Wood for deals, oars, &c., 218; £6 10s. to William Woodfield, *Smith*, for iron hoops, 219; £29 18s. to Thomas Robinseon for cables and skeytes, 219; £92 10s. to Mr. Skelton, *Chaundler*, for butter, candles, powder, &c., 219; £11 6s. 8d. to Mr. Johnson for bay salt, 219; £143 to Thomas Barber for canvas for sails for the two flyboats for the North

INDEX 327

Warrants per Mr. Cambell —*continued*.
West voyage, 220; £32 10s. to Robert Hewhes, *Sailmaker*, for making sails, 221; £9 10s. to Arnold Mahancke for pullies, 221; £13 6s. 8d. to Thomas Tyler, *Painter*, for work done on the pinnaces, 221; £19 to Roger Frythe, *Smith*, for iron work for ships' stores, 221; £26 to Richard Hall, *Blacksmith*, for iron work, 221; £3 8s. to George Gryce, *Carriage Maker*, 221; £22 6s. to Xpofer Thompson, *Smith*, for iron work, 221; £12 to William Denham, for pullies, 221; £120 3s. to Abraham Campion for beer, 221; £58 13s. to Nic. Symonson, *Carpenter*, for work on the "Discovery," 221; £13 to do. do. for timber and a boat, 221; £7 11s. to Mr. Skelton for powder for the pinnaces, 221; £4 15s. to Richard Wright for charges on procuring the Queen's letters, 222; £34 7s. 10d. to Xpofer and Thomas Nicholls for cordage, 222; £3 to Mr. Savage for a spare mast, 222; £40 15s. 8d. to Richard Stapers, due to him, as appears by his audited account, 222; 30s. 8d. to William Deyns, *Ironmonger*, for spits, &c., 222; £17 17s. to John Makesfield, *Brasier*, for pots of brass, copper kettles, &c., 222; £41 8s. to Joseph Page for biskett and biskett bags, 222; £42 to Alderman Watts for iron hoops, 222; £4 7s. to Tristram Eldrich for mariners' lodgings, &c., 222; £2 3s. to Peter Wright for lanthorns, &c., 223; 26s. to William Thomas for lanthorns, &c., 223; 37s. to William Smalwood for locks, staples, &c., 223; £52 to Joseph Pett, *Shipwright*, for work on the "Godspeed," 223; 28s. 8d. to Richard Stapers, amount disbursed by him to John Franklyn for carrying a letter to Captain Waymouth in the Downs, 223; £6 to Richard Staper, the amount disbursed to one Stace, a pilot hired to go with the captain to Newcastle, 223; £5 10s. to William Hedger of Wapping for a boat for the "Discovery," 223; £51 3s. 3d. to Nicholas Leat for money laid out in merchandise, 223; £129 9s. to John Fletcher for cordage, 224; £3 to William Kymber for wharfage, 224; 30s. to Faith May, wife of John May, master's mate on the "Susan," 224; 13s. 10d. to Xpofer Thomson for plates for the pinnaces, 224; £8 8s. to William Edward, *Plumber*, for lead, &c., 224; £42 to John Watts for iron hoops, 224; 46s. 8d. to Mr. Rumney for boat hire, &c., 224.
Warrants per Mr. Chamberlaine: £6 13s. 4d. to Tristram Eldred, purser, for his pains taken on the Company's affairs, 226; £6 to John Bowen for six quarters' rent of Founders Hall for the Company's meetings, 227; to pay mariners hired at Dartmouth to bring the pinnaces to London, 231; 24s. to Thomas Smith for keeping the pinnaces, 234; £5 to John Drew, Master of the "Godspeed," for wages in the late North West voyage, 234; 30s. to John Lane for wages in the late North West voyage, 234; £3 to Thomas Boarne for wages in the late North West Voyage, 234; £2 6s. 8d. to Thomas Branskom for wages in the late North West voyage, 234; £6 13s. 4d. to Thomas Verworth, *Purser*, for wages and expenses, 235; £23 6s. 8d. to Thomas Stevens, *Accountant*, for three quarters' salary, 235; £4 to the porters for landing and housing of stores from the North West ships, 238; 25s. 7d. to Thomas Evesed for disbursements, 238; 24s. to Thomas Smith for keeping the pinnaces two months, 240; £6 to Edward Pullyson, *Purser*, in full of his account and for wages, 240; 20s. to the wife of Thomas Bowrne, steward of the "Godspeed," in full of all demands, 240; 24s. to Thomas Smith for keeping the pinnaces two months, 241; 24s. to Thomas Smith for keeping the pinnaces two months, 242.
Warrants per Mr. Chambers: 34s. 3d. to Captain Mydleton as by a bill of particulars, 142.
Warrants per Mr. Holliday, Treasurer: £100 to the purser of the "Scourge," 45; £700 to the Earl of Cumberland on account of the "Mare Scurge," 45; £200 to Sergeant Hill for a bill of exchange on Plymouth, 55; £30 to Philip Grove on account of his wages, 56; £120 to Francis Evington on a bill of exchange from the West Country, 56; £50 to Nicholas Holway on a bill of exchange from Robert Pope, 58; £1,000 to Robert Stephens on a bill of exchange from John Ellacott of Exeter, 58; £44 to Peter Sampson on a bill of exchange from John Sandy of Exeter, 58; £200 to George Speake on a bill of exchange from Robert Pope, 66; £500 to Mr. Allabaster for the provision of royals of plate, 68; £400 to Sir Hugh Portman on bill of exchange from Robert Pope, 68; £200 to Ellys Cryspe on bill of exchange from Plymouth, 68; £70 to Peter Grove in full of his agreement, 71; £50 to William Harvy on bill of exchange from Robert Pope, 73; £100 to James Prockter on bill of exchange from Robert Pope, 73; £100 to Edward Stephens for timber for the "Malice Scurge," 74; £200 to Mr. Burrell for the preparation of the shipping, 74; £50 to Richard Stratford on a bill of exchange from Exeter, 83; £500 to John Ellecott on a bill of exchange from Exeter, 83; £100 to Edward Highlord, purser, for the preparation of the "Scourge," 84; £40 to Richard Walton on a bill of exchange from Exeter, 84; £60 to Richard Rudd on a bill of exchange from Exeter, 84; £50 to Nicholas Ranton on a bill of exchange from Exeter, 84; £40 to Richard Gregory on a bill of exchange from Robert Pope, 84; £70 to William Mallett on a bill of exchange from Robert Pope, 85; £200 to William Garway for the preparation of the "Assention," 85; £100 to William Burrell for timber and necessaries for the ships, 86; £50 to Edward Stephens, Carpenter, for repairs to the "Scourge," 87; £200 to John Portman, to be paid to Robert Pope in the West Country, 87; £100 to the purser of the "Hector" on account of repairs, 88; £4 in recompence to a poor man for bulging his crane with the "Scourge's" anchor, 88; £100 to John Colles, to be repaid to Robert Pope in the West Country, 88; £100 to Captain Lancaster, on account for his entertainment in the voyage, 89; £172 7s. 9d. for meal bought of Mr. Gawldsmith, 90; £500 to Mr. Allabaster for Royals; £100 to Mr. Garway for the provision of the "Assention," 91; £100 to Mr. Chambers for the provision of caske, 92; £80 to Mr. Burrell for timber and other necessaries, 93; £500 to Mr. Allabaster for royals, 95; £50 to Edward Stephens, Carpenter, on account of repairs of the "Scourge," 95; £32 to Raphe Salter, Surgeon, for his medicine chest, 95; £28 14s. to William and George Cater for

Warrants per Mr. Holliday, *continued.*
roan cloths, 97; £36 0s. 4d. to Roger Hankin, Master of the "Assention," for ballast and charges on two hoyes to go to the ships, 97; £100 to the purser of the "Assention" for repairs and preparations, 99; £600 to Robert Stevens and Roger Howe on a bill of exchange from John Ellacott, 102; £241 to Francis West on a bill of exchange from John Sandy, 102; £100 to Richard Hart for smithery for the "Assention," 104; £100 to William Garway for the "Assention," 105; £150 to William Candish on account of lead, 105; £25 to Laurence Waldo on a bill of exchange from Exeter, 106; £50 to William Starky, a factor, for his entertainment and preparation, 106; £100 and £50 to Richard Wright for gratuities and charges for the patent, &c., 107; £100 to William Dyckes, purser of the "Red Dragon," on account of necessaries, 108; £100 to Robert Stephens on a bill of exchange from John Ellicott, 108; £100 to Robert Stephens on a bill of exchange from John Ellicott, 109; £194 5s. 6d. to William Garway for candy oil, 114; £150 to William Garway for the repairs to the "Assention," 114; £150 to William Dixsy, purser of the "Red Dragon," for repairs, 114; £500 to Sir Hugh Portman on bill of exchange from Robert Pope, 115; £100 to William Burrell for boats and other necessaries, 115; £25 10s. to Anthony Moseley for vinegar, 115; £20 to Humfrey Phipps for wine-vinegar, 115; £14 12s. to John Combe for wine-vinegar, 116; £69 8s. 2d. to Christopher Wasse for a silver fountain and case, 116; £26 13s. 4d. to Thomas Pulleyn, preacher, for his provision to sea, 116; £250 to William Dixson, purser of the "Red Dragon," 117; £6 13s. 4d. to Thomas S monds, 117; £250 to Richard Wyseman for the purser of the "He tor," 117; £150 to William Leake, purser of the "Assention," for men's wages, 117; £250 to John Havard for men's wages on the "Susan," 118; £19 6s. 3d. to George Davies for chests for cloth, 118; £100 to Widowe Bennett for iron, 119; £20 to Percival Stradling, *factor,* for his preparation, 119; £500 to Sergeant Helle for exchange at Exeter, 119; £50 to Thomas Salterne, *factor,* for his entertainment, 120; £20 to Phillip Winchecomb, *factor,* for his preparation for sea, 121; £100 to George Persons, purser of the "Hector," for provisions, 121; £8 to Patrick Johnson for salt, 121; £126 13s. 4d. to Symon Furner for powder, 121; £20 to Thomas Tudd, factor, to make his provision, 122; £100 to John Havard, *factor,* for his entertainment, 123; £60 to Thomas Shere of Exeter for so much paid to John Sandy, 125; £100 to William Brunde, *factor,* for his entertainment, 125; £100 to Mr. Garway, purser of the "Assention," for necessaries, 126; £90 10s. to Mr. Robert Bell for paper, 126; £38 16s. 3d. to George Smithyes for plate, 127; £100 to William Brodebent, Master of the "Dragon," an advance on mortgage, 128; £200 to the assignee of Thomas Billett on a bill of exchange from Robert Pope, 129; £68 18s to Thomas Lieth for pewter, 129; £43 16s. 6d. to Robert Warner for glasses, 129; £40 to Derick Lypson for steel, 138; £11 to Phillip Grove for travelling expenses, 138; £30 to Nathaniel Jamryn, *factor,* as per agreement, 139; £100 to Mr. Wyseman for the purser of the "Hector," for men's wages, 139; £23 7s. 7d. to William Dove, *Cooper,* for work done, 139; £13 7s. 8d. to William Segar, *Herald,* for writing the Queen's letters to the Kings of the East Indies, 139; £100 to Captain Mydleton for his entertainment in the voyage, 140; £100 to William Garway on account for the provision of the "Assention," 140; £8 3s. 7d. to Captain Mydleton for disbursements, 140; £400 to William Harvey on a bill of exchange from Robert Pope, 141; £2 13s. to Mr. Pope, Sergeant of the Admiralty, on a bill of charges for the burial of those slain in the "Hector," 141; £50 to Henry Mydleton, *factor,* for his entertainment in the voyage, 141; £371 15s. to Simon Furnor for powder, brimstone, and saltpetre, 142; £61 5s. 9d. to Simon Yomans for butter and cheese, 142; £86 to William Uffington for wax candles, 142; £100 to Mr. Wiseman for the purser of the "Hector" for charges, 142; £49 to William Candishe for lead, 143; £30 to James Emerson for aquavitæ, 143; £11 10s. to Mr. Hacklett for advice and maps, 143; £100 to William Dixon, purser of the "Red Dragon," for the clearing of the ship, 144; £50 to the purser of the "Hector" for the clearing of the ship, 144; to take 4, 5, or £600 to Gravesend for the payment of harbor-wages and other expenses in clearing the ships, 146; £61 to Henry Ryvelles, *Cooper,* for caske, 147; £57 15s. to John Hardway, *Cooper,* for caske, 147; £40 12s. to Leonard Onnyslowe, *Cooper,* for caske, 148; £36 19s. to George Chapman, *Cooper,* for caske, 148; £20 to Thomas Duck for ancients and streamers for the "Dragon," 149; £80 to Josephe Page, Baker, for bread, 149; £7 10s. to John Pywell for head pieces and morrens, 149; £100 to Christopher Thomson, *Smith,* for iron, 149; £30 10s. to Richard Hall, *Smith,* for two anchors for the "Hector," 150; £100 to William Leake, purser of the "Assention," for wages and clearing expenses, 154; £100 to George Parsons, purser of the "Hector," for wages and clearing expenses, 154; £100 to Joseph Salbanck, purser of the "Susan," for wages and clearing expenses, 154; £180 to William Dixon, purser of the "Red Dragon," for wages and clearing expenses, 154; £15 7s. to Anthonie Duffeilde for beer, 154; £300 to Robert Golding for the ship "Guift," 154; £24 19s. to James Dover and Richard Vale for spectacles and boxes, 155; £200 to Abraham Campion, part of his account for beer, 155; £100 to Lewys Tyght, *Blacksmith,* for iron work for the "Red Dragon," 157; £50 to Joseph Page, *Baker,* for biskett, 157; £30 to Francis Caudell, *Painter,* for painting the "Red Dragon," 157; £161 13s. 1 d. to Richard Hart, *Smith,* for nails and iron work for the "Assention," 157; £18 to Edmond Saunderson for Turner's work for the "Red Dragon," 157; £100 to William Burrell for money owing, 157; £16 0s. 10d. to William Bacon for masts and stores, 157; £30 12s. 4d. to James Waters, Ironmonger, for gunners' stores for the "Susan," 157; £31 16s. 8d. to William Kymber, *Wharfinger,* for lighterage and porterage, 158; £34 13s. 4d. to various porters for portage and lading of the ships, 158; £11 6s. 8d. to Robert Wood, *Wharfinger,* for wharfage and lighterage, 158; £42

Warrants per Mr. Holliday, *continued*.
8s. 11d. to Mr. Rumney for disbursements, 158; £12 8s. 6d. to Thomas Hewys, *Clothworker*, for work done, 159; £30 to Arnold Mabanck, *Pullymaker*, for work done, 163; £34 4s. 2d. to Christopher Thomson, *Smith*, for work done, 163; £16 1s. 8d. to John Hedland for carriages for the ships, 163; £100 to Lewis Tate, *Smith*, for iron-work, 163; £100 to Thomas Barbor for canvas, 163; £11 to John Maxfield, *Brasier*, for copper vessels, 164; £42 15s. to Robert Heighoo for canvas, 164; £22 4s. to Francis Covell, *Channeller*, for provisions, 164; £45 10s. 11d. to Joseph Page, *Baker*, for biskett, 167; £200 to Thomas Barber for canvas, 167; £6 to William Hedger for building a pinnace for the "Hector," 167; £49 to Robert Huse, *Sailmaker*, for sails, 167; £40 to John Bowden, *Sailmaker*, for sails, 168; £42 5s. 4d. to Adam Wood, *Carpenter*, in full of his account, 168; £86 15s. 4d. to Robert Bradbury, *Sailmaker*, for sails for the "Dragon" and "Hector," 168; £42 15s. to Robert Highhoe for *canvas* for the "Assention," 168; £27 to James Waters, *Ironmonger*, for iron-work, 168; £13 to Hildebrand Sprusen, *Sailmaker*, in full of his bill, 168; £17 12s. 6d. to Peter Pett, *Shipwright*, for work and charges, 169; £14 to Mr. Crosse for a pipe of Malaga wine, 169; 20 merkes to the King of Heralds for assigning the Company's arms, 171; £102 to Robert Savadge for wastes and deales, 171; £29 1s. 4d. to Justice Mullett, *Smith*, for iron work for the "Dragon," 172; £300 to Thomas Barbar on account of canvas, 172; £90 to Elizabeth Bennett for nails, &c., 172; £3 15s. to Peter Hiller for caske for the "Hector," 172; £48 to Francis Caudell, *Painter*, for work done on the "Dragon," 172; £10 to William Allom, *Lighterman*, for lighterage of goods, 173; £27 to Lewis Tate, *Blacksmith*, for iron work for the "Red Dragon," 173; £2 to Agnes Haselton to relieve her husband, hurt in the "Hector," 173; £29 10s. to Charles Anthony for stamps made for the East India monies, 174; £13 3s. 2d. to Robert Bell for disbursements for wharfage and cutting of lead, 203; £4 7s. 5d. to Alderman Bannyng, *Treasurer*, for so much disbursed by him beyond his receipts, 203; £109 16s. 8d. to Benjamin Deycro, agent of the Muskovia Company for cordage, 204.

Warrants per Thomas Stephens: £2 16s. to the wife of John May, master's mate in the "Susan," for a month's wages, 248; £6 for pilotage of the "Assention" into the river, 248.

Warwicke, *see* Heale.

Washer, Richard, assembly, 60; bill of adventure sealed, £240, p. 252.

Wasse, Christopher, warrant £69 8s. 2d. for silver plate, 116.

Wasse, Thomas, desires to be employed as a factor, 56.

Wastall, ⎱ William, adventurer, assembly 59;
Wastell, ⎰ will bring in his money in dollars, 63; committee, 246; bill of adventure sealed, £240, p. 260.

Watches, 218.

Water caske, 150 tonnes of caske required, whereof 40 tonnes of hogsheads, 30, 36; committee to provide 150 tonnes, 76; committee to provide for the North West Voyage, 209.

Waters, James, *Ironmonger*, warrant £30 12s. 4d. for gunner's stores, 157; do. £27 for iron work, 168.

Wattes, John, Alderman, assemblies, 68, 69, 71, 78, 79, 80, 82, 83, 85, 87, 89, 91, 96, 99, 100, 102, 104, 106, 109, 112, 115, 127, 124, 128, 138, 140, 143, 144, 148, 151, 155, 159, 164, 167, 168, 170, 171, 172, 173, 174, 175, 176, 180, 181, 182, 183, 184, 185, 186, 187, 190, 192, 193, 194, 203, 204, 205, 206, 208, 214, 215, 216, 217, 219, 224, 225, 244, 248; committees, 57, 67, 69, 70, 71, 72, 73, 77, 90, 99, 115, 147, 155, 183, 186, 191, 194, 209; warrant £36 10s. 10d. for shirts of mail, 123; to confer as to the damage done to a ship by the anchor of the "Scourge," 125; elected governor, 166, 179; the oath of office, 179; to examine the charters as to authority for compelling contributions for a second voyage, 183; conference with Lord Admiral and Mr. Secretary (Herbert) as to the delay in the second voyage, 189; advice from Middleboroughe of the return of two Dutch ships from the East Indies, 194; an Englishman returned from the East Indies to be conferred with as to the state of trade, &c., 194; signatures to treasurer's warrant, 206, 210; warrant £42 for iron hoops, 222; do. £42, p. 224; general committee and sworn, 225; requested to give his bond with Mr. Bannyng for £1,000 as security for money to be taken up at interest for the payment of wages of mariners returned in the "Assention," 249; bill of adventure sealed, £600, p. 256; do. £240, p. 261.

Waymoth, ⎱ Captain George, *see also North*
Waymouth, ⎰ *West Passage*; assemblies,
Waymouthe, ⎰ 183, 204, 208; letter from him proposing the Company should undertake a voyage for the discovery of a North West passage to the East Indies, 182; conference and resolutions that the voyage be made, 183-4; the terms agreed on with Waymouth, 185; report of the committee, 185; warrant £30 for instruments, 204; do. £30, p. 204; do. £20, p. 204; £60 taken up at Exeter for the hiring of mariners, 209; warrant £100 for men's wages, 211; formal agreement with Waymouth containing his commission and instructions, 211-14; *see North West Passage*; John Cartwright, *Preacher*, engaged to go in the voyage, 216; the articles of agreement read, 217; warrant £30 for expenses prior to sailing, 218; return to Dartmouth; his journal read; ordered to bring ships round to London, 227; delay in coming to London, 229; arrival in London, 229; Mr. Cartwright accused of being the main persuader for the return of the expedition, 232; proceedings before the Privy Council as to his return; his hope of discoveries in a second voyage, and a second and final voyage resolved on; re-appointed chief in command, confident of success in finding a passage, 233; proposed conference as to a second voyage, 236-7; his demands for charges and expenses in the voyage referred to arbitration, 240; *see his Agreement*, 211-14.

Webbe, Thomas, admitted as an extra factor, 102.

Welbye, Richard, adventurer with Giles Doncomb, £200, p. 4.

Wellington, Peter, being the assign of Peter Helms, deceased, he desires the transfer of his stock and the freedom of the Company, 226; stock transferred but the freedom denied, 227.

West, Francis, warrant £241 on bill of exchange, 102.
West Country ; Mr. Howe requested to travel there to make provision for dollars and victuals for the ships, 15 ; he agrees to go with Captain Davies, 21 ; a commission to be prepared, 28 ; committee appointed to purchase, 29 ; letter from the Lord Treasurer to Her Majesty's receivers of Devon and Cornwall, authorizing credit to be given to the agents of the Company, 38 ; Captain Baker's commission for the purchase of victuals, 38, 40, 48-50 ; the quantities of provisions to be purchased, 41 ; money and bills of exchange, 45, 47, *see Warrants*, commissions for the purchase of provisions, 48-54 ; letters of advice respecting the providing of victuals, money, &c., 61 ; provisions to be bought to carry the ships to the West Country, 67 ; committee to solicit the Lord Treasurer's warrant to transport provisions, 78 ; the warrant sent, 79 ; poll davies to be bought and made up into bags, 86 ; order for no more biscuit or meal to be bought, 88 ; instructions for shipping the Spanish money, 119 ; committee to see the discharge of the ships, 128, 140 ; Mr. Howe's and Mr. Combe's commission, 147 ; Mr. Howe and Mr. Combe to bring in their accounts, 172-3 ; letters sent down for the purser and officers of the "Assention," 243.
Westray, } Thomas, adventurer with others,
Westrow, } £300, p. 3 ; bill of adventure sealed, £240, p. 254.
Westwray, John, made free though not named in the patent, 177 ; bill of adventure sealed, £360, p. 256.
Wethrall, Larance, adventurer with Thomas Wheeler, £200, p. 2.
Wharfage, 203, 224.
Wharfingers, *see William Kynber, Robert Wood*.
Wharfs, Gully Key, 158 ; Wiggens Key, 203 ; Wooll Key, 158.
Wheat, estimate of quantity and price, 35 ; revised estimate, 46, 54-5 ; quantity to be bought in the West Country, 41, 52.
Wheeler, Ambrose, committees, 246 ; bill of adventure sealed, £240, p. 257.
Wheeler, Thomas, adventurer with Larance Wethrall, £200, p. 2 ; assembly, 4.
White, Leonarde, adventurer, £200, p. 2 ; assemblies, 5, 59 ; bill of adventure sealed, £240, p. 259.
White, Thomas ; assembly, 59 ; committee, 245 ; to keep a note of the weight of the goods from the "Assention" received at the Exchange vaults, 248 ; bill of adventure sealed, £240, p. 255.
Whitehall, 112, 164.
Whitmore, George, adventurer with Henrye Poalstedd, £200, p. 4 ; bill of adventure sealed, £240, p. 252.
Whyte, *see White*.
Wiggens Key, *Wharf*, 203.
Wilford, nominated factor, 77 ; elected factor of the third sort, 83 ; to sail in the "Susan," 101 ; warrant £30 for salary, 103 ; bill of adventure sealed, £50, p. 150.
Willoughby, Lord, warrant to buy the Spanish meal taken prize by his ship, 88.
Wilson, Francis, offers as a purser, 27.
Winchcomb, } Phillip, nominated factor, 77 ;
Winchcombe, } elected factor of the fourth sort, 83 ; to sail in the "Assention," 101 ; warrant £20 for his preparation, 121 ; bill of adventure sealed, £40, p. 149.
Wine, an estimate to be made, 26 ; to be in good casks iron bound, 30 ; estimate of quantity and price, 34 ; quantity and price in the West Country to be ascertained, 49 ; wine out of a prize ship to be purchased at Plymouth and price, 50 ; committee to provide 66 tuns, 75 ; warrant £100 for Canary, 95 ; do. £231 10s., £378, and £160, p. 103 ; do. £210, p. 104 ; do. £14 10s. for a pipe of Malaga wine given to the Lord Admiral in lieu of the deodand claimed for the "Hector," 169 ; do. £18 for a tun of claret for the like purpose, 169.
Wiseman, Richard, *Goldsmith*, adventurer, £200, p. 2 ; assemblies, 4, 9, 14, 20, 22, 24, 26, 28, 30, 31, 39, 44, 46, 47, 56, 57, 58, 67, 68, 69, 73, 74, 76, 78, 79, 80, 82, 83, 86, 88, 89, 90, 91, 93, 94, 95, 96, 98, 99, 100, 102, 103, 104, 106, 109, 112, 123, 124, 125, 126, 138, 140, 142, 144, 155, 156, 158, 160, 162, 163, 164, 167, 168, 170, 171, 172, 174, 175, 176, 177, 180, 182, 183, 184, 185, 192, 203, 214, 216, 217, 218, 224, 225, 227, 231, 232, 241, 242, 244 ; committees, 6, 8, 9, 12, 27, 68, 75, 76, 80, 91, 99, 107, 114, 115, 117, 124, 155, 156, 183, 186, 203, 209, 214 ; views ships, 13 ; surveyor for the "Hector," 14 ; warrant £100 for provisioning the "Hector," 25 ; signatures to the West Country commissions, 52, 54, 55 ; general committee, 63 ; warrant £100 for the use of the "Hector," 65 ; compounds with William Tavernor, mariner, 68 ; order to use a mast for the "Hector," 71 ; warrant £100 for the preparation of the "Hector," 79 ; do. £100, p. 96 ; do. £200, p. 104 ; do. £100, p. 111 ; do. £250, p. 117 ; do. £100, p. 139 ; do. £100, p. 142 ; to pay dock charges, 80 ; to clear accounts with Mr. Burrell, 127 ; appointed auditor, 166 ; general committee and sworn, 179 ; do. 225 ; allows the chests of merchandise returned from the North West voyage to be stored and viewed at his house, 231 ; bill of adventure sealed, £600, p. 255.
Wollastone, William, bill of adventure sealed, £240, p. 252.
Wollstenham, John, bill of adventure sealed, £240, p. 255.
Wood, committee to provide for the North West voyage, 209 ; warrant for wood, 211.
Wood, Adam, warrant £50 for masts and timber, 164 ; do. £42 5s. 4d., p. 168 ; do. £7 8s. for deals, &c., 218.
Wood, Robert, Wharfinger, warrant £11 6s. 8d. for wharfage, 158.
Woodfield, William, *Smith*, warrant £6 10s. for iron hoops, 219.
Woodwarde, John, *Ironmonger*, adventurer, £300, p. 2.
Wooll Key, *Wharf*, 158.
Woolwich, committee to inspect ships lying there, 13 ; the use of the docks requested, 13 ; the "Mare Scourge" in dock there, 27 ; a committee to lie at Woolwich to superintend the preparation of the "Mare Scourge," 39 ; Justice Mullett, a smith, to be employed, 40 ; timber borrowed from Her Majesty's storehouse, 71.
Worsenham, Mr., *The Searcher*, warrant £2 for the clearing of the ships, 156.
Wragge, John, bill of adventure sealed, £240, p. 201.

INDEX

Wragge, Richard, adventurer £200, p. 2; bill of adventure sealed, £240, p. 261.
Wray, John, nominated factor, 77.
Wright, Peter, warrant 43s. for lanthorns, &c., 223.
Wright, } Richard, *Secretary of the Company:*
Wryght, } assemblies, 228, 249; committees, 31, 33, 65, 75, 87, 91, 106, 115, 124, 141, 152; elected secretary, 38; ordered to request the Queen's Attorney to finish the patent, 88; warrant £100 and £50 for the expenses of the patent, &c., 107; do. £39 16s. 6d. for disbursements, 173; order to make out bills of adventure for every adventurer, 175; sixpence to be paid for every bill of adventure, 175; warrant 20 marks for his services, 203; to make out new bills of adventure, embodying all supplies, &c., in one lump sum, 220; warrant £4 15s. for charges in procuring the Queen's letters, 222; re-elected secretary, 226.
Wryte, Hugh, nominated factor, 77.
Wich, }
Wiche, } *see Wyche.*
Witche, }
Wyche, James, adventurer with Richard Wyche, £200, p. 2.
Wyche, } Richard, adventurer with James
Wycke, } Wyche, £200, p. 2; assemblies, 4, 7, 9, 10, 14, 20, 24, 26, 27, 29, 31, 33, 37, 39, 46, 56, 57, 64, 67, 69, 71, 74, 76, 78, 80, 82, 83, 85, 86, 88, 89, 95, 98, 99, 100, 104, 108, 109, 112, 113, 116, 119, 121, 122, 123, 124, 128, 129, 139, 140, 143, 144, 148, 150, 151, 152, 154, 155, 160, 168, 170, 175, 181, 192, 193, 197, 204, 205, 225, 228, 232, 235, 236, 238, 240, 241, 244, 247; committees, 6, 8, 12, 31, 33, 40, 65, 75, 120, 124, 128, 147, 156, 229, 230, 240, 248; views ships, 13; feoffee in trust for ships bought, 32; surveyor of the "Malice Scurge," 33; money in the West Country, 45; signature to West Country commissions, 52; general committee, 63; to buy oatmeal, 75; do. mustard seed, 76; order to provide ship's stores for the "Red Dragon," 117; expenses at Gravesend, 158; general committee, 179; do. and sworn, 225; bill of adventure sealed, £240, p. 259.
Wymers, Humfrey, adventurer with Richard Edmonds, £200, p. 3.
Wynchcomb, *see Winchcomb.*
Wyndham, John, warrant £40 on bill of exchange, 79.

Yerworth, Thomas, *purser of the "Discovery,"* appointed purser of one of the ships for the North West Voyage, 205; salary contingent on the discovery of the passage, 205; to give a bond of £100 for his good behaviour, 205; warrant £80 for carpenters' wages, 206; do. £30 for mariners' wages, &c., 208; do £100 for anchors and stores for the "Discovery," 210; do. £100 for coals, &c., 210; his account, £210, to be audited, 214; warrant £100 for provisions, 215; dislike taken to him, but his employment continued, 219; warrant £6 13s. 4d. for wages, 235.
Yemans, Simon, *Chandler,* warrant £61 5s. 9d. for butter and cheese, 142.
Yonson, Richard, *Goldsmith,* adventurer £200, and will pay in Spanish money, 31.

CHISWICK PRESS:—C. WHITTINGHAM AND CO. TOOKS COURT,
CHANCERY LANE, LONDON, 1885.

www.ingramcontent.com/pod-product-compliance
Lightning Source LLC
Chambersburg PA
CBHW020244240426
43672CB00006B/632